SELF-HELP POST-CONVICTION HANDBOOK

JOE ALLAN BOUNDS

∞INFINITY
PUBLISHING

Copyright © 2011 by Joe Allan Bounds

ISBN 978-0-7414-6814-7

Printed in the United States of America

The author, Joe Allan Bounds, is not an attorney. The motions, petitions, memorandum briefs, appellate briefs, and other pleadings were not drafted by attorneys. The publisher and author take no responsibility for the use of any materials or methods described in this book. This book is not a replacement for an attorney.

No claim of copyright is made to any official government work, rules, regulations, statutes, or any court holdings or findings.

Cover Illustration by: Jane Eichwald of Ambler Document Processing

Published November 2011

INFINITY PUBLISHING

Toll-free (877) BUY BOOK
Local Phone (610) 941-9999
Fax (610) 941-9959
Info@buybooksontheweb.com
www.buybooksontheweb.com

Introduction and Foreword

My name is Joe Allan Bounds. I am not an attorney. However, I did legal work for twenty three (23) years in the federal prison system and have been very successful. I watched other prisoners struggle or wait to the last minute to take care of legal problems related to post-conviction pleading or a detainer. I never could understand how a person would let a detainer be lodged against them for several years and then wait until a month or days before their scheduled release to attempt to take care of the matter. On the other hand, why would a person not take the time out of their prison schedule to research the applicable law related to their own case and make a determination whether their conviction and sentence were valid.

This book provides form letters and sample motions and memorandum briefs covering most of the scenario's a prisoner will encounter doing legal work in the system and is designed to improve the quality of legal work that comes out of the state and federal prison systems. This book will assist state and federal prisoners with obtaining documents and to understand how to format your pro se pleading and will guide them in the right direction on how to format your constitutional claims. For example, a state or federal prisoner can raise a Fourth Amendment claim straight up in a habeas corpus proceeding and will lose because the claim is procedurally barred for not being raised at trial or on direct appeal. **See Stone v. Powell, 428 U.S. 465, 493 (1976); Sanna v. Dipaolo, 265 F.3d 1, 10 (1st Cir. 2001)***(review of Fourth Amendment claim barred because petitioner had an opportunity to litigate claim in state court)*. However, that same prisoner might have prevailed or at least had the merits of the claim addressed had he/she raised the claim that: *"Counsel was constitutionally ineffective for failure to file a motion to suppress the illegal obtained evidence,"* which would provide cause for procedural default. See **Kimmelman v. Morrison, 477 U.S. 365, 382-83 (1986)**. In **Kimmelman**, the petitioner asserted an ineffective assistance of counsel claim in reference to the litigation of his Fourth Amendment claim. **See id. at 371**. The **Kimmelman** court found that Stone's reasoning could not be applied in this situation because the Sixth Amendment right to counsel is a fundamental constitutional right whereas the Fourth Amendment exclusionary rule is merely a prophylactic measure. **Id. at 375-76**. The **Kimmelman** court concluded that "no meaningful opportunity exists for the full and fair litigation of a habeas petitioner's ineffective-assistance [of counsel] claims at trial or on direct appeal." **Id. at 378 n. 3**. Generally, the prisoner must establish cause for procedural default and actual prejudice. **See United States v. Frady, 456 U.S. 152 (1979)**.

If you need assistance on post-conviction legal research, it's strongly recommended that you purchase my other book entitled: **"The Post-Conviction Citebook,"** from **Infinity Publishing.Com, 1094 Dehaven Street, Suite 100, West Conshohocken, PA 19428-2713**, Or buy online @ www.BuyBooksOnTheWeb.com. Or @ www.bbotw.com. **The Post-Conviction Citebook** is a research reference book with favorable case law on almost any subject in the field of post-conviction remedies. The contents have been designed to assist the individual user in finding favorable case law by topic and in chronological order as a criminal trial or proceeding may unfold. The book provides the user with a 16 page Table of Contents and over 740 quick reference topics.

Good luck on your quest for post-conviction relief!

ACKNOWLEDGEMENT

I am grateful to have the opportunity to publish this book which I know will assist a lot of state and federal prisoners for many years to come. I am also thankful to have met and worked with some real good people with brilliant minds down through the years. For example, Kamal Patel, Micha Rudisill, and Donnie Dyer, are all great people with brilliant legal minds. I want to thank my editor Jimmy Barkley and typist and cover designer Jane Eichwald.

I am thankful to all the individuals that I assisted down through the years. A lot of those individuals were successful in their litigation and some were not. Facts either win or lose a case. For some reason, I never liked losing. I am thankful to the many attorneys that I have had the privilege meeting and working with down through the years.

INSTRUCTIONS ON USE OF BOOK (IMPORTANT)

These instructions and form letters and sample pleadings were designed to assist prisoners who are proceeding in forma pauperis and without the assistance of counsel. This book is not a replacement for counsel. Rather, its for individuals who cannot afford an attorney and believe that they were not treated fairly by the judicial system. The TABLE OF CONTENTS list everything in this book. Read the Table of Contents to locate what you are looking for. Flip to that specific page number and then read the entire document to make a determination whether that is the document you're looking for.

This book provides numerous Form Letters which have all been previously successful. However, I am sure not saying that they will be successful in every situation because lets keep it real that won't happen. Locate the specific Form Letter and retype the letter and change the tone to fit your specific criteria. Try to keep your letters and pleading professional. Check your emotions at the door. As a general rule, most letters are single spaced.

On the other hand, most motions, petitions, memorandum briefs and pleadings are double spaced except for indented quotations which are generally singled space. **See, e.g., Rules of the Supreme Court of the United States, Rule 33(h)(2).** The only reason the pleadings in this book are single spaced is to compact the book. Check your local court rules because various courts have different rules and requirements for pleading. Therefore, it is a must to read your local court rules. Most state pleadings requires that a "Verification" be attached to the pleading. Additionally, most state and federal pleadings require a "Certificate of Service" be attached to them. Most of the pleadings in this book do not have a "Verification" or "Certificate of Service" in order to keep the book compact. Nevertheless, you will find both the Verification and Certificate of Service located separately somewhere in this book.

At the bottom of some of these pleadings you will notice a line and then under the line: PRO SE REPRESENTATION. It should have under the line, NAME, PRO SE REPRESENTATION, ADDRESS, TOWN, STATE & ZIP CODE. However, to compact the book I cut out the name, address, town, state, & zip code.

Applying common sense goes a long ways in using this book. There are a lot of fill in the blank form letters which only requires a little common sense to figure out what goes into the blanks. In order to compact this book I left out the answers to the blanks. If you have any trouble figuring out what goes in a blank ask someone who does legal work.

TABLE OF CONTENTS

CONTENTS	**PAGES**

Chapter I
Gathering Documents and Transcripts

❑ Preparing for Post-Conviction Relief

❑ Basic Documents required to collateral attack the validity of a criminal conviction and sentence

❑ How to obtain the documents:

➢ *Form* letters for case file (attorney)

➢ *Form letter to state bar* (case file)

➢ Motion to compel attorney to surrender case file (state & federal)

➢ *Form* letter for transcripts

➢ *Form* letters for docket entry sheets

➢ *Form* letters for appellate docket

➢ *Form* letters to order documents from the docket entry sheet and appellate docket

➢ *Form* letters for Freedom of information act request and appeals

PREPARATION FOR POST-CONVICTION RELIEF

This section deals with the preparation for filing a post-conviction relief motion. In order to properly prepare a post-conviction relief motion challenging the constitutionality of your conviction or sentence it is extremely important to gather all necessary and available documents to properly analyze the case.

1.   GATHERING DOCUMENTS AND TRANSCRIPTS

Gather all available documents and transcripts to properly analyze issues, arguments of error and to discover all issues that may exist in order to prepare a post-conviction motion. As a general rule, a criminal defendant has never been afforded the opportunity to review all the discovery material obtained by his/her attorney. A few prime examples why you need the necessary documents to prepare your post-conviction motion are set forth below:

- The Criminal Docket Sheet should show all documents, motions and exhibits filed for record, in your case. You may learn valuable information which supports an ineffective assistance of counsel claim etc. The Criminal Docket Sheet may show that your attorney never filed pretrial motions for discovery or to suppress evidence (although he assured you that he had). The Criminal Docket Sheet may show that the jury sent a note to the court while in deliberations for further instructions, which went to your guilt or innocence and supports a constitutional claim that you were denied the right to be present at a critical stage of the proceedings, or that your attorney rendered ineffective assistance by failing to inform you about the jury note (even through you were waiting in the hall of the courthouse). It could further show that your attorney did not know about the jury note and that the court and the prosecution discussed the note and submitted further instructions, without you or your attorney's knowledge and presence, which may constitute a violation of the Fifth and Sixth Amendment right to be present and represented by counsel at a critical stage of the proceeding.

- The transcript will assist you in finding errors during the course of the proceeding in your case, regardless as to whether your case is a guilty plea or trial. For example, if you pled guilty, (a) the court may have failed to establish a factual basis for the plea; (b) the court may have failed to insure that the plea was voluntarily entered; (c) the court may have failed to advise you of the nature of the charge you were pleading guilty to, and (d) the court may have failed to advise you of the minimum or maximum penalty provided by law. If your case was a trial, the transcripts could possibly show that your attorney conceded your guilty during opening statements, allowed highly inflammatory inadmissible evidence in your trial without objection, failed to present evidence in your behalf, the indictment was constructively amended by proof at trial, or your attorney failed to request a curative or limiting jury instruction based on inadmissible evidence.

- The sentencing transcript could show numerous errors made by the court, your attorney or the prosecution.

- An indictment or information might show that the court was without jurisdiction to proceed over the case to start with.

- A DEA 6 report may show that the actual amount of drugs involved in the case was 1–kilogram of cocaine; but yet the sentence was based on 15–kilograms of cocaine, which resulted in a much harsher sentence.

- A police report, DEA 6 report, or FBI report may show that the suspect in the case was 5'11", weighed approximately 200 lbs., red hair with a receding hair line (not fitting your description).

- As a general rule, your previous attorney should have the majority of the documents that you will need. Trial and sentencing transcripts can be obtained from the court reporter whose name and address you will be able to obtain from the Clerk of the Court or from your Appellate Attorney. It is important to utilize the use of the Freedom of Information Act (for the Federal system) in order to obtain government agents' reports, such as FBI reports, DEA 6 reports and ATF reports, etc.

It is important to utilize the following steps to gather the documents, case file and transcripts in order to properly prepare your post-conviction motion.

2. BASIC DOCUMENTS REQUIRED TO COLLATERALLY ATTACK THE VALIDITY OF A GUILTY PLEA

(1) Police reports; DEA 6 reports; FBI reports (302's) (whatever the case may be);

(2) Warrant, search warrant, arrest warrant, and affidavit used to obtain warrant;

(3) Indictment or Information (whichever the case may be);

(4) All pretrial motions, responses, and orders;

(5) Letters from attorney concerning plea offers etc.;

(6) Plea agreements; Guilty plea transcripts; Factual basis for the plea;

(7) Presentence Report; Objections to presentence report;

(8) Sentencing Transcripts, and judgment and commitment order;

(9) Apellant and Appellee Briefs (if any); and

(10) Judgment (opinion) of Court of Appeals.

The above mentioned documents are the basic documents necessary to properly prepare a post-conviction relief motion challenging the constitutionality of a guilty plea.

3. BASIC DOCUMENTS REQUIRED TO COLLATERALLY ATTACK A CRIMINAL CONVICTION AND SENTENCE SUSTAINED BY A TRIAL

(1) The investigative reports; whether Police reports; ATF reports; DEA 6 reports; FBI reports (whatever the case may be);

(2) Arrest warrants; search warrants; and affidavit used to obtain said warrants;

(3) Indictment or Information (whichever the case may be);

(4) Docket entry sheet;

(5) All pretrial motions; motion to suppress; suppression and motions hearing transcript (if possible);

(6) Proposed jury instruction by defense and the government;

(7) Trial transcripts including but not limited to: jury selection; opening arguments, trial, motions hearing held during the course of the trial, jury charge conference, and closing arguments;

(8) Jury instructions charged;

(9) Verdict forms requested and verdict form actually used;

(10) Motions for new trial, judgment of acquittal, or arrest of judgment;

(11) Transcripts related to hearing on motions for new trial, judgment of acquittal or arrest of judgment, etc.

(12) Presentence Report and objections to presentence report;

(13) Sentencing transcript and judgment and commitment order;

(14) Notice of appeal;

(15) Appellant and Appellee briefs (if any);'

(16) Court of Appeals decisions (opinion) rendered in your case;

(17) Any and all post-conviction motions which may have been filed (if any);

(18) Any and all letters from you to your attorney; letters from your attorney to you; and

(19) Affidavits from witnesses who were not called detailing what their testimony would have been, if possible;

(20) Affidavits from expert witnesses that weren't used during trial, but whose testimony would have made a difference if they had testified.

The above listed documents are generally needed in order to properly prepare a post-conviction relief motion challenging your conviction and sentence. Preparing a post-conviction without proper documents your relying on sheer speculations and wishful thinking that may result in the denial of your post-conviction relief motion.

4.   POST-CONVICTION INVESTIGATION

A post-conviction investigation proceeds in virtually the same manner and has the same scope as a conscientious pretrial investigation during the original criminal proceeding. This investigation includes reading all available documents, interviewing witnesses, taking the witnesses deposition, affidavits in the form of their testimony, gather documents, etc. It's extremely important to conduct a thorough post-conviction investigation in order to properly analysis your claims and to present valid arguments. Without conducting a proper post-conviction investigation your relying on sheer speculations and wishful thinking or collusionary allegations which may result in the denial of your post-conviction relief motion.

CRIMINAL DOCKET SHEET

A Criminal Docket Sheet lists all documents, motions, minute entries, orders, referrals, and exhibits etc. filed with the clerk of the court in that specific docket number. As a general rule, the clerk of the court will list the documents filed with the court on the docket entry sheet in chronological order as they were filed. **See Sample, Criminal Docket Sheet**. The clerk of the court files each document by criminal docket number and the parties names. Each document filed is assigned a docket **entry** number and a filing date.

How to Obtain the Criminal Docket Sheet

In order to obtain a copy of the docket entry sheet in a specific case use **Form Letter No. 1** and customize the letter using the correct docket number and the parties names. Mail the letter to the clerk of the court with a self-addressed stamped envelope enclosed for the return of the docket entry sheet. To obtain an appellate docket sheet use **Form Letter 2** and customize it by using the correct appellate court number and list the parties names. Generally, there is a small charge (fee) per page for the docket sheet from the clerk's office.

How to Order Documents From a Criminal Docket Sheet

To order a document that has been filed with the Clerk of the court you should state the parties name, docket number, and the docket entry number listed for that specific document your requesting. **See Form Letter No.3**. To order documents that have been filed with the appellate court use **Form Letter No.4**.

How to Obtain a Transcript Order Form

To obtain a transcript order form (federal) use **Form Letter No. 5** and customize the letter by using the correct docket number and parties names and the court reporter's name, if known, and mail to the clerk of the court with a self-addressed stamped envelope enclosed for the return of the transcript order form. **See Form Letter No.5.**

Form Letter No. 1

[Your Name & Prison Number]
[Institution]
[Your Address]
[Town, State & Zip Code]

[Date]

Office of the Clerk
Attn: [Clerk's Name]_____
Address_____
Town, State & Zip Code_____

Re:_____ v. _____,
Docket Number _____

Dear Clerk:

At this time, I am requesting a copy of the **Criminal Docket Sheet**, in the above styled and numbered cause. I have enclosed a self-addressed stamped envelope for your convenience. If there is a cost for the **Criminal Docket Sheet**, please advise me of such so I can have the necessary funds forwarded to your office.

Thank you.

Sincerely,

_____
[Your Name]

CC:
        p/file.

Certified Mail No. _____

7

Form Letter No. 2

[Your Name & Prison Number]
[Institution]
[Your Address]
[Town, State & Zip Code]

[Date]

Office of the Clerk
Court of Appeals
Attn: [Clerk's Name]_____
Address_____
Town, State & Zip Code_____

Re:_____ v. _____,
    Docket Number _____

Dear Clerk:

At this time, I am requesting a copy of the **Appellate Docket Sheet**, in the above styled and numbered cause. I have enclosed a self-addressed stamped envelope for your convenience. If there is a cost for the **Appellate Docket Sheet**, please advise me of such so I can have the necessary funds forwarded to your office.

Thank you.

Sincerely,

_____
[Your Name]

CC:
    p/file.

Certified Mail No. _____

Form Letter No. 3

[Your Name & Prison Number]
[Institution]
[Your Address]
[Town, State & Zip Code]

[Date]

Office of the Clerk
Attn: [Clerk's Name]_____
Address_____
Town, State & Zip Code____

Re:_____ v. _____,
    Docket Number _____

Dear Clerk:

At this time, I am requesting to purchase a copy of the following documents listed on the **Criminal Docket Sheet**, in the above styled and numbered cause to wit:

Doc. No. [Insert No.] [Insert Document name]
Doc. No. [Insert No.] [Insert Document name]; and
Doc. No. [Insert No.] [Insert Document name]

I have arranged payment for those documents through _____.
Please contact _____, phone number _____, for prompt payment of the above listed documents.

Thank you in advance.

Sincerely,

_____
[Your Name]

CC:
    p/file.

Certified Mail No. _____

9

Form Letter No. 4

[Your Name & Prison Number]
[Institution]
[Your Address]
[Town, State & Zip Code]

[Date]

Office of the Clerk
Court of Appeals
Attn: [Clerk's Name]_____
Address_____
Town, State & Zip Code____

Re:_____ v. _____,
    Docket Number _____

Dear Clerk:

    At this time, I am requesting to purchase a copy of the following documents listed on the **Appellate Docket Sheet**, in the above styled and numbered cause to wit:

    Doc. No. [Insert No.] [Insert Document name]
    Doc. No. [Insert No.] [Insert Document name]; and
    Doc. No. [Insert No.] [Insert Document name]

    I have arranged payment for those documents through _____.
Please contact _____, phone number _____, for prompt payment of the above listed documents.

    Thank you in advance.

                     Sincerely,

                     _____

                     [Your Name]

CC:
    p/file.

Certified Mail No. _____

Form Letter No. 5

[Your Name & Prison Number]
[Institution]
[Your Address]
[Town, State & Zip Code]

[Date]

Office of the Clerk
Attn: [Clerk's Name]_____
Address_____
Town, State & Zip Code_____

Re:_____ v. _____,
    Docket Number _____

Dear Clerk:

This letter is in reference to the above styled and numbered cause. At this time, I am requesting a **Transcript Order Form** from your office. I have enclosed a self-addressed stamped envelope for the return of the transcript order form.

Thank you.

Sincerely,

_____
[Your Name]

CC:
    p/file.

Certified Mail No. _____

Sample Criminal Docket Sheet
U.S. District Court
_____ **District of** _____
CRIMINAL DOCKET CASE #_____ **All Defendants**

Case title: USA v. _____   Date Filed _____
Magistrate judge case number: _____

Assigned to Judge _____
Referred to: Magistrate Judge _____

Appeals court case numbers: _____
5th Cir. USCA, not available 5th Cir.

Defendant

_____   **Represented by:** _____
                                    Federal Public Defender
                                    Address _____
                                    Town, State & Zip Code

Pending Counts   **Disposition**

Manufacturing of a   **Dismissed**
controlled substance schedule
II, amphetamine and phenylacetone.

Plaintiff

USA   **Represented by:** _____
                           Assistant United States Attorney
                           _____
                           _____

Date Filed	#	Docket Text
07/21/1988	1	**CRIMINAL COMPLAINT** as to _____ (Entered 7/21/1988)
07/23/1988	2	**ARREST WARRANRT** for _____ (Entered: 7/23/1988)
07/25/1988	3	**Arrest** of _____ (Entered 7/25/1988)
07/25/1988	4	**Initial Appearance** of _____ held before Magistrate Judge
07/25/1988	5	**ORDER OF TEMPORARY DETENTION** as to _____. Detention hearing set for _____ before Magistrate _____.
08/01/1988	6	**Preliminary Hearing and Detention Hearing, ORDER granting detention** of _____ pending trial. Signed by Magistrate _____. (Entered _____)

08/03/1988	7	**INDICTMENT** one count charging _____ with manufacturing a schedule II controlled substance amphetamine and phenylacetone (Entered on 08/03/1988)
08/06/1988	8	**NOTICE** of Arraignment as to _____ set for 09/11/1988 before Magistrate _____
08/11/1988	9	Minute Entry for proceedings held before Magistrate Judge _____ Arraignment of _____. (Entered 08/11/1988)
08/12/1988	10	**ORDER** on Arraignment as to _____. Jury selection set for 10/03/1988. Pretrial motions due by (09/04/1988) by Mag. _____.
08/22/1988	11	**MOTION TO SUPPRESS AND DISMISS** by _____ (Entered on 08/22/1988) by defense counsel.
08/30/1988	12	**RESPONSE BY USA TO MOTION TO SUPPRESS AND DISMISS** by the United States. (Entered on 08/30/1988)
09/05/1988	13	**ORDER** setting hearing on motion to suppress and dismiss. Hearing set for 9/16/1988 before Magistrate Judge _____.
09/16/1988	14	**HEARING** on motion to suppress and dismiss. (Court Reporter _____) Hearing continued to September 21, 1988 to locate witness.
09/21/1988	15	**HEARING** on motion to suppress and dismiss. Testimony of witnesses. Court to take motion under advisement.
09/30/1988	16	**REPORT AND RECOMMENDATION** of Magistrate Judge _____, recommending that the evidence be suppressed and charges dismissed.
10/06/1988	17	**OBJECTIONS by the USA to** the Magistrate Judge _____ Report and recommendation. (Entered 10/06/1988)
11/01/1988	18	**ORDER** overruling **USA objections** to **REPORT AND RECOMMENDATION** of Magistrate Judge _____.
11/01/1988	19	**ORDER AND JUDGMENT adopting Magistrate Judge _____ Report and Recommendation. The Court orders that the evidence is suppressed and the charges are hereby DISMISSED.** The Clerk is directed to close this case.

THE CASE FILE

A case file is created during the representation of a criminal defendant and retained by the attorney. A case file may consist of: All the discovery material, motions, responses, orders, minute entries, exhibits, investigative reports, police reports, research, case law, notes, correspondence from the prosecutor to your lawyer concerning plea offers, letters from your lawyer to the prosecutor, experts, or letters to and from the client. There is no way to state exactly what will be in each case file.

How to Obtain the Case File From Your Attorney

In order to obtain the case file from your trial or appellate counsel write a letter designed to obtain the case file. As a general rule, state law requires the attorney to provide a copy of the case file to his/her client, if the client offers to pay for the cost of copying and shipping. This varies from state to state so it is best to always offer to pay for copying and shipping cost.

First Letter: The first letter is designed to obtain a copy of the entire case file from the attorney, that is, in his/her possession. **See Form Letter No.6**. Send this letter by Certified Mail, if possible. Customize the letter by using the correct criminal or appellate docket number and the parties names and tone the letter to fit your specific situation.

Second Letter: In the event that your attorney failed to respond to your first letter requesting a copy of the entire case file then mail him/her the second letter as used in **Form Letter No.7**. Send this letter by Certified Mail, if possible. This letter is designed to trigger a prompt response.

The State Bar Letter: In the event that your first and second letters failed to generate a response from your attorney then that forces you to write to the State Bar Association. **See Form Letter No.8**. See State Bar Associations listing for the address. As a general rule most State Bar Associations have an Attorney/Consumer Assistant Program and they will assist you in obtaining your case file from your attorney.

MOTION TO COMPEL ATTORNEY _____
TO SURRENDER THE CASE FILE IN _____

In the event that you do not receive the case file after mailing your letters then file a Motion to compel attorney _____ to surrender the case file. A **Form** Motion to compel attorney _____ to surrender the case file has been created using the first and second letters as exhibits. This motion is filed with the clerk of the sentencing court. **See Form Motions**. All form letters and motions should be customized to fit the specific criteria of the case.

14

Form Letter No. 6

[Your Name & Prison Number]
[Institution]
[Your Address]
[Town, State & Zip Code]

[Date]

[Your Attorney's Name] _____
Attorney At Law
Address _____
Town, State & Zip Code _____

Re: **Case File:**

_____ v. _____,

Docket Number _____

Dear [Your Attorney's Name]:

     This letter is in reference to the above styled and numbered cause, where you represented me in the district court proceedings. At this time, I am requesting that you or your office <u>forward me</u> the entire case file in your possession including all discovery material, pretrial motions, responses, and orders. I am willing to pay cost of copying and shipping.

     I am entitled to the case file for several reasons. You nor your office no longer represents me and I plan to pursue a habeas corpus petition attacking the constitutionality of the conviction or sentence. As your aware the 1996 Antiterrorism and Effective Death Penalty Act placed time limitations on filing habeas petitions. Hopefully, you will act consistent with the American Bar Association standards and not impede my rights to challenge the constitutionality of my conviction and sentence, and forward the case file to me.

     Please forward the case file in large envelopes, addressed to the defendant, _____ _____ #_____, address, Town, State & Zip Code.

     I anxiously await the transmission of the case file.

Sincerely,

_____
[Your Name]

CC:

    p/file

Form Letter No. 7

[Your Name & Prison Number]
[Institution]
[Your Address]
[Town, State & Zip Code]

[Date]

[Your Attorney's Name]
Attorney At Law
Address
Town, State & Zip Code

Re: _____ v. _____,
 Case Number _____ **(Case File)**

Dear _____:

    This is my second letter concerning the case file in the above entitled action. You represented me in the _____ court proceedings. I am requesting that you <u>forward</u> the entire case file in your possession, including but not limited to: all discovery material, pretrial motions, responses, orders, telephone records/recordings, CD's and video tapes. Enclosed find a courtesy copy of the _____ Legal Material Authorization Form for mailing such materials.

    I am entitled to the case file for several reasons. First, because the case file was created during the period of time you represented me, it is my property. **See, e.g., Hiatt v. Clark, Ky. No. 2002-SC-000455-MR (6/15/06)**. Second, both the law and the American Bar Association recognize that you have a duty not to <u>impede</u> my attempt to challenge my conviction and/or sentence. **See, ABA Standards for Criminal Justice, Defense Functions Standards and Commentary** ("the resounding message is that defense attorneys, because of their intimate knowledge of the trial proceedings and their possession of unique information regarding possible post-conviction claims, have an obligation to cooperate with their client's attempt to challenge their convictions.") **United States v. Dorman, 58 M.J. 295 (C.A.A.F. 2003); Hiatt v. Clark, supra. See also Maxwell v. Florida, 479 U.S. 972, 93 L.Ed.2d 418, 107 S.Ct. 474 (1986)** ("The right to effective assistance fully encompasses the client's right to obtain from trial counsel the work files generated during and pertinent to that client's defense. It further entitles the client to utilize materials contained in these files in any proceeding at which the adequacy of trial counsel's representation may be challenged") ; **Spivey v. Zant, 683 F.2d 881, 885 (5th Cir. 1982)** (Habeas corpus petitioner is entitled to former trial attorneys file and the work-product doctrine does not apply to situation in which the client seeks access to documents or other tangible things created during course of attorney's representation).

    I plan to pursue a habeas corpus petition attacking the constitutionality of the conviction, sentence and your performance. You are currently impeding my right to make a habeas petition by retaining the case file.

In the event you fail to comply with my request, I will do the following:

1.   File a complaint with the _____ State Bar for your failure to surrender my case file and conscious efforts to impede my habeas petition;

2.   File a motion to compel you to surrender the case file with the sentencing court; and

3.   Pursue any other lawful and ethical method to seek my case file.

Hopefully, you will act consistently with your obligations. I look forward to hearing from you (but not more than **TEN (10) DAYS** from your receipt of this letter) (FCI _____ requires that all legal material be mailed in large envelopes) marked special legal mail open in front of inmate.

Sincerely,

_____
Your Name

CC:
p/file

LEGAL MATERIAL AUTHORIZATION FORM

Inmate Name: (Last, First, MI)		BOP Register Number:	Federal Case Number:
Number of Compact Discs:	Number of Cassettes:		Trial Date:
Number of VCR Tapes:			
Requesting Attorney's Name: State & Bar No.:	Business Address:		Phone: Fax:

Package Requirements:
- CD's must be in a paper sleeve
- Documents and/or images on CD should be in PDF format for compatibility purposes
- All media must be clearly labeled as "Legal" with the inmate's name, register number, and case number and must consist of ongoing litigation
- All media must be numbered in a manner indicating the total number of electronic media being mailed in the package (e.g., 1 of 10)
- Cassettes should be clear in color
- No items other than CDs, VCR Tapes, or Cassettes will be accepted in the package
- Personal CD players and cassette players are **not** permitted.

ATTORNEY CERTIFICATION OF LEGAL MATERIAL:

I, _____, hereby declare that the items contained in this package consist
      (Attorney's Name)
solely of my client's legal material and no sexually explicit material is included in this package. I

understand that any unauthorized material contained in this package will result in the entire package being

returned undeliverable. I also certify that all of the information contained on this form is true and correct to the

best of my knowledge.

_____   _____
Attorney's signature   Date

BOP USE ONLY
Inmate Acknowledgment of Receipt of Property:

The above referenced attorney has produced _____ CDs _____ VCR Tapes, and/or _____ cassettes (please circle those that apply), which are pertinent to your case for your review. All removable media will be stored in the Education Department and must be checked out. You should direct any questions about these materials to your attorney.

_____   _____   _____
Inmate's signature   Register Number   Date

Form Letter No. 8

[Your Name & Prison Number]
[Institution]
[Your Address]
[Town, State & Zip Code]

[Date]

THE _____ BAR
ATTORNEY/CONSUMER ASSISTANT PROGRAM
Address_____
Town, State & Zip Code____

Re: Attorney's Name, Address, Town, State & Zip Code

Dear ACAP:

This letter is in reference to the above entitled attorney, Mr. _____, refusal to release my case file created during Mr. _____'s representation of me in the matter of United States v. _____, Case No. _____ (__.__. _____ 200___), and his impediment of my statutory and constitutional rights to file a timely post-conviction motion.

On _____, 200 ___, I wrote Mr. _____ a letter requesting my case file in his possession created during Mr. _____ representation of me in the above entitled action. Mr. _____ failed to respond to my letter.

On _____, 200 ___, I mailed Mr. _____ a second letter requesting the case file and offered to pay for the cost of copying and mailing. Mr. _____ failed to respond to the second letter.

I seek the assistance of the Attorney/Consumer Assistant Program to obtain my case file. Mr. _____ no longer represents me and has no need to retain the case file and I am entitled to the case file for several reasons. See Maxwell v. Florida, 479 U.S. 972, 93 L.Ed.2d 418, 107 S.Ct. 474 (1986); and Spivey v. Zant, 683 F.2d 881, 885 (5th Cir. 1982).

Your assistance in this matter is greatly appreciated. Thank you.

Sincerely,

_____
Your Name

CC:
     p/file.

19

IN THE UNITED STATES DISTRICT COURT
FOR THE _____ DISTRICT OF _____

UNITED STATES OF AMERICA

VS.   Case No. _____

_____,

      Defendant.

MOTION TO COMPEL ATTORNEY _____
TO SURRENDER THE CASE FILE IN NO. _____

TO THE HONORABLE JUDGE _____:

    COMPES NOW _____, the defendant, pro se, and respectfully moves this Honorable Court to issue an order compelling Attorney _____ _____, to surrender the case file he created in representing _____ _____, in the above entitled criminal case. In support, Mr. _____ avers:

    1.   Attorney _____, is currently employed at _____ _____, _____, _____, as an attorney. Mr. _____ resides in _____ area.

    2.   On _____ _____, 200_, the defendant, _____, mailed Mr. _____ a letter requesting that Mr. _____ and/or his office forward him a complete copy of the case file in his possession. This letter was mailed to Mr. ____ _____ _____, Attorney At Law, _____ Street, _____, _____ _____. **See Exhibit "A"** attached hereto a copy of said letter. Mr. _____ never responded to this letter.

    3.   On _____ _____, 200__the defendant, _____, mailed Mr. _____, a second letter requesting the entire case file in the above entitled case in Mr. _____ possession. This letter was mailed by Certified Mail No. ____ _____. **See Exhibit "B"** attached hereto a copy of said letter with Certified Mailing Number. Once again, Mr. _____ never responded to this letter.

    4.   Mr. _____ intends to file a motion to vacate, set aside or correct sentence under 28 U.S.C. §2255. For such motion to be timely, Mr. _____ must file within one year of his criminal conviction becoming final, or before _____ _____, 200__. The records Mr. _____ seeks are necessary for preparation of such pleadings and his property, in any event.

    5.   To this date, Attorney _____ _____, has not surrendered Mr. ____ _____'s case file nor has he responded to Mr. _____ letters. Mr. _____ asserts based on facts he has recently discovered that Mr. _____ is aware of the reason Mr. _____ seeks these records and is attempting to frustrate his attempt to prepare a

meritorious §2255 motion attacking Mr. _____ ineffectiveness during pretrial, trial and sentencing.

6.   Mr. _____ seeks the active protection of this Court through a Court order directing Attorney _____ _____ to surrender the case file to Mr. _____.

7.   The Court may order Attorney _____ _____ to   surrender Mr. _____'s case file. First, Mr. _____ is entitled to the case file because it was created during the time period Mr. _____ represented Mr. _____.   Second, both the law and the American Bar Association recognize that Mr. _____ has a duty not to impede Mr. _____'s attempt to challenge his conviction and/or sentence. **See ABA Standards for Criminal Justice, Defense Functions Standards and Commentary** ("the resounding message is that defense attorneys, because of their intimate knowledge of the trial proceedings and their possession of unique information regarding possible post-conviction claims, have an obligation to cooperate with the client's attempt to challenge their convictions."); **United States v. Dorman, 58 M.J. 295 (C.A.A.F. 2003); Hiatt v. Clark, Ky. No. 2005-SC-000455-MR (6/15/06). See also Maxwell v. Florida, 479 U.S. 972, 93 L.Ed.2d 418-420, 107 S.Ct. 474 (1986)** ("The right to effective assistance fully encompasses the client's right to obtain from trial counsel the work files generated during and pertinent to that client's defense. It further entitles the client to utilize materials contained in these files in any proceeding at which the adequacy of trial counsel's representation may be challenged"); **Spivey v. Zant, 683 F.2d 881, 885 (5th Cir. 1982)** (Habeas corpus petitioner is entitled to former trial attorneys file and the work-product doctrine does not apply to situation in which the client seeks access to documents or other tangible things created during course of attorney's representation).

8.   Finally, the exhibits Mr. _____ submits with this motion establish that Attorney _____ _____ recognizes Mr. _____ right to his case file. Mr. _____ appears to be attempting to stall Mr. _____ until his AEDPA deadline passes.

WHEREFORE, premised considered, Mr. _____ respectfully   urges this Honorable Court to issue an order compelling Attorney _____ _____ to surrender the complete case file created during his representation of Mr. _____ in Case No. _____, by placing these material in <u>large</u> envelopes clearly marked "<u>Legal Mail: Open in Presence of Inmate</u>" and mailing the large package (large envelopes only) to: Mr. _____ _____ # ____,   Federal   Correctional Institution, ___ _____, _____, _____, via registered mail, within ten (10) days of service of said order.

Respectfully submitted on this ____ day of _____ 2008.

_____
Your Name   Prison Number
PRO SE REPRESENTATION
Address
Town, State and Zip Code

21

[CAPTION]

<u>ORDER</u>

Upon consideration of the defendant, _____, motion to compel attorney _____ _____ to surrender the case file in the above captioned number the Court finds that the motion should be **GRANTED**.

IT IS HEREBY ORDERED that attorney _____ is directed to produce and release the case file to the defendant _____ in the above entitled action.

Done on this _____ day of _____ 200__.

_____

IN THE _____ COURT OF _____ COUNTY

FOR THE STATE OF _____

THE STATE OF _____

VS.   **Case No. _____**

_____,

      Defendant.

**MOTION TO COMPEL ATTORNEY _____
TO SURRENDER THE CASE FILE IN NO. _____**

TO THE HONORABLE JUDGE _____:

    COME NOW _____, the defendant, pro se, and respectfully moves this Honorable Court to issue an order compelling Attorney _____ _____ _____, to surrender the case file he created in representing _____ _____, in the above entitled criminal case. In support, Mr. _____ avers:

    1.   Attorney _____ _____, is currently employed at _____ _____, _____, _____, as an attorney. Mr. _____ resides in _____ area.

    2.   On _____ _____, 200__, the defendant, _____ _____, mailed Mr. _____ a letter requesting that Mr. _____ and/or his office forward him a complete copy of the case file in his possession. This letter was mailed to Mr. _____ _____, Attorney At Law, _____ Street, _____ _____, _____, **See Exhibit "A"** attached hereto a copy of said letter. Mr. _____ never responded to this letter.

    3.   On _____ _____, 200__, the defendant, _____, mailed Mr. _____, a second letter requesting the entire case file in the above entitled case in Mr. _____ possession. This letter was mailed by Certified Mail No. _____. **See Exhibit "B"** attached hereto a copy of said letter with Certified Mailing Number. Once again, Mr. _____ never responded to this letter.

    4.   Mr. _____ intends to file a post-conviction relief motion challenging the constitutionality of his conviction and sentence. For such motion to be timely, Mr. _____ must file within one year of his criminal conviction becoming final, or before _____ _____, 200__. The records Mr. _____ seeks are necessary for preparation of such pleadings and his property, in any event.

    5.   To this date, Attorney _____ _____, has not surrendered Mr. _____ case file nor has he responded to Mr. _____'s letters. Mr. _____

_____asserts based on facts he has recently discovered that Mr. _____ is aware of the reason Mr. _____ seeks these records and is attempting to frustrate his attempt to prepare a meritorious post-conviction relief motion attacking Mr. _____ _____'s ineffectiveness during pretrial, trial and sentencing.

      6. Mr. _____ seeks the active protection of this Court through a Court order directing Attorney _____ _____to surrender the case file to Mr. _____ _____.

      7. The Court may order Attorney _____ _____ to surrender Mr. _____ _____'s case file. First, Mr. _____ is entitled to the case file because it was created during the time period Mr. _____ represented Mr. _____. Second, both the law and the American Bar Association recognize that Mr. _____ has a duty not to impede Mr. _____'s attempt to challenge his conviction and/or sentence. See **ABA Standards for Criminal Justice, Defense Functions Standards and Commentary** ("the resounding message is that defense attorneys, because of their intimate knowledge of the trial proceedings and their possession of unique information regarding possible post-conviction claims, have an obligation to cooperate with the client's attempt to challenge their convictions."); **United States v. Dorman, 58 M.J. 295 (C.A.A.F. 2003); Hiatt v. Clark, Ky. No. 2005-SC-000455-MR (6/15/06). See also Maxwell v. Florida, 479 U.S. 972, 93 L.Ed.2d 418-420, 107 S.Ct. 474 (1986)** ("The right to effective assistance fully encompasses the client's right to obtain from trial counsel the work files generated during and pertinent to that client's defense. It further entitles the client to utilize materials contained in these files in any proceeding at which the adequacy of trial counsel's representation may be challenged"); **Spivey v. Zant, 683 F.2d 881, 885 (5th Cir. 1982)** (Habeas corpus petitioner is entitled to former trial attorneys file and the work-product doctrine does not apply to situation in which the client seeks access to documents or other tangible things created during course of attorney's representation).

      8. Finally, the exhibits Mr. _____ submits with this motion establish that Attorney _____ _____ recognizes Mr. _____ right to his case file. Mr. _____ appears to be attempting to stall Mr. _____ until his AEDPA deadline passes.

      WHEREFORE, premised considered, Mr. _____ respectfully urges this Honorable Court to issue an order compelling Attorney _____ _____ to surrender the complete case file created during his representation of Mr. _____ in Case No. _____, by placing these material in <u>large</u> envelopes clearly marked "**Legal Mail: Open in Presence of** Inmate" and mail the large package (large envelopes only) to:_____ _____ # _____, Institution, __ _____, _____ _____, _____, via registered mail, within ten (10) days of service of said order.

      Respectfully submitted on this ____ day of _____ 200___.

_____
Your Name   Prison Number
PRO SE REPRESENTATION
Address
Town, State and Zip Code

[CAPTION]

<u>ORDER</u>

Upon consideration of the defendant, _____, motion to compel attorney _____ _____ to surrender the case file in the above captioned number the Court finds that the motion should be **GRANTED**.

IT IS HEREBY ORDERED that attorney _____ is directed to produce and release the case file to the defendant _____ in the above entitled action.

Done on this _____ day of _____ 200___.

_____

FREEDOM OF INFORMATION ACT/PRIVACY ACT REQUEST

The Freedom of Information Act (FOIA), Title 5, United States Code, Section 552, is to establish general philosophy of full agency disclosure unless information is exempted under clearly delineated statutory language, and as the Act is structured, virtually every document generated by the agency is available to the public in one form or another, unless it falls within one of the Act's exemptions. The FOIA allows you to request documents relating to you and all public documents. The Privacy Act allows you access to your personal files and to inspect them. If the records are inaccurate about you then you can request the records be corrected or amended.

READ: Title 5 of United States Code, Sections 552 and 552a

The FOIA/Privacy Act are set forth in Title 5 United States Code, Sections 552 and 552a. Reading those two Sections will provide you with a good understanding of the Act and its exemptions.

Procedures for disclosure of records under the Freedom of Information Act are set forth in 28 CFR (Code of Federal Regulations) Part 16.1 through 16.12. The procedures for disclosure of records under the Privacy Act are set forth in 28 CFR Part 16.40 through 16.55.

FREEDOM OF INFORMATION ACT REFERENCE GUIDE

The Department of Justice provides a "Freedom of Information Act Reference Guide," which is available electronically at the Department's World Wide Web site, and also available in paper form which is designed to assist you in your FOIA/Privacy request.

1. How to request documents through FOIA/Privacy Act

In order to obtain documents from a government agency through the Freedom of Information Act a person has to write a request letter to the main agency and request the required documents. See **Form Letter No. 9. Sample FOIA Request Letter**. The request letter must contain a **"Certification of Identity**. See **Sample: "Certification of Identity" form** attached to form letter.

APPEALS FROM DENIAL OF FOIA/PRIVACY REQUEST

Appeals from the denial of FOIA request are governed by **28 CFR Part 16.9 Appeals**. Additionally, appeals are governed by **5 U.S.C. §§552(a)(4) and 552(a)(6)(A)-(C)**. If you are dissatisfied with a component's response to your request, you may appeal an adverse determination denying all or part of your request to: FREEDOM OF INFORMATION ACT APPEAL, OFFICE OF INFORMATION AND PRIVACY, U.S. DEPARTMENT OF JUSTICE, FLAG BUILDING, SUITE 570, WASHINGTON, DC 20530-0001. Your appeal must be in writing and must be received by the "Office of Information and Privacy" within 60 days from the date that the agency letter denied your request.

2. How to Appeal the denial of FOIA/Privacy Act Request

To appeal the denial of a FOIA/Privacy Act Request you can use a simple letter stating the facts and arguments in support of your claim that the agency erred denying your request. **See FOIA Appeal Form Letter No. 10**. In the event that you're not successful in your appeal then you can file a civil suit in federal court under 28 U.S.C. §1331 and 5 U.S.C. §552(a)(4)(B).

FOIA/PRIVACY ACT CONTACT LIST (ABRIDGED)

A complete list of all agency contacts can be obtained online "www.usdoj.gov/04foia" under "Department Components," for offices of the Justice Department, or "Principal FOIA Contacts at Federal Agencies," for other government agencies.

DEPARTMENT OF JUSTICE COMPONENTS

Offices of the Attorney General, Deputy Attorney General or
Associate Attorney General

Requests for records of these Offices should be addressed to:

Deputy Director
Office of Information and Privacy
Suite 570, Flag Building
Department of Justice
Washington, DC 20530-0001

Civil Division
Freedom of Information/Privacy Act
Officer
Civil Division
Room 808, 901 E Street, N.W.
Department of Justice
Washington, DC 20530-0001

Civil Rights Division
Chief, FOIA/PA Branch
Civil Rights Division
Box 65310
Department of Justice
Washington, DC 20035

Drug Enforcement Administration Chief
Freedom of Information Operations Unit
Drug Enforcement Administration
Department of Justice
700 Army Navy Drive
Arlington, VA 22202

Executive Office for United States
Attorneys
Assistant Director, FOIA/Privacy Unit
Executive Office for United States
Attorneys
Room 7200, 600 E Street, N.W.
Department of Justice
Washington, DC 20530-0001

Federal Bureau of Investigation
Chief, FOIPA Section
Federal Bureau of Investigation
935 Pennsylvania Avenue, N.W.
Department of Justice
Washington, DC 20535-0001

Request For Criminal History Records (Rap Sheets) only.
Requests for Rap Sheets should be sent to the FBI, Criminal Justice Information Services Division, Attn: SCU, MOD. D-2, 1000 Custer Hollow Road, Clarksburg WV 36306. Requests must be accompanied by the subject's full name, date and place of birth and a set of rolled ink fingerprint impressions placed upon fingerprint cards or forms

commonly utilized for applicant or law enforcement purposes by law enforcement agencies. A fee of $18 in the form of a certified check or money order payable to the Treasury of the United States must also be enclosed. Further information appears at 28 C.F.R. §§16.32-16.33.

Federal Bureau of Prisons
Chief, FOIA Section
Office of the Director
FOIA/Privacy Act Requests
Room 738, HOLC Building
Bureau of Prisons
Department of Justice
Washington, DC 20534

Immigration and Naturalization Service
Processing of Immigration and Naturalization Service (INS) FOIA/PA record requests is decentralized and should be directed to the INS field office nearest your place of residence. If you do not know which office has the records you seek, you may obtain the appropriate address by writing to:

Director
Freedom of Information Act/Privacy Act Program
Immigration and Naturalization Service
2nd floor, 425 Eye Street, N.W.
Department of Justice
Washington, DC 20536

INTERPOL-United States National Central Bureau
FOIA/PA Specialist
INTERPOL-United States National Central Bureau
Department of Justice
Washington, DC 20530-0001

Office of the Inspector General
FOIA Paralegal Specialist
Office of the Inspector General
Room 4261, 950 Pennsylvania Avenue, N.W.
Department of Justice
Washington, DC 20530-0001

Office of Justice Programs
FOIA Legal Technician
Office of Justice Programs
Room 5400, 810 7th street, N.W.
Department of Justice
Washington, DC 20531

Tax Division
Senior Division Counsel for FOIA and PA Matters
Tax Division
950 Pennsylvania Avenue, N.W.
Department of Justice
Washington, DC 20530-0001

United States Marshals Service
FOIA/PA Officer
Office of General Counsel
United States Marshals Service
Suite 1250, 600 Army Navy Drive
Department of Justice
Arlington, VA 22202-4210

United States Parole Commission
FOIA Officer
United states Parole Commission
Suite 420, 5550 Friendship Boulevard
Department of Justice
Chevy Chase, Maryland 20815

OTHER FEDERAL AGENCIES

Bureau of Alcohol, Tobacco, and Firearms
Chief, Disclosure Division, Room 8400
650 Massachusetts Avenue, N.W.
Washington, D.C. 20226

Central Intelligence Agency
FOIA and Privacy Coordinator
Washington, D.C. 20505

Department of State
Director, Office of IRM Programs,
SA- 2, 5th Floor
Washington, D.C. 20522-6001

Internal Revenue Service
Director, Freedom of Information
Office of Disclosure
1111 Constitution Avenue, N.W.
Washington, D.C. 20224

National Archives
FOIA Officer
Office of the General Counsel
8601 Adelphi Road
College Park, MD 20740-6001

United States Customs Service
FOIA Paralegal Specialist, ORR
Room 3. 4A
1300 Pennsylvania Avenue, N.W.
Washington, D.C. 20229

United States Secret Service
FOIA/PA Officer
Suite 3000, 950 H Street, N.W.
Washington, D.C. 20001

Form Letter No. 9

[Your Name & Prison Number]
[Institution]
[Your Address]
[Town, State & Zip Code]

[Date]

U.S. Department of Justice
Freedom of Information & Privacy Staff
Address
Washington, DC 20530

Re: Freedom of Information Act Request

Dear (Agency Name):

Under the Freedom of Information Act, 5 U.S.C. subsection 552, and the Privacy Act, 5 U.S.C. subsection 552a, I am requesting access to all records related to: _____ _____ (State specifically the records you are requesting and the location of those records).

Pursuant to 5 USCS §552(a) (6) (A) (i), I request that you make a determination regarding the release of this information within the 20 day statutory period.

I also request a fee waiver pursuant to 5 USCS §552(a) (4) (A) (111).

If you deny all or any part of this request, please cite each specific exemption you think justifies your refusal to release under the law.

If you have any questions about handling this request, you may contact me at the above address.

Sincerely,

_____
[Your Name]

CC:
    p/file.

Certification of Identity

Privacy Act Statement. In accordance with 28 CFR Section 16.41(d) personal data sufficient to identify the individuals submitting requests by mail under the Privacy Act of 1974, 5 U.S.C. Section 552a, is required. The purpose of this solicitation is to ensure that the records of individuals who are the subject of U.S. Department of Justice systems of records are not wrongfully disclosed by the Department. Failure to furnish this information will result in no action being taken on the request. False information on this form may subject the requester to criminal penalties under 18 U.S.C. Section 1001 and/or 5 U.S.C. Section 552a(i)(3).

Public reporting burden for this collection of information is estimated to average 0.50 hours per response, including the time for reviewing instructions, searching existing data sources, gathering and maintaining the data needed, and completing and reviewing the collection of information. Suggestions for reducing this burden may be submitted to Director, Facilities and Administrative Services Staff, Justice Management Division, U.S. Department of Justice, Washington, DC 20530 and the Office of Information and Regulatory Affairs, Office of Management and Budget, Public Use Reports Project (1103-0016), Washington, DC 20503.

Full Name of Requester [1] _____

Citizenship Status [2] _____ Social Security Number [3] _____

Current Address _____

Date of Birth _____ Place of Birth _____

I declare under penalty of perjury under the laws of the United States of America that the foregoing is true and correct, and that I am the person named above, and I understand that any falsification of this statement is punishable under the provisions of 18 U.S.C. Section 1001 by a fine of not more than $10,000 or by imprisonment of not more than five years or both, and that requesting or obtaining any record(s) under false pretenses is punishable under the provisions of 5 U.S.C. 552a(i)(3) by a fine of not more than $5,000.

Signature [4] _____ Date _____

OPTIONAL: Authorization to Release Information to Another Person

This form is also to be completed by a requester who is authorizing information relating to himself or herself to be released to another person.

Further, pursuant to 5 U.S.C. Section 552a(b), I authorize the U.S. Department of Justice to release any and all information relating to me to:

Print or Type Name

[1] Name of individual who is the subject of the record sought.

[2] Individual submitting a request under the Privacy Act of 1974 must be either "a citizen of the United States or an alien lawfully admitted for permanent residence," pursuant to 5 U.S.C. Section 552a(a)(2). Requests will be processed as Freedom of Information Act requests pursuant to 5 U.S.C. Section 552, rather than Privacy Act requests, for individuals who are not United States citizens or aliens lawfully admitted for permanent residence.

[3] Providing your social security number is voluntary. You are asked to provide your social security number only to facilitate the identification of records relating to you. Without your social security number, the Department may be unable to locate any or all records pertaining to you.

[4] Signature of individual who is the subject of the record sought.

[Your Name & Prison Number]
[Institution]
[Your Address]
[Town, State & Zip Code]

[Date]

FOIA APPEAL
DEPARTMENT OF JUSTICE

_____

WASHINGTON, DC _____

Re: FOIA Appeal from Case No. _____

To The Administrator:

   This is an appeal under the Freedom of Information Act, 5 U.S.C. §552. On _____ _____, 20 __, I made an FOIA request to your agency for information and data related to: _____ that is in the _____ _____ _____ Agencies possession. On _____ _____, 20 ___, your agency denied my request in part because: [Describe the reasons for the denial]. Please find copies of my FIOA request and your agencies responds attached hereto.

   The requested material is clearly releasable under the FOIA and I consider your agency's blanket denial policy to be arbitrary and capricious.

   [Present your arguments in support of disclosure] The denial of FOIA request in this case is clearly a violation of President Obama's Executive Order 2009.

   Upon reconsideration I expect that you will reverse the decision to deny my request. In the event, that you do deny this appeal, I intend to proceed with a lawsuit to compel disclosure.

Respectfully submitted,

_____

[Your Name]

CC:
  p/file.

32

Chapter II
Detainers and Extradition

❑ How to deal with Detainers and Extradition

- ➤ Effects of Detainers
- ➤ Interstate Agreement on Detainers Act
- ➤ Extradition
- ➤ Motion's to dismiss (with memorandum brief)
- ➤ Motion for fast and speedy trial (with memorandum brief)
- ➤ Motion to reinstate probation
- ➤ Motion to terminate probation as unsatisfactorily completed
- ➤ Motion to revoke probation & impose sentence in absentia
- ➤ Guilty plea in absentia
- ➤ Motion to enforce terms of plea agreement (with memorandum)
- ➤ Motion to impose sentence in absentia
- ➤ Request to invoke interstate agreement on detainers act
- ➤ Motion for appointment of counsel
- ➤ Sample negotiation letters

33

DETAINERS AND EXTRADITION

This Chapter deals with Detainers and Extradition. Many times prisoners are wanted in other jurisdictions because of an outstanding criminal charge, warrant, sentence, and for parole, probation, or supervised release violation. The jurisdiction where said charges are pending may place a detainer on the prisoner with the Warden of the institution. A detainer is a written request from the prosecuting authority of another jurisdiction requesting the Warden to detain the prisoner upon release from incarceration so that they may prosecute him/her.

1.   Effects of a Detainer

Once a detainer is lodged against a prisoner, he/she will be released to the custody of the demanding jurisdiction to dispose of the outstanding criminal charges. His/her release to the other jurisdiction may occur during the current term of imprisonment or upon his/her release. Prison Staff at the records office or the Warden's Office will mark the prisoner's file to show that a detainer has been filed against the individual. Prison Officials should notify the prisoner that a detainer against them has been lodged for a pending charge.

A detainer and the delay of the final disposition of the underlying charges can adversely affect a prisoner because:

1   He/she will suffer psychological pressure from the uncertainties presented by a detainer and underlying pending charges against him/her. **See Smith v. Hooey, 393 U.S. 374, 379 , 21 L. Ed. 2 d 607, 89 S. Ct 575 (1969); Strunk v. United States, 412 U.S. 434, 439, 37 L.Ed.2d 56, 93 S.Ct. 2260 (1973).**

2.   He/she probably will be unable to present a valid defense to the charges underlying the detainer because the prisoner will not be able to keep track of witnesses. **See United States v. Ewell, 15 L.Ed.2d 627, 383 U.S., 116, 122, 86 S Ct. 773 (19 8 5).**

3.   He/she will lose the opportunity to have at least a partially concurrent sentence on the underlying criminal charges of the detainer with his/her present term of imprisonment. **Smith v. Hooey, 393 U.S. at 379.**

4.   He/she will probably be housed in a higher security prison because the detainer will increase their custody classification level.

5.   He/she will be prevented from receiving benefits from rehabilitation programs like educational, halfway house, home confinement, work release, and lower security institutions. **See Article I** of the Interstate Agreement on Detainers Act (IADA).

There are many ways to dispose of a detainer which will be discussed herein.

2.   Interstate Agreement On Detainers Act

The Interstate Agreement on Detainers (IADA) creates uniform procedure for lodging and executing a detainer, i. e., a legal order that requires a State to hold a currently imprisoned individual when he/she has finished serving his sentence so that he may be tried by a different State for a different crime. A prisoner who has a detainer based on untried indictments, information, or complaints and difficulties in securing speedy trial of persons already incarcerated in other jurisdictions, produce uncertainties which obstruct programs of prisoner treatment and rehabilitation. It is the policy of the States and the purpose of this agreement to encourage the expeditious and orderly disposition of such charges and determination of the proper status of any and all detainers based on untried indictments, information, or complaints. The party States also find that proceedings with reference to such charges and detainers, when emanating from another jurisdiction, cannot properly be had in the absence of cooperative procedures. It is further purpose of this agreement to provide such cooperative procedures. See **Article I of** the IADA.

The IADA is a statutory provision authorizing "party States" to enter an agreement, for the disposition of "untried" charges, indictments, information or complaints, which form the basis of a detainer. The agreement applies to all detainers based on pending charges lodged against the prisoner by a "party State," no matter when the detainer was lodged. However, the IADA does not apply to parole/probation/supervised release violations. **See Carchman v. Nash, 473 U.S. 716, 105 S.Ct. 340, 87 L.Ed.2d 516 (1985).**

3.   Detainers Under the IADA

The IADA applies to federal and state prisoners who have entered upon a term of imprisonment for service of the sentence. Resolution of any untried charges may be obtained through the provisions of the IADA. A State or local authority can lodge a detainer against a prisoner with the Warden or Prison Officials. **Article III(c)**, of the IADA provides that the prison is required to inform the prisoner of all sources and contents of any detainer lodged.

4.   Prisoner's Right To Request For Final Disposition

Article III (d) provides that once the prisoner has been notified of the source and content of the detainer he/she has the right to request a final disposition of the charges. **See United States v. Johnson, 196 F.3d 1000 (9th Cir. 1999); United States v. Mason, 372 F.Supp. 651 (DC Ohio 1973).** Once he/she request a final disposition of the charges, the Warden, commissioner of corrections, or other official having custody of the prisoner shall forthwith notify all appropriate prosecuting officers and courts in the several jurisdictions within the state to which the prisoner's request for final disposition is being sent of the proceedings being initiated by the prisoner. Any notification sent pursuant to this paragraph shall be accompanied by copies of the prisoner's written notice, request, and the certificate. If trial is not had on any indictment, information, or complaint contemplated hereby prior to the return of the prisoner to the original place of imprisonment, such indictment, information, or complaint shall not be of any further force or effect, and the court shall enter an order dismissing the same with prejudice. **See Article III (d) of the IADA. See also Alabama v. Bozeman, 533 U.S. 146, 150 L.Ed.2d 188,121 S.Ct. 2079 (2001).**

5. Waiver of Extradition.

Any request by the prisoner for final disposition of the charges under the IADA constitutes a waiver of extradition. **See Article III(e)**. A waiver of extradition means that the receiving state may take custody of the prisoner directly from the prison, for the charges that the IADA is based upon, regardless of whether the state in which the prison is located would require that the prisoner be released to its jurisdiction to satisfy the extradition rules for its state. **See <u>Franks v. Johnson</u>, 401 F.Supp. 669 (ED Mich. 1975).**

6. Prison Officials Notifying Prosecuting Authority

After receiving the prisoner's request for final disposition of the charges, the Prison Official or Warden must send the prisoner's written notice, request, and the certificate for final disposition of the charges to: The Clerk of the Court, via certified mail return receipt, to the Prosecuting Officer, via certified mail return receipt, and IADA Compact Administrator, first class mail. Copies of the forms, along with the cover letter are forwarded to each of them and placed into the prisoner's file and forwarded to the prisoner. **See Federal Bureau of Prisons, Program Statement 5130.06. See Attached Bureau of Prisons Sample Letters to the Interstate Agreement on Detainers Act** herein.

7. Prisoner's Copy Of All IADA Letters Etc.

The prisoner should keep his copy of all letters and documents sent by prison officials to the receiving State authorities in reference to the IADA. These letters and documents will be used as an Exhibit to a motion to dismiss for failure to prosecute and violation of the interstate agreement on detainers act.

8. Receiving State Has A 180-Days To Take Custody of And Try the Prisoner or Dismiss The Charges

Article III (a) provides: Whenever a person has entered upon a term of imprisonment in a penal or correctional institution of a party State, and whenever during the continuance of the term of imprisonment there is pending in any other party State any untried indictment, information, or complaint on the basis of which a detainer has been lodged against the prisoner, he shall be brought to trial within one hundred and eighty (180) days after he shall have caused to be delivered to the prosecuting officer and the appropriate court of the prosecuting officer's jurisdiction written notice of the place of his imprisonment and his request for a final disposition to be made of the indictment, information, or complaint. Id. Failure of the receiving State to try the case within 180 days warrants dismissal unless the prisoner or his counsel requests a continuance. See **<u>Gibson v. Klevenhagen</u>, 777 F.2d 1056 (5th Cir. 1976).**

9. Motion To Dismiss

After the prisoner has completed the requirements of the IADA and the prison has mailed by certified mail the IADA package to the Clerk of the Court, the Prosecuting

Officer, and IADA Compact Administrator, the State has 180 days to try the case or dismiss it. Once the 180 days time limit has expired the prisoner should file a **"MOTION TO DISMISS FOR FAILURE TO PROSECUTE, VIOLATION OF THE SPEEDY TRIAL AND INTERSTATE AGREEMENT ON DETAINERS ACTS; AND MEMORANDUM BRIEF IN SUPPORT OF SAID MOTION."** See Form Motion.

10. State Refusal To Issue A Detainer On Pending Charge

A lot of times a State which has pending charges will refuse to lodge a detainer against the prisoner. The IADA does not apply where no detainer has been lodged against the prisoner. **See <u>Gray v. Benson</u>, 443 F.Supp. 1284 (DC Kan. 1978)**. In the event that this occurs the prisoner should to write a letter to the Clerk of the Court, Sheriff's Department, and the Prosecuting Officer requesting that they file a detainer so that he can invoke the IADA and request a speedy and final disposition charges. See **Form Letter No. 1.** The prisoner should send the letter by certified mail if affordable. If the prisoner does not hear from the Court, Sheriff's Department or the Prosecuting Officer within thirty (30) days then the prisoner should file a **"MOTION FOR A FAST AND SPEEDY TRIAL WITH MEMORANDUM BRIEF IN SUPPORT,"** and attach a copy of all the letters as Exhibits. **See Form Motion**. This will not always work, but it gives you a valid argument at a later date that the State knew of the prisoners whereabouts and failed to prosecute in a timely manner and the charges should be dismissed.

11. Interstate Parole Compact

The Interstate Parole Compact, which has been adopted by all·50 states, provides that all legal requirements to obtain the extradition of fugitives from justice are expressly waived by states that are a party to this compact. See **N.Y. Exec. Law § 2S9-m**. When a parolee or probationer live outside of their jurisdiction, they are generally asked to sign a waiver of extradition from the sending jurisdiction to the receiving jurisdiction. When a prisoner has a detainer for a parole violation it is generally a losing proposition to fight the detainer.

12. Probation Violation Warrants

A lot of prisoners are faced with probation revocation warrants because they violated the terms and conditions of the probation. The IADA does not apply in probation violation cases. **See <u>Carchman v. Nash</u>, 473 U.S. 716, 105 S.Ct. 340, 87 L.Ed.2d 516 (1985)**. Nevertheless, if the probation is for some minor charge this should play a factor in getting the case disposed of. When a prisoner receives a probation he/she generally either plead guilty or was found guilty and the court placed the prisoner on probation. Once the prosecutor files a "Motion To Revoke/Revocation of Probation" a warrant will be issued· and a detainer lodged against that prisoner. The prisoner cannot force the prosecutor's hand in this type of cases. However, there is several ways to deal with the matter. For example, if the alleged violations are for technical violations the prisoner can file a **"MOTION TO REINSTATE PROBATION."** See **Form Motion**. If the original offense was for a minor charge the prisoner can propose to the prosecutor that he be allowed to enter a **"PLEA IN ABSENTIA WITH A WAIVER OF RIGHTS"** with a **SENTENCE RECOMMENDATION**. See **Form Motion**. See also **Cover Letter No. 2**. In the event, that the initial charge was for a more serious offense the prisoner can file a **"MOTION TO TERMINATE PROBATION AS UNSATISFACTORY COMPLETED"** See **Form Motion**. Alternatively, the prisoner can file a **"MOTION TO REVOKE PROBATION AND IMPOSE SENTENCE IN ABSENTIA"** requesting that the sentence be ordered to be served concurrently with his instant offense. See **Form Motion**.

13.   Sentence

Sometimes a prisoner will either plead guilty or go to trial and then fail to appear for sentencing. A warrant will be issued for his/her arrest. A detainer will be lodged against the prisoner for the un-sentenced case. In this type of case the IADA does not apply. **See Article I** of the IADA. On a rare occasion, if the charge was a petit offense the State might refuse to lodge a detainer against the prisoner because it does not want to go through the extradition proceedings and will just keep an open warrant for his/her arrest should he/she appear back in that jurisdiction. In this type of case it is almost a losing proposition to get the case disposed of. However, the prisoner can try to negotiate with the prosecuting attorney on the case. **See Form Letter No. 3**. In the event that this fails, the prisoner should try a second letter to the prosecuting attorney attempting to dispose of the case. **See Form Letter No. 4**. If the prosecuting attorney fails to respond to the prisoner's request he/she can file numerous motions. For example, he/she can file a **"PETITION FOR WRIT OF HABEAS CORPUS AD TESTIFICANT AND AD PROSEQUENDUM."** See **Form Motion**. Most likely the prisoner was represented by counsel during the guilty plea or trial whose still the attorney of record. He/She may need to get rid of that attorney before the Court would rule on any pro se motions by filing a **"MOTION TO RELIEVE APPOINTED COUNSEL OF HIS DUTIES BECAUSE OF A CONFLICT OF INTEREST."** See **Form Motion**. The prisoner should then file a **"NOTICE OF APPEARANCE."** See **Form Motion**. If the prisoner entered a guilty plea that the State failed to comply with the terms of the plea agreement he/ she would need to file a **"MOTION TO ENFORCE TERMS OF PLEA; MEMORANDUM BRIEF IN SUPPORT OF MOTION TO ENFORCE TERMS OF PLEA AGREEMENT."** See **Form Motion**. Alternatively, if the prisoner wants the Court to impose sentence he/ she could file a **"MOTION TO IMPOSE SENTENCE IN ABSENTIA."** See **Form Motion**.

14.   Detainer Strategies

There are numerous ways to deal with a detainer:

1.   Retain counsel or seek Appointed counsel;

2.   Invoke The Interstate Agreement on Detainers Act;

3.   Negotiate with The Prosecutor;

4.   Take No Action At All; and

5.   File Motions Seeking Dismissal of the Detainer based on whatever valid legal arguments available.

Making a decision on a detainer is one of the most important decision made by the prisoner who has already been sentenced. His/her decision could result in the prisoner serving an additional amount of time incarcerated.

Set forth below are at least ten different factual scenarios which should be taken into consideration while making a decision on how to resolve a detainer. Applying a comprehensive understanding of the facts of the pending criminal charge to the applicable law for the crime charged will afford the prisoner an opportunity to understand his/her available options and possible consequences, in order to make a conscientious decision to dispose of the detainer.

Studying the fact and applicable criminal law and applying common sense will generally allow the prisoner to make the correct decision on how to resolve a detainer.

The decision on how to handle a detainer should depend on all the below mentioned factors as well as the independent facts of the underlying charge of the detainer.

First, if the detainer is based on a parole, probation, or supervised release violation more than likely the detaining agency will prosecute after the prisoner serves the term of imprisonment he/she is currently serving. It should be noted that the IADA does not apply to parole, probation, or supervised release violations. As a general rule, the prisoner will want to write a nice letter to his parole, probation, or supervised release officer or the parole board and attempt to resolve this matter by having the parole, probation or supervised release reinstated to be served upon release from his/her present term of imprisonment. **See Form Letter No. 5**. Alternatively, revoke the parole, probation, or supervised release and have it ordered to be served concurrently with the prisoner's instant term of imprisonment. **See Form Letters No. 6** . It is best to deal with a detainer for violation of parole, probation, or supervised release as soon as possible and hope for at least a partial concurrent sentence with the term of imprisonment the prisoner is currently serving.

Second, if the prisoner is serving a lengthy term of imprisonment for a serious offense and the detainer is for a minor charge the State agency with the detainer will probably dismiss the charges. The question remains whether to take action on the detainer are let things ride as they are. Is the detainer causing the prisoner to be placed into a higher security prison? If the detainer is removed will it affect the prisoner custody classification? If the prisoner invokes the Interstate Agreement on Detainers what are the chances that the prosecutor will prosecute or dismiss? This depends on a lot of facts. For example, the distance of the detainer jurisdiction? Whether it's worth the expense of the detaining jurisdiction to prosecute? What type of evidence the prosecutor has? Sometimes the prosecution will dismiss the detainer because of the length of the sentence the prisoner is serving.

Third, if the prisoner is serving a lengthy prison sentence and will remain in a higher security for several years then it might be wise to leave the detainer alone for a few years and then move to dismiss it.

Fourth, if the detainer is for a serious offense and the prisoner is serving a sentence on a minor offense, and soon to be released, the decision must be made based on the independent facts. Under these circumstances the prisoner may need to seek the assistance of an attorney. If he/she can not afford an attorney, file a **"MOTION FOR APPOINTMENT OF COUNSEL." See Form Motion**.

Fifth, the length of the prisoner's present sentence will play a major factor on how the detainer will be handled by both the prisoner and state jurisdiction which has the detainer.

Sixth, the adverse impact of the detainer itself on the prisoner's custody classification and rehabilitation efforts will play a factor in deciding how to handle the detainer.

Seventh, the distance of the demanding state jurisdiction which placed the detainer will play a factor in whether that state is willing to prosecute the prisoner on that charge.

Eighth, the legal arguments to dispose of the detainer are based on the independent facts of each case and will play a factor in the disposition of the detainer.

Ninth, negotiation with the prosecutor can be a double edge sword which can be used against the prisoner. Any statements made by the prisoner during the negotiations might assist the prosecutor in obtaining a conviction. This is an area that the prisoner must be real careful. One mistake can mean additional prison time and the loss of a valid defense or strategy. A lot of times the prisoner can have his/her prison counselor or case manager contact the district attorney and advise him/her that the prisoner seeks to resolve the detainer and request some type of offer to dispose of the matter without placing the prisoner in harms way. The prisoner can offer to make restitution to resolve the matter.

Tenth, determine whether to invoke the Interstate Agreement on Detainers Act; seek appointment of counsel; Retain Counsel; negotiate with the prosecutor, take no action at all, or file motions seeking dismissal of the detainer and charges are all decision that should be made by the prisoner in a timely manner.

15. How to invoke the Interstate Agreement on Detainers Act

Prison Officials should promptly inform the prisoner of any detainer and his/her right to request a final disposition of the underlying charges under the IADA. **See Article III(c)**. However, some prison officials are lazy and fail to adequately do their jobs. The prisoner should check with the Unit Team, Case Manager, or Counselor concerning whether he/she has any detainers or pending charges. If the prisoner learns he/she has a detainer the prisoner should send to the warden, commissioner of corrections, or other official having custody of him/her a written request for a final disposition of the charge and to invoke the Interstate Agreement on Detainers Act on said detainer. The prison officials will have the prisoner sign the Interstate Agreement on Detainers Act, who shall promptly forward it together with the certificate to the appropriate prosecuting official and court by registered or certified mail, return receipt requested. **See Article III(b)**.

The easiest way to invoke the Interstate Agreement on Detainers Act is to send a written Inmate Request to Staff. **See Form Letter No. 7. Inmate Request to Staff**. The Inmate Request to Staff requests that the prison officials invoke Interstate Agreement on Detainers on his/her pending detainer. The prisoner should keep a copy of the Inmate Request to Staff and should verify that Staff received and processed his/her request. Additionally, the prisoner should obtain a copy of the IADA mailed to the prosecuting official and a copy of the certified mail receipt for his/her records. Generally, most institutions will supply you with a copy of these documents.

EXTRADITION

Extradition is defined as: "The official surrender of an alleged criminal by one state or nation to another having jurisdiction over the crime charged; the return of a fugitive from justice, regardless of consent, by the authorities where the fugitive is found. Cf. RENDITION(2)." **Black's Law Dictionary, p. 665 (9th Ed. 2009)**.

Extradite is defined as: "1. To surrender or deliver (a fugitive) to another jurisdiction . . . . 2. To obtain the surrender of (a fugitive) from another jurisdiction." **Black's Law Dictionary, p. 665 (9th Ed. 2009)**.

Rendition is defined as: "1. The action of making, delivering, or giving out, such as a legal decision. 2. The return of a fugitive from one state to the state where the fugitive is accused or was convicted of a crime." **Black's Law Dictionary, p. 1410 (9th Ed. 2009)**.

The "Demanding State" means the state in which the fugitive is wanted for a crime extraditable.

The "Asylum State" is the state where the fugitive is found. The asylum state must delivery the fugitive upon proper demand. Federal courts can compel performance of this duty. See *Puerto Rico v. Barnstad*, **483 U.S. 219, 107 S.Ct. 2802, 2809, 97 L.Ed.2d 187 (1987)**.

Constitutional and Federal Statutory Bases

Extradition is the surrender of a person from one state to another, country, territory, Commonwealth, or nation for the purpose of a criminal prosecution. A person charged in any state with treason, felony, or other crime, who shall flee from justice, and then be found in another state, shall on demand of the executive authority of the state from which he fled, be delivered up to be removed to the state having jurisdiction of the crime. See **U.S. Const. art. IV, §2, cl. 2**. The United States Constitution gives one state the right to demand extradition from another state the delivery of a person who has been charged in any state with either treason, a felony, or any other crime, who then flees from justice and is found in another state, must on proper demand of the requesting state from where the person fled, be surrendered by the state in where the person is found and returned to the requesting state. Congress enacted the Extradition Act **18 U.S.C. §§3182-3185 (2009)**, to implement the extradition clause set forth in the Constitution. The Extradition Act requires asylum states to extradite fugitive upon proper demand of the requesting/demanding state. See **18 U.S.C. §§3182-3185 (2009)**.

The Uniform Criminal Extradition Act (UCEA)

The Uniform Criminal Extradition Act (UCEA), which was created to streamline extradition proceedings. This act was approved by the American Bar Association and the National Conference of Commissioners on Uniform State Laws. Forty seven (47) states have adopted the UCEA, into their state legislation as well as the Commonwealth of Puerto Rico, the territories of Guam, and the Virgin Islands. Three states Louisiana, Mississippi and South Carolina refused to adopt the UCEA. The UCEA requires that the accused fugitive has been charged with a crime in the demanding state or jurisdiction, or has been convicted of a crime in the demanding state or either escaped confinement, or violated the terms of release on bond, probation or parole.

State Law

State law generally governs the extradition process in that specific state. The fugitive is entitled to a hearing and presentment of the alleged crime charged.

Arrest of the Fugitive

The extradition process begins with an arrest of the fugitive on a warrant, bench warrant, indictment, or information issued in the demanding state. An arrest may be made without a warrant upon reasonable information that the accused is charged in the demanding state. The criminal charge must be a felony which carries a term of imprisonment exceeding one year. Extradition is a two step process involving the executive authority (governor) and judicial authorities.

The Hearing

The fugitive may demand an extradition hearing or waive the proceedings. If the hearing is waived, the court will sign an order returning the fugitive to the demanding state. If the fugitive demands a hearing then a hearing will be conducted. The fugitive can present a defense to the extradition to wit: (1) the defendant is not the person named as the fugitive; (2) the defendant is not charged with a crime; (3) the defendant has never been to the demanding state; (4) the defendant was not in the demanding state when the alleged crime was committed; and (5) the governor's papers are not in order on their face. Extradition is a procedure which only requires a showing of probable cause in which the asylum state may ascertain whether the requisites of the Extradition Act have been complied with. The court must order the return of the fugitive to the demanding state upon finding that the fugitive (1) is the person named in the requisition; (2) is substantially charged with a crime in the demanding state; and (3) is a fugitive from justice from the demanding state. The court may base its findings based on a certified papers from the governor.

Bail

Bail is generally a slim option but in some cases it may be granted under certain conditions and stipulations.

Appeal

If the fugitive is extradited he/she can appeal the court's findings under the applicable state law governing appeals of extradition proceedings.

**IN THE _____ COURT OF _____ COUNTY
STATE OF _____**

THE STATE OF _____

       Plaintiff

VS.   **Docket No. _____**

_____,

       Defendant.

MOTION TO DISMISS FOR FAILURE TO PROSECUTE, VIOLATION OF THE SPEEDY TRIAL AND INTERSTATE AGREEMENT ON DETAINERS ACTS

TO THE HONORABLE JUDGE _____:

     COMES NOW _____, the defendant, pro se, and respectfully moves this Honorable Court to dismiss the charges because of the State's failure to prosecute, violation of the speedy trial and interstate agreement on detainers act. In support thereof, the defendant will show this Honorable Court as follows:

     1.   On _____ _____, 200__, the defendant, _____, was arrested in _____ County, and subsequently charged with _____ and __ _____. The defendant was released on bond and subsequently re-arrested by federal authorities.

     2.   The defendant has been in federal custody since_____ 200__, and the State of _____, County of _____, has known of the defendant's whereabouts at all times.

     3.   The County of _____, State of _____, has lodged a detainer against the defendant. **See Exhibit "A"** (a copy of the detainer).

     4.   On _____ _____, 200__, the defendant invoked the Interstate Agreement on Detailers Act at the _____ Institution requesting the State of _____ County of _____, to prosecute the instant charges within 180 days. Alternatively, to dismiss the charges. **See Exhibit "B"** (a copy of the Interstate Agreement of Detailers Act Request).

     A memorandum brief in support of this motion is attached hereto and made part of this motion by reference herein.

     Respectfully submitted on this ___ day of _____ 200__.

                            _____

                             Name
                             PRO SE REPRESENTATION
                             Address
                             Town, State and Zip Code

IN THE _____ COURT OF _____ COUNTY
STATE OF _____

THE STATE OF _____

        Plaintiff

VS.   **Docket No.** _____

_____,

        Defendant.

MEMORANDUM BRIEF IN SUPPORT OF MOTION TO DISMISS FOR FAILURE TO PROSECUTE, VIOLATION OF THE SPEEDY TRIAL AND INTERSTATE AGREEMENT ON DETAINERS ACTS

COMES NOW _____, the defendant, pro se, and respectfully files this memorandum brief in support of his motion to dismiss for failure to prosecute, violation of the speedy trial and interstate agreement on detainers acts. **See 18 U.S.C. Appx. Art. V(c)**.

On _____, 200__, the State of _____ County of _____, placed a detainer on the defendant. **See Exhibit "A"** attached hereto.

On _____ _____, 200__, the defendant invoked the Interstate Agreement on Detainers Act through the _____ institution. **See Exhibit "B"** attached hereto. **See also 18 U.S.C. Appx. Art III (a)**. The State of _____ County of _____, had 180 days to bring the defendant to trial. **See United States v. Mauro, 436 U.S. 340, 349-53, 98 S.Ct. 1834, 1841-44, 56 L.Ed.2d 329 (1978)**. The Act places the following burden on the government.

> **(c)** The warden, commissioner of corrections, or other official having custody of the prisoner shall promptly inform him of the source and contents of any detainer lodged against him and shall also inform him of his right to make a request for final disposition of the indictment, information, or complaint on which the detainer is based.

18 U.S.C. Appx. Art. III (c).
Once the request for trial is made, the prosecuting jurisdiction must bring the prisoner to trial within 180 days. **18 U.S.C. Appx. Art. III(a)**. Failure to do so requires that the indictment against the prisoner be dismissed. **See Mauro, supra.**

45

The State of _____, County of _____, had a continuing constitutional duty as the charging authority to provide a prompt trial. See **Dickey v. Florida, 398 U.S. 30, 37- 38, 26 L.Ed.2d 26, 90 S.Ct. 1564 (1970)** ("...the right to a prompt inquiry into criminal charges is fundamental and the duty of the charging authority is to provide a prompt trial"). See also **Strunk v. United States, 412 U.S. 434, 438 (1973).**

The Sixth Amendment guarantee of the right to a speedy trial recognizes that a prolonged delay may subject the accused to an emotional stress that can be presumed to result in the ordinary person from uncertainties in the prospect of facing public trial or of receiving a sentence longer than, or consecutive to, the one he is presently serving- uncertainties that prompt trial removes. See **Smith v. Hooey, 393 U.S , 374, 379, 21 L.Ed 607 (1969).** "[T]he possibility that the defendant already in prison might receive a sentence at least partially concurrent with the one he is serving may be forever lost if trial of the pending charge is postponed." See **Smith, 393 US at 378; Strunk v. United States, 412 U.S. 434, 37 L.Ed.2d 56, 93 S.Ct. 2260 (1973).** The Sixth Amendment guaranty of the speedy trial is made applicable to the states through the Fourteenth Amendment due process clause. See **Klopfer v. North Carolina, 386 U.S. 213, 18 L.Ed.2d 1, 87 S. Ct 988 (1967).**

The State of _____, County of _____, has failed to exercise due diligence in providing the defendant a prompt trial. Even after the defendant invoked the Interstate Agreement on Detainers Act. Therefore, the defendant is entitled to dismissal of the instant charges. See **Dickey, Strunk, Smith,** and **Mauro,** all supra.

WHEREFORE based on the foregoing the defendant, _____ urges this Honorable Court to issue an order to **DISMISS** the charges.

Respectfully submitted on this ___ day of _____ 200__.

_____
Name   Prison Number
PRO SE REPRESENTATION
Address
Town, State and Zip Code

Form Letter No. 1

Your Name & Prison Number
_____ Correctional Institution
Address
Town, State & Zip Code

[Date]

_____ Court
Clerk of the Court
Address
Town, State & Zip Code

Re:_____ v. _____,
    Case Number _____

Dear Judge:

This letter is in reference to the above entitled action. At this time, I am requesting a final disposition of the above entitled action. This case has been pending since _____ and the State of _____, County of _____ has taken no action whatsoever on the matter. Therefore, I am requesting a final disposition of this case as soon as possible.

Sincerely,

_____
[Your Name]

CC:
    Assistant District Attorney, _____
    _____ Sheriff
    p/file.

IN THE _____ COURT OF _____ COUNTY

STATE OF _____

THE STATE OF _____

               Plaintiff

VS.   **Docket No.** _____

_____,

               Defendant.

MOTION FOR A FAST AND SPEEDY TRIAL

TO THE HONORABLE JUDGE _____:

      COMES NOW _____, the defendant, pro se, and respectfully moves this Honorable Court for a fast and speedy trial pursuant to _____ § _____; the Sixth and Fourteenth Amendments of the United States Constitution. In support thereof, the defendant will show this Honorable Court as follows:

      1.   On _____ _____, 200__, the defendant, _____, was arrested in _____ County, and subsequently charged with _____ and _____. The defendant was released on bond and subsequently re-arrested by federal authorities.

      2.   The defendant has been in federal custody since_____ 200__, and the State of _____, County of _____, has known of the defendant's whereabouts at all times.

      3.   The County of _____, State of _____, has lodged a detainer against the defendant. **See Exhibit "A"** (a copy of the detainer).

      4.   The defendant,_____, hereby moves this Court for a fast and speedy trial pursuant to _____ § _____, or in the alternative for dismissal of the charges.

      A memorandum brief in support of this motion is attached hereto and made part of this motion by reference herein.

      Respectfully submitted on this ___ day of _____ 200__.

_____
Name   Prison Number
PRO SE REPRESENTATION
Address
Town, State and Zip Code

IN THE _____ COURT OF _____ COUNTY
STATE OF _____

THE STATE OF _____

Plaintiff

VS.   **Docket No. _____**

_____,

Defendant.

MEMORANDUM BRIEF IN SUPPORT OF MOTION
FOR FAST AND SPEEDY TRIAL

TO THE HONORABLE JUDGE _____ :

COMES NOW _____, the defendant, pro se, and respectfully files this memorandum brief in support of his motion for a fast and speedy trial pursuant to _____ § _____. On _____, 200__, the defendant _____, was arrested in the County of _____ State of _____, and subsequently charged with _____ and _____.

The defendant, _____, hereby demands a fast and speedy trial pursuant to _____ § _____; and the Sixth and Fourteenth Amendments. Alternatively, the defendant moves this Honorable Court for an order dismissing the charges. The Sixth Amendment guaranty of speedy trial is applicable to the states through the Fourteenth Amendment's due process clause. **See <u>Dickey v. Florida</u>, 398 U.S. 30, 37, 26 L.Ed.2d 26, 31-32, 90 S.Ct. 1564 (1970).**

The Sixth Amendment of the United States Constitution provides that: "In all criminal prosecutions, the accused shall enjoy the right to a speedy trial and public trial, by an impartial jury of the State and district wherein the crime shall have been committed, which shall have previously ascertained by law, and to be informed of the nature and cause of the accusation; to be confronted with witnesses against him; to have compulsory process for obtaining witnesses in his favor, and to have the Assistance of Counsel for his defence." **See <u>Barker v. Wingo</u>, 407 U.S. 574, 92 S.Ct. 2182, 33 L.Ed.2d 101 (1972).**

An accused's right to a prompt inquiry into criminal charges is fundamental and the duty of the charging authority is to provide a prompt trial. **See <u>Strunk v. United States</u>, 412 U.S. 434, 436-37, 37 L.Ed.2d 56, 93 S.Ct. 2260 (1973).** The Sixth Amendment guarantee of the right to a speedy trial recognizes that a prolonged delay may subject the accused to an emotional stress that can be presumed to result in the ordinary person from uncertainties in the prospect of facing public trial or of receiving a sentence longer than, or consecutive to, the one he is presently serving–uncertainties that a prompt trial removes. **<u>Strunk</u>, 412 U.S. at 439; <u>Smith v. Hooey</u>, 393 U.S. 374, 379, 21 L.Ed.2d 607, 89 S.Ct. 575 (1969)** ("the possibility that the defendant already in

49

prison might receive a sentence at least partially concurrent with the one he is serving may be forever lost if trial of the pending charge is postponed").

In light of the policies which underlie the right to a speedy trial, dismissal of the charges is the proper remedy. **See <u>Strunk</u>, 312 U.S. at 440; <u>Barker</u>, 407 U.S. at 522**.

WHEREFORE based on the above,_____, urges this Honorable Court to **GRANT** this motion and schedule this case for a fast and speedy trial, or in the alternative **DISMISS** the charges.

Respectfully submitted on this ____ day of _____ 200__.

_____

Name   Prison Number
PRO SE REPRESENTATION
Address
Town, State and Zip Code

[CAPTION]

MOTION TO REINSTATE PROBATION

TO THE HONORABLE JUDGE OF SAID COURT:

    COME NOW _____, the defendant, pro se, and respectfully moves this Honorable Court to reinstate probation, in this cause. The defendant will show this Court as follows:

    1.   On _____ ____, 20____, this Court sentenced the defendant to: _____ (__) years Probation.

    2.   On _____ ____, 20____, the State of _____, County of _____, filed a Motion for revocation of probation for ____ technical violations. The ____ violations were as follows:

[State the violations charged].

    3.   The Defendant has been in federal custody since _____ 20____, serving a federal _____ month sentence. The State of _____, County of _____, has known of the defendant's whereabouts since _____ 20____.

    4.   The Defendant has attempted to resolve the instant revocation of probation on numerous occasions without any success. The Defendant will be released on _____ ____, 20____, to serve a _____ (__) year term of federal supervised release.

    5.   The Defendant had to be placed in a higher federal security prison because of the warrant for the technical violations. While placing the defendant in a higher security prison because of the instant detainer is not punishment in and of itself it has had a bearing on the Defendant.

    6.   The Defendant moves this Honorable Court to reinstate probation and provide him with an opportunity to complete the _____ years probation. The Defendant moves this Court to order that the violation of probation warrant for his arrest be dismissed and his probation reinstated to be completed upon his release from federal prison. The Defendant will report into the State of _____, County of _____, Probation Department within 72 hours upon release from federal prison.

    WHEREFORE based on the above, _____ , urges this Honorable Court to issue an order reinstating the probation and dismissing/withdrawing the warrant for his arrest and allow him the opportunity to report into the State of _____, County of _____, Probation Department within 72 hours upon his release from federal prison.

    Respectfully submitted on this ____ day of _____ 200__.

                            Name   Prison Number

                          PRO SE REPRESENTATION

                                     Address

                            Town, State and Zip Code

Form Letter No. 2

Your Name & Prison Number
_____ Correctional Institution
Address
Town, State & Zip Code

[Date]

_____ COUNTY COURT
OFFICE OF THE CLERK
Address
Town, State, & Zip Code

Re: The State of _____ v. _____,
       Case No. _____

Dear Clerk:

Please find enclosed the original and one copy of my: PLEA IN ABSENTIA WITH A WAIVER OF RIGHTS, for filing with the Court.

Your assistance on this matter is greatly appreciated. Thank you.

Sincerely,

_____
Your Name

CC:

    p/file.

THE STATE OF _____   _____ **COUNTY**

VS.   **Docket No.** _____

_____ ,

      Defendant.

GUILTY PLEA IN ABSENTIA WITH A WAIVER OF RIGHTS

THE HONORABLE JUDGE OF SAID COURT:

    COME NOW _____, the defendant, pro se, and respectfully enters a guilty plea in absentia to: "Failure to stop at accident causing minor damage."

FACTUAL BASIS FOR PLEA

    The defendant states that the facts for a factual basis for the plea are: "I, _____, was backing my vehicle out of my driveway and bumped into the back of the neighbor's vehicle. I got out of my vehicle and looked at both vehicles and noticed a small crack in the neighbor's tail light." I then got back into my vehicle and went to the store. I was subsequently arrested and charged with "Failure to stop at accident causing minor damage." The defendant made bond. This Court has set a Court date, NOTICE OF TRIAL FOR _____ ____, 200___, at _____:00 AM, requiring the defendant's presence. The defendant is currently incarcerated by federal authorities at the Federal Correctional Institution, _____, _____, _____ serving a _____ month term of imprisonment making it impossible for the defendant to appear. Therefore, the defendant requests to enter a Guilty Plea In Absentia With A Waiver of Rights to resolve this cause.

WAIVER OF RIGHT TO BE PRESENT

    I, _____, state that I make this plea in absentia knowingly, voluntarily, and intelligently, and hereby waive my rights to be present and to have counsel.

SENTENCE RECOMMENDATION

    The defendant, _____, moves this Honorable Court to impose a jail sentence of _____ to be served concurrently with his federal sentence. Alternatively, impose a _____ term of probation and a fine of $_____.

    WHEREFORE, based on the above, _____, urges this Honorable Court to grant this motion and allow him to enter into this Guilty Plea in Absentia to resolve this matter and to impose sentence according to defendant's sentence recommendation.

_____

Your Name   Prison Number
PRO SE REPRESENTATION
Address
Town, State and Zip Code

STATE OF TENNESSEE   _____ **COUNTY**

VS.   **GENERAL SESSIONS COURT**

_____   **Docket No.** _____

ORDER AND JUDGMENT

The defendant _____, plea in absentia with a waiver of rights came before this Court this date seeking final disposition of "Failure to stop at accident causing minor damages." The Court finds that said pleadings should be granted. The defendant _____, is sentenced to a six month jail sentence to be served concurrently and coterminous with his federal sentence.

IT IS HEREBY ORDERED that the defendant _____ is sentenced to _____ days in jail to be served concurrently with his federal sentence he is currently serving. The Clerk of this Court is directed to close this case.

Thus, done in chambers on this ____ day of _____, 20 ____.

_____
General Sessions Judge

IN THE _____ COURT OF _____ COUNTY

STATE OF _____

_____

THE STATE OF _____ ,

Respondent,

VS.   Docket No. _____

_____ ,

Defendant.

_____

MOTION TO TERMINATE PROBATION
AS UNSATISFACTORILY COMPLETED

_____

TO THE HONORABLE JUDGE OF SAID COURT:

  COMES NOW _____ the defendant, pro se, and respectfully moves this Honorable Court to terminate probation as unsatisfactorily completed. In support thereof, defendant avers:

I.
STATEMENT OF THE FACTS

  1. On _____ ____, 200___, the defendant was arrested by the _____ County Sheriff's Department and charged with _____ .

  2. On _____ ____, 200___, the defendant appeared before this Court with counsel and entered a guilty plea to a criminal charge of _____ and this Court imposed a ____ year term of probation and a $_____ fine.

  3. The defendant has paid the $_____ fine and served a year and a half of the term of probation.

  4. On _____ ____, 200___, the defendant was arrested by federal authorities and charged with _____ .

  5. On _____ ____, 200___, the defendant pled guilty in federal court. On _____ ____, 200___, the United States District Court for the _____ District of _____ imposed a _____ month term of imprisonment to be followed by a ____ year term of supervised release.

  A more precise set of facts are set forth throughout this motion.

II.
THE TERM OF PROBATION EXPIRED

The defendant submits that the _____ year term of probation has expired and should be terminated. Nevertheless, because of the defendant's conduct stated in ¶¶4-5 the probation should be terminated on the grounds of unsatisfactorily completed. The State of _____ has stated that it does not intend on revoking the defendant's probation.

WHEREFORE based on the above, (defendant's name), respectfully moves this Honorable Court to grant this motion and to terminate the probation.

Respectfully submitted on this ____ day of _____ 200__.

_____

Name   Prison Number
PRO SE REPRESENTATION
Address
Town, State and Zip Code

STATE OF _____

_____ **COUNTY**

SWORN AND SUBSCRIBED TO BEFORE me the undersigned, a person known to be _____, who swears and declares under penalty of perjury pursuant to 28 U.S.C. §1746 that he has read the above document and that the facts stated therein are true and correct.

Executed on this _____ day of _____, 200____.

_____
Notary Public

IN THE _____ **COURT OF** _____ **COUNTY**

STATE OF _____

THE STATE OF _____ ,

        Respondent,

VS.   **Docket No.** _____

_____ ,

        Defendant.

ORDER AND JUDGMENT

The matter of <u>(defendant's name)</u>, Motion to terminate probation as unsatisfactorily completed is currently pending before this Court and came under consideration on this date. This Court finds that the motion should be **GRANTED**.

IT IS HEREBY ORDERED that the ____ year term of probation is terminated. The Clerk of this Court is directed to close this case.

Thus, done on this ____ day of _____ , 200___ .

_____
Presiding Judge

IN THE _____ COURT OF _____ COUNTY

STATE OF _____

THE STATE OF _____,

        Respondent,

VS.   **Docket No.** _____

_____,

        Defendant.

MOTION TO REVOKE PROBATION AND
IMPOSE SENTENCE IN ABSENTIA

TO THE HONORABLE JUDGE OF SAID COURT:

COMES NOW _____, the defendant, pro se, and respectfully moves this Honorable Court to revoke probation and impose sentence in absentia to be served concurrently with the federal term of imprisonment in **United States v.** _____, **Case No.** _____ ( ). In support thereof, defendant avers:

I.
STATEMENT OF THE FACTS

1.   On _____ ____, 200____, the defendant was arrested by the _____ County Sheriff's Department and charged with _____.

2.   On _____ ____, 200____, the defendant appeared before this Court with counsel and entered a guilty plea to a criminal charge of _____ and this Court imposed a ____ year term of probation and a $_____ fine.

3.   The defendant has paid the $_____ fine and served a year and a half of the term of probation.

4.   On _____ ____, 200____, the defendant was arrested by federal authorities and charged with _____.

5.   On _____ ____, 200____, the defendant pled guilty in federal court. On _____ ____, 200____, the United States District Court for the _____ District of _____ imposed a _____ month term of imprisonment to be followed by a ____ year term of supervised release.

A more precise set of facts are set forth throughout this motion.

II.
<u>REVOCATION OF PROBATION</u>

The defendant submits that his conduct stated in ¶¶4 and 5 violates the terms and conditions of his probation. Therefore, this Court should make a finding of fact that the defendant violated the terms of his probation.

III.
<u>WAIVER OF THE RIGHT TO BE PRESENT</u>

The defendant hereby knowingly, voluntarily, and intelligently waives his right to be present at the revocation and sentencing hearings provided that this Court orders the term of imprisonment to be served concurrently with the federal sentence imposed in **United States v.** _____, **Case No.** _____ ( ).

IV.
<u>IMPOSE SENTENCE IN ABSENTIA</u>

The defendant hereby moves this Court to impose sentence in absentia to be served concurrently with the _____ month term of imprisonment in **United States v.** _____ _____, **Case No.** _____ ( ).

WHEREFORE based on the above, (defendant's name), respectfully moves this Honorable Court to grant this motion, revoke the probation and impose sentence in absentia to be served concurrently with the term of imprisonment imposed in the matter of **United States v.** _____, **Case No.** _____ ( ), commencing on _____ the date that the federal sentence was imposed.

Respectfully submitted on this _____ day of _____, 200____.

_____
PRO SE REPRESENTATION

STATE OF _____

_____ COUNTY

SWORN AND SUBSCRIBED TO BEFORE me the undersigned, a person known to be _____, who swears and declares under penalty of perjury pursuant to 28 U.S.C. §1746 that he has read the above document and that the facts stated therein are true and correct.

Executed on this _____ day of _____, 200____.

_____
Notary Public

IN THE _____ COURT OF _____ COUNTY

STATE OF _____

THE STATE OF _____,

        Respondent,

VS.   **Docket No. _____**

_____,

        Defendant.

ORDER AND JUDGMENT

The matter of, <u>(defendant's name)</u>, Motion to revoke probation and to impose sentence in absentia to be served concurrently with the federal term of imprisonment in **United States v. _____, Case No. _____ ( ),** is currently pending before this Court and came under consideration on this date. This Court finds that the motion should be **GRANTED.**

IT IS HEREBY ORDERED that the _____ year term of probation is revoked and that a _____ term of imprisonment is imposed to be served concurrently with the federal sentence in **United States v. _____, Case No. _____ ( ),** commencing on the _____ day of _____, 200____, the same date that the federal sentence was imposed.

Thus, done on this _____ day of _____, 200____.

_____
Presiding Judge

Form Letter No. 3

Your Name & Prison Number
Prison Institution
Address
Town, State & Zip Code

Date

Prosecutor Name_____
_____DISTRICT ATTORNEY
Address_____
Town, State, & Zip Code

Re: _____ v. _____
       Case No. _____

Dear Mr. _____

This letter is in reference to the above entitled action. At this time, I am requesting for a final resolution of this matter. Please advise me of the State's position on the case. I plead guilty to Counts 1 and 7 with an agreement to: No more than one year county jail with felony probation. However, when the state probation department got through the one year county jail become two years county jail and I filed a motion to withdraw the guilty plea. Subsequently, I failed to appear at the withdrawal of the plea hearing and a warrant was issued for my arrest.

A final resolution in this matter will save judicial resources and clear the Court's crowded docket. I am currently serving a ____ month federal term of imprisonment without parole and a ____ year term of supervised release.

I am requesting for a final resolution of this case and willing to make restitution. Please advise me of the State's position on this matter.

Your consideration on this matter will be greatly appreciated.

Sincerely,

_____
Your Name

CC:

p/file.

Form Letter No. 4

Your Name & Prison Number
Prison Institution
Address
Town, State & Zip Code

Date

Prosecutor Name_____
_____DISTRICT ATTORNEY
Address_____
Town, State, & Zip Code

Re: _____ v. _____
     Case No. _____

Dear Mr. _____

    This is my second letter to you requesting to resolve the above entitled action. On _____ ____, 200____ I mailed you the first letter. As of this date, I have not heard from you nor your office.

    Once again, I am requesting to resolve this matter and to know the State's position. Resolving this matter will save the State judicial resources and clear the court's docket. The State initially offered me one year in the county jail with a felony probation. I accepted the State's offer in good faith. The State breached its plea offer through the Presentence Report by attempting to have the court impose a two year county jail sentence instead of the one year county jail sentence, which forced me to file a motion to withdraw my guilty plea.

    I am requesting to hear from your office on this matter within the next twenty working days. In the event that you or you office fail to respond to this request I will be forced to do the following:

1. File a motion for sentence in absentia;

2. File a motion for specific performance of the plea;

3. File a motion to relieve counsel of his duties because of a conflict of interest; and a notice of appearance through self-representation; and

4. File a writ of habeas corpus ad testificant and ad prosequendum.

Your consideration on this matter will be greatly appreciated. Thank you.

                Sincerely,

                _____
                Your Name

CC:

    p/file.

IN THE _____ COURT OF _____ COUNTY
FOR THE STATE OF _____

_____

THE STATE OF _____,

VS.   Docket No. _____

_____,

Defendant-Petitioner

_____

PETITION FOR WRIT OF HABEAS CORPUS
AD TESTIFICANT AND AD PROSEQUENDUM

_____

IN THE MATTER OF THE APPLICATION OF _____, THE DEFENDANT FOR WRIT OF HABEAS CORPUS AD TESTIFICANT AND AD PROSEQUENDUM TO WARDEN _____ AT THE FEDERAL CORRECTIONASL INSTITUTION ___, _____, TO PRODUCE ONE, _____, UPON THE TRIAL/SENTENCE OF THE ABOVE ENTITLED ACTION.

TO THE HONORABLE JUDGE OF THE _____ COURT:

_____, pro se, and respectfully shows:

1. _____, is the defendant in this criminal action.

2. There is now pending in the _____ Court of _____ County, _____, a criminal action against the above named defendant, who is charged with crimes of _____.

3. The defendant's presence is required so he can present his defense to the crime charged.

4. The testimony of one _____ is material and necessary on the trail of the indictment, as your petitioner believes.

5. The said _____ is now confined at the Federal Correctional Institution, _____, _____, _____.

6. The above-entitled criminal action against _____ is noticed for a hearing at the said _____ Court of _____ County, _____, for the ____ day of _____, 200___.

7. No previous application has been made for a Writ of Habeas Corpus ad testificant or ad prosequendum herein.

WHEREFORE, I ask that a Writ of Habeas Corpus ad testificant or ad prosequendum issue out of this Honorable Court to the Warden of the Federal Correctional Institution, ____, _____, to: produce the said _____, at the aforesaid Court.

Respectfully submitted on this ____ day of _____, 20 ____.

_____ ____

Name   Prison Number

PRO SE REPRESENTATION

Address

Town, State and Zip Code

IN THE _____ COURT OF _____ COUNTY
FOR THE STATE OF _____

THE STATE OF _____,

VS.   Docket No. _____

_____,

Defendant.

MOTION TO RELIEVE APPOINTED COUNSEL OF HIS DUTIES BECAUSE OF A CONFLICT OF INTEREST

TO THE HONORABLE JUDGE OF THE _____ COURT:

COMES NOW _____, the defendant, pro se, and respectfully moves this Honorable Court to relieve appointed counsel, _____, of his duties because of a conflict of interest. The defendant will show this Court as follows:

1.   The Defendant filed a motion to withdraw his guilty plea based on breach of plea. Appointed counsel _____ will become a witness on Mr. _____'s behalf, or a witness against Mr. _____. Either way would require that appointed counsel _____ withdraw from the case because of a conflict of interest. Therefore, this motion should be granted.

2.   The Defendant submits that, if counsel _____ disputes Mr. _____'s facts then he represents conflicting interest, and if he agrees with Mr. _____'s facts then he failed to perform his official duties constituting ineffective assistance of counsel.

WHEREFORE based on the above, _____, urges this Court to grant this motion and relieve counsel _____ of his duties.

Respectfully submitted on this ____ day of _____, 20 ____.

_____
PRO SE REPRESENTATION

64

IN THE _____ COURT OF _____ COUNTY
FOR THE STATE OF _____

THE STATE OF _____,

VS.   Docket No. _____

_____,

Defendant.

NOTICE OF APPEARANCE

TO THE HONORABLE JUDGE OF THE _____ COURT:

COMES NOW _____, the defendant, pro se, and respectfully files notice of appearance. The defendant hereby places all parties on notice that he exercises his Sixth and Fourteenth Amendment rights to self-representation pursuant to **Farrett v. California, 422 U.S. 806, 45 L.Ed.2d 562, 95 S.Ct. 2525 (1975)**, and will appear herein through pro se representation.

Respectfully submitted on this ____ day of _____, 20 ____.

_____
PRO SE REPRESENTATION

IN THE _____ COURT OF _____ COUNTY
FOR THE STATE OF _____

THE STATE OF _____,

VS.   Docket No. _____

_____,

Defendant.

MOTION TO ENFORCE TERMS OF PLEA AGREEMENT

TO THE HONORABLE JUDGE OF THE _____ COURT:

COMES NOW _____, the defendant, pro se, and respectfully moves this Court to enforce terms of plea agreement. The Defendant will show this Honorable Court as follows:

I.
<u>STATEMENT OF THE FACTS</u>

1.   On _____ ____, 200 ____, Mr. _____ was arrested and charged with _____ counts of _____ in the above entitled action.

2.   On _____ ____, 200 ____, Mr. _____ posted a $_____ bond and was released from custody.

3.   On _____ ____, 200 ____, Mr. _____ entered into a plea agreement with the State on ____ counts of _____ before a magistrate judge in _____, _____, for ____ year in the county jail with a felony probation.

4.   In _____, 200 ____ Mr. _____ expressed his desire to withdraw his plea before the honorable judge of the _____ Court of _____ County because the State of _____ failed to honor its plea agreement. The State attempted to raise the ____ year county jail to _____ years county jail, which forced Mr. _____ to move to withdraw his plea. Said judge scheduled a hearing for _____ ____, 200 ____ before a magistrate judge for the withdrawal of Mr. _____ plea.

5.   On _____ ____, 200 ____, Mr. _____ failed to appear in the lower court for the hearing on withdrawal of his plea. Consequently, the lower court issued a bench warrant for the arrest of Mr. _____.

6.   On _____ ____, 200 ____, Mr. _____ was arrested by the _____ Police Department for being a fugitive from justice from _____ County, _____. The _____ Police Department and court officials at the arraigning courthouse repeatedly contacted the _____ County Prosecutor's Office, requesting extradition of Mr. _____. The _____ County Prosecutor's Office did not respond.

7. On _____ ____, 200 ____, Mr. _____ was sentenced to a term of ____ months imprisonment in federal prison. See **Exhibit "A"** (Federal Judgment and Commitment order).

8. In _____, 200 ____, the Federal Bureau of Prisons officials at the Federal Correctional Institution _____ contacted the _____ County Prosecutor's Office attempting to resolve Mr. _____'s pending charges. The _____ County Prosecutor's Office declined to extradite, preventing resolution of this matter.

II.
TERMS OF PLEA AGREEMENT

The terms of the plea agreement as explained to Mr. _____ by counsel. Mr. _____ would plead guilty to counts ____ and ____ and the remainder of the counts would be dismissed at sentencing. Mr. _____ faced no more than ____ (__) year in the county jail, with a felony probation to follow. See REGISTER OF ACTIONS/DOCKET Page ___ and ___.

III.
STATE'S BREACH OF TERMS OF PLEA AGREEMENT

The State of _____ through the Presentence Report attempted to breach the terms of the plea agreement by recommending that Mr. _____ receive ____ (__) years in the county jail. This type of action violates the terms of the plea. See REGISTER OF ACTIONS/DOCKET Pages ___ and ___.

Mr. _____ urges this Court to issue an order enforcing the terms of the plea agreement. This Court should impose a sentence of ____ (__) year in the county jail, with a felony probation, to be served concurrently with the federally imposed sentence in **Exhibit "A"**.

A memorandum brief in support of this motion is attached hereto and made part of this motion herein.

Respectfully submitted on this ____ day of _____, 20 ____.

_____
PRO SE REPRESENTATION

IN THE _____ COURT OF _____ COUNTY
FOR THE STATE OF _____

THE STATE OF _____,

VS.   **Docket No. _____**

_____,

   Defendant.

MEMORANDUM BRIEF IN SUPPORT OF
MOTION TO ENFORCE TERMS OF PLEA AGREEMENT

TO THE HONORABLE JUDGE OF THE _____ COURT:

The defendant, _____, respectfully files this Memorandum Brief in support of motion to enforce terms of plea agreement.

TERMS OF PLEA AGREEMENT

The terms of the plea offer required Mr. _____ to plead guilty to counts ___ and ___ and he would be sentenced to: no more than ___ year in the county jail, with a felony probation. See REGISTER OF ACTIONS/DOCKET at Pages ___ and ___. The agreement that Mr. _____ would waive his constitutional rights in exchange for: No more than ___ (___) year in the county jail with a felony probation which was accepted and final the moment that the magistrate judge made the requisite factual findings and accepted the plea. **See _____ Penal Code §_____.** In **Brown v. Poole, 337 F.3d 1155, 1159 (9th Cir. 2003),** the court explained that: "The terms of oral plea agreements are enforceable, as are those of any other contracts, even though oral plea agreements are not encouraged by reviewing courts." **Id. See also e.g., United States v. Monreal, 301 F.3d 1127, 1133 (9th Cir. 2002).**

Mr. _____ due process rights conferred by the federal constitution allow him to enforce the terms of the plea agreement. **See Santobello v. New York, 404 U.S. 257, 262, 92 S.Ct. 495, 30 L.Ed.2d 427 (1971)** ("[W]hen a plea rests in any significant degree on a promise or agreement of the prosecutor, so that it can be said to be a part of the inducement or consideration, such promise must be fulfilled."); see also **United States v. Hallam, 472 F.2d 168, 169 (9th Cir. 1973)** ("It is clear from **Santobello** . . . that due respect for the integrity of plea bargains demands that once a defendant has carried out his part of the bargain the Government [State of _____] must fulfill its part.").

THE BREACH OF PLEA AGREEMENT

Mr. _____ argues that the terms of the plea offer were breached by the State of _____ when it recommended through the Presentence Report to the Court to impose a sentence of _____ (___) years in the county jail, with a felony probation. **See United States v. Boatner, 966 F.2d 1575, 1580 (11th Cir. 1992).** This is the sole reason that Mr. _____ sought to withdraw his plea. See REGISTER OF ACTIONS/DOCKET at Page _____.

ENFORCEMENT OF PLEA AGREEMENT TERMS

There are two remedies available to rectify the government's breach of its plea agreement. **Santobello, 404 U.S. at 263, 92 S.Ct. at 499.** Because Mr. _____ is entitled to specific performance of the agreement, this Court should impose a sentence of: **no more than one year in the county jail, with a felony probation. See United States v. Tobon-Hernandez, 845 F.2d 277, 280 (11th Cir. 1988) (citing Santobello, 404 U.S. at 263.** Additionally, the court may permit Mr. _____ to withdraw his plea. The choice of remedies lies within this Court's discretion. **Tobon-Hernandez, 845 F.2d at 281.** Mr. _____ requests specific performance which is justified by the fact that he entered into his plea agreement freely and intelligently, and adhered to his part of the bargain.

WHEREFORE, PREMISES CONSIDERED, Mr. _____ urges this Court to enforce the terms of the plea agreement and impose a sentence of: **no more than one year in the county jail, with a felony probation.** Additionally, Mr. _____ requests that this Court order that sentence to be served concurrent with the federal sentence imposed in **Exhibit "A".**

Respectfully submitted on this _____ day of _____, 20 ____.

_____
PRO SE REPRESENTATION

IN THE _____ **COURT OF** _____ **COUNTY**
FOR THE STATE OF _____

THE STATE OF _____ ,

VS.   **Docket No.** _____

_____ ,

     Defendant.

MOTION TO IMPOSE SENTENCE IN ABSENTIA

TO THE HONORABLE JUDGE OF THE _____ **COURT:**

    COMES NOW _____ , the defendant, pro se, and respectfully moves this Court to impose sentence in absentia. The Defendant will show this Honorable Court as follows.

I.
STATEMENT OF THE FACTS

    1.   On _____ ____, 200 ____, Mr. _____ was arrested and charged with _____ counts of _____ in the above entitled action.

    2.   On _____ ____, 200 ____, Mr. _____ posted a $_____ bond and was released from custody.

    3.   On _____ ____, 200 ____, Mr. _____ entered into a plea agreement with the State on ____ counts of _____ before a magistrate judge in _____, _____, for ____ year in the county jail with a felony probation.

    4.   In _____, 200 ____ Mr. _____ expressed his desire to withdraw his plea before the honorable judge of the _____ Court of _____ County because the State of _____ failed to honor its plea agreement. The State attempted to raise the ____ year county jail to _____ years county jail, which forced Mr. _____ to move to withdraw his plea. Said judge scheduled a hearing for _____ ____, 200 ____ before a magistrate judge for the withdrawal of Mr. _____ plea.

    5.   On _____ ____, 200 ____, Mr. _____ failed to appear in the lower court for the hearing on withdrawal of his plea. Consequently, the lower court issued a bench warrant for the arrest of Mr. _____.

    6.   On _____ ____, 200 ____, Mr. _____ was arrested by the _____ Police Department for being a fugitive from justice from _____ County, _____. The _____ Police Department and court officials at the arraigning courthouse repeatedly contacted the _____ County Prosecutor's Office, requesting extradition of Mr. _____. The _____ County Prosecutor's Office did not respond.

70

7.	On _____ ____, 200 ____, Mr. _____ was sentenced to a term of ____ months imprisonment in federal prison. See **Exhibit "A"** Federal Judgment and Commitment order.

8.	In _____, 200 ____, the Federal Bureau of Prisons officials at the Federal Correctional Institution _____ contacted the _____ County Prosecutor's Office attempting to resolve Mr. _____'s pending charges. The _____ County Prosecutor's Office declined to extradite, preventing resolution of this matter.

II.
WAIVER OF THE RIGHT TO BE PRESENT
AND
WAIVER OF RIGHT TO COUNSEL

The Defendant, _____, hereby knowingly, voluntarily, and intelligently waives his right to be present during sentencing and waives his right to counsel, provided the Court imposes sentence in accordance with the plea agreement to one year in the county jail, with a felony probation, to be served concurrently with the federal sentence already imposed.

WHEREFORE, PREMISES CONSIDERED, Mr. _____ urges this Court to impose sentence in absentia to the one year county jail, with a felony probation to be served currently with the federal sentence already imposed in **Exhibit "A"**.

Respectfully submitted on this ____ day of _____, 20 ____.

_____
PRO SE REPRESENTATION

Form Letter No. 5

Your Name & Prison Number
Federal Correctional Institution
Address
Town, State & Zip Code

Date

Pardon & Parole Board
Address
Town, State & Zip Code

Re: Detainer For Parole Violation
       Your Name & DCO# _____

Dear Pardons & Parole Board

      This letter is in reference to the above detainer that has been lodged against me based on a Parole Revocation warrant issued by your agency. A parole violation warrant was issued against me for absconding.

      On _____ ____, 20 ____, I complete the federal term of imprisonment and will be released to a _____ (___) year of supervised release. While on federal supervised release I will be drug tested twice a week and have to attend drug classes (AA & NA), work a regular job, and comply with the Probation Officer's requirements.

      At this time, I would respectfully request that your agency reinstate my parole so that I can serve it along with the _____ year term of supervised release. I plan on returning to _____, _____, (_____ County), when I am released by the federal government so that I can be close to my family and kids. I ask that your agency reinstate the parole and lift its detainer against me as soon as possible. I will be released from federal supervised release on 20___, while I discharge the _____ Parole in 20___. Therefore, I request that the Parole Board reinstate my parole.

      Your assistance on this matter is greatly appreciated. Thank you.

Sincerely,

_____
Your Name

CC:

      p/file.

Form Letter No. 6

Your Name & Prison Number
Federal Correctional Institution
Address
Town, State & Zip Code

Date

Pardon & Parole Board
Address
Town, State & Zip Code

Re: Detainer For Parole Violation
         Your Name & DCO# _____

Dear Pardons & Parole Board

     This letter is in reference to the above detainer that has been lodged against me based on a Parole Revocation warrant issued by your agency. A parole violation warrant was issued against me for absconding.

     On _____ ____, 20 ____, I complete the federal term of imprisonment and will be released to a _____ (___) year of supervised release. While on federal supervised release I will be drug tested twice a week and have to attend drug classes (AA & NA), work a regular job, and comply with the Probation Officer's requirements.

     At this time, I would respectfully request that your agency revoke my parole and order that it be served concurrently with the federal term imprisonment that I am currently serving. I plan on returning to _____, _____, (_____ County), when I am released by the federal government so that I can be close to my family and kids. I ask that your agency revoke the _____ parole and order it to be served concurrently with the federal term of imprisonment. This will provide me with the opportunity to assist my kids and family who are now struggling because of my mistakes related to this case.

     Your assistance on this matter is greatly appreciated. Thank you.

Sincerely,

_____
Your Name

CC:

     p/file.

73

[Caption]

MOTION FOR APPOINTMENT OF COUNSEL

TO THE HONORABLE JUDGE OF SAID COURT:

      COMES NOW _____, the defendant, pro se, and respectfully moves this Honorable Court pursuant to the Sixth and Fourteenth Amendments of the United States Constitution to appoint counsel to represent him in this above entitled action. The defendant _____ will show this Honorable Court as follows:

      1.   The State of _____ has charged the defendant with _____ and _____ and the defendant faces a possible _____ term of imprisonment if convicted.

      2.   The defendant, _____, is currently serving a _____ term of imprisonment and housed at _____ Federal Correctional Institution. The State of _____ has lodged a detainer against the defendant for the above charges. **See Exhibit "____".**

      3.   The defendant has filed an Interstate Agreement on Detainers Act requesting final disposition of the instant charges and seeks appointment of counsel to prepare for trial in this matter. **See Exhibit "____".**

      4.   The defendant _____, has no funds to retain counsel and has been in the federal prison system for _____ years. The defendant was appointed counsel in the federal system because of his indigence. The defendant, _____, still remains in the in forma pauperis status and request counsel.

      WHEREFORE based on the above, _____, urges this Honorable Court to appoint counsel to represent him on the entitled action.

      Respectfully submitted on this _____ day of _____, 200 _____.

                                _____

                                PRO SE REPRESENTATION
                                Address
                                Town, State & Zip Code

Form Letter No. 7

INMATE REQUEST TO STAFF

FEDERAL BUREAU OF PRISONS

TO: Warden   DATE: 11/20/2010

FROM: John A. Doe   REGISTER NO.: 99999-997

WORK ASSIGNMENT: LAW LIBRARY   UNIT: CA

SUBJECT: (State briefly your question and the solution you're requesting).

I am requesting to invoke the Interstate Agreement on Detainers Act on the two detainers that has been lodged against me from Atlanta, Georgia and Miami, Florida, through your office or the Records Office. Your assistance on this matter is greatly appreciated. Thank you.

Form Letter No. 8

Your Name & Prison Number
Federal Correctional Institution
Address
Town, State & Zip Code

Date

Mr. _____
Assistant District Attorney
___rd Judicial District
P.O. Box _____

_____, _____

Re: State of Tennessee v. _____
        Docket No. _____

Dear Mr. _____:

      Please find enclosed a "Plea In Absentia with a Waiver of Rights" that I propose to resolve the March 3, 3000, "Revocation of Probation" for Driving on Suspended License.

      I seek the assistance of you or your office to resolve this matter. If this matter can be resolved in this manner, then I would request for you or your office to approve this "Plea In Absentia with a Waiver of Rights," or to make any changes to the document necessary for approval. This DWLS has been hanging over my head for nine years. I do not intend on coming back to the State of Tennessee unless I am just passing through.

      I would like to file the proposed "Plea In Absentia with a Waiver of Rights" within the next thirty days.

      Your assistance on this matter is greatly appreciated. Thank you.

Sincerely,

_____
Your Name

CC:

      p/file.

INTERSTATE AGREEMENT ON DETAINERS ACT

Title 18 United States Code, Appendix 2 provides:

Sec. 1. This Act may be cited as the "Interstate Agreement on Detainers Act."

Sec. 2. The Interstate Agreement on Detainers is hereby enacted into law and entered into by the United States on its own behalf and on behalf of the District of Columbia with all jurisdictions legally joining in substantially the following form:

"The contracting States solemnly agree that:

"Article I

"The party States find that charges outstanding against a prisoner, detainers based on untried indictments, informations, or complaints and difficulties in securing speedy trial of persons already incarcerated in other jurisdictions, produce uncertainties which obstruct programs of prisoner treatment and rehabilitation. Accordingly, it is the policy of the party States and the purpose of this agreement to encourage the expeditious and orderly disposition of such charges and determination of the proper status of any and all detainers based on untried indictments, informations, or complaints. The party States also find that proceedings with reference to such charges and detainers, when emanating from another jurisdiction, cannot properly be had in the absence of cooperative procedures. It is the further purpose of this agreement to provide such cooperative procedures.

"Article II

"As used in this agreement:

(a) 'State' shall mean a State of the United States; the United States of America; a territory or possession of the United States; the District of Columbia; the Commonwealth of Puerto Rico.

(b) 'Sending State' shall mean a State in which a prisoner is incarcerated at the time that he initiates a request for final disposition pursuant to article III hereof or at the time that a request for custody or availability is initiated pursuant to article IV hereof.

(c) 'Receiving State' shall mean the State in which trial is to be had on an indictment, information, or complaint pursuant to article III or article IV hereof.

"Article III

(a) Whenever a person has entered upon a term of imprisonment in a penal or correctional institution of a party State, and whenever during the continuance of the term of imprisonment there is pending in any other party State any untried indictment, information, or complaint on the basis of which a detainer has been lodged against the prisoner, he shall be brought to trial within one hundred and eighty days after he shall have caused to be delivered to the prosecuting officer and the appropriate court of the prosecuting officer's jurisdiction written notice of the place of his imprisonment and his request for a final disposition to be made of the indictment, information, or complaint: Provided, That, for good cause shown in open court, the prisoner or his counsel being present, the court having jurisdiction of the matter may grant any necessary or reasonable continuance. The request of the prisoner shall be accompanied by a certificate of the appropriate official having custody of the prisoner, stating the term of commitment under which the prisoner is being held, the time already served, the time remaining to be served on the sentence, the amount of good time earned, the time of parole eligibility of the prisoner, and any decision of the State parole agency relating to the prisoner.

(b) The written notice and request for final disposition referred to in paragraph (a) hereof shall be given or sent by the prisoner to the warden, commissioner of corrections, or other official having custody of him, who shall promptly forward it together with the certificate to the appropriate prosecuting official and court by registered or certified mail, return receipt requested.

(c) The warden, commissioner of corrections, or other official having custody of the prisoner shall promptly inform him of the source and contents of any detainer lodged against him and shall also inform him of his right to make a request for final disposition of the indictment, information, or complaint on which the detainer is based.

(d) Any request for final disposition made by a prisoner pursuant to paragraph (a) hereof shall operate as a request for final disposition of all untried indictments, informations, or complaints on the basis of which detainers have been lodged against the prisoner from the State to whose prosecuting official the request for final disposition is specifically directed. The warden, commissioner of corrections, or other official having custody of the prisoner shall forthwith notify all appropriate prosecuting officers and courts in the several jurisdictions within the State to which the prisoner's request for final disposition is being sent of the proceeding being initiated by the prisoner. Any notification sent pursuant to this paragraph shall be accompanied by copies of the prisoner's written notice, request, and the certificate. If trial is not had on any indictment, information, or complaint contemplated hereby prior to the return of the prisoner to the original place of imprisonment, such indictment, information, or complaint shall not be of any further force or effect, and the court shall enter an order dismissing the same with prejudice.

(e) Any request for final disposition made by a prisoner pursuant to paragraph (a) hereof shall also be deemed to be a waiver of extradition with respect to any charge or proceeding contemplated thereby or included therein by reason of paragraph (d) hereof; and a waiver of extradition to the receiving State to serve any sentence there imposed upon him, after completion of his term of imprisonment in the sending State. The request for final disposition shall also constitute a consent by the prisoner to the production of his body in any court where his presence may be required in order to effectuate the purposes of this agreement and a further consent voluntarily to be returned to the original place of imprisonment in accordance with the provisions of this agreement. Nothing in this paragraph shall prevent the imposition of a concurrent sentence if otherwise permitted by law.

(f) Escape from custody by the prisoner subsequent to his execution of the request for final disposition referred to in paragraph (a) hereof shall void the request.

"Article IV

(a) The appropriate officer of the jurisdiction in which an untried indictment, information, or complaint is pending shall be entitled to have a prisoner against whom he has lodged a detainer and who is serving a term of imprisonment in any party State made available in accordance with article V(a) hereof upon presentation of a written request for temporary custody or availability to the appropriate authorities of the State in which the prisoner is incarcerated: Provided, That the court having jurisdiction of such indictment, information, or complaint shall have duly approved, recorded, and transmitted the request: And provided further, That there shall be a period of thirty days after receipt by the appropriate authorities before the request be honored, within which period the Governor of the sending State may disapprove the request for temporary custody or availability, either upon his own motion or upon motion of the prisoner.

(b) Upon request of the officer's written request as provided in paragraph (a) hereof, the appropriate authorities having the prisoner in custody shall furnish the officer with a certificate stating the term of commitment under which the prisoner is being held, the time already served, the time remaining to be served on the sentence, the amount of good time earned, the time of parole eligibility of the prisoner, and any decisions of the State parole agency relating to the prisoner. Said authorities simultaneously shall furnish all other officers and appropriate courts in the receiving State who has lodged detainers against the prisoner with similar certificates and with notices informing them of the request or custody or availability and of the reasons therefor.

(c) In respect of any proceeding made possible by this article, trial shall be commenced within one hundred and twenty days of the arrival of the prisoner in the receiving State, but for good cause shown in open court, the prisoner or his counsel being present, the court having jurisdiction of the matter may grant any necessary or reasonable continuance.

(d) Nothing contained in this article shall be construed to deprive any prisoner of any right which he may have to contest the legality of his delivery as provided in paragraph (a) hereof, but such delivery may not be opposed or denied on the ground that the executive authority of the sending State has not affirmatively consented to or ordered such delivery.

(e) If trial is not had on any indictment, information, or complaint contemplated hereby prior to the prisoner's being returned to the original place of imprisonment pursuant to article V(e) hereof, such indictment, information, or complaint shall not be of any further force or effect, and the court shall enter an order dismissing the same with prejudice.

"Article V

(a) In response to a request made under article III or article IV hereof: the appropriate authority in a sending State shall offer to deliver temporary custody of such prisoner to the appropriate authority in the State where such indictment, information, or complaint is pending against such person in order that speedy and efficient prosecution may be had. If the request for final disposition is made by the prisoner, the offer of temporary custody shall accompany the written notice provided for in article III of this agreement. In the case of a Federal prisoner, the appropriate authority in the receiving State shall be entitled to temporary custody as provided by this agreement or to the prisoner's presence in Federal custody at the place of trial, whichever custodial arrangement may be approved by the custodian.

(b) The officer or other representative of a State accepting an offer of temporary custody shall present the following upon demand:

(1) Proper identification and evidence of his authority to act for the State into whose temporary custody this prisoner is to be given.

(2) A duly certified copy of the indictment, information, or complaint on the basis of which the detainer has been lodged and on the basis of which the request for temporary custody of the prisoner has been made.

(c) If the appropriate authority shall refuse or fail to accept temporary custody of said person, or in the event that an action on the indictment, information, or complaint on the basis of which the detainer has been lodged is not brought to trial within the period provided in article III or article IV hereof: the appropriate court of the jurisdiction where the indictment, information, or complaint has been pending shall enter an order dismissing the same with prejudice, and any detainer based thereon shall cease to be of any force or effect.

(d) The temporary custody referred to in this agreement shall be only for the purpose of permitting prosecution on the charge or charges contained in one or more untried indictments, informations, or complaints which form the basis of the detainer or detainers or for prosecution on any other charge or charges arising out of the same transaction. Except for his attendance at court and while being transported to or from any place at which his presence may be required, the prisoner shall be held in a suitable jail or other facility regularly used for persons awaiting prosecution.

(e) At the earliest practicable time consonant with the purposes of this agreement, the prisoner shall be returned to the sending State.

(f) During the continuance of temporary custody or while the prisoner is otherwise being made available for trial as required by this agreement, time being served on the sentence shall continue to run but good time shall be earned by the prisoner only if, and to the extent that, the law and practice of the jurisdiction which imposed the sentence may allow.

(g) For all purposes other than that for which temporary custody as provided in this agreement is exercised, the prisoner shall be deemed to remain in the custody of and subject to the jurisdiction of the sending State and any escape from temporary custody may be dealt with in the same manner as an escape from the original place of imprisonment or in any other manner permitted by law.

(h) From the time that a party State receives custody of a prisoner pursuant to this agreement until such prisoner is returned to the territory and custody of the sending State, the State in which the one or more untried indictments, informations, or complaints are pending or in which trial is being had shall be responsible for the prisoner and shall also pay all costs of transporting, caring for, keeping, and returning the prisoner. The provisions of this paragraph shall govern unless the States concerned shall have entered into a supplementary agreement providing for a different allocation of costs and responsibilities as between or among themselves. Nothing herein contained shall be construed to alter or affect any internal relationship among the departments, agencies, and officers of and in the government of a party State, or between a party State and its subdivisions, as to the payment of costs, or responsibilities therefor.

"Article VI

(a) In determining the duration and expiration dates of the time periods provided in articles III and IV of this agreement, the running of said time periods shall be tolled whenever and for as long as the prisoner is unable to stand trial, as determined by the court having jurisdiction of the matter.

(b) No provision of this agreement, and no remedy made available by this agreement shall apply to any person who is adjudged to be mentally ill.

"Article VII

Each State party to this agreement shall designate an officer who, acting jointly with like officers of other party States, shall promulgate rules and regulations to carry out more effectively the terms and provisions of this agreement, and who shall provide, within and without the State, information necessary to the effective operation of this agreement.

"Article VIII

This agreement shall enter into full force and effect as to a party State when such State has enacted the same into law. A State party to this agreement may withdraw herefrom by enacting a statute repealing the same. However, the withdrawal of any State shall not affect the status of any proceedings already initiated by inmates or by State officers at the time such withdrawal takes effect, nor shall it affect their rights in respect thereof.

"Article IX

This agreement shall be liberally construed so as to effectuate its purposes. The provisions of this agreement shall be severable and if any phrase, clause, sentence, or provision of this agreement is declared to be contrary to the constitution of any party State or of the United States or the applicability thereof to any government, agency, person, or circumstance is held invalid, the validity or the remainder of this agreement and the applicability thereof to any government, agency, person, or circumstance shall not be affected thereby. If this agreement shall be held contrary to the constitution of any State party hereto, the agreement shall remain in full force and effect as to the remaining States and in full force and effect as to the State affected as to all severable matters."

Sec 3. The term "Governor" as used in the agreement on detainers shall mean with respect to the United States, the Attorney General, and with respect to the District of Columbia, the Commissioner of the District of Columbia the Mayor of the District of Columbia.

Sec 4. The term "appropriate court" as used in the agreement on detainers shall mean with respect to the United States, the courts of the United States, and with respect to the District of Columbia, the courts of the District of Columbia, in which indictments, informations, or complaints, for which disposition is sought, are pending.

Sec 5. All courts, departments, agencies, officers, and employees of the United States and of the District of Columbia are hereby directed to enforce the agreement on detainers and to cooperate with one another and with all party States in enforcing the agreement and effectuating its purpose.

Sec 6. For the United States, the Attorney General, and for the District of Columbia, the Commissioner of the District of Columbia, the Mayor of the District of Columbia, shall establish such regulations, prescribe such forms, issue such instructions, and perform such other acts as he deems necessary for carrying out the provisions of this Act.

Sec 7. The right to alter, amend, or repeal this Act is expressly reserved.

Sec 8. This Act shall take effect on the ninetieth day after the date of its enactment.

Sec 9. Special Provisions when United States is a Receiving State

Notwithstanding any provision of the agreement on detainers to the contrary, in a case in which the United States is a receiving State--

(1) any order of a court dismissing any indictment, information, or complaint may be with or without prejudice. In determining whether to dismiss the case with or without prejudice, the court shall consider, among others, each of the following factors: The seriousness of the offense; the facts and circumstances of the case which led to the dismissal; and the impact of a reprosecution on the administration of the agreement on detainers and on the administration of justice; and

(2) it shall not be a violation of the agreement on detainers if prior to trial the prisoner is returned to the custody of the sending State pursuant to an order of the appropriate court issued after reasonable notice to the prisoner and the United States and an opportunity for a hearing.

(Dec. 9, 1970, P. L. 91-538, § 9, as added Nov. 18, 1988, P. L. 100-690, Title VII, Subtitle S, § 7059, 102 Stat. 4403.)

PROSECUTOR'S NOTIFICATION (SAMPLE LETTER)

(DATE)

PROSECUTOR'S NAME
TITLE
STREET ADDRESS
CITY, STATE   ZIP CODE

RE: INMATE NAME
      INMATE REGISTER NO.
      STATE CASE/REFERENCE NO.

Dear **PROSECUTOR'S NAME:**

The above referenced defendant has requested disposition of pending charges in your jurisdiction pursuant to the Interstate Agreement on Detainers Act (IADA). Necessary forms are enclosed.

We request action be taken under Article III of the IADA and IADA Forms VI, "Evidence of Agents' Authority to Act for Receiving State" and VII, "Prosecutor's Acceptance of Temporary Custody Offered in Connection with a Prisoner's Request for Disposition of a Detainer" be submitted to us, as necessary. The two (2) persons who are the designated agents to return the prisoner to your State must also be the persons whose signatures appear on the Form VI, BP-S564. It would be advisable to designate alternate agents whose signatures must also appear on the IADA Form VI, BP-S564, in the event the primary agents are unable to make the trip. Also be advised that the designated agents must have in their possession a copy of the IADA Form VI, BP-S564, proper identification, and a certified copy of the warrant when assuming custody of the prisoner. Any questions regarding this procedure may be directed to the individual listed below or the Agreement Administrator for your State.

Inmates who are temporarily transferred pursuant to the IADA remain under the primary jurisdiction of federal authorities. Should you accept temporary custody of this inmate, we wish to remind you that under Article V(e) of the IADA, you are required to return the above named inmate to this institution after prosecution on all pending charges. While this inmate is in your temporary custody, he or she will be held in a suitable jail that meets the level of security required by the Bureau of Prisons. In addition, security requirements for the inmate (e.g., type of restraints, number of escorting staff, who may transport, etc.) must be met. Any problems associated with this inmate must be reported to the individual listed below. This inmate may not be released on bail or bond while in your custody. Additionally, this inmate is not to be committed to a state correctional institution for service of any state sentence(s) that may be imposed because of your prosecution.

PROSECUTOR'S NOTIFICATION
Page Two
RE: INMATE'S NAME

To help us with processing, please fill out the enclosed certification form and return to us before scheduling a date for assuming custody. Upon completion of the State proceedings contact this office to schedule a date for the inmate's return to federal custody.

If you have any question on this matter, please call: **ISM NAME AND TELEPHONE NUMBER**.

Sincerely,

CEO'S NAME

/S/
NAME
INMATE SYSTEMS MANAGER

Enclosures: BP-Forms S236, S238, S239
               BP-S565, Prosecutor's Certification Form

cc: Clerk of Court
       State IADA Administrator

OTHER PROSECUTOR'S NOTIFICATION (SAMPLE LETTER)

(DATE)

PROSECUTOR'S NAME
TITLE
STREET ADDRESS
CITY, STATE   ZIP CODE

RE: **INMATE NAME**
       INMATE REGISTER NO.
       STATE CASE/REFERENCE NO.

Dear **OTHER PROSECUTOR'S NAME:**

The above referenced defendant has requested disposition of pending charges in **(ORIGINAL JURISDICTION)** pursuant to Article III of the Interstate Agreement on Detainers Act (IADA). According to Article III(d), the inmate's request also is a request for disposition of the charges in your jurisdiction lodged as a detainer. Consistent with the same Article, copies of the appropriate forms are enclosed. You should contact the prosecuting official named above to arrange for a transfer of custody once trial is had in their jurisdiction. Any questions regarding this procedure may be directed to the individual listed below or the Agreement Administrator for your state.

Inmates who are temporarily transferred pursuant to the IADA remain under the primary jurisdiction of federal authorities. Should you accept temporary custody of this inmate, and are the last to prosecute the inmate among those eligible to do so, you will be required to return him or her to this institution after prosecution of all pending charges that form the basis for your detainer (Article V9e)). While in your temporary custody, the inmate must be held in a suitable jail that meets the level of security required by the Bureau of Prisons. **In addition, security requirements for the inmate (e.g., type of restraints, number of escorting staff, who may transport, etc.) must be met**. Any problems encountered with this inmate must be reported to the individual listed below. This inmate may not be released on bail or bond while in your custody. Additionally, this inmate is not to be committed to a state correctional institution for service of any state sentence(s) that may be imposed because of your prosecution.

To help us with processing, please fill out the enclosed certification form and return to us before scheduling a date for assuming custody.

If you have any question on this matter, please call: **ISM NAME AND TELEPHONE NUMBER**.

Sincerely,

CEO'S NAME

/S/
NAME
INMATE SYSTEMS MANAGER

Enclosures: BP-Forms S236, S238, S239
                BP-S565, Prosecutor's Certification Form

cc: Clerk of Court **(COUNTy)**
        (ORIGINAL PROSECUTOR'S NAME)
        State IADA Administrator

ARTICLE III FOLLOW-UP (SAMPLE LETTER)

(DATE)

PROSECUTOR'S NAME
TITLE
STREET ADDRESS
CITY, STATE   ZIP CODE

RE: **INMATE NAME**
      INMATE REGISTER NO.
      STATE CASE/REFERENCE NO.

Dear **PROSECUTOR'S NAME:**

The above named subject applied for final disposition of pending charges pursuant to the Interstate Agreement on Detainers Act (IADA) which application was received in your office on **(DATE)**. As you are aware, under Article III of the IADA, Inmate **(NAME)** is to be brought to trial on these charges within 180 days from the date the forms were received in your office as noted on the certified mail receipt. It appears that Inmate **(NAME)** has not been brought to trial on the charges specified in your detainer and the 180-day period will lapse on **(DATE)**.

I would appreciate hearing from you at your earliest convenience as to your state's intentions in this case. Further arrangements may be made by contacting me at **(TELEPHONE NUMBER)**.

Sincerely,

/S/
NAME
INMATE SYSTEMS MANAGER

PROSECUTOR'S REQUEST FOR TEMPORARY CUSTODY
(SAMPLE LETTER)

(DATE)

PROSECUTOR'S NAME
TITLE
STREET ADDRESS
CITY, STATE   ZIP CODE

RE: **INMATE NAME**
        INMATE REGISTER NO.
        STATE CASE/REFERENCE NO.

Dear **PROSECUTOR'S NAME:**

In response to your request for temporary custody pursuant to the Interstate Agreement on Detainers Act (IADA), applicable forms are enclosed. Please be advised subject has been notified of your Request and has been given 30 days in which to contact the Warden of this institution as to any reasons why he should not be produced in your State pursuant to the Agreement. This 30-day period, provided under Article IV(a), expires on **(DATE)** any court proceedings must occur after this date. Please remit to this office completed Forms VII, "Prosecutor's Acceptance of Temporary Custody Offered" and VI, "Evidence of Agent's Authority to Act for Receiving State." The persons designated as agents to return the prisoner to your State must also be the persons whose signatures appear on the IADA Form VI, BP-S564. Naming alternative agents would be advisable in case your primary agents cannot make the trip. The alternate agent's signatures should also appear on the IADA Form VI, BP-S564. Also be advised that the designated agents must have in their possession a copy of the warrant when assuming custody of the prisoner.

Inmates who are temporarily transferred pursuant to the IADA remain under the primary jurisdiction of federal authorities. Should you accept temporary custody of this inmate, we wish to remind you that under Article V(e) of the IADA, you are required to return the above named inmate to this institution after prosecution on all pending charges. While this inmate is in your temporary custody, he/she will be held in a suitable jail that meets the level of security required by the Bureau of Prisons. **In addition, security requirements for the inmate (e.g., type of restraints, number of escorting staff, who may transport, etc.) must be met**. Any problems associated with this inmate must be reported to the individual listed below. This inmate may not be released on bail or bond while in your custody. Additionally, this inmate is not to be committed to a state correctional institution for service of any state sentence(s) that may be imposed because of your prosecution.

To help us with processing, please fill out the enclosed certification form and return to us before scheduling a date for assuming custody.

If you have any question on this matter, please call: **ISM NAME AND TELEPHONE NUMBER**.

Sincerely,

CEO'S NAME

/S/
NAME
INMATE SYSTEMS MANAGER

Enclosures: BP-Forms S236, S238, S239
              BP-S565, Prosecutor's Certification Form

cc: Clerk of Court
      State IADA Administrator

Chapter III
How To Analyze Your Case

- ❑ How to analyze your case
  - ➢ Pretrial claims
  - ➢ Guilty plea claims
  - ➢ Trial claims
  - ➢ Sentencing claims
  - ➢ Appellate claims
  - ➢ Case law reference for claims
  - ➢ State & federal form motions
  - ➢ How to fill out state & federal *form* motions
- ❑ How to obtain state & federal *forms*
  - ➢ Objections to magistrate's report and recommendations
  - ➢ Reply Brief/Traverse/Response
  - ➢ Addresses:
    - ➢ State & Federal Supreme Courts
    - ➢ State Court of Criminal Appeals
    - ➢ United States Court of Appeals
    - ➢ List of State Bar Associations

HOW TO ANALYZE YOUR CASE

The steps set forth herein provide a simple guide of how to analyze a federal criminal conviction for possible errors. This guide is based on the applicable Federal statutes and Federal Rules of Criminal Procedure. While this guide is based on a federal case the exact same scenario should apply to most state cases.

1. Obtain all available documents. This includes: affidavits for search warrants, arrest warrants, criminal complaints, indictment, information, discovery material, Freedom of Information Act material, pretrial motions, response motions, orders, docket entry sheet, suppression or motion hearing transcripts, plea offers, plea agreements, guilty plea transcripts, trial transcripts, presentence report (if available the federal systems requires Presentence Reports to be reviewed in the case manager's office), objections to the presentence report, sentencing transcripts, notice of appeal, appellant and appellee briefs, court of appeals opinion or decision, petition for writ of certiorari and any other available document etc. Most of the documents will be in the attorney's case file.

2. Organize all the documents in chronological order as the criminal proceedings unfolded. This will allow review of the file in a chronological order.

3. Review and evaluate all the available documents to determine their accuracy and then compare them to the applicable law and rules to make a determination whether law enforcement or the court complied with the applicable law.

4. **Pretrial claims**. After reading all the available documents compare those documents to the applicable rules or law governing those proceeding. For example, lets say that after reading the available documents you make a determination that the arrest was made without a warrant and the evidence might have been obtained illegal. Read the applicable Federal Rules of Criminal Procedure governing pretrial proceedings. Federal pretrial motions are governed by Federal Rules of Criminal Procedure, Rule 12. Rule 12 (a) Entitled: "Pleadings and Pretrial Motions." Rule 12(a) limits motions challenging the indictment, the information, and the pleas of not guilty, guilty, and nolo contendere. Rule 12 (b) "Pretrial motions," provides that a party may raise by pretrial motion any defense, objection, or request that the court can determine without a trial of the general issue. Rule 12 (b) requires that the following *claims* must be raised before trial: (1) motion alleging defect in instituting the prosecution; (2) motion alleging defect in the indictment or information, but at any time the case is pending; (3) *motion to suppress evidence. See Rule 41*; (4) a Rule 14 motion to sever charges or defendants; and (5) a Rule 16 motion for discovery. Rule 12.1 "Notice of an Alibi Defense." Read the applicable rules and law governing: "arrest, search and seizures." See Federal Rules of Criminal Procedure, *Rules 4, 9, 40, and 41, and Fourth Amendment case law relevant to illegal arrest and seizure of evidence*.

5. After reading the applicable rules and governing law make a determination whether the arrest and seizure of evidence was illegal, then check the docket entry sheet to determine whether defense counsel filed a motion to suppress evidence. Under Federal habeas corpus law a prisoner cannot raise the claim that the arrest and seizure of evidence was illegal. See ***Stone v. Powell, 428 U.S. 465, 49 L.Ed.2d 1067,96 S.Ct. 3037 (1976)***, the Court concluded "that where the state has provided an opportunity for full and fair

litigation of a Fourth Amendment claim, a state prisoner may not be granted federal habeas corpus relief on the ground that evidence obtained in an unconstitutional search or seizure was introduced at his trial." Id. at 494-95. See also ***United States v. Hearst*, 638 F.2d 1190, 1196 (9th Cir. 1980)** (4th Amendment claim not available on collateral attack because federal prisoner had full and fair opportunity to litigate issue at trial). However, a claim would be cognizable that: "Counsel was constitutionally ineffective for failure to move to suppress illegally seized evidence." See ***Kimmelman v. Morrison*, 477 U.S. 365, 91 L.Ed.2d 305, 106 S.Ct. 2574 (1986)**. Therefore, it's important to find the err and evaluate that err under post-conviction case law and make a determination of how to frame the claim.

6. **Guilty Plea claims**. In order to properly analyze the case where the defendant pleaded guilty a person would need a copy of the plea agreement, guilty plea transcripts, presentence report, objections to the presentence report and sentencing transcripts. Compare the documents to the requirements of Rule 11 and 32 and the United States Sentencing Guidelines. Rule 11 governs guilty plea's in the federal court system. Rule 11 requires that the district court advise the defendant of: (1) the nature of the charge; (2) the mandatory minimum penalty; (3) the maximum possible penalty; (4) applicable fines and restitution; (5) the right to trial by jury; (6) the right to counsel; (7) the right to confront and cross-examine adverse witnesses, and the right against compelled self-incrimination; (8) insure that the guilty plea is voluntarily; (9) determine the accuracy of the plea; and (10) establish a factual basis for the plea. A comparison of the plea agreement and guilty plea transcript to Rule 11 will allow you to make a determination of whether the district court complied with the core concerns of Rule 11 while accepting the guilty plea. A review of post-conviction case law relating to Rule 11 will show you how to frame your claim to meet the requirements of the post-conviction case law to obtain the necessary relief you desire.

7. **Trial claims.** In order to properly analyze the case where the defendant proceeded to trial a person would obtain all available documents. This includes all available pretrial documents, trial transcripts, jury instructions, verdict forms, jury notes, verdict, motions for judgment of acquittal or arrest of judgment, presentence report, sentencing transcripts, appellate briefs, appellate court opinions and petition for writ of certiorari documents. Review all pretrial documents to make sure everything was properly done in compliance with the applicable rules and law. If an error is located in the pretrial proceeding make a determination whether said claim would have made a difference in the outcome of the trial. Some pretrial claims such as counsel's failure to communicate the government's plea offer to defendant would not necessary make a difference in the trial, but the defendant can still show a constitutional violation and that the result of the proceedings would have been different, absent counsel's unprofessional errors and omissions. When reading the trial transcripts evaluate the jury selections, voir dire proceedings, opening statements, introduction of relevant evidence, inadmissible evidence, trial objections, proposed jury instructions, jury instructions, closing arguments, jury notes, proposed verdict form, verdict form, verdict, motions for judgment of acquittal or arrest of judgment. If a error is located during any of these proceedings make a determination whether the error would have changed the outcome of the trial or appellate proceedings had the claim been objected to and raised at the proper times.

Review post-conviction case law applicable to the err and make a determination how to raise the claim.

8. **Sentencing claims**. In order to properly analyze a sentencing claim a person would need the presentence report, objections to the presentence report (PSR) and the sentencing guidelines. Review the presentence report and compare it to the United States Sentencing Guidelines. In each numbered paragraph of the PSR where points/levels are added such as the calculation of criminal history points, or base offense levels, the PSR will list a Section/Provision of the Guidelines as reference for that specific enhancement. Review the presentence report and the applicable guidelines and make a determination whether the guidelines were misapplied. If a determination is made that the guidelines were misapplied then read and review the sentencing transcript to determine whether the claim was objected to at sentencing or raised on direct appeal. After locating an error during sentencing, review the applicable post-conviction case law and make a determination how to raise the claim in a post-conviction proceeding. For example, an error in the application of Sentencing Guidelines is not cognizable in §2255 proceeding, absent a complete miscarriage of justice. ***Jones v. United States*, 178 F.3d 790, 796 (6th Cir. 1999)**; ***United States v. Williamson*, 183 F.3d 458, 462 (5th Cir. 1999)**. However, the same claim can be framed differently and be cognizable. See ***United States v. Williamson*, 183 F.3d 458, 463-64 (5th Cir. 1999)** (Appellate counsel's failure to raise the ***Bellazerius*** issue which held that drug conspiracy conviction could not serve as trigger for career offender sentence enhancements constituted ineffective assistance of counsel and warranted resentencing without the use of the career offender enhancement); ***Glover v. United States*, 531 U.S. 198, 148 L.Ed.2d 607, 611, 121 S.Ct. 696 (2001)** (claim that ineffective assistance of counsel led to sentencing error were cognizable §2255 constitutional violation).

9. **Appellate claims**. In order to properly analyze whether an appellate claim exists a person has to read and review the entire record. If an error is located make a determination whether the error had been objected to and preserved for review on direct appeal, but not raised on direct appeal. The question then is: If the claim would have been raised on direct appeal would it have required reversal of the conviction or a remand for resentencing?

10. In a lot of cases a claim may exist that are not located in the available documents. For example, the defendant committed the offense and advised counsel that he committed the offense and he was guilty, but counsel failed to seek a plea offer. The government never made a plea offer. So counsel assumed that there were no plea offers and the defendant had to proceed to trial. Under these type of situations counsel may have failed to advise the defendant that he could still plead guilty to the charge and receive a lesser sentence by accepting responsibility for his actions. See USSG §3El.l. Whereas the same defendant proceeds to trial knowing he is going to be convicted and will loses the opportunity to receive a three (3) level reduction for acceptance of reasonability. See USSG §3El.l. The defendant would have a claim that: Counsel was constitutionally ineffective for failure to advise defendant he could pled guilty to an open plea and receive a reduction in sentence for acceptance of responsibility. **See *United States v. Booth*, 432 F.3d 542, 550 (3rd Cir. 2005)**.

11. **Case law reference for claims**. If you locate a claim of error that is related to the Rules violation then use the Case Annotation Version for the Rules to review for post-conviction case law. Once you find applicable case law, that gives you a starting point. Shepardize the case law which will lead you to other cases. The Case Annotation version of the Statute for the crime will provide other case law. Alternatively, get a quick reference citebook. **"The Post-Conviction Citebook"** *has a 16 page Table of Contents with over 740 quick reference topics with favorable case on almost any subject in the field of post-conviction relief.* A review of the "Table of Contents" will assist the individual user in finding and recognizing errors which occurred in his/her case with favorable case law supporting that specific constitutional claim. See Page 426.

12. **Procedural bar**. The Federal Court system has created an extremely narrow road in the field of post-conviction for State and Federal prisoners designed to prevent an individual from obtaining relief from a constitutional violation based on the procedural default rule. The pitfalls created by the procedural default rule require a criminal defendant to show "cause" for failure to raise the issue at trial or on direct appeal and "actual prejudice" resulting from the error. Prejudice must be shown based on the individual facts of each case.

STATE & FEDERAL FORM MOTIONS

As a general rule, most state and federal courts require the use of the appropriate state or federal habeas corpus/post-conviction form motion or forms that were promulgated by the Administrative Office of the Courts. The Clerk's Office could reject or return the prisoner documents (not filed), if he/ she did not use the appropriate "Form Motion." So it's important to gather the necessary form motions well in advance and make additional copies of the forms.

A prisoner must fill out the appropriate Form(s) Motion if required by the Court. The Form Motions were designed to assist the prisoner and courts. A prisoner can take advantage of the Forms if he/she is about to miss his filing deadline by filling out and filing the form motion in order to meet the filing deadline. The prisoner can submit a "Memorandum Brief In Support of the Motion," at a later date.

The form is your Motion for relief.

How to fill out State & Federal Form Motions

A prisoner should study the Form carefully. All questions must be answered concisely in the proper space on the form. As a general rule, if you do not have enough space you may submit additional pages if necessary. Remember the prisoner is swearing under penalty of perjury that his/her statements in the Form are true and correct. Any false statement of a material fact may serve as the basis for prosecution for perjury.

Answer every item that applies to you on the form. If a question or items does not apply to you, put Not Applicable or "N/A" in the blank. Use additional pages if the Instructions that come with the form allows you to do so.

It's strongly recommended that prior to filling out the Form motion that you review the relevant post-conviction/habeas corpus law related to your claim and to make a determination of how to frame your claim as a "Ground" for relief. For example, a state prisoner cannot claim a Fourth Amendment violation as a "Ground" because of illegal search and seizure without showing cause for procedural default. See, e.g., ***Stone v. Powell*, 428 U.S. 465, 49 L.Ed.2d 1067, 96 S.Ct. 3037 (1976).** However, that same prisoner would have been able to raise his "*Ground*" for relief as: "Counsel was constitutionally ineffective for failure to move to suppress the evidence from the illegal search and seizure." See ***Kimmelman v. Morrison,*' 477 U.S. 365, 91 L.Ed.2d 305, 106 S.Ct. 2574 (1986)**.

Facts are what wins cases. It's important to properly plead your facts which support your Constitutional claims.

This Form is your motion for relief.

If you fail to set forth all the grounds in the form motion, you may be procedurally barred from presenting additional grounds at a later date.

How to obtain State & Federal Form Motions

First, check with the prison law library to see what Form motions are available at the institution level. Request a copy of their forms that you know that you are going to use. If the prison law library does not have a copy of the Form motion submit an "Inmate Request To Staff" generally to the "Educational Supervisor" or the "Warden" and request that they supply you with the necessary forms. While your waiting for a response on your "Inmate Request To Staff" use the "Form Letters" in Chapter IV of this book as sample letters and write letters to the: (1) sentencing Court; (2) Court of Criminal Appeals; (3) State Supreme Court; (4) United States District Court; and (5) your lawyer. If you write enough letters and inmate requests you will obtain the necessary Form motions.

Objections To Magistrate Judge's Report and Recommendation

In the federal court system the Magistrate Judge pursuant to Federal Rule of Civil Procedure, Rule 72 (b)(1), will issue a "**Findings and Recommendations**" (The Magistrate's Report and Recommendations may be named differently), on a prisoner's petition. The parties have 14 days to file written objections to the magistrate's report. See Rule 72 (b)(2). Failure to make timely objections to the magistrate's report prior to the district court adopting the magistrate's report may constitute a waiver of appellate review of the district judge's order. See ***United States v. Walters, 638 F.2d 947 (6th Cir. 1981)***. On the other hand, filing timely objections requires the district judge to whom the case is assigned to make a de novo review of the record and determination of those portions of the report, findings or recommendations to which timely objections is made. See **Fed. R. Civ. P. Rule 72(b)(3)**. A lot of state courts have a similar system.

Objections to the magistrate's report does not have to be lengthy. See Sample: Objections in Chapter VI. Rather, most objections to the magistrate's report are based on an inaccurate determination of the facts or an incorrect conclusion of the law.

Reply Brief/Traverse/Response

A prisoner should file a "Reply Brief," "Traverse," or "Response" regardless of its label to the government's response/answer. Why should you file a reply? The answer to this is simple. **28 U.S.C. §2248** Return or answer' conclusiveness. §2248 provides: "The allegation of a return [Government's Response] to an order to show cause in a habeas corpus proceeding, if not traversed, shall be accepted as true except to the extent that the judge finds from the evidence that they are not true." (emphasis added).

A strong reply to the government's response/answer in a lot of cases will create the winning argument. If the government concedes your argument is correct on one of your claims be sure and point it out up front in your "Reply Brief" that the government conceded this claim.

Alabama Supreme Court
Office of the Clerk
300 Dexter Ave.
Montgomery, AL 36104-3741
Phone (334)242-4609

Alaska Supreme Court
Office of the Clerk
303 K Street
Anchorage, AK 99501
Phone (907)264-0612

Arizona Supreme Court
Office of the Clerk
Arizona State Courts Building
1501 W. Washington, Suite 402
Phoenix, AZ 85007
Phone (602)542-9396

Arkansas Supreme Court
Office of the Clerk
Justice Building
Little Rock, AR 72201
Phone (501)682-6841

California Supreme Court
Office of the Clerk
State Building
350 McAllister St.
San Francisco, CA 94102
Phone (415)865-7000

Colorado Supreme Court
Office of the Clerk
Judicial Building
2 East 14th Ave., 4th Fl.
Denver, CO 80203
Phone (303)861-1111 ext. 277

Connecticut Supreme Court
Office of the Clerk
Supreme Court Building
231 Capitol Ave.
Hartford, CT 06106
Phone (860)757-2200

Iowa Supreme Court
Office of the Clerk
111 E. Court Ave.
Des Moines, IA 50319
Phone (515)281-5911

Delaware Supreme Court
Office of the Clerk
55 The Green
Dover, DE 19903
Phone (302)739-4155

Florida Supreme Court
Office of the Clerk
Supreme Court Building
500 S. Duval St.
Tallahassee, FL 32399-1925
Phone (850)488-0125

Georgia Supreme Court
Office of the Clerk
244 Washington St. S.W.
Atlanta, GA 30334
Phone (404)656-3470

Hawaii Supreme Court
Office of the Clerk
Ali'iolani Hale
417 S. King Street
Honolulu, HI 96813
Phone (808)539-4919

Idaho Supreme Court
Office of the Clerk
Supreme Court Bldg.
P.O. Box 83720
451 W. State Street
Boise, ID 83720-0100
Phone (208)334-2210

Illinois Supreme Court
Office of the Clerk
200 E. Capitol Ave.
Springfield, IL 62701-1721
Phone (217)782-2035

Indiana Supreme Court
Office of the Clerk
217 State House
Indianapolis, IN 46204
Phone (317)232-1930

Kansas Supreme Court
Office of the Clerk
Kansas Judicial Center
301 S.W. 10th Street
Topeka, KS 66612
Phone (785)296-3229

Kentucky Supreme Court
Office of the Clerk
State Capitol Bldg.
Frankfort, KY 40601
Phone (502)564-4720

Louisiana Supreme Court
Office of the Clerk
Supreme Court Bldg.
400 Royal St., Suite 4200
New Orleans, LA 70112
Phone (504)310-2300

Maine Supreme Court
Office of the Clerk
Supreme Judicial Court
142 Federal St., P.O. Box 368
Portland, ME 04112-0368
Phone (207)822-4148

Maryland Court of Appeals
Court of Appeals Bldg.
Office of the Clerk
361 Rowe Blvd.
Annapolis, MD 21401
Phone (410)260-1500

Massachusetts Supreme Court
Supreme Judicial Court
Office of the Clerk
One Pemberton Square
Boston, MA 02108
Phone (617)557-1187

Michigan Supreme Court
Office of the Clerk
P.O. Box 30052 (48909)
925 W. Ottawa
Lansing, MI 48915
Phone (517)373-0120

Minnesota Supreme Court
Office of the Clerk
25 M.L.K. Blvd.
St. Paul, MN 55155
Phone (651)292-2581

Mississippi Supreme Court
Office of the Clerk
Carroll Gartin Justice Bldg.
P.O. Box 249
Jackson, MS 39205
Phone (601)359-3697

Missouri-Supreme Court
Office of the Clerk
Supreme Court Bldg.
High & Washington Sts.
P.O. Box 150
Jefferson City, MO 65102
Phone (573)751-4144

Montana Supreme Court
Office of the Clerk
Justice Bldg., Rm 323
215 N. Sanders
Helena, MT 58620
Phone (406)444-3858

Nebraska Supreme Court
Office of the Clerk
2413 State Capitol
P.O. Box 98910
Lincoln, NE 68509-8910
Phone (402)471-3731

Nevada Supreme Court
Office of the Clerk
Supreme Court Bldg.
Carson City, NV 89701
Phone (775)684-1600

New Hampshire Supreme Court
Office of the Clerk
Noble Drive
Concord, NH 03301
Phone (603)271-2646

New Jersey Supreme Court
Justice Complex, CN-970
Trenton, NJ 08625
Phone (609)984-7791

New Mexico Supreme Court
Office of the Clerk
Supreme Court BLdg.
237 Don Gaspar, RM 104
P.O. Box 848
Santa FE, NM 87503
Phone (505)827-4860

New York Court of Appeals
Office of the Clerk
Courthouse
20 Eagle Street
Albany, NY 12207-1095
Phone (518)455-7700

North Carolina Supreme Court
Office of the Clerk
P.O. Box 2170 (27602-2170)
227 S. Fayetteville Mall
Raleigh, NC 27601
Phone (919)733-3723

North Dakota Supreme Court
Office of the Clerk
State Capitol
Mismarck, ND 58505
Phone (701)328-2221

Ohio Supreme Court
Office of the Clerk
65 S. Front St.
Columbus, OH 43215
Phone (614)387-9530

Oklahoma Supreme Court
Office of the Clerk
State Capitol, Room 1
Oklahoma City, OK 73105
Phone (405)521-2164

Oregon Supreme Court
Office of the Clerk
Supreme Court Bldg.
1163 State Street
Salem, OR 97301-2563
Phone (503)986-5555

Pennsylvania Supreme Court
Eastern District
468 City Hall
Philadelphia, PA 19107
Phone (215)560-6370

Pennsylvania Supreme Court
Office of the Clerk
Middle District
434 Main Capitol Bldg.
Harrisburg, PA 17120
Phone (717)787-6181

Pennsylvania Supreme Court
Western District
Office of the Clerk
801 City-County Bldg.
414 Grant St.
Pittsburgh, PA 15219
Phone

Puerto Rico Supreme Court
Office of the Clerk
Ponce De Leon Ave.
Stop 8, Puerta De Tierra,
Box 9022392
San Juan, PR 00902-2392
Phone (787)723-6033

Rhode Island Supreme Court
Office of the Clerk
250 Benefit St.
Providence, RI 02903
Phone (401)222-3272

South Carolina Supreme Court
Clerk's Office, Courthouse
1231 Gervais St.
Columbia, SC 29211
Phone (803)734-1080

South Dakota Supreme Court
500 E. Capital
Pierre, SD 57501
Phone (605)773-3511

Tennessee Supreme Court
Eastern Grand Division
Supreme Court Bldg.
P.O. Box 444
Knoxville, TN 37901
Phone (865)594-6700

Tennessee Supreme Court
Office of the Clerk
Western Grand Division
Supreme Court Bldg.
P.O. Box 909
Jackson, TN 38202
Phone (731)423-5840

Texas Supreme Court
Office of the Clerk
Supreme Court Bldg.
P.O. Box 12248
201 W. 14th St.
Austin, TX 78711
Phone (512)463-1312

Utah Supreme Court
Office of the Clerk
450 South State
P.O. Box 14021
Salt Lake City, UT 84114-0210
Phone (801)578-3900

United States Supreme Court
Supreme Court Bldg.
Office of the Clerk
One First Street
N.E. Washington, DC 20543
Phone (202)479-3000

Vermont Supreme Court
Office of the Clerk
109 State St.
Montpelier, VT 05609-0801
Phone (802)828-3278

Virginia Supreme Court
Office of the Clerk
100 N. Ninth St., 5th Floor
Richmond, VA 23219
Phone (804)786-2251

Washington Supreme Court
Temple of Justice
P.O. Box 40929
Olympia, WA 98504-0929
Phone (360)357-2102

West Virginia Supreme Court
Supreme Court of Appeals
State Capitol
Charleston, WV 25305
Phone (304)558-2601

Wisconsin Supreme Court
Office of the Clerk
110 E. Main St., Room 215
P.O. Box 1688
Madison, WI 53701-1688
Phone (608)266-1880

Wyoming Supreme Court
Office of the Clerk
Supreme Court Bldg.
2301 Capitol Ave.
Cheyenne, WY 82002
Phone (307)777-7316

Alabama Court of Appeals
300 Dexter Ave.
Montgomery, AL 36104-3741
Phone No. 334-242-4095

Alaska Court of Appeals
303 K. St.
Anchorage, AK 99501
Phone No. 907-264-0612

Arizona Court of Appeals
Division One
Arizona State Court Bldg.
1501 W. Washington St.
Phoenix, AZ 85007
Phone No. 602-542-4821

Arizona Court of Appeals
Division Two
State Office Bldg.
400 West Congress, RM 200
Tucson, AZ 085701-1374
Phone No. 520-628-6954

Arkansas Court of Appeals
Justice Bldg.
Little Rock, AR 77201
Phone No. 501-682-6841

California Court of Appeals
1st Appellate District
350 McAllister St.
San Francisco, CA 94101
Phone No. 415-865-7200
(Coveirng these counties: Alameda, Contra Costa, Del Norte, Humbodlt, Lake Marin, Mendocino, Napa, San Francisco, San Mateo, Solano and Sonoma).

California Court of Appeals
2nd Appellate District
300 S. Spring St. 2nd Fl.
Lost Angeles, CA 90013
Phone No. 213-830-7000

OR

200 E. Santa Clara
Ventura, CA 93001
Phone No. 805-641-4700
(Covering these counties: Angeles, San Luis, Obispo, Santa Barbara and Ventura).

California Court of Appeals
3rd Appellate District
914 Capitol Mall
Sacramento, CA 95814
Phone No. 916-654-0209
(Covering these counties: Alpine, Amado, Butte, Calaveras, Colusa, El Dorado, Glenn, Lassen, Modoc, Mono, Nevada, Placer, Plumas, Sacramento, San Joaquin, Shasta, Sierra, Siskiyou, Sutter, Tehama, Trinity, Yolos and Yuba).

California Court of Appeals
4th Appellate District
750 "B" St., #300
San Diego, CA 92101
Phone No. 619-645-2760

OR

328 13th Street
Riverside, CA 92501
Phone No. 951-248-0200

OR

925 N. Spurgeon St.
Santa Ana, CA 92701
Phone No. 714-558-6777
(Covering these counties: Imperial, Inyo, Orange, Riverside, San Bernardino and San Diego.

California Court of Appeals
5th Appellate District
2525 Capitol St.
Fresno, CA 93721
Phone No. 559-445-5491
(Covering these counties: Fresno, Kern, Kings, Madera, Mariposa, Merced, Stanislaus, Tulare and Tuolumne).

California Court of Appeals
6th Appellate District

333 W. Santa Clara, Ste. 1061
San Jose, CA 95113
Phone No. 408-277-1004
(Covering these counties: Monterey, San Benito, Santa Clara and Santa Cruz).

Colorado Court of Appeals
Judicial Bldg. 3rd Fl
2 East 14th Ave.
Denver, CO 80203
Phone No. 303-837-3785

Connecticut Appellate Court
Supreme Court Bldg.
231 Capitol Ave.
Hartford, CT 06106
Phone No. 860-757-2200

The State of Delaware Has No
Intermediate Appellate Court

District of Columbia
Court of Appeals
500 Indiana Ave. N.W.
6th Floor
Washington, DC 20001
Phone No. 202-879-2725

Florida:
District Court of Appeals
1st District
301 M.L. King Blvd.
Tallahassee, FL 32399-1850
Phone No. 850-488-6151
(Covering these counties: Alachua, Baker, Bay, Bradford, Calhoun, Clay, Columbia, Dixie, Duval, Escambia, Franklin, Gadsden, Gilchrist, Gulf, Hamilton, Holmes, Jackson, Jefferson, Lafayette, Leon, Levy, Liberty, Madison, Nassau, Okaloosa, Santa Rosa, Suwanee, Taylor, Union, Wakulla, Walton and Washington).

Florida:
District Court of Appeals
2nd District
P.O. Box 327

Lakeland, FL 33802-0327
Phone No. 863-499-2290
(Covering these counties: Charlotte, Collier, DeSoto, Glades, Hardee, Hendry, Highlands, Hillsborough, Lee, Manatee, Pasco, Pinellas, Polk and Sarasota).

Florida:
District Court of Appeals
3rd District
2001 S.W. 117th Ave.
Miami, FL 33175-1716
Phone No. 305-229-3200
(Covering these counties: Dade and Monroe).

Florida:
District Court of Appeals
4th District
P.O. Box 3315
W. Palm Beach, FL 33402-3315
Phone No. 561-242-2000
(Covering these counties: Broward, Indina River, Martin, Okeechobee, Palm Beach and St. Lucie).

Florida:
District Court of Appeals
5th District
300 South Beach St.
Dayton, Beach, FL 32114
Phone No. 386-255-8600
(Covering these counties: Brevard, Citrus, Flaglar, Henando, Lake Marion, Orange, Osceola, Putnam, St. Johns, Seminole, Sumter and Volusia).

Georgia Court of Appeals
334 State Judicial Bldg.
Atlanta, GA 30334
Phone No. 404-656-3450

Hawaii Court of Appeals
426 Queen St.
Honolulu, HI 96813
Phone No. 808-539-4919

Idaho Court of Appeals
Supreme Court Bldg.
P.O. Box 83720
Boise, ID 83720-0101
Phone No. 208-334-2210

Illinois Appellate Court
1st District
160 N. La Salle St.
Chicago, IL 60601
Phone No. 312-793-5501
(Covering Cook County).

Illinois Appellate Court
2nd District
Appellate Court Bldg.
Elgin, IL 60120
Phone No. 847-695-3750
(Covering these counties: Boone, Garroll,
DeKalb, Du Page, Jo Daviess, Kane,
Kendall, Kake, Lee, McHenry, Ogle,
Stephenson and Winnebago).

Illinois Appellate Court
3rd District
1004 Columbus St.
Ottawa, IL 61350
Phone No. 815-434-5050
(Covering these counties: Bureau, Fulton,
Grundy, Hancock, Henderson, Henry,
Iroquois, Kankakee, Knox, La Salle,
Marshall, McDonough, Mercer, Peoria,
Putnam, Rock Island, Stark, Tazewell,
Warren, Whiteside and Will).

Illinois Appellate Court
4th District
201 W. Monroe St.
P.O. Box 19206
Springfield, IL 62794-9206
Phone No. 217-782-2586

(Covering these counties: Adams, Brown,
Calhoun, Cass, Champaign, Clark, Coles,
Cumberland, DeWitt, Douglas, Edgar,
Ford, Greene, Jersey, Livingston, Logan,
Macon, Macoupin, Mason, McLean,

Menard, Morgan, Moultrie, Piatt, Pike,
Sangamon, Schuyler, Scott, Vermilion and
Woodford).

Illinois Appellate Court
5th District
14th & Mains St.
P.O. Box 867
Mount Vernon, IL 62844-0018
Phone No. 618-242-3120
(Covering these counties: Alexander,
Bond, Christian, Clay, Clinton, Crawford,
Edwards, Effingham, Fayette, Franklin,
Gallatin, Hamilton, Hardin, Jackson,
Jasper, Jefferson, Johnson, Lawrence,
Madison, Marion, Massac, Monroe,
Montgomery, Perry, Rope, Rulaski,
Randolph, Richland, Saline, Shelby, St.
Clair, Union, Wabash, Washington,
Wayne, White and Williamson).

Indiana Court of Appeals
1st District
217 State House
Indianapolis, IN 46204
Phone No. 317-232-1930
(Covering these counties: Barholomew,
Boone, Brown, Clark, Clay, Crawford,
Daviess, Dearborn, Decatur, Dubois,
Fayette, Floyd, Fountain, Franklin, Gibson,
Greene, Hancock, Harrison, Hendricks,
Herny, Jackson, Jefferson, Jennings,
Johnson, Knox, Lawrence, Martin,
Monroe, Montgomery, Morgan, Ohio,
Orange, Owen, Parke, Perry, Pike, Posey,
Putnam, Shelby, Spencer, Sullivan,
Switzerland, Union, Vanderburgh,
Vermillion, Vigo, Warrick, Washington
and Wayne).

Indiana Court of Appeals
2nd District
217 State House
Indianapolis, IN 46204
Phone No. 317-232-1930
(Covering these counties: Adams,
Blackford, Carroll, Cass, Clinton,

STATE COURT OF CRIMINAL APPEALS

Delaware, Grant, Hamilton, Howard,
Huntington, Jay, Madison, Marion, Miami,
Tippecanoe, Tipton, Wabash, Wells and
White).

Indiana Court of Appeals
3rd District
217 State House
Indianapolis, IN 46204
Phone No. 317-232-1930
(Covering these counties: Allen, Benton,
DeKalb, Elkhart, Fulton, Jasper,
Kosciusko, LaGrange, Lake, LaPorte,
Marshall, Newton, Noble, Porter, Pulaski,
St. Joseph, Starke, Steuben, Warren and
Whitely).

Indiana Court of Appeals
4th District
217 State House
Indianapolis, IN 46204
Phone No. 317-232-1930
(Covering these counties: Every fourth
case from each of the other three districts).

Indiana Court of Appeals
5th District
217 State House
Indianapolis, IN 46204
Phone No. 317-232-1930
(An at large district).

Iowa Court of Appeals
1111 E. Court Ave.
Des Moines, IA 50319
Phone No. 515-281-5911

Kansas Court of Appeals
Kansas Judicial Center
301 S.W. 10th St.
Topeka, KS 66612
Phone No. 785-296-3229

Kentucky Court of Appeals
360 Democrat Drive
Frankfort, KY 40601
Phone No. 502-573-7920

Louisiana Court of Appeals
1st Circuit
P.O. Box 4408
Baton Rouge, LA 70821
Phone No. 225-382-3000
(Covering these Parishes: Ascension,
Assumption, East Baton Rouge, East
Feliciana, Iberville, Lafourche, Livingston,
Point Coupee, St. Helena, St. Mary, St.
Tammany, Tangipahoa, Terrebonne,
Washington, West Baton Rouge and West
Feliciana).

Louisiana Court of Appeals
2nd Circuit
430 Fannin St.
P.O. Box 1528
Shreveport, LA 71165-1528
Phone No. 318-227-3702
(Coveirng these Parishes: Bienville,
Bossier, Caddo, Caldwell, Claiborne,
DeSoto, East Carroll, Franklin, Jackson,
Lincoln, Madison, Morehouse, Ouachita,
Red River, Richland, Tensas, Union,
Webster, West Carroll and Winn).

Louisiana Court of Appeals
3rd Circuit
Calcasieu Parish Courthouse
P.O. Box 16577
Lake Charles, LA 70616
Phone No. 337-433-9403
(Covering these Parishes: Acadia, Allen,
Avoyelles, Beauregard, Calcasieu,
Cameron, Catahoula, Concordia,
Evangeline, Grant, Iberia, Jefferson Davis,
Lafayette, La Salle, Natchtoches, Rapides,
Sabine, St. Landry, St. Martin, Vermilion
and Vernon).

Louisiana Court of Appeals
4th Circuit
410 Royal St.
New Orleans, LA 70130
Phone No. 504-412-6019
(Covering these Parishes: Orleans,
Plaquemines and St. Bernard).

Louisiana Court of Appeals
5th Circuit
P.O. Box 489
Courthouse Annex
Gretna, LA 70054
Phone No. 504-376-1400
(Covering these Parishes: Jefferson, St. Charles, St. James and St. John the Baptist).

Maine has no Intermediate Appellate Court

Maryland Court of Appeals
Courts of Appeal Bldg.
361 Rowe Blvd.
Annapolis, MD 21401
Phone No. 410-260-1500

Massachusetts Court of Appeals
Appeals Court
John Adams Courthouse
One Pemberton Square
Boston, MA 02108
Phone No. 617-725-8106

Michigan Court of Appeals
1st District
Cadillac Place
3020 W. Grand Blvd.
Detroit, MI 48202
Phone No. 313-972-5678
(Covering these counties: Calhoun, Hillsdale, Lenawee, Monroe and Wayne).

Michigan Court of Appeals
2nd District
201 W. Big Beaver Rd. Ste. 800
Troy, MI 48084
Phone No. 248-542-8700
(Covering these counties: Genesee, Macomb, Oakland and Shiawassee).

Michigan Court of Appeals
3rd District
Michigan Office Bldg.
350 Ottawa, N.W.
Grand Rapids, MI 49503-2349

Phone No. 616-456-1167
(Covering these counties: Allegan, Bary, Berrien, Branch, Cass, Eaton, Jackson, Ionia, Kalamazoo, Kent, Muskegon, Newaygo, Ottawa, St. Joseph, Van Buren and Washtenaw).

Michigan Court of Appeals
4th District
Hall of Justice
925 W. Ottawa
P.O. Box 30022
Lansing, MI 48909-7522
Phone No. 517-373-0786

Minnesota Court of Appeals
25 M.L.K. Blvd.
St. Paul, MN 55155
Phone No. 651-296-2581

Mississippi Court of Appeals
656 N. State St.
P.O. Box 22847
Jackson, MS 39255
Phone No. 601-354-7410

Missouri Court of Appeals
Eastern District
Old Post Office Sq.
815 Olive St.
St. Louis, MO 63101
Phone No. 314-539-4300
(Covering these counties: Audrain, Cape Girardeau, Clark, City of St. Louis, Franklin, Gasconade, Jefferson, Knox, Lewis, Lincoln, Madison, Marion, Monroe, Montgomery, Osage, Perry, Pike, Ralls, St. Charles, St. Francois, Ste. Genevieve, St. Louis, Scotland, Shelby, Warren and Washington).

Missouri Court of Appeals
Southern District
University Plaza
300 Hammons Parkway
Springfield, MO 65806
Phone No. 417-895-6811

(Covering these counties: Barry, Barton, Bollinger, Butler, Camden, Carter, Cedar, Christian, Crawford, Dade, Dallas, Dent, Douglas, Dunklin, Greene, Hickory, Howell, Iron, Jasper, Laclede, Lawrence, McDonald, Maries, Mississippi, New Madrid, Newton, Oregon, Ozark, Pemiscot, Phelps, Polk, Pulaski, Reynolds, Ripley, Scott, Shannon, St. Clair, Stoddard, Stone, Taney, Texas, Wayne, Webster and Wright).

Missouri Court of Appeals
Western District
1300 Oak Street
Kansas City, MO 64106
Phone No. 816-889-3600
(Covering these counties: Adair, Andrew, Atchison, Bates, Benton, Boone, Buchanan, Caldwell, Callaway, Cass, Chariton, Clay, Clinton, Carroll, Cole, Cooper, Daviess, DeKalb, Gentry, Grundy, Henry, Holt, Howard, Harrison, Jackson, Johnson, Lafayette, Linn, Livingston, Macon, Mercer, Miller, Moniteau, Morgan, Nodaway, Platte, Putnam, Pettis, Randolph, Ray, Saline, Schuyler, Sullivan, Vernon and Worth).

Montana has no Appellate Courts

Nebraska Court of Appeals
2413 State Capitol
P.O. Box 98910
Lincoln, NE 68509-8910
Phone No. 402-471-3731

Nevada has no Intermediate Appellate Court.

New Hampshire has no Intermediate Appellate Court.

New Jersey Court of Appeals
Superior Court
Appellate Division
Justice Complex

CN-006
Trenton, NJ 08625
Phone No. 609-292-6995

New Mexico Court of Appeals
Supreme Court Bldg.
237 Don Gaspar, RM 116
P.O. Box 2008
Santa Fe, NM 87503
Phone No. 505-827-4925

New York Court of Appeals
Courthouse
20 Eagle St.
Albany, NY 12207-1095
Phone No. 518-455-7700

New York Court of Appeals
Appellate Division, 1st Department
Courthouse
27 Madison Ave. & 25th
New York, NY 10010
Phone No. 212-240-0400
(Covering these counties: Bronx and New York).

New York Court of Appeals
Appellate Division, 2nd Department
Supreme Court Bldg.
45 Monroe Place
Brooklyn, NY 11201
Phone No. 718-722-6307
(Covering these counties: Dutchess, Kings, Nassau, Orange, Putnam, Queens, Richmond, Rockland, Suffolk and Westchester).

New York Court of Appeals
Appellate Division, 3rd Department
Justice Bldg.
P.O. Box 7288
Capitol Station
Albany, NY 12224
Phone No. 518-474-3609
(Covering these counties: Albany, Broome, Chemung, Chenango, Clinton, Columbia, Cortland, Delaware, Essex, Franklin,

Fulton, Greene, Hamilton, Madison, Montgomery, Ostego, Rensselaer, St. Lawrence, Saratoga, Schenectady, Schoharie, Schuyler, Sullivan, Tioga, Tompkins, Ulster, Warren and Washington).

New York Court of Appeals
Appellate Division, 4th Department
50 East Ave. Ste. 200
Rochester, NY 14604
Phone No. 585-530-3100
(Covering these counties: Allegany, Cattaraugus, Cayuga, Chautauqua, Erie, Genesee, Herkimer, Jefferson, Lewis, Livingston, Monroe, Niagara, Oneida, Onondaga, Ontario, Orleans, Oswego, Seneca, Steuben, Wayne, Wyoming and Yates).

North Carolina Court of Appeals
P.O. Box 2779
Raleigh, NC 27602-2779
Phone No. 919-733-3561

North Dakota has no Intermediate Appellate Court.

Ohio has twelve (12) District Court of Appeals. The Clerk of each County operates as the Appellate Clerk for said county.

Ohio Court of Appeals
1st District
(Covers Hamilton county).

Ohio Court of Appeals
2nd District
(Covering these counties: Champaign, Clark, Darke, Greene, Miami and Montgomery).

Ohio Court of Appeals
3rd District
(Covering these counties: Allen, Auglaize, Crawford, Defiance, Hancock, Hardin,

Herny, Logan, Marion, Mercer, Paulding, Putnam, Seneca, Shelby, Union, Van Wert and Wyandot).

Ohio Court of Appeals
4th District
(Covering these counties: Adams, Athens, Gallia, Highland, Hocking, Jackson, Lawrence, Meigs, Pickaway, Pike, Ross, Scioto, Vinton and Washington).

Ohio Court of Appeals
5th District
(Covering these counties: Ashland, Coshocton, Delaware, Fairfield, Guernsey, Holmes, Knox, Licking, Morgan, Morrow, Muskingum, Perry, Richland, Stark and Tuscarawas).

Ohio Court of Appeals
6th District
(Covering these counties: Erie, Fulton, Huron, Lucas, Ottawa, Sandusky, Williams and Woods).

Ohio Court of Appeals
7th District
(Covering these counties: Belmont, Carroll, Columbiana, Harrison, Jefferson, Mahoning, Monroe and Noble).

Ohio Court of Appeals
8th District
(Covers Cuyahoga County).

Ohio Court of Appeals
9th District
(Covering these counties: Lorain, Medina, Summit and Wayne).

Ohio Court of Appeals
10th District
(Covers Franklin County).

Ohio Court of Appeals
11th District
(Covering these counties: Ashtabula, Geauga, Lake, Portage and Trumbull).

Ohio Court of Appeals
12th District
(Covering these counties: Brown, Bulter, Clermont, Clinton, Fayette, Madison, Preble and Warren).

Oklahoma Court of Appeals
Criminal Appeals
State Capitol, RM 230
Oklahoma City, OK 73105
Phone No. 405-521-2163

Oregon Court of Appeals
1163 State St.
Supreme Court Bldg.
Salem, OR 97301-2563
Phone No. 503-986-5555

Pennsylvania Court of Appeals
Commonwealth Court
Harrisburg
S. Office Bldg. 6th FL
Harrisburg, PA 17120
Phone No. 412-255-1600

Pennsylvania Commonwealth Court
Philadelphia
Widener Bldg. Ste. 990
One South Penn Sq.
Philadelphia, PA 19107
Phone No. 215-560-5742

Puerto Rico Court of Appeals
Circuit Court of Appeals
115 Eleanor Roosevelt Ave.
P.O. Box 191067
Hato Rey, PR 00919-1067
Phone No. 787-281-4329

Rhode Island has no Intermediate
Appellate Court.

South Carolina
Court of Appeals
1015 Sumter St. 5th Fl.
P.O. Box 11629

Columbia, SC 29211
Phone No. 803-734-1890

South Dakota has no Intermediate
Appellate Court.

Tennessee Court of Appeals
Middle Grand Division Supreme Court
Bldg.
401 7th Ave. N.
Nashville, TN 37219
Phone No. 615-741-2681

Tennessee Court of Appeals
Eastern Grand Division Supreme Court
Bldg.
P.O. Box 444
Knoxville, TN 37901
Phone No. 865-594-6700

Tennessee Court of Appeals
Western Grand Division
Supreme Court Bldg.
#6 Hwy 45 Bypass
P.O. Box 909
Jackson, TN 38302
Phone No. 731-432-5840

Texas Court of Criminal Appeals
Supreme Court Bldg.
201 W. 14th St.
P.O. Box 12308
Capitol Station
Austin, TX 78711
Phone No. 512-463-1551

Texas Court of Appeals
1st District
S. Tex. Col. of Law Bldg.
1307 San Jacinto, 10th FL
Houston, TX 77002
Phone No. 713-655-2700
(Covering these counties: Austin, Brazoria, Chambers, Colorado, Fort Bend, Galveston, Grimes, Harris, Waller and Washington).

Texas Court of Appeals
2nd District
Tarrant C. Justice Cntr.
401 W. Belknap St. Ste. 9000
Fort Worth, TX 76196
Phone No. 817-884-1990
(Covering these counties: Archer, Clay,
Cooke, Denton, Hood, Jack, Montague,
Parker, Tarrant, Wichita, Wise and
Young).

Texas Court of Appeals
3rd District
209 W. 14th St. RM 101
P.O. Box 12547
Austin, TX 78711-2547
Phone No. 512-463-1709
(Coveirng these counties: Bastrop, Bell,
Blanco, Burnet, Caldwell, Coke, Comal,
Concho, Fayette, Hays, Irion, Lampasas,
Lee, Llano, McCulloch, Milam, Mills,
Runnels, San Saba, Schleicher, Sterling,
Tom Green, Travis and Williams).

Texas Court of Appeals
4th District
Bexar Co. Justice Ctr.
300 Dolorosa St. Ste. 3200
San Antonio, TX 78205-3037
Phone No. 210-335-2635
(Covering these counties: Atascosa,
Bandera, Bexar, Brooks, Dimmit, Duval,
Edwards, Frio, Gillespie, Guadalupe, Jim
Hogg, Jim Wells, Karnes, Kendall, Kerr,
Kimble, Kinney, La Salle, Mason,
Maverick, McMullen, Medina, Menard,
Real Starr, Sutton, Uvalde, Val Verde,
Webb, Wilson, Zapata and Zavala).

Texas Court of Appeals
5th District
600 Commerce St. 2nd FL
Dallas, TX 75202-4658
Phone No. 214-712-3400
(Covering these counties: Collin, Dallas,
Grayson, Hunt, Kaufman and Rockwall).

Texas Court of Appeals
6th District
Bi-State Justice Bldg. #2A
100 N. State Line Ave.
Texarkana, TX 75501-5666
Phone No. 903-798-3046
(Covering these counties: Bowie, Camp,
Cass, Delta, Fannin, Franklin, Gregg,
Harrison, Hopkins, Hunt, Lamar, Marion,
Morris, Panola, Red River, Rusk, Titus,
Upshur and Wood).

Texas Court of Appeals
7th District
501 S. Fillmore St. #2A
P.O. Box 9540
Amarillo, TX 79105-9540
Phone No. 806-342-2650
(Covering these counties: Armstrong,
Bailey, Briscoe, Carson, Castro, Childress,
Cochran, Collingsworth, Cottle, Crosby,
Dallam, Deaf Smith, Dickens, Donley,
Floyd, Foard, Garza, Gray, Hale, Hall,
Hansford, Hardeman, Hartley, Hemphill,
Hockley, Hutchinson, Kent, King, Lamb,
Lipscomb, Lubbock, Lynn, Moore,
Motley, Ochiltree, Oldham, Parmer, Potter,
Randal, Roberts, Sherman, Swisher, Terry,
Wheeler, Wilbarger and Yoakum).

Texas Court of Appeals
8th District
500 E. San Antonio, Ste. 1203
El Paso, TX 79901
Phone No. 915-546-2240
(Covering these counties: Andrews,
Brewster, Crane, Crockett, Culberson, El
Paso, Hudspeth, Jeff Davis, Loving, Pecos,
Presido, Reagan, Reeves, Terrell, Upton,
Ward and Winkler).

Texas Court of Appeals
9th District
1001 Pearl St. Suite 330
Beaumont, TX 77701
Phone No. 409-835-8402
(Covering these counties: Hardin, Jasper,

Jefferson, Liberty, Montgomery, Newton, Orange, Polk, San Jacinto and Tyler).

Texas Court of Appeals
10th District
501 Washington Ave.
Waco, TX 76701-1327
Phone No. 254-757-5200
(Covering these counties: Bosque, Brazos, Burleson, Coryell, Ellis, Falls, Freestone, Hamilton, Hill, Johnson, Leon, Limestone, McLennan, Madison, Navarro, Robertson, Somervell and Walker).

Texas Court of Appeals
11th District
100 W. Main St.
P.O. Box 271
Eastland, TX 76448-0271
Phone No. 254-629-2638
(Covering these counties: Baylor, Borden, Brown, Callahan, Coleman, Comanche, Dawson, Eastland, Ector, Erath, Fisher, Gaines, Glascock, Kaskell, Howard, Jones, Knox, Martin, Midland, Mitchell, Nolan, Palo Pinto, Scurry, Shackelford, Stephens, Stonewall, Taylor and Throckmorton).

Texas Court of Appeals
12th District
1517 W. Front, Ste. 354
Tyler, TX 75702
Phone No. 903-593- 8471
(Covering these counties: Anderson, Angelina, Cherokee, Gregg, Henderson, Houston, Nacogdoches, Rains, Rusk, Sabine, San Augustine, Shelby, Smith, Trinity, Upshur, Van Zandt and Wood).

Texas Court of Appeals
13th District
901 Leopard St. 10th FL.
Corpus Christi, TX 78401
Phone No. 361-888-0416
(Covering these counties: Aransas, Bee, Calhoun, Cameron, De Witt, Goliad, Gonzalez, Hidalgo, Jackson, Kenedy,

Kleberg, Lavaca, Live Oak, Matagorda, Nueces, Refugio, San Patricio, Victoria, Wharton and Willacy).

Texas Court of Appeals
14th District
S. Tex. Col. of Law Bldg.
1307 San Jacinto St.
Houston, TX 77002-7006
Phone No. 713-655-2800
(Covering these counties: Austin, Brazoria, Chambers, Colorado, Fort Bend, Galveston, Grimes, Harris, Waller and Washington).

Utah Court of Appeals
405 South State
P.O. Box 140230
Salt Lake City, UT 84114-0230
Phone No. 801-578-3907

Vermont has no Intermediate Appellate Court.

Virginia Court of Appeals
109 N. 8th St.
Richmond, VA 23219
Phone No. 804-371-8428

Washington Court of Appeals
Division One
One Union Sq.
600 University St.
Seattle, WA 98101-1176
Phone No. 206-464-5871
(Covering these counties: Island, King, San Juan, Skagit, Snohomish and Watcom).

Washington Court of Appeals
Division Two
950 Broadway Ste. 300
MS TB-06
Tacoma, WA 98402-4427
Phone No. 253-593-2970
(Covering these counties: Clallam, Clark, Cowlitz, Grays Harbor, Jefferson, Kitsap,

Lewis, Mason, Pacific, Pierce, Skamania,
Thurston and Wahkiakum).

Washington Court of Appeals
Division Three
500 N. Cedar St.
P.O. Box 2159
Spokane, WA 99201-2159
Phone No. 509-456-3082
(Covering these counties: Adams, Asotin,
Benton, Chelan, Columbia, Douglas, Ferry,
Franklin, Garfield, Grant, Kittitas, Klicktat,
Lincoln, Okanogan, Pend Oreille, Spokane,
Stevens, Walla Walla, Whitman and
Yakima).

West Virginia has no Intermediate
Appellate Court.

Wisconsin Court of Appeals
District One
110 E. Main Street, RM 215
P.O. Box 1688
Madison, WI 53701-1688
Phone No. 608-266-1880
(Covering Milwaukee County)

Wisconsin Court of Appeals
District Two
110 E. Main St. RM 215
P.O. Box 1688
Madison, WI 53701-1688
Phone No. 608-266-1880
(Covering these counties: Calument, Fond
du Lac, Green Lake, Kenosha, Manitowoc,
Ozaukee, Racine, Sheboygan, Walworth,
Washington, Waukesha and Winnebago).

Wisconsin Court of Appeals
District Three
110 E. Main St. RM 215
P.O. Box 1688
Madison, WI 53701-1688
Phone No. 608-266-1880
(Covering these counties: Ashland, Barron,
Bayfield, Brown, Buffalo, Burnett,
Chippewa, Door, Douglas, Dunn, Eau

Claire, Florence, Forest, Iron, Kewaunee,
Langlade, Lincoln, Marathon, Marinette,
Menominee, Oconto, Oneida, Outagamie,
Pepin, Pierce, Polk, Price, Rusk, Sawyer,
Shawano, St. Croix, Taylor, Tempealeau,
Vilas and Washburn).

Wisconsin Court of Appeals
District Four
110 E. Main St. RM 215
P.O. Box 1688
Madison, WI 53701-1688
Phone No. 608-266-1880
(Covering these counties: Adams, Clark,
Columbia, Crawford, Dane, Dodge, Grant,
Green, Iowa, Jackson, Jefferson, Juneau,
LaCrosse, Lafayette, Marquette, Monroe,
Portage, Richland, Rock, Sauk, Vernon,
Waupaca, Waushara and Wood).

Wyoming has no Intermediate Appellate
Court.

UNITED STATES COURT OF APPEALS ADDRESSES

United States Court of Appeals
First Circuit
Richard C. Donovan, Clerk
Office of the Clerk
Moakley U.S. Courthouse
1 Courthouse Way Ste. 2500
Boston, MA 02210
Phone No. 617-748-9057

United States Court of Appeals
Second Circuit
Catherine O'Hagan Wolfe
Thurgood Marshall U.S. Courthouse
40 Foley Sq.
New York, NY 10007
Phone No. 212-855-7850

United States Court of Appeals
Third Circuit
Marcia Waldron, Clerk
21400 U.S. Courthouse
601 Market St.
Philadelphia, PA 19106-1790
Phone No. 215-597-2992

United States Court of Appeals
Fourth Circuit
Patrick Connor, Clerk
Power Courthouse Annex
1100 E. Main St. Ste 501
Richmond, VA 23219-3517

United States Court of Appeals
Fifth Circuit
Charles Fulburge III
600 S. Maestri Place
New Orleans, LA 70130-3408
Phone No. 504-310-7700

United States Court of Appeals
Sixth Circuit
Leonard Gren, Clerk
540 Potter Stewart Courthouse
100 E. Fifth St.
Cincinnati, OH 45202-3988
Phone No. 513-564-7000

United States Court of Appeals
Seventh Circuit
Gino Agnello, Clerk
Dirksen Courthouse
219 S. Dearborn St. RM 2722

Chicago, IL 60604
Phone No. 312-435-5850

United States Court of Appeals
Eighth Circuit
Michael Gans, Clerk
Eagleton Courthouse
111 S. 10th St. RM 24.329
St. Louis, MO 63102
Phone No. 314-244-2400

500 Federal Bldg.
St. Paul, MN 55101
Phone No. 651-848-1300

United States Court of Appeals
Ninth Circuit
Molly Dwyer, Clerk
95 Seventh St. (94103-1526)
P.O. Box 193939
San Francisco, CA 94119-3939
Phone No. 415-355-8000

Richard Chambers Bldg.
125 S. Grand Ave.
Pasadena, CA 91105-1652
Phone No. 626-229-7250

Park Place Bldg.
1200 Sixth Ave., 3rd FL
Seattle, WA 98101
Phone No. 206-553-2937

Pioneer Courthouse
700 S.W. 6th Ave.
Portland, OR 97204
Phone No. 833-5311

United States Court of Appeals
Tenth Circuit
Elizabeth Shumaker
U.S. Court of Appeals
Byron White Courthouse
1823 Stout St.
Denver, CO 80257
Phone No. 303-844-3147

United States Court of Appeals
Eleventh Circuit
Thomas Kahn, Clerk
Tuttle Bldg.
56 Forsyth St. N.W.
Atlanta, GA 30303-3147
Phone No. 335-6535

LIST OF STATE BAR ASSOCIATIONS

The following is a list of State Bar Associations addresses and PO Box (Zip Code for PO Box is next to PO Box) and phone number.

Alabama State Bar
P.O. Box 671 (36101)
415 Dexter St.
Montgomery, AL 36104
(334) 269-1515

Alaska Bar
P.O. Box 100279 (99510)
510 K St. #602
Anchorage, AK 99501
(907) 272-7469

State Bar of Arizona
4201 N. 24th Street
Phoenix, AZ 85016-6288
(602) 252-4804

Arkansas Bar
400 W. Markham, Ste 401
Little Rock, AR 72201
(501) 375-4606

State Bar of California
180 Howard St.
San Francisco, CA 94105
(415) 538-2000

The Colorado Bar
1900 Grant St. 9th FL
Denver, CO 80203
(303) 860-1115

Connecticut State Bar
30 Bank St.
P.O. Box 350
New Britain, CT 06050-0350
(860) 223-4400

Delaware State Bar
301 N. Market Street
Wilmington, DE 19801
(302) 658-5279

District of Columbia Bar
1101 K. Street N.W. Ste 200
Washington, DC 20005
(202) 737-4700

District of Columbia Bar
1225 19th Street Ste. 800
Washington, DC 20036
(202) 293-3388

The Florida Bar
651 E. Jefferson St.
Tallahassee, FL 32399-2300
(850) 561-5600

State Bar of Georgia
104 Marietta Street NW, Ste 100
Atlanta, GA 30303
(404) 527-8700

Hawaii State Bar
First Hawaiian TWR
1132 Bishop St. Ste. 906
Honolulu, HI 96813
(808) 537-1868

Idaho State Bar
P.O. Box 895 (83701)
525 W. Jefferson
Boise, ID 83702
(208) 334-4500

Illinois State Bar
424 S. Second St.
Springfield, IL 62701
(217) 525-1760

Indiana State Bar
One Indiana Square, Ste. 530
Indianapolis, IN 46204
(317) 639-5465

Iowa State Bar
521 E. Locust, Ste 300
Des Moines, IA 50309-1939
(515) 243-3179

Kansas State Bar
P.O. Box 1037 (66601-1037)
1200 Harrison St.
Topeka, KS 66612
(785) 234-5696

Kentucky State Bar
514 West Main St.
Frankfort, KY 40601-1883
(502) 564-3795

Louisiana State Bar
601 St. Charles Ave.
New Orleans, LA 70130
(504) 566-1600

Maine State Bar
P.O. Box 788 (04332-0788)
124 State St.
Augusta, ME 04330
(207) 622-7523

Maryland State Bar
520 W. Fayette St.
Baltimore, MD 21201
(410) 685-7878

Massachusetts State Bar
20 West St.
Boston, MA 02111-1204
(617) 338-0500

State Bar of Michigan
306 Townsend St.
Lansing, MI 48933-2083
(517) 346-6330

Minnesota State Bar
600 Nicollect Mall, Ste 380
Minneapolis, MN 55402
(612) 333-1183

Mississippi State Bar
P.O. Box 2168 (39225-2168)
643 N. State St.
Jackson, MS 39202
(601) 948-4471

Missouri State Bar
P.O. Box 119 (65102)
326 Monroe
Jefferson City, MO 65101
(573) 635-4128

State Bar of Montana
P.O. Box 577 (59624)
7 West Sixth Ave. Ste. 2B
Helena, MT 59624
(406) 442-7660

Nebraska State Bar
P.O. Box 81809 (68501)
635 S. 14th Street, 2nd FL
Lincoln, NE 68508
(402) 475-7091

State Bar of Nevada
600 E. Charleston Blvd.
Las Vegas, NV 89104
(702) 382-2200

New Hampshire Bar
112 Pleasant St.
Concord, NH 03301
(603) 224-6942

New Jersey State Bar
One Constitution Sq.
New Brunswick, NJ 08901-1500
(732) 249-5000

State Bar of New Mexico
P.O. Box 92860
5121 Masthead NE
Albuquerque, NM 87109
(505) 797-6000

New York State Bar
One Elk St.
Albany, NY 12207
(518) 463-3200

North Carolina State Bar
P.O. Box 25908 (27611)
208 Fayetteville St. Mall
Raleigh, NC 27601
(919) 828-4620

North Carolina Bar
P.O. Box 3688
Cary, NC 27519
(919) 677-0561

State Bar of North Dakota
P.O. Box 2136
Bismarck, ND 58502
(701) 255-1404

Ohio State Bar
P.O. Box 16562
1700 Lake Shore Drive
Columbus, OH 43216-6562
(614) 487-2050

Oklahoma State Bar
P.O. Box 53036 (73152)
1901 N. Lincoln
Oklahoma City, OK 73105
(405) 416-7000

Oregon State Bar
P.O. Box 1689
5200 S.W. Meadows Rd.
Lake Oswego, OR 97035
(503) 620-0222

Pennsylvania Bar
P.O. Box 186 (17108)
100 South Street
Harrisburg, PA 17108-0186
(717) 238-6715

Puerto Rico Bar
808 Stop II
P.O. Box 9021900
San Juan, PR 00902-1900
(787) 721-3358

Rhode Island Bar
115 Cedar Street
Providence, RI 02903
(401) 421-5740

South Carolina Bar
P.O. Box 608
950 Taylor St.
Columbia, SC 29202
(803) 799-6653

State Bar of South Dakota
222 E. Capitol
Pierre, SD 57501-2596
(605) 224-7554

Tennessee State Bar
221 Fourth Ave. N
Nashville, TN 37219
(615) 383-7421

State Bar of Texas
P.O. Box 12487 (78711)
1414 Colorado
Austin, TX 78701
(512) 463-1483
(800) 204-2222

Utah State Bar
645 S. 200 East, Ste 310
Salt Lake City, UT 84111-3834
(801) 531-9077

Vermont State Bar
P.O. Box 100 (05601)
35-37 Court Street
Montpelier, VT 05602
(802) 223-2020

Virgin Island Bar
P.O. Box 4108
Christianstead, VI 00822
(340) 778-7497

Virginia State Bar
707 East Main St. Ste. 1500
Richmond, VA 23219-2800
(804) 775-0500

Virginia Bar
7th & Franklin Bldg.
701 E. Franklin St. #1515
Richmond, VA 23219
(804) 644-0041

Washington State Bar
2101 Fourth Ave. 4th FL
Seattle, WA 98121-2599
(206) 443-9722

West Virginia State Bar
2006 Kamawha Blvd. E.
Charleston, WV 25311
(304) 558-2456

West Virginia Bar
1111 Sixth Ave.
Huntington, WV 25701
(304) 522-2652

State Bar of Wisconsin
P.O. Box 7158 (53707)
5302 E. Park Blvd.
Madison, WI 53718
(608) 257-3838

Wyoming State Bar
P.O. Box 109 (82003-0109)
500 Randall Ave.
Cheyenne, WY 82001
(307) 632-9061

Chapter IV
State Habeas Corpus or Post-Conviction Motions

❑ State Habeas Corpus or Post-Conviction Relief Statute Citations

> ➤ *Form* letter requesting local habeas corpus statute

> ➤ *Form* letter requesting copies of specific state statutes

> ➤ *Form* letters requesting habeas corpus or post-conviction relief *Form* motions

> ➤ Petition for writ of habeas corpus

> ➤ Verification for petition

> ➤ Traverse To State's Return And Answer

> ➤ Notice Of Appeal (State)

> ➤ Memorandum brief in support of motion for post-conviction relief pursuant to Fla. R. Criminal P. 3.850 (Florida)

> ➤ Motion for permission to file a motion for Writ of Error Coram Nobis (Arkansas)

> ➤ *Form* affidavit for petition

STATE HABEAS CORPUS/POST-CONVICTION
RELIEF STATUTE CITATIONS

The State habeas corpus/post-conviction relief statute citations are listed below. The Federal habeas corpus statutes are set forth in Chapters V, VI, and VII. The State statutes can be obtained online at the State's website or from the State Court system.

Form Letter No. 1 has been predrafted to the State Supreme Court, Law Librarian, and **Form Letter No. 2** has been predrafted to the State Criminal Court of Appeals both letters requesting a copy of the State habeas corpus/post-conviction relief statute. **Form Letter No. 3** has been predrafted to the State Sentencing Court requesting a copy of the **State Habeas Corpus Form Motion**. **Form Letter No. 4** has been predrafted to a State Court's Law Librarian requesting specific copies of various state statutes. **Form Letter No. 5** has been predrafted requesting specific copies of the State's habeas corpus/post-conviction relief statute and applicable Time Limits for filing a habeas petition. **Enclose a self-addressed stamped envelope for the return of said statute or information**. Check the Table Of Contents for the Supreme Court's and Criminal Court of Appeals address listings. The Sentencing Court's addresses are not listed herein.

Generally, the Supreme Court, Criminal Court of Appeals, or the Sentencing Court Clerk's Office or Law Librarian will forward you a copy of the State Habeas Corpus **Form Motion** and applicable habeas statute. Alternatively, they will advise you where your family or a friend can download said documents online and print them and mail to you.

Alabama: Ala. Code §15-21-1 et seq.
Alaska: Alaska Stat. §12.75.010 et seq.
Arizona: Ariz. R. Crim. P. 32; Ariz. Rev. Stat. §13-4021 et seq.
Arkansas: Ark.R.Crim.P.37; Ark. Code Ann. §16-112-101 et seq.
California: Cal. Penal Code §1473 et seq.
Colorado: Colo.R.Crim.P.35; Colo. Rev. Stat. §13-45-101 et seq.
Connecticut: Conn. Gen. Stat. Ann. §52-466 et seq.
Delaware: Delaware Superior Court Criminal Rule 61; Rule 35 (Modification
    of sentence)
District of Columbia: D.C. Code §23-110; D.C. Code §16-1901 et seq.
Florida: Fla. R. Crim. 3.850; Fla. R. Crim. 3000 correct illegal sentence.
Georgia: O.G.G.A. §9-14-1 et. seq.
Hawaii: Haw. Rev. Stat. §660-3 et. seq. Haw. R. Penal Pro. 40
Idaho: Idaho Code Ann. §19-4901 et seq.
Illinois: 725 Ill. Com. Stat. 5/122-1 et seq.
Indiana: Ind. Code Ann. §34-25.5-1-1 et seq.; Ind: R.P. for Post-Conviction
    Remedies R. 1
Iowa: Iowa Code Ann. §663A.1 et seq.
Kansas: Kan. Stat. Ann. §60-1501 et seq.
Kentucky: Ky. R. Crim. P. 11.42; Ky. Rev. Stat. Ann. §419.020 et seq.
Louisiana: La. Code Crim. Proc. Ann. art. 924 et seq.

Maine: Me. Rev. Stat. Title 15, §2121 et seq.
   Me. Rev. Stat. Ann. Title 14, §5501 et seq.
Maryland: Md. Ann. Code art. 27, §645A et seq.
   Md. Ann. Ann. Cts. & Jud. Proc. §3-701 et seq.
Massachusetts: Mass. R. Crim. P. 30
Michigan: Mich. Compo Laws Ann. §600.4307 et seq.
Minnesota: Minn. Stat. Ann. §590.01 et. seq.
Mississippi: Miss. Code. Ann.§99-39-1 et seq.
Missouri: Mo. S.Ct. R. Crim. P. 29.12 §548.101 R.S.MO
Montana: Mont. Code Ann. §46-21-101 et seq.
   Mont. Code Ann. §46-22-101 et seq.
Nebraska: Neb. Rev. Stat. §29-3001 et seq.
Nevada: Nev. Rev. Stat. §34-360 et seq.
New Hampshire: N.H. Rev. Stat. §534:1 et. seq.
New Jersey: N.J. Ct. R. ann. 3-22.
New Mexico: N.M. Stat. Ann. §31-11-6; N.M. Crim. Proc. Rule 5-802
New York: N.Y. Crim. Proc. Law §440.10 et seq.
North Carolina: N.C. Gen. Stat. 15A-1411 et seq. id. 17-1 et seq.
North Dakota: N.D. Ct. R. Ann. 29-32.1-02.
Ohio: Ohio Rev. Code Ann. §2953.21 et seq.
Oklahoma: Okla. Stat. Rev. Title 22, §1080 et seq.
Oregon: Or. Rev. Stat. §138.510 et seq.
Pennsylvania: 42 Pa. Cons. Stat. Ann. §§9541-9546.
Puerto Rico Crim. Proc. Rule 192.1; P.R. Laws Ann. tit. 34, §1741(c).
Rhode Island: R.I. Gen. Laws §10-9.1-1 et seq. id. 10-903 et seq.
South Carolina: S.C. Code Ann. §17-27-10 et seq.
South Dakota: S.D. Code Ann. §21-27-1 et. seq.
Tennessee: Tenn. Code Ann. §40-30-102 et. seq. Tenn. S.Ct. Rule 39
Texas: Tex. Crim. P. Code Ann. art. §11.01 et seq.
Utah: Utah Code Ann. §78-35a-101 to 106.
Vermont: 13 V.S.A. §7131 et. seq.
Virginia: Va. Code Ann. §8.01-654 et seq.
Washington: Wash. Rev. Code Ann. §7.36.010 et seq.
West Virginia: W. Va. Code §53-4A-1 et seq.
Wisconsin: Wis. Stat. Ann. §974.06 et seq.
       Wyoming: Wyo. Stat. Ann. §7-14-101 et seq.

Form Letter No. 1

[Your Name & Prison Number]
[Your Institution]
[Your Address]
[Town, State & Zip Code]

[Date]

_____ SUPREME COURT
ATTN: LAW LIBRARIAN
Address
Town, State & Zip Code

Re: _____ Post-Conviction Relief/Habeas Corpus Statute

Dear Law Librarian:

At this time, I am requesting a copy of the _____ Post-Conviction Relief statute _____ § _____ for filing a post-conviction motion challenging the constitutionality of my criminal conviction or sentence. I am currently incarcerated at the _____ Correctional Institution, _____, _____, which does not have _____ Statutes or law books.

I have enclosed a self-addressed stamped envelope for the return of a copy of the _____ Post-Conviction Relief/Habeas corpus statute.

Your assistance on this matter is greatly appreciated. Thank you.

Sincerely,

_____
[Your Name]

CC:
        p/file.

120

Form Letter No. 2

[Your Name & Prison Number]
[Your Institution]
[Your Address]
[Town, State & Zip Code]

[Date]

_____ CRIMINAL COURT OF APPEALS
LAW LIBRARIAN
Address
Town, State & Zip Code

Re: _____ Post-Conviction Relief/Habeas Corpus Statute

Dear Law Librarian:

At this time, I am requesting a copy of the _____ Post-Conviction Relief statute _____ § _____ for filing a post-conviction motion challenging the constitutionality of my criminal conviction or sentence. I am currently incarcerated at the _____ Correctional Institution, _____, _____, which does not have _____ Statutes or law books.

I have enclosed a self-addressed stamped envelope for the return of a copy of the _____ Post-Conviction Relief/Habeas corpus statute.

Your assistance on this matter is greatly appreciated. Thank you.

Sincerely,

_____
[Your Name]

CC:
p/file.

Form Letter No. 3

[Your Name & Prison Number]
[Your Institution]
[Address]
[Town, State & Zip Code]

[Date]

Clerk of the Court

_____

_____

Address
Town, State & Zip Code

Re: **<u>Request For Habeas Corpus Form Motion</u>**

Dear Clerk:

 I am requesting for your office to provide me with a copy of the _____ State Habeas Corpus Form Motion required by the Court for prisoners to use to file an application for Habeas Corpus challenging the constitutionality of a conviction and sentence in this Court.

 I have enclosed a self-addressed stamped envelope for the return of the Habeas Corpus Form Motion.

 Your assistance on this matter is greatly appreciated. Thank you.

Sincerely,

_____

Your Name

CC:
 p/file.

Form Letter No. 4

[Your Name & Prison Number]
[Your Institution]
[Your Address]
[Town, State & Zip Code]

[Date]

_____ COURT
ATTN: LAW LIBRARIAN

Dear Law Librarian:

    In _____ and _____ I was charged and subsequently convicted in _____ of violating the following statutes: _____ §§ _____ _____ and _____. I need a copy of those statutes to make a determination whether those convictions can properly be used as predicate offenses under the federal Armed Career Criminal Act. The FCI _____ Law Library does not have any _____ State Law Books. Would your office be kind enough to please forward me a copy of the _____ _____ statutes stated above.

    I have enclosed a self-addressed stamped envelope for the return of a copy of those statutes.

    Your assistance on this matter is greatly appreciated. Thank you.

Sincerely,

_____
[Your Name]

CC:
    p/file.

Form Letter No. 5

[Your Name & Prison Number]
[Your Institution]
[Address]
[Town, State & Zip Code]

[Date]

_____COURT
ATTN: LAW LIBRARIAN
Address
Town, State & Zip Code

Dear Law Librarian:

I am requesting a copy of the _____ State Habeas Corpus Post-Conviction Statute and applicable Time Limits for filing a habeas corpus petition challenging the constitutionality of a criminal conviction. I am currently incarcerated at the _____ Correctional Institution, _____, _____, and they do not have _____ State Statutes or law books.

I have enclosed a self-addressed stamped envelope for the return of the _____ State Habeas Corpus statute for challenging the constitutionality of a conviction.

Your assistance on this matter is greatly appreciated. Thank you.

Sincerely,

_____
Your Name

CC:
p/file.

Form Letter No. 6

Name & Prison Number
_____ Correctional Institution
Address
Town, State & Zip Code

Date

_____County Superior Court
Office of the Clerk
Address
Town, State & Zip Code

Re: Petition For Writ of Habeas Corpus

Dear Clerk:

Please find enclosed the original and two copies of my: "Petition For Writ of Habeas Corpus and Exhibits," for filing with the Court. Once I receive a Docket Number from your office, I will make the necessary arrangements to have the filing fee sent to your office in reference to that specific Docket Number.

Additionally, I have enclosed a third copy of the Petition For Writ of Habeas Corpus to be stamped filed for record and returned to me in the enclosed self-addressed stamped envelope.

Your assistance on this matter is greatly appreciated. Thank you.

Sincerely,

_____
Your Name

CC:
p/file.

IN THE SUPERIOR COURT OF _____ COUNTY
STATE OF GEORGIA

_____
                  Petitioner,

VS.   Civil Action _____
                                           Case No. _____

THE STATE OF GEORGIA
_____ **, Warden**
_____ **Correctional Institution,**
_____ **, Georgia**

                  Respondent.

PETITION FOR WRIT OF HABEAS CORPUS

Petitioner, _____, pro se, respectfully petitions this Court, pursuant to **O.C.G.A. §9-14-41** (2003), to issue a Writ of Habeas Corpus.

I.
THE CONVICTION AND SENTENCE FROM WHICH PETITIONER SEEKS RELIEF

1. Petitioner is currently incarcerated at the _____ Correctional Institution _____, Georgia, by Respondent _____ the Warden.

2. The conviction and sentence from which Petitioner seeks relief was imposed by this Court in the case styled **State of Georgia v.** _____, Case No. _____ (_____ County, Ga. _____).

3. Petitioner has sought no other review of the conviction and sentence challenged herein nor has Petitioner brought the Claims for Relief asserted herein in any appeal or in any other post-conviction proceeding.

II.
SUMMARY OF CLAIMS FOR RELIEF

4. Petitioner asserts the following five Claims for Relief, as described more fully below:

   a. Petitioner was denied his Sixth Amendment right to effective of counsel due to trial counsel's conflict of interest;

   b. Petitioner was denied his Sixth Amendment right to effective assistance of counsel because:

   (i) Failure to investigate and file a motion to suppress illegal seized evidence without a warrant;

   (ii) Induced Petitioner's guilty plea based on faulty and erroneously legal advice;

126

(iii) Failure to file Petitioner's requested motion to withdraw guilty plea; and

(iv) Failure to file a requested notice of appeal.

Based on the Claims for Relief asserted herein, Petitioner seeks to vacate or set aside the conviction and sentence. Such conviction and sentence being imposed in violation of the constitutions and laws of the State of Georgia and the United States of America.

III.
FACTS APPLICABLE TO ALL CLAIMS FOR RELIEF

Petitioner Arrest:

5. On _____ ___, 20___, Petitioner and co-defendant _____ were living together at _____ _____, Georgia. On that same day, _____ County Sheriff's Department raided that residence and arrested Petitioner and co-defendant _____. The _____ County Sheriff's Department searched the residence and seized five pounds and nine ounces of marijuana. The _____ County Sheriff's Department did not have a search warrant or an arrest warrant.

6. On _____ ___, 20___, after law enforcement personnel arrested Petitioner and _____ at their residence and seized five (5) pounds and nine (9) ounces of marijuana. Later, that same day, a second group of law enforcement officers obtained a search warrant for that residence and conducted a second search finding no new evidence.

Trial Court Proceedings:

7. On _____ ___, 20___, the State of Georgia, charged Petitioner and co-defendant _____ with possession of marijuana with intent to distribute (Count One); Petitioner was charged in Count Two with selling of 9 ounces of marijuana to _____. Count Three charged both Petitioner and co-defendant _____ with possession of marijuana. On that same day, co-defendant _____ posted bail and the following day co-defendant _____ posted Petitioner's bond.

8. Codefendant _____ subsequently retained defense counsel _____ to represent her and Petitioner. Co-defendant _____ and Petitioner explained to counsel _____ that law enforcement did not have a search or arrest warrant when they raided their residence and seized the marijuana. **See Exhibit "__"** co-defendant _____ affidavit and Petitioner's affidavit **Exhibit "___".**

9. On _____ ___, 20___, the grand jury for _____ County, returned a three count indictment. Count One charged that on _____ ___, 20___, Petitioner possessed more than one ounce to wit: Five (5) pounds and nine (9) ounces of cannabis sativa L, commonly known as marijuana. Count Two charged Petitioner with unlawfully selling five (5) pounds and nine (9) ounces of cannabis sativa L, commonly known a marijuana, to _____; and, Count Three charged Petitioner and _____ with possession of cannabis sativa L, commonly known as marijuana, of more than one ounce, to wit: (24 ounces) six (6) pounds of marijuana, in violation of the Georgia Controlled Substance Act.

10. On _____ ___, 20___, Petitioner selected a jury and a recess was taken. Defense counsel _____ explained to Petitioner that he had negotiated a plea agreement for co-defendant _____ which required her testimony against Petitioner if he proceeded to trial and she would receive a 12 month probation. **See Exhibit "___"** Petitioner's Affidavit.

11. Defense counsel _____ advised Petitioner that he could plead guilty to two misdemeanor's and the felony offenses would be dismissed and he would have to serve 12 months at the _____ County Public Work Camp. On that same day, Petitioner pled guilty to two counts. See **Exhibit "___"** Petitioner's affidavit.

12. On that same day, the Court sentenced Petitioner on Count Two to five (5) years probation and on Count Three to 12 months at the _____ County Public Work Camp to be served consecutively to count two and a fine of $2,000.00. At that time, Petitioner specifically informed defense counsel _____ to file a motion to withdraw his guilty plea because the Court sentenced him to a felony and file a notice of appeal. See **Exhibit "___"** Petitioner's Affidavit. See also **Exhibit "___"** Codefendant _____ affidavit.

13. The State of Georgia dismissed the indictment against co-defendant _____ and the record reflects that she entered a plea of guilty to a misdemeanor in a separate action. Ms._____ was sentenced to 12 months probation.

Petitioner's Appeal:

14. On _____ ___, 20___, Petitioner instructed defense counsel _____ to file an appeal. Defense counsel abandoned Petitioner and failed to file his requested notice of appeal and his motion to withdraw guilty plea. See _____ ___, 20___, **Exhibit "___"** Petitioner's affidavit. See also **Docket Entry Sheet**.

15. But for Mr. _____ advice based upon his actual conflict of interest in representing co-defendant _____, Petitioner would not have pled guilty and instead would have insisted on going to trial. See **Exhibit "___"**.

_____ § _____

IV.
CLAIMS FOR RELIEF

All previous paragraphs of this Petition are incorporated herein by reference.

1. **Ineffective Assistance of Counsel Due To An Actual Conflict of Interest**

Petitioner was deprived of his constitutional right to effective assistance of counsel because trial counsel represented actual conflicting interests throughout the trial court proceedings. **U.S. Const. Amendments VI** and **XIV; Cuyler v. Sullivan, 466 U.S. 335, 100 S.Ct. 1708, 64 L.Ed.2d 333 (1980)**. In order to find a Sixth Amendment violation based on a conflict of interest, the reviewing court must find: (1) that counsel actively represented conflicting interests; and (2) that an actual conflict of interest adversely affected the attorney's performance. **Id. at 348, 100 S.Ct. at 1718.** Under **Cuyler**, the court must presume prejudice if the conflict of interest adversely affected the attorney's performance. **Id.**

128

Petitioner is entitled to Relief on this Claim because (1) trial counsel's duel representation of Petitioner and co-defendant _____ created an actual conflict of interest which adversely affected trial counsel's performance. **See Fact No. 10.** Trial counsel ambushed Petitioner after jury selections with the fact that he had negotiated a plea agreement for co-defendant _____, which required her testimony against Petitioner if he proceeded to trial and she would receive a 12 month probation for a misdemeanor charge. **See Fact No. 10.** These actions by counsel violated Petitioner's Sixth and Fourteenth Amendment right to effective assistance of counsel. **See Tarwater v. State, 259 Ga. 516, 383 S.Ed.2d 883 (1989).**

In **Tarwater**, the Georgia Supreme Court, held that "when counsel representing multiple defendants negotiates a plea bargain conditioned upon more than one pleading guilty, that attorney has suffered a conflict of interest which per se adversely affects his representation of each defendant affected." **id., at 885.** From the undisputed documentary evidence in the record of Petitioner's case, it is clear that this is precisely what happened. **See Wood v. Georgia, 450 U.S. 261, 67 L.Ed.2d 220, 101 S.Ct. 1097 (1981); Ford v. Ford, 749 F.2d 681, 683 (11th Cir. 1985); Trejo v. United States, 66 F.Supp.2d 1274, 1285 (S.D. Fla. 1999).**

Defense counsel induced Petitioner's guilty plea based on two misdemeanor offenses and that the felony charges would be dismissed, and advised Petitioner that if he continued to proceed to trial that co-defendant _____ was going to testify against him. **See Facts No. 10 and 11.** Because Petitioner detrimentally relied upon this advice in deciding to change his plea to guilty, said plea must be set aside on the grounds of prejudicially inadequate representation. **See Trejo, 66 F.Supp.2d at 1285.**

Adverse Performance:

The conflict adversely affected counsel's performance because counsel:

(1)   Failed to seek a favorable plea agreement for Petitioner requiring Petitioner to testify for the State. **See Tarwater, supra; Holloway v. Arkansas, 435 U.S. 475, 490, 98 S.Ct. 1173, 1181, 55 L.Ed.2d 426 (1978); Baty v. Balkcom, 661 F.2d 391, 395 (5th Cir. 1981) (Unit B), cert. denied, 456 U.S. 1011, 102 S.Ct. 2307, 73 L.Ed.2d 1308 (1982).**

(2)   Failed to investigate the illegal search and seizure and file a motion to suppress the illegal seized evidence without a warrant or probable cause. **Huynh v. King, 95 F.3d 1052, 1056 (11th Cir. 1996); Kimmelman v. Morrison, 477 U.S. 365, 382-83, 106 S.Ct. 2574, 2587, 91 L.Ed.2d 305 (1986).**

(3)   Induced Petitioner's guilty plea based on faulty and erroneous legal advise that Petitioner would be pleading guilty to two misdemeanor offenses which was untrue. **See Slicker v. Wainwright, 809 F.2d 768, 769 (11th Cir. 1987)** (evidentiary hearing required to determine whether lawyer mislead petitioner to plead guilty based on faulty information); **United States v. Scott, 625 F.2d 623, 625 (5th Cir. 1981)** (A conviction on a guilty plea that is tendered solely as a result of faulty legal advice is a miscarriage of justice);

(4)   Failed to advise the trial court that he was burdened with a conflict of interest. See **Mickens v. Taylor, 535 U.S. 162, 152 L.Ed.2d 291, 122 S.Ct. 1237 (2002)**;

(5)   Failed to file Petitioner's requested motion to withdraw guilty plea because he was erroneously induced Petitioner's to plead guilty based on two misdemeanor offense. See **United States v. Segatta-Rivera, 473 F.3d 381, 383 (1st Cir. 2007)** (Evidentiary hearing warranted to determine whether counsel was burdened with a conflict of interest because the defendant accused counsel of failing to file his requested motion to withdraw guilty plea based on counsel concealing exculpatory evidence, manipulated defendant into signing plea agreement to avoid trial for which counsel failed to prepare, used improper means to obtain defendant's signature on plea); **Lewis v. Johnson, 359 F.3d 646, 660-662 (3rd Cir. 2004)**; and

(6)   Failed to file Petitioner's requested notice of appeal. See **Roe v. Flores-Ortega, 528 U.S. 470, 120 S.Ct. 1029, 145 L.Ed.2d 985 (2000)**.

Once it is established that both prongs of the **Cuyler** test: (1) actual conflict; and (2) adverse impact on representation, have been met, a defendant need not show prejudice in order to obtain reversal of his conviction. **Porter v. Singletary, 14 F.3d 554, 560 (11th Cir. 1994)**. Petitioner is entitled to relief based on the actual conflict of interest.

2.   Ineffective Assistance Of Counsel

A.   Failure to Investigate and File a Motion to Suppress Illegally Seized Evidence

Defense counsel's performance fell below an objective standard of reasonableness because he failed to investigate the illegal search and seizure and file a motion to suppress the illegally seized evidence. See **Huynh v. King, 95 F.3d 1052, 1056 (11th Cir. 1996)**; **Kimmelman v. Morrison, 477 U.S. 365, 382-83, 106 S.Ct. 2574, 2587, 91 L.Ed.2d 305 (1986)**.

The _____ County Sheriff's Department busted into Petitioner's residence and searched the residence without a warrant. This action by law enforcement violated Petitioner's Fourth Amendment right. See **Katz v. United States, 389 U.S. 347, 19 L.Ed.2d 576, 88 S.Ct. 507 (1967)**. Searches conducted without warrants have been held unlawful "notwithstanding facts unquestionably showing probable cause." **Agnello v. United States, 269 U.S. 20, 33, 70 L.Ed. 145, 149, 46 S.Ct. 4, 51 ALR 409**, for the Constitution requires "that the deliberate, impartial judgment of a judicial officer . . . be interposed between the citizen and the police . . ." **Wong Sun v. United States, 371 U.S. 471, 481-82, 9 L.Ed. 2d 441, 451, 83 S.Ct. 1076**. "Over and again this Court has emphasized that the mandate of the [Fourth] Amendment requires adherence to judicial processes," **United States v. Jeffers, 342 U.S. 48, 51, 96 L.Ed. 59, 64, 72 S.Ct. 93**, and that searches conducted outside the judicial process, without prior approval by judge or magistrate, are per se unreasonable under the Fourth Amendment—subject only to a few specifically established and well-delineated exceptions. See **Katz, 389 U.S. at 357**.

Had counsel investigated the illegal search and seizure and filed a motion to suppress; there exists more than a reasonable probability that the result of the proceedings would have been different and the evidence would have been suppressed. **See Kimmelman, 477 U.S. at 383, n.7, 106 S.Ct. at 2587 n.7.**

B.   Induced Petitioner's Guilty Plea based on Faulty and Erroneous Legal Advice

Defense counsel induced Petitioner's guilty plea based on faulty and erroneous legal advice that Petitioner would be pleading guilty to two misdemeanor offenses. **See Fact No. 11.** A plea induced by the misrepresentation of counsel is ineffective. **See United States v. French, 719 F.2d 387, 390 (11th Cir. 1983), cert. denied, 466 U.S. 960, 104 S.Ct. 2174, 80 L.Ed.2d 557 (1984); Slicker v. Wainwright, 809 F.2d 768, 769 (11th Cir. 1987)** (Evidentiary hearing required to determine whether lawyer mislead petitioner to plead guilty based on faulty information).

In **Ford v. Ford, 749 F.2d 681 (11th Cir. 1985)**, the Court addressed the question of whether a defendant whose counsel had a conflict of interest could enter a valid plea of guilty. In that opinion, the court, first, noted its holding in **Scott v. Wainwright, 698 F.2d 427, 429 (11th Cir. 1983)**, that a "guilty plea cannot have been knowing and voluntary, however, if a defendant does not receive reasonably effective assistance of counsel in connection with the decision to plead guilty, because the plea does not then represent an informed choice." **Ford, 749 F.2d at 683.** Accordingly where a court has determined that the defendant has been deprived of effective assistance of counsel and the guilty plea cannot have been knowing or voluntary, or the product of an informed choice. **id.**

Petitioner is entitled to relief because his guilty plea was not voluntarily or intelligently entered due to faulty and erroneous legal advice by counsel. **See United States v. Scott, 625 F.2d 623, 625 (5th Cir. 1981)** (A conviction on a guilty plea that is tendered solely as a result of faulty legal advice is a miscarriage of justice). In this case, Petitioner had already picked a jury and was proceeding to trial. **See Fact No. 10.** Absent counsel's faulty and erroneously legal advice that Petitioner could plead to two misdemeanors offenses he would not have pleaded guilty but would have continued to proceed with the jury trial. Thus, prejudice under **Strickland** has been shown. **See Hill v. Lockhart, 474 U.S. 52, 88 L.Ed.2d 203, 106 S.Ct. 366 (1985).**

C.   Failure to File Petitioner's requested Motion to Withdraw Guilty Plea

After the Court imposed sentence, Petitioner requested counsel to file a motion to withdraw his guilty plea because counsel misinformed him that he would be pleading guilty to two misdemeanor offenses not a felony. **See Fact No. 12.** Counsel failed to file Petitioner's requested motion to withdraw guilty plea because it was based on faulty and erroneous legal advice because of a conflict of interest. **See United States v. Segarra-Rivera, 473 F.3d 381, 383 (1st Cir. 2007)** (Evidentiary hearing warranted to determine whether counsel was burned with a conflict of interest because the defendant accused counsel of failing to file his _requested_ motion to withdraw guilty plea based on counsel concealing exculpatory evidence, manipulated defendant into signing plea agreement to avoid trial for which counsel failed to prepare, used improper means to obtain defendant's signature on plea); **United States v. Ellison, 798 F.2d 1102 (7th Cir. 1986)**

131

(Ellison filed a motion to withdraw his guilty plea in the context of a letter form. Ellison claimed his guilty plea were the result of psychological pressures of solitary confinement, the exclusion from family and friends, and the erroneous advice of his court appointed attorney "that an immediate guilty plea would place [him] in better and more humane living conditions and renew [my] contract with family and friends." The court concluded an evidentiary hearing on defendant's motion. Counsel testified against Ellison at the hearing. The court denied the motion to withdraw guilty plea. The Seventh circuit reversed and remanded, holding that there was no doubt that a conflict of interest existed, where counsel testified against Ellison, but without counsel Ellison was deprived of his right to cross-examine counsel, in violation of the Sixth Amendment) (Emphasis added). See also **Beckan v. Wainwright**, **639 F.2d 262 (5th Cir. 1981)**.

There exists more than a reasonable probability that the Court would have afforded Petitioner an opportunity to withdraw his guilty plea, had counsel filed Petitioner's requested motion to withdraw guilty plea and the facts had been developed concerning the inducements counsel used to obtain the plea. See **Segarra-Rivera**, **473 F.3d at 383**.

D.   Failure to File Petitioner's Requested Notice of Appeal

Petitioner asserts that counsel failed to file his requested notice of appeal. **See Fact No. 12**. Petitioner attaches hereto his affidavit detailing the facts related to his claim. **See Exhibit "___"**. Petitioner maintains that such unprofessional errors and omissions by counsel constitutes ineffective assistance of counsel because it deprived him of an opportunity to obtain appellate review. See **Roe v. Flores-Ortega**, **528 U.S. 470, 120 S.Ct. 1029, 145 L.Ed.2d 985 (2000)**.

The Supreme Court in **Flores-Ortega** reaffirmed the well settled rule that an attorney who fails to file an appeal on behalf of a client who specifically requests it acts in a professional unreasonable manner per se. **Id. at 477, 120 S.Ct. at 1035 (citing Rodriguez v. United States, 395 U.S. 327, 89 S.Ct. 1715, 23 L.Ed.2d 340 (1969))**. The **Flores-Ortega** Court went on to hold that, even if a client has not made a specific request of his attorney to file an appeal, a court must inquire whether the attorney consulted with the client regarding the advantages and disadvantages of appealing and made a reasonable effort to determine the client's wishes. **id. at 478, 120 S.Ct. at 1035**. If so, the attorney has only acted unreasonably if he ignored the client's wishes to appeal the case. **id.** If not, the court must further inquire whether the attorney had the affirmative duty to consult. **id.** An attorney has this duty when either (1) any rational defendant would want to appeal, or (2) his particular client reasonably demonstrated an interest in appealing. **id. at 480, 120 S.Ct. at 1036**. Petitioner requested counsel to file a notice of appeal.

As to the second prong of the **Strickland**, test, the **Flores-Ortega** court held that the failure to file an appeal that the defendant wanted to file denies the defendant his constitutional right to counsel at a critical stage. **id. at 483, 120 S.Ct. at 1038**. In such cases, prejudice is presumed because rather than being denied the opportunity for a fair proceedings, the defendant is denied the opportunity for a proceeding at all. **id. (citing Smith v. Robbins, 528 U.S. 259, 286, 120 S.Ct. 746, 765, 145 L.Ed.2d 756 (2000); Penson v. Ohio, 488 U.S. 75, 88-89, 109 S.Ct. 346, 354, 102 L.Ed.2d 300 (1988);**

United States v. Cronic, 466 U.S. 648, 659, 104 S.Ct. 2039, 2047, 80 L.Ed.2d 657 (1984)); **Gomez-Diaz v. United States**, 433 F.3d 788, 792 (11th Cir. 2005). Accordingly, to satisfy the prejudice prong of **Strickland** test, a defendant who shows that his attorney has ignored his wishes and failed to appeal his case need only demonstrate that, but for the attorney deficient performance, he would have appealed. **Floes-Ortega**, 528 U.S. at 484, 120 S.Ct. at 1038. Petitioner is entitled to an out-of-time appeal. **See Gomez-Diaz, 433 F.3d at 793.**

—————— § ——————

The cumulative effect of the constitutional infirmities described herein deprived Petitioner of his right to a fair trial proceeding, in violation of the Due Process Clauses of the Constitutions of the United States and the State of Georgia. U.S. Const. XIV.

V.
<u>VERIFICATION</u>

STATE OF _____

COUNTY OF _____

    Petitioner, _____, being first sworn under oath, states that I have signed the above Petition, that I have read and understand the contents of the Petition, and that the statements therein are true and correct to the best of my knowledge and belief.

_____
Petitioner,

Subscribed and sworn to before me this _____ day of _____ 20__.

_____
Notary Public

My Commission Expires:

_____

V.
PRAYER FOR RELIEF

Petitioner respectfully requests this Court vacate and set aside Petitioner's conviction and sentence and order Respondents to release or remove any and all restraint, confinement or other legal infirmity currently placed upon Petitioner as a result of the challenged conviction and sentence.

Respectfully submitted on this _____ day of _____ 20__.

_____

Name   Prison Number
PRO SE REPRESENTATION
Address
Town, State and Zip Code

Form Letter No. 7

Name & Prison Number
_____ Correctional Institution
Address
Town, State & Zip Code

Date

_____County Superior Court
Office of the Clerk
Address
Town, State & Zip Code

Re: Traverse To State's Return And Answer

Dear Clerk:

Please find enclosed the original and two copies of my: "Traverse To State's Return And Answer," for filing with the Court.

Additionally, I have enclosed a third copy of the Traverse To State's Return And Answer to be stamped filed for record and returned to me in the enclosed self-addressed stamped envelope.

Your assistance on this matter is greatly appreciated. Thank you.

Sincerely,

_____
Name

CC:
      p/file.

IN THE SUPERIOR COURT OF _____ COUNTY
STATE OF GEORGIA

_____
                          Petitioner,
VS.

                                    Case No. _____

THE STATE OF GEORGIA
_____, **Warden**
_____ **Correctional Institution,**
_____, _____
                          Respondent.

TRAVERSE TO STATE'S RETURN AND ANSWER

TO THE HONORABLE JUDGE OF SAID COURT:

COMES NOW _____, the petitioner, pro se, and respectfully files this Traverse to State's Return and Answer to his Petition For Writ of Habeas Corpus, pursuant to **O.C.G.A. §9-14-41 (2003)**. All references to paragraphs referred to in Petitioner's initial petition are incorporated herein by reference. This traverse addresses only the parts of the State's Return and Answer that requires a reply.

I.
FACTS APPLICABLE TO ALL CLAIMS

The respondent admits and denies in part the facts applicable to all claims. Petitioner maintains that all his factual allegations stated in the Facts Applicable To All Claims For Relief are true and correct and have been verified under penalty of perjury. See VERIFICATION. The Court should appoint counsel and conduct an evidentiary hearing to resolve the factual disputes, pursuant to **O.C.G.A. §9-14-14**, which provides: "If the return denies any of the material facts stated in the petition or alleges other facts upon which issue is taken, the judge hearing the return may in a summary manner hear testimony as to the issue. To that end, he may compel the attendance of witnesses and the production of papers, may adjourn the examination of the question, or may exercise any other power of a court which the principles of justice may require." **id.**

II.
CLAIMS FOR RELIEF

1. Ineffective Assistance of Counsel Due To An Actual Conflict of Interest

The respondent erroneously claims that Petitioner waived his conflict of interest claim. Contrary to the Respondent's position, there is absolutely nothing in the record to support that Petitioner waived his conflict of interest claim. The trial court failed to inquiry into the conflict of interest when it knew prior to jury selections that defense counsel _____ represented both _____ and Petitioner and that there was a potential conflict. **See Mickens v. Taylor, 535 U.S. 162, 152 L.Ed.2d 291, 122 S.Ct. 1237 (2002).** It is axiomatic that a defendant may waive his right to conflict-free representation. **United States v. Garcia, 517 F.2d 272, 277 (5th Cir. 1975).** However, the effective of waiver of a constitutional right requires that the waiver must be an " 'intentional relinquishment of or abandonment of a known right.' " **Garcia, 517 F.2d at 276, quoting Johnson v. Zerbst, 304 U.S. 458 (1938).**

An effective waiver requires three things. First, the defendant must be told there is a conflict. Second, the defendant must be informed of the possible consequences to his defense that a conflict may have. Finally, the defendant must be informed of his or her right to other counsel. **Duncan v. Alabama, 881 F.2d 1013 (11th Cir. 1989).** The State has the burden of establishing that a knowing and intelligently waiver of the right to conflict-free representation was executed by the defendant. **Freund v. Butterworth, 117 F.3d 1543, 1583 (11th Cir. 1997).** This burden has not been met, as the record is uncontroverted that none of these three steps were taken by the prosecution, defense counsel or the court. See **Docket Entry Sheet.** Additionally, the waiver of a constitutional right cannot be inferred from a silent record, and the courts must indulge in every reasonable presumption against a waiver of fundamental rights. **United States v. Auerbach, 420 F.2d 921, 924 (5th Cir. 1969).**

In the face of the unrebutted contents of Petitioner, his conviction cannot stand. "When there are indications in the record that stir doubts about the effectiveness of joint representation, those doubts should be resolved in favor of the defendant, particularly where, as here, the record fails to indicate whether in assigning counsel the danger of prejudice from joint representation was considered." **Lollar v. United States, 370 F.2d 243, 247 (D.C. Cir. 1967).**

Petitioner is entitled to Relief on this Claim.

2. Ineffective Assistance of Counsel

A. Failure to investigate and File A Motion to Suppress Illegally Seized Evidence

The respondents admit that the first search was conducted without a warrant because the Officers felt that Petitioner was going to destroy the evidence. The respondents position is baseless and ridiculous. First, the respondent has not shown that Petitioner planned to destroy the marijuana. Second, the _____ County Sheriff's Department had Petitioner's residence under surveillance and could have detained Petitioner if he left. Third, the _____ County Sheriff's Department had an informant inside Petitioner's residence for over three hours which was ample time to obtain a search warrant. Finally, the _____ County Sheriff's Department had plenty of time to obtain a search warrant before entering the residence. Next, the respondent attempts to argue that the second search was conducted by a warrant and that somehow covers the initial illegal search and seizure. However, the respondent has pointed to no authority to support its position.

138

B. Induced Petitioner's Guilty Plea Based On Faulty and Erroneous Legal Advice

The State claims that it does not have sufficient information to admit or deny Petitioner's factual allegations concerning this claim. **See Fact Nos. 10, 11, and 12.** Because the State failed to admit or deny the Court should conduct an evidentiary hearing to resolve the factual disputes, pursuant to **O.C.G.A. §9-14-14; Tower v. Phillips, 979 F.2d 807 (11th Cir. 1992)** (An evidentiary hearing required because defendant alleged that his attorney misrepresented the degree of the offense to which Petitioner pled guilty and that he did not understand the charges he pled guilty to, and the record does not resolve the disputed facts based on attorney-client communication); **Holmes v. United States, 878 F.2d 1545 (11th Cir. 1989).**

Petitioner supported his claims with affidavits under penalty of perjury. The State failed to dispute these facts which entitles Petitioner to relief.

——————— § ———————

C. Failure to file Petitioner's Requested Motion To Withdraw Guilty Plea At Sentencing

The State denies Petitioner's factual allegations concerning Petitioner requested counsel _____ to file a Motion To Withdraw His Guilty Plea. The State failed to produce an affidavit from counsel _____ and has failed to submit any proof concerning its denial of the facts stated in **Fact No. 12** and this claim for relief. The State claims that Petitioner couldn't file a motion to withdraw his guilty plea on the day of sentencing. The State proposition is contrary to Georgia Criminal Procedure and is not supported by any authority. Contrary to the State's response Petitioner's claim is supported by two affidavits. Once again the court is faced with disputed facts which warrants an evidentiary hearing. **See O.C.G.A. §9-14-14.**

The State submitted its **Exhibit "B"** which is transcript of Petitioner entering his plea of guilty, he claimed to be satisfied with his attorney, understood what he was charged with, and that no one made any promises or threats to influence him to plead guilty. The State's **Exhibit "B"** does not dispute Petitioner's factual allegations. At no time, during the guilty plea colloquy did the court inform Petitioner of the specific charges he was pleading guilty to. See the State's **Exhibit "B".** As the United States Supreme Court in **Kimmelman v. Morrison, 477 U.S. 365, 378, 91 L.Ed.2d 305, 321, 106 S.Ct. 2574 (1986)**, stated: "A laymaqn will ordinarily be unable to recognize counsel's errors and to evaluate counsel's professional performance, consequently a criminal defendant will rarely know that he has not been represented competently until after trial or appeal, usually when he consults another lawyer about his case. Indeed, an accused will often not realize that he has a meritorious ineffectiveness claim until he begins collateral review proceedings, particularly if he retained trial counsel on direct appeal." **Id. (citations omitted).** Like, **Morrison,** Petitioner was not qualified to know or understand whether he had been represented competently at the time he answered those questions in **Exhibit "B".** Likewise, the sworn statement provided in **Exhibit "B"** does not meet the criteria set forth in **Bazemore v. State of Georgia, No. SOOA1100 (Ga S. Ct.)** (The State has the burden to show that the pleas were voluntarily, knowingly, and intelligently made. To meet this burden the State must preserve on the record that the defendant was cognizant of his rights and waiver of those rights, or by using evidence that shows that the guilty pleas were entered knowingly and voluntarily"). Like **Bazemore**, the Court in Petitioner's case failed to conduct an on the record review of Petitioner and failed to read the charges to Petitioner that he was allegedly pleading guilty to. Thus, under **Bazemore**, Petitioner's conviction should be vacated.

——————— § ———————

D.   Failure to File Petitioner's Requested Notice of Appeal

The State denies that counsel's failure to file Petitioner's requested notice of appeal constitutes ineffective assistance of counsel. The State claims that Petitioner waived his right to appeal by pleading guilty. Contrary to the State's proposition, the State's **Exhibit "B"** does not show that the court advised Petitioner that he was waiving his right to appeal. Contrary to the State's position, there is no written plea agreement and no waiver of appeal in the record. Thus, counsel's failure to file Petitioner's requested notice of appeal constitutes ineffective assistance of counsel. **See Roe v. Flores-Ortega, 528 U.S. 470, 120 S.Ct. 1029, 145 L.Ed.2d 985 (2000); Gomez-Diaz v. United States 433, F.3d 788, 792-93 (11th Cir. 2005).**

——————— § ———————

PRAYER FOR RELIEF

Petitioner respectfully requests the Court to vacate and set aside Petitioner's guilty plea, conviction, and sentence, and order a retrial within ninety (90) days.

Respectfully submitted on this ____ day of _____ 20__ .

_____
Name   Prison Number
PRO SE REPRESENTATION
Address
Town, State, and Zip Code

IN THE SUPERIOR COURT OF _____ COUNTY
STATE OF GEORGIA

_____

Defendant-Petitioner,

VS.

Civil Action
Case No. _____

_____, **Warden**

STATE OF GEORGIA,

Respondent.

_____

NOTICE OF APPEAL

_____

PLEASE TAKE NOTICE that the above named Defendant-Petitioner, pro se, appeals to: The Georgia State Supreme Court, from the Superior Court of _____ County, order denying Petitioner's habeas corpus petition, pursuant to **O.C.G.A. §9-14-14**, entered for record on _____ ____, 20___. **See Exhibit "1"** the Superior Court of _____ County, order denying Petitioner's habeas corpus petition, entered for record on _____ ____, 20___.

I.
STATEMENT REGARDING TRANSCRIPTS

TRANSCRIPTS: Petitioner requests that the _____ ____, 20___, revocation of probation and sentencing hearing be transcribed for appellate purposes. All other records on file at the Clerk of the Superior Court for _____ County, in Case No. _____, to be transferred to the Georgia State Supreme for appellate purposes.

II.
NAME OF APPELLANT AND APPELLEE

The Appellant is _____. The Appellee is the State of Georgia.

All parties are hereby placed on notice that the above named Defendant-Petitioner's intends to appeal the denial of his habeas corpus petition, pursuant to **O.C.G.A. §9-14-14**, to the Georgia State Supreme Court.

Respectfully submitted on this ____ day of _____ 20 ___.

Name
PRO SE REPRESENTATION
Address
Town, State, and Zip Code

IN THE SUPERIOR COURT OF _____ COUNTY
STATE OF GEORGIA

_____

Defendant-Petitioner,

VS.

Civil Action
Case No. _____

_____, Warden

STATE OF GEORGIA,

Respondents.

MOTION TO PROCEED IN FORMA PAUPERIS ON APPEAL

COMES NOW _____, the Defendant-Petitioner, pro se, and respectfully moves the Court to grant him permission to proceed through in forma pauperis status on appeal. The Court, previously granted Petitioner permission to proceed through in forma pauperis status on his habeas corpus petition. Nothing has changed concerning Petitioner's financial status since the Court granted him permission to proceed in forma pauperis on the habeas corpus petition.

Petitioner states that because of his poverty he is unable to pay the costs of said proceeding or to give security thereof.

WHEREFORE, based on the above, _____, prays that the Court **GRANTS** this motion and authorizes him to proceed on appeal through in forma pauperis status.

Respectfully submitted on this ____ day of _____ 20 ___.

_____
Name
PRO SE REPRESENTATION
Address
Town, State, and Zip Code

IN THE CIRCUIT COURT OF THE _____ JUDICIAL CIRCUIT
IN AND FOR THE _____ COUNTY, FLORIDA CRIMINAL ACTION

_____

_____,

Petitioner,

VS.   **Docket No. _____**

STATE OF FLORIDA, and
_____, Warden
Federal Correctional Institution,
_____, _____,

Respondent.

_____

MEMORANDUM BRIEF IN SUPPORT OF MOTION FOR
POST-CONVICTION RELIEF PURSUANT TO FLA. R. CRIM. P. 3.850

_____

TO THE HONORABLE JUDGE OF SAID COURT:

COMES NOW_____ _____, the petitioner, pro se, and respectfully files this memorandum brief in support of his motion for post-conviction relief pursuant to Florida Rules of Criminal Procedure, Rule 3.850, seeking to vacate the conviction based on constitutional grounds.

I.
MR. _____ IS BEING RESTRAINED OF LIBERTY AS
A RESULT OF THE UNCONSTITUTIONAL CONVICTION IN THIS CASE

1. Mr. _____ was arrested by federal authorities; plead guilty, and subsequently sentenced by the federal court system. The United States Probation Department for the Southern District of _____, _____ Division, used the conviction in the above entitled action for aggravated assault with a deadly weapon as a predicate offense to enhance Mr. _____'s federal sentence. See Exhibit "___" page ___ of the Presentence Report prepared by the United States Probation Department, which was adopted by the federal court. Mr. _____ is currently being restrained of his liberty as a result of the conviction in the above entitled action because it was used as a predicate offense to enhance his federal sentence.

II.
PARTIES TO THE PROCEEDINGS

The respondent, State of Florida, County of _____, obtained the illegal and unconstitutional conviction against Mr. _____. The respondent, _____ _____, is the Warden at the Federal Correctional Institution, _____, _____, and the custodian of Mr. _____.

III.
STATEMENT OF THE CASE

On August 3, 2000, the _____ County Sheriff's Office arrested Mr. _____ and charged him with aggravated assault with a firearm. The facts stemming from Mr. _____ arrest are: (1) Mr. _____ and his girlfriend lived in the _____ Mobile Home Park; (2) Mr. _____ and his girlfriend got into a screaming match; (3) Mr. _____'s neighbor, _____, sent her drunk boyfriend and another man over to Mr. ___'s residences to check on Mr. _____'s girlfriend; (4) one of these individuals had a hammer in his hand. They knocked on Mr. _____'s door and when Mr. _____ answered the door they told him that they needed to see him outside; (5) as Mr. _____ walked outside he noticed that one of these individuals was holding a hammer in a threatening manner. Mr. _____ opened his pickup truck door and pulled out his baseball bat; (7) as soon as Mr. _____ pulled out the baseball bat the two individuals run off; (8) Mr. _____ girlfriend left in a pickup truck with one of their friends to go to his mother-n-law house; (9) Upon Mr. _____ and his girlfriend returning from his mother-n-laws the _____ County Sheriff's Department showed up at Mr. _____'s residence.

On June 27, 2001, Mr. _____ appeared before the court with counsel. Mr. _____ on the advice of counsel entered a plea of guilt to the charge of aggravated assault with a deadly weapon. The court assessed punishment by imposing a two year probation with a three (3) year suspended sentence in the Florida Department of Corrections.

On April 4, 2005, the State of Florida filed a motion to revoke probation and this Court held a hearing. After the hearing the court revoked the probation and sentenced Mr. _____ to three (3) years in the Florida Department of Corrections. Mr. _____ requested counsel to file an appeal. Counsel assured Mr. _____ he would file his appeal.

Mr. _____ filed a motion for an belated appeal in the District Court of Appeal of Florida Second District.

On or about February 6, 2008, and in Appeal Number _____, the District Court of Appeal of Florida Second District issued an order granting Mr. _____'s petition for belated appeal: (1) subsequent to the report and recommendation by the commissioner upon petition for belated appeal, and (2) pending consideration by the lower court of Mr. _____ eligibility for appointment of appellate counsel.

On or about March 19, 2008, the Honorable _____ _____, Circuit Judge, entered an order denying Appellant's request to be declared indigent and appointed counsel. On or about April 27, 2008, and in "new" appeal No. _____, the Appellant renewed his motion for appointment, which motion Judge _____ granted by order dated June 3, 2008.

On or about October 2, 2008, and in Appeal No. _____, the Court entered the following order: "Appellant's motion to reinstate appeal is granted." An appeal followed this order.

On July 10, 2009, the District Court of Appeals of Florida Second District in Case No. 2D08-729, affirmed the lower court's decision revoking probation.

_____ § _____

IV.
STATEMENT OF THE FACTS

Mr. _____ submits that the following facts support his constitutional claim that he was deprived of effective assistance of counsel as guaranteed by the Sixth and Fourteenth Amendment of the United States Constitution during a crucial stage of the proceeding.

1. Mr. _____ advised counsel that he never saw or talked to his neighbor, _____ _____, on August 3, 2000, as she claimed in the report to the police.

2. Mr. _____ explained to counsel that him and his girlfriend _____ _____ lived in the _____ Mobile Home Park on August 3, 2000. Mr. _____ and his _____ _____ got into a screaming match.

3. Mr. _____'s neighbor, _____ _____, sent her drunk boyfriend and another man over to Mr. _____'s residence to check on _____ _____. One of these individuals carried a claw hammer in his hands in a threatening manner. These individuals knocked on Mr. _____'s front door and when Mr. _____ opened the door they told him they needed to see him outside. Mr. _____ noticed that one of these individuals were holding a claw hammer in his hand in a threatening manner. Mr. _____ opened his pickup truck door and pulled out his baseball bat and these two individuals took off running. Mr. _____ never said anything to these two individuals.

4. Mr. _____ went back inside his trailer and _____ _____ told him that she was going to her mother's house and for him to pick her up in a couple of hours. Mr. _____ and _____ _____ friend arrived and _____ _____ went outside and got in the vehicle and left. Shortly after that, Mr. _____ got in his pickup truck and left. Mr. _____ went shopping and then approximately a hour and half later went by his mother-n-law house and picked up _____ _____ and they returned to Mr. _____'s trailer house.

5. Upon _____ _____ and Mr. _____ returning to his trailer house the _____ County Sheriff's Department showed up. The _____ County Deputy Sheriff explained to Mr. _____ that his neighbor, _____ _____, made a complaint against him and asked him his version of the facts. Mr. _____ and _____ _____ told the officer what occurred as outlined above. The _____ County Deputy Sheriff asked Mr. _____, if he wanted to file charges and he said no. The _____ County Deputy Sheriff arrested Mr. _____.

6. Defense counsel refused to investigate the alleged crime or to interview _____ _____ even when Mr. _____ brought Ms. _____ to his office.

7. Defense counsel never advised Mr. _____ that he had a right to protect his property and that he has an affirmative defense of self-defense to the charge, and that

he would be entitled to a jury instruction, and there is a reasonable probability that he would get a not guilty verdict prior to induce Mr. _____'s guilty plea.

A more precise set of facts are set forth in this memorandum brief.

———————— § ————————

ISSUE I

THE CONVICTION IS UNCONSTITUTIONAL BECAUSE PETITIONER DID NOT RECEIVE EFFECTIVE ASSISTANCE OF COUNSEL AS GUARANTEED BY THE SIXTH AND FOURTEENTH AMENDMENTS

Claims of ineffectiveness of counsel in criminal cases are evaluated under a two-prong test set forth in **Strickland v. Washington, 466 U.S. 668, 687-88, 694, 104 S.Ct. 2052, 80 L.Ed.2d 674 (1984)**, and its progeny. "To succeed on any claim of ineffective assistance of counsel, a defendant must show that: (1) the attorney's representation fell below an objective standard of reasonableness, and (2) there is a reasonable probability that except for the attorney's unprofessional errors, the result of the proceedings would have been different." **United States v. Arteca, 411 F.3d 315, 320 (2d Cir. 2005)**. In the plea bargaining context, a petitioner seeking to establish ineffective assistance of counsel must demonstrate that: (1) counsel's advice and performance fell below an objective standard of reasonableness; and (2) the petitioner would not have pleaded guilty and would have insisted on going to trial in the absence of his attorney's errors. **Hill v. Lockhart, 477 U.S. 52, 58-59, 106 S.Ct. 366, 370-71, 88 L.Ed.2d 203 (1985)**.

In **Hill, 474 U.S. at 59**, the Court further explained that in many guilty plea cases, the "prejudice" inquiry would closely resemble the injury engaged in by courts reviewing ineffective assistance challenges to convictions obtained through a trial. For example, where the alleged error of counsel is failure to investigate or discovery potentially exculpatory evidence, the determination whether the error "prejudiced" the defendant by causing him to plead guilty rather than to go to trial will depend on the likelihood that discovery of the evidence would have led counsel to change his recommendation as to the plea. This assessment, in turn, will depend in large part on a prediction whether the evidence likely would have changed the outcome of a trial. Similarly, where the alleged error of counsel is a failure to advise the defendant of a potential affirmative defense to the crime charged, the resolution of the "prejudice" inquiry will depend largely on whether the affirmative defense likely would have succeeded at trial. **Id.**

In this case, defense counsel committed several unprofessional errors and omissions which amounted to performance at a level below the acceptable objective standard of reasonableness for counsel in a criminal case. Petitioner asserts the following errors and omissions as grounds for relief:

A.   **Counsel was constitutionally ineffective for to investigate the crime charged and to advise Mr. _____ of the affirmative defense of self-defense and that the defense could request a self-defense instruction prior to inducing**

Petitioner's guilty plea which rendered the plea not voluntarily or intelligently entered.

Defense counsel's performance fell well below an objective standard of reasonableness for counsel in a criminal case for failure to investigate the crime charged and to advise Mr. _____ of his affirmative defense of self-defense, and that he could request a self-defense jury instruction prior to inducing Petitioner's guilty plea, which renders the guilty plea not voluntary and intelligently entered. See **Dando v. Yukins, 461 F.3d 791, 798-800 (6th Cir. 2006); Woodard v. Collins, 898 F.2d 1027, 1029 (5th Cir. 1990); Smith v. Dretke, 417 F.3d 438, 442-444 (5th Cir. 2005); United States v. Span, 75 F.3d 1383 (9th Cir. 1996); and Weidner v. Wainwright, 708 F.2d 614 (11th Cir. 1983)**. In this case, Mr. _____ had a valid affirmative defense of self-defense which counsel failed to investigate and advise Mr. _____ of prior to inducing his guilty plea rendering the plea involuntary.

Fla. Stat. §784.021(1)(a) provides, in relevant part: (1) An "aggravated assault" is an assault: (a) With a deadly weapon without intent to kill; or (b) With an intent to commit a felony. (2) Whoever commits an aggravated assault shall be guilty of a felony of the third degree. Id. To prove the crime of aggravated assault, the State was required to prove the following four elements beyond a reasonable doubt: (1) Petitioner intentionally and unlawfully threatened, either by word or act, to do violence to the victim; (2) at the time, Petitioner appeared to have the ability to carry out the threat; (3) Petitioner's act created in the mind of the victim a well-founded fear that the violence was about to take place, and (4) the assault was made with a deadly weapon. Florida Standard Jury Instructions, Chapter 8.2 Aggravated Assault. The jury instructons state that it is not necessary for the State to prove that Petitioner had an intent to kill. Id. The instructions define a deadly weapon as a weapon that is used or threatened to be used in a way likely to produce death or great bodily harm. Id. See **Garland v. McDonough, 2006 U.S. Dist. LEXIS 95993 (June 28, 2006)**.

Had counsel advised Mr. _____ that he could testify to the facts and call _____ _____ to testify to the same facts as outlined above and Mr. _____ would be able to argue self-defense he would have proceeded to trial. See **Exhibit "___"** (Mr. _____'s affidavit). See also **Exhibit "___"** (_____ _____ affidavit). There is a right to a self-defense instruction where there has been sufficient evidence to support it. See **Dames v. State, 773 So. 2d 563 (Fla. 2d DCA 2000)**. Therefore, counsel would have been ineffective for failure to request an instruction on self-defense under the circumstances of this case and failure to advise Mr. _____ of such defense. See **Dando v. Yukins, 461 F.3d at 798-800**.

In Florida, "[u]pon request, a defendant is entitled to a jury instruction on any theory of defense the substantive evidence supports, however weak or improbable his testimony may have been. **Mathews v. State, 799 So.2d 265, 266 (Fla. 1st DCA 2001)**. There is evidence that one of the alleged victims was armed with a claw hammer holding it in a threatening manner when he knocked on Mr. _____'s door and demanded that Mr. _____ step outside so they could talk to him. Counsel's failure to advise Mr. _____ of the self-defense and its instruction renders the guilty plea involuntarily and unintelligently entered as a result of ineffective assistance of counsel. See, e.g., **Mathis v. State, 973 So. 2d 1153, 2006 App. LEXIS 17642, at *8 (Fla. V DCA Oct. 25,**

2006)("[A]rguing that the jury should find appellant not guilty because he was acting in self-defense and then failing to request an instruction on that theory was patently unreasonable and, thus, subject to collateral attack."). **Harris v. State, 104, So.2d 739 (Fla. 3d DCA 1980)**(holding that in a self-defense claim, the danger must be only apparent, not real); **Davis v. State, 387 So.2d 978 (Fla. 3d DCA 1980)**(conviction reversed where defendant believed victim was armed); **Andrews v. State, 577 So.2d 650 (Fla. 1st DCA 1991)**(holding that the State has the burden of providing the defendant did not act in self-defense); **Cox v. State, 555 So.2d 352 (Fla. 1989)**(holding that state's proof must be inconsistent with any reasonable hypothesis of innocence).

Had Mr. _____ been advised of his available self-defense and that he could receive a jury instruction and request for an acquittal on the charge, he would not have plead guilty, rather he would have proceeded to trial. Thus, prejudice has been shown. **See Hill, 477 U.S. at 59**.

_____ § _____

CONCLUSION

Petitioner, _____ _____, has been deprived of basic fundamental rights guaranteed by the Sixth and Fourteenth Amendments of the United States Constitution and seeks to restore those rights in this Court. Mr. _____ prays that this Honorable Court will set aside his guilty plea and schedule this case for trial. Justice demands nothing less.

Respectfully submitted on this ____ day of _____ 2010.

_____
PRO SE REPRESENTATION

IN THE _____**COURT OF** _____ **COUNTY**
STATE OF _____

THE STATE OF _____

           Plaintiff,

VS.   Case No. _____

_____
           Petitioner.

MOTION FOR WRIT OF ERROR CORAM NOBIS AND A
MEMORANDUM OF LAW IN SUPPORT OF SAID MOTION

TO THE HONORABLE JUDGE OF SAID COURT:

    COMES NOW_____, the petitioner, pro se, and respectfully moves this Honorable Court to: issue a writ of error coram nobis and to vacate or set aside the conviction because it was sustained in violation of the Sixth and Fourteenth Amendment right to counsel. In support thereof, petitioner states:

I.
STATEMENT OF THE FACTS

    1.   On _____ ___, 20___, the petitioner was arrested by an Officer of the _____ Police Department and charged with _____.

    2.   On _____ ___, 20___, petitioner appeared before this Court without counsel and was informed by the prosecution, that if he pleaded guilty that he would get time served and ____ year probation. This Court advised petitioner of his right to counsel, but failed to inform petitioner of the dangers and disadvantages of self-representation prior to accepting petitioner's guilty plea. Additionally, this Court failed to advise petitioner of his available options and possible defenses.

    3.   This Court assessed punishment at ___ day in jail and ___ year probation.

    A more precise set of facts are set forth throughout this motion for writ of error coram nobis.

II.
MEMORANDUM OF LAW

        The guilty plea was not voluntarily or intelligently entered where this court failed to advise the petitioner of the dangers and disadvantages of self-representation prior to accepting the guilty plea in violation of <u>Faretta</u> and

Argersinger and the Sixth and Fourteenth Amendments of the United States Constitution

Petitioner argues that his guilty plea was not voluntarily or intelligently entered where he was not advised of the dangers and disadvantages of self-representation and did not understand the consequences of his waiver of the right to counsel, and the plea must be set aside. **See United States v. Akins, 276 F.3d 1141, 1146 (9th Cir. 2002); Faretta v. California, 422 U.S. 806, 835, 95 S.Ct. 2525, 45 L.Ed.2d 562 (1975); and Argersinger v. Hamlin, 407 U.S. 25, 37, 92 S.Ct. 2006, 32 L.Ed. 530 (1972)**,

To knowingly and intelligently waive the Sixth Amendment right to counsel, a defendant must be made aware of (1) the nature of the charges against him, (2) the possible penalties, and (3) the dangers and disadvantages of self-representation. **Faretta v. California, 422 U.S. 806, 835, 95 S.Ct. 2525, 45 L.Ed.2d 562 (1975); Akins, 276 F.3d at 1146.** In evaluating whether a waiver is invalid, courts adopt "every reasonable presumption against waiver." **Johnson v. Zerbst, 304 U.S. 458, 464-465, 58 S.Ct. 1019, 82 L.Ed. 1461 (1938).**

A.   Waiver of Counsel in misdemeanor proceedings.

A misdemeanor defendant must be informed of "the nature of the charges and possible penalties, as well as the dangers and disadvantages of self-representation." **See United States v. Rylander, 714 F.2d 996, 1005 (9th Cir. 1983) (internal quotations omitted)** (holding that a defendant charged with criminal contempt did not knowingly and intelligently waive the right to counsel because he was not informed of the nature of the charges and possible penalties); **United States v. Carpenter, 91 F.3d 1285 (9th Cir. 1996)** (criminal contempt is a Class A misdemeanor for sentencing purposes). Nowhere is counsel more important than at a plea proceeding. "[A]n intelligent assessment of the relative advantages of pleading guilty is frequently impossible without the assistance of an attorney." **Brady v. United States, 397 U.S. 742, 748 n. 6, 90 S.Ct. 1463, 25 L.Ed.2d 747 (1970); Von Moltke v. Gillies, 332 U.S. 708, 721, 68 S.Ct. 316, 92 L.Ed 309 (1948)(Black, J., plurality opinion)** ("A waiver of the constitutional right to the assistance of counsel is of no less moment to an accused who must decide whether to plead guilty then to an accused who stands trial.").

Because a guilty plea serves as a conviction and relieves the state of its burden of proof in a criminal case, ensuring the validity of the plea is of vital importance. **See Von Moltke, 332 U.S. at 719, 68 S.Ct. 316.** It may be difficult for a defendant, whether charged with a misdemeanor or a felony, to assess accurately his own guilt without the assistance of counsel. "Substantive criminal law contains many complexities—intent standards, jurisdictional provisions, defenses, and so forth. The defendant may be 'guilty' in a layman's sense, and so be willing to confess, and yet may have a viable defense that he ought to invoke, or may be pleading guilty to the wrong grade of crime." **See Akins, 276 F.3d at 1147-1148 (citing William J. Stuntz, Waiving Rights in Criminal Procedure, 75 Va. L. Rev. 761, 830 (1989); United States ex rel. McDonald v. Pennsylvania, 343 F.2d 447, 451 (3rd Cir. 1965)** ("The exercise of judgment on the factual issues, the legal problems of evidence by which facts may be proven, the elements and ingredients of the crime charged, all these are matters which no layman, however intelligent or how often embroiled in legal proceedings, can be presumed to comprehend adequately, especially when, because his own freedom is at stake, it would be impossible to except of him the detached, impersonal judgment which is unique contribution of a professional advisor.") Another threat to the accuracy of a guilty plea entered without the assistance of counsel is the danger that "innocent men pitted against trained prosecutorial forces may waive counsel and plead guilty to crimes they have not committed, if they think that by doing so they will avoid the publicity of trial, secure a break at the sentencing stage, or simply get the whole thing over with." **Molignaro v. Smith, 408 F.2d 795, 801 (5th Cir. 1969)**.

B. The Sixth Amendment knowingly and intelligently waiver standard

The **Akins** Court found that: Under the Sixth Amendment, a criminal defendant has a constitutional right to be represented by counsel at all critical stages of the prosecution, **Mempa v. Rhay, 389 U.S. 128, 134, 88 S.Ct. 254, 19 L.Ed2d 336 (1967)**, including the plea proceeding. **United States v. Fuller, 941 F.2d 993, 995 (9th Cir. 1991)**. The right to counsel applies in any offense, misdemeanor or felony, for which a term of imprisonment is imposed. **Argersinger v. Hamlin, 407 U.S. 25, 37, 92 S.Ct. 2006, 32 L.Ed.2d 530 (1972)**.

Although a defendant has a constitutional right to represent himself, in order to do so he must knowingly and intelligently waive the right to counsel. **United States v. Balough, 820 F.2d 1485, 1487 (9th Cir. 1987)**. "A waiver is knowing and intelligently only if it comes after the defendant has been 'made aware of the dangers and disadvantages of self-representation, so that the record will establish that he knows what he is doing and his choice is made with eyes open.'" **Faretta v. California, 422 U.S. 806, 835, 956, S.Ct. 2525, 45 L.Ed.2d 562 (1975)(internal quotations omitted); Akins, 276 F.3d at 1146**.

C. Petitioner did not knowingly and intelligently waive his right to counsel and the writ of error should be granted

Petitioner argues that the harmless error analysis does not apply to a situation in which a defendant waived his right to counsel without being advised of the dangers and disadvantages of self-representation. See **United States v. Allen, 895 F.2d 1577, 1580 (10th Cir. 190); United States v. Dawes, 895 F.2d 1581 (10th Cir. 1990)**. The United States Supreme Court has held that the writ of error **coram nobis** is available to correct errors "'of the most fundamental character.'" **United States v. Morgan, 346 U.S. 502, 512, 74 S.Ct. 247, 253, 98 L.Ed. 248 (1954)(quoting United States v. Mayer, 235 U.S. 55, 69, 35 S.Ct. 16, 19-20, 59 L.Ed. 129 (1912))**. **Morgan** held the district court had power under the All-Writs Act, 28 U.S.C. §1651(a), to issue a writ of error **coram nobis** to vacate a conviction on the ground that the defendant had been deprived of counsel without his knowing waiver of his constitutional right to counsel. Although this writ is an "'extraordinary remedy [available] only under circumstances compelling such action to achieve justice,'" **346 U.S. at 511**, we believe circumstances here justify its issuance.

See <u>Dawes</u>, 895 F.2d at 1582. The exact same applicable law applies to the facts of this case.

WHEREFORE, based on the above facts, arguments, and authorities, _____, urges this Honorable Court to grant this motion and vacate the judgment of conviction and order that the charges be dismissed.

Respectfully submitted on this ___ day of _____, 200___.

_____
PRO SE REPRESENTATION

IN THE _____**COURT OF** _____ **COUNTY**
STATE OF _____

THE STATE OF _____

VS.   Case No. _____

_____

ORDER AND JUDGMENT

The matter of _____, Motion for writ of error coram nobis, currently pending before this Court came under consideration on this date. The Court finds that the guilty plea was sustained in violation of the Sixth and Fourteenth Amendment of the United States Constitution because _____ was not advised of the dangers and disadvantages of proceeding through self-representation.

IT IS HEREBY ORDERED that the guilty plea is set aside and the conviction is **VACATED** and the charge is hereby dismissed.

Thus, done on this _____ day of _____, 200___.

_____
Judge

IN THE
ARKANSAS SUPREME COURT

_____

Petitioner,

VS.   Case No. _____
                                           Docket _____

STATE OF ARKANSAS, and
_____, Warden,
Federal Correctional Institution,
_____, _____,

Respondents.

MOTION FOR PERMISSION TO FILE A MOTION FOR
WRIT OF ERROR CORAM NOBIS AND MEMORANDUM OF LAW

TO THE ARKANSAS SUPREME COURT JUSTICES:

 COMES NOW_____, the petitioner, pro se, and respectfully moves this Honorable Court for permission to file a motion for writ of error coram nobis and memorandum of law, in the Circuit Court of _____, Arkansas, _____ District Criminal Division, Docket No. _____. Petitioner is currently being restrained of his liberty, in violation of the constitution and laws of the State of Arkansas and the United States as a result of the _____ County unlawful conviction.

I.
<u>STATEMENT OF JURISDICTION</u>

 This Court has jurisdiction to grant Petitioner permission to file a motion for writ of error coram nobis under Arkansas law based on newly discovered evidence, in the Circuit Court of _____, Arkansas, _____ District District Criminal Division. See **Edgemon v. State, 292 Ark. 465, 473 S.W.2d 898 (Ark. 1987); McDaniel v. State, 286 Ark. 246, 691 S.W.2d 153, 154 (1985); Hill v. State, 289 Ark. 387, 398-99, 713 S.W.2d 233, 239 (1986).** There is no specific time limit for seeking a writ of error coram nobis under Arkansas law. **Echols v. State, 369 Ark. 332, 201 S.W.3d 890, 2005 WL 107133, at *3 (Arkansas Supreme Court 2005).** A writ of error coram nobis is an exceeding narrow remedy under state law, appropriate only when "there existed some fact which would have prevented [a judgment's] rendition if it had been known to the trial court and which, through no negligence or fault, of the defendant was not brought forward before rendition of judgment." **Echols, 360 Ark. 337, [WL] at *3.**

II.
THE CONVICTION AND SENTENCE

1.   Petitioner is currently incarcerated at the Federal Correctional Institution (FCI) in _____, _____, by the respondent, _____ _____, who is the Warden of FCI _____, _____. The State of Arkansas is the respondent for the conviction and sentence under collateral attack.

2.   The conviction and sentence from which Petitioner seeks relief was imposed in the case styled, <u>State of Arkansas v.</u> _____,_Docket No. _____, in the Circuit Court of _____, Arkansas, _____ District Criminal Division. See Exhibit <u>"A"</u> Judgement and Disposition Order in the Circuit Court of _____, Arkansas, _____ District Criminal Division. Petitioner is currently incarcerated as a result of this conviction because his federal sentence was enhanced from _____ months to _____ **months** under the Career Offender provision as a result of the _____ County conviction. **See <u>United States v.</u> _____, Criminal No. _____ (2003).** See also Exhibit <u>"B"</u> (_____ affidavit).

III.
STATEMENT OF THE FACTS

3.   Petitioner was arrested in _____ County, Arkansas, with _____ _____ and _____. The _____ County Sheriff's Department seized from _____ _____'s pickup truck stolen property from a burglary in _____, Arkansas.

4.   Petitioner was subsequently brought to _____, Arkansas, and charged with Theft of Property and burglary. This Court appointed _____ _____ to represent the Petitioner.

5.   Petitioner advised counsel _____ that he did not commit any burglary in _____, Arkansas. Petitioner advised counsel _____ that he went to sleep in the Motel Room in _____, Arkansas. See Exhibit <u>"B"</u> (Affidavit of _____). _____ and _____ woke Petitioner up and told him its time to leave. After Petitioner got into _____'s pickup truck he noticed that there was some property in the bed of the pickup. Petitioner asked _____ _____ and _____ where they got that property and they said they got it while he was sleeping in the motel room. See Exhibit <u>"C"</u> (_____ affidavit).

6.   _____ made a statement to _____ County Detectives that Petitioner _____ did not have anything to do with the theft and burglary because he was asleep in the Motel Room. The detectives wrote down the information. See Exhibit <u>"C"</u> (_____ affidavit).

7.   Petitioner went back to sleep in the pickup and woke up in _____ County, Arkansas, and was subsequently arrested.

8.   Petitioner was subsequently transferred to _____, Arkansas, and charged with Burglary and Theft of property.

9.   Defense counsel _____ _____ advised the Petitioner that it did not matter that he wasn't involved in the burglary because the stolen property was seized

155

from the pickup truck that he was riding when they were arrested and that made him guilty of burglary. See Exhibit "B" (Affidavit of _____).[1]

A more precise set of facts are set forth throughout this motion.

_____ § _____

IV.
MEMORANDUM OF LAW

ISSUE I

The guilty plea was not a voluntary or intelligently entered as a result of ineffective assistance of counsel and incompetent legal advice and must be set aside.

Petitioner argues that his guilty plea was not knowingly, intelligently, or voluntarily entered as a result of ineffective assistance of counsel and counsel's incompetent legal advice. **See Tollet v. Henderson, 411 U.S. 258, 93 S.Ct. 1602, 36 L.Ed.2d 235 (1973)**(A criminal defendant can only attack the voluntary and intelligent character of the guilty plea based on the advice of counsel). See also **Scott v. Wainwright, 698 F.2d 427, 429-30 (11th Cir. 1983)**(counsel's failure to learn the facts and familiarize himself with the law in relation to the plea constitutes ineffective assistance and renders the guilty plea invalid); **Herring v. Estelle, 491 F.2d 125, 128 (5th Cir. 1974)**.

Defense counsel _____ advised Petitioner that it did not matter that he was asleep at the motel room when _____ _____ and ____ _____ committed the burglary or that he had no prior knowledge that they were going to commit the burglary because he was riding in Mr. _____'s truck where the stolen property was sized from and that made him guilty of burglary. See Exhibit "B" (_____ _____ affidavit). See Exhibit "C" (_____ _____ affidavit).

"A person comits burglary if he enters or remains unlawfully in a occupiable structure of another person with the purpose of committing therein any offense punishable by imprisonment." **Ark. Stat. Ann. §41-2002(1)(Repl. 1977), Amended and recodified at Ark. Code Ann. §5-39-201 (1987)**. Both entry into a building and specific criminal intent are essential elements of the crime of burglary. **Norton v. State, 271 Ark. 451, 609 S.W.2d 1, 3 (1980); Selph v. State, 264 Ark. 197, 570 S.W.2d 256, 259 (1978)**.

It is well established that the due process clause of the fourteenth amendment require that the prosecution prove beyond a reasonable doubt every essential element of

---

[1] This motion is based on newly discovered evidence in the form of affidavits based on facts that Petitioner just discovered. See Newly Discovered Evidence on page ___. Had petitioner knew that _____ made exculpatory statements to _____ county detectives he would have never plead guilty to a crime he was innocent of.

156

the crime charged. **In re Winship, 397 U.S. 358, 364, 25 L.Ed.2d 368, 90 S.Ct. 1068 (1970); Patterson v. New York, 432 U.S. 197, 215, 53 L.Ed.2d 28, 97 S.Ct. 2319 (1977); Small v. State, 5 Ark. App. 87, 632 S.W.2d 448, 449-50 (1982).** In Petitioner's case, in order to prove the crime of burglary, the State would have been required to prove beyond a reasonable doubt that Petitioner unlawfully entered the residence in question with intent to commit an offense punishable by imprisonment, **Ark. Stat. Ann. §41-2002(1).** Or that he was an accomplice in the commission of the same. **Bradley v. State, 8 Ark. App. 300, 651 S.W.2d 113, 116 (1983).** Thus, the question before this Court is whether after viewing the evidence in light most favorable to the prosecution, any rational trier of fact could have found beyond a reasonable doubt that Petitioner made the unlawful entry into the residence and that he did so with the intent to commit theft, or that he acted as another accomplice. **See Ward v. Lockhart, 841 F.2d 844, 847 (8th Cir. 1988); Jackson v. Virginia, 443 U.S. 307, 319, 61 L.Ed.2d 560, 99 S.Ct. 2781 (1979).**

A review of the evidence in Petitioner's case, reveals that he was asleep in the motel room when _____ _____ and _____ committed the burglary. See Exhibit "C" (Affidavit of _____ _____). Mr. _____ did not have any knowledge that _____ _____ and _____ _____ were going to commit the burglary nor did Petitioner entry the residence. See Exhibits "B" and "C". The evidence is insufficient to convict Petitioner _____ of burglary under Arkansas law. See **Jackson, supra.**

Petitioner submits that based on the above facts, arguments, and authority his guilty plea was not voluntary or intelligently entered and it must be set aside. This Court should set aside the guilty plea and dismiss the charges. There exists more than a reasonable probability that Petitioner would have plead not guilty and proceeded to trial, absent counsel _____'s erroneous legal advice. Thus, prejudice under **Strickland** has been shown. **See Hill v. Lockhart, 474 U.S. 52, 59, 88 L.Ed.2d 203, 106 S.Ct. 366 (1985).**

_____ § _____

ISSUE II

Counsel failed to investigate, provide proper legal advice, induced the guilty plea based on erroneous and faulty legal advice rendering the plea involuntary

Petitioner argues that counsel failed to investigate the crime charged, failed to research the applicable law in relation to Arkansas burglary statute, and erroneously induced petitioner to plead guilty to a crime that Petitioner is actually innocent of. Counsel _____'s unprofessional legal advice renders Petitioner's guilty plea involuntary entered as a result of ineffective assistance of counsel and must be set aside. See **Woodward v. Collins, 898 F.2d 1027, 1029 (5th Cir. 1990); Scott v. Wainwright, 698 F.2d 427, 429-30 (11th Cir. 1983); Norton v. State, 271 Ark. 451, 609 S.W.2d 1, 3 (1980); Selph v. State, 264 Ark. 197, 570 S.W.2d 256, 259 (1978).**

Petitioner submits that had counsel _____ correctly advised him that his conduct did not constitute the crime of burglary he would not have pled guilty, rather he would have proceeded to trial. See Exhibit "B" (_____ affidavit). Thus, prejudice has been shown. **See Hill, 474 U.S. at 59.**

_____ § _____

ISSUE III

The guilty plea was not knowingly, voluntarily, or intelligently entered because the State failed to disclose Brady material, which would have proved petitioner's innocence; and counsel was constitutional ineffective for failing to seek discovery material that would have shown his client's innocence

The State of Arkansas failed to disclose to the defense statements made by _____ that Petitioner, _____, did not have anything to do with the burglary or theft from _____ County, Arkansas, as he was asleep in the motel room when those crimes occurred. See Exhibit "C" (_____ affidavit). The Supreme Court in **Brady v. Maryland, 373 U.S. 83, 87 (1963),** held that "due process requires the prosecution to disclose evidence favorable to an accused upon his request when such evidence is material to guilt or punishment." **Id. at 87.**

In **Tate v. Wood, 963 F.2d 20, 24-25 (2nd Cir. 1992),** found that Tate was entitled to an evidentiary hearing on **Brady** claim concerning failure to disclose evidence that victim was initial aggressor. The test materiality in the context of a guilty plea is whether there is a reasonable probability that, but for the failure to produce such information, the defendant would not have entered the plea but instead would have insisted on going to trial. The inquiry is an objective one that is resolved largely on the basis of the persuasiveness of the withheld evidence. **See Miller v. Angliker, 848 F.2d 1312, 1322 (2nd Cir.), cert. denied, 488 U.S. 890, 109 S.Ct. 224, 102 L.Ed.2d 214 (1988).** Petitioner submits that if the State would have disclosed _____ _____'s statement and counsel would have explained the true essential elements of the crime to Petitioner he would not have pled guilty, but would have demanded to proceed to trial.

Petitioner further argues that counsel's performance fell well below an objective standard of reasonableness for failing to seek discovery prior to inducing petitioner to plead guilty. **See Stano v. Dugger, 889 F.2d 962, 964 (11th Cir. 1992).** Petitioner is prejudiced by counsel _____'s unprofessional errors because had counsel obtained discovery and read _____'s statement he would not have recommended that Petitioner plead guilty to a crime he did not commit. See **United States v. Briggs, 939 F.2d 222, 228 (5th Cir. 1991).** In **Stano** trial counsel advised the judge that he had not received full discovery from the state and he could not advise defendant of wisdom of whether state had sufficient evidence to convict defendant or not. The trial judge accepted defendant's guilty plea anyway, which violated Stano's Sixth Amendment right to counsel. The exact same scenario applies to Petitioner. There exists more than a reasonable probability that Petitioner would have plead not guilty, absent counsel's unprofessional errors and omissions. **See Tate, and Stano, both supra.**

158

_____ § _____

NEWLY DISCOVERED EVIDENCE

Petitioner just recently discovered that his conduct in this case did not constitute the crime of burglary or theft under Arkansas law. See Exhibit "B" _____ affidavit. Petitioner was researching his federal case at the Federal Correctional Institution, _____, _____, and asked inmate _____ a jailhouse lawyer to review his federal case and tell him if he had any type of errors that he could obtain relief on his federal case. Petitioner learned after talking with ____ _____ that his conduct in the _____ County case did not constitute the crime to what he pled guilty of. See Exhibit "B". Thereafter, petitioner obtained an affidavit from _____. See Exhibit "C" (_____ affidavit). These affidavits constitute the newly discovered evidence that Petitioner's claims are based on. Additionally, petitioner's federal sentence was enhanced because of the _____ County burglary conviction and has restrained petitioner of liberty as a result of the unlawful conviction.

_____ § _____

CONCLUSION

WHEREFORE based on the above, _____, prays that this Honorable Court grants this motion for permission to file a motion for writ of error coram nobis, in the Circuit Court of _____, Arkansas, _____ District Criminal Division, Docket No. _____.

Respectfully submitted on this ____ day of _____ 2010.

_____
PRO SE REPRESENTATION

VERIFICATION

I, _____, hereby verify that I have read this motion and the facts stated therein are true and correct under penalty of perjury pursuant to 28 U.S.C. §1746.

CERTIFICATE OF SERVICE

I HEREBY CERTIFY that a true and correct copy of this foregoing instrument has been mailed postage prepaid on this ___ day of _____ 2010, to the: The Prosecuting Attorney's Office, _____ _____, _____, _____ _____.

Executed under penalty of perjury on this ____ day of _____ 2010.

_____

IN THE STATE OF _____

COUNTY OF _____

AFFIDAVIT OF _____

Before me, the undersigned authority, on this day of _____ personally appeared _____ who first being duly sworn, states that the following facts are true and correct to wit:

    1.

    2.

Executed on this _____ day of _____ 2010.

_____

SWORN TO AND SUBSCRIBED to before me this _____ day of _____ 20 _____.

_____
Notary Public

Chapter V
Federal Habeas Corpus for State & Federal Prisoners

❑ 28 U.S.C. §§2241 through 2254. Federal Habeas Corpus Statutes

> ➤ Rules governing 28 U.S.C. §2254 proceedings

> ➤ (Sample) *Form* to be used by federal prisoner in filing a petition for writ of habeas corpus under 28 U.S.C. §2241

> ➤ Memorandum brief in support of petition for writ of habeas corpus (§2241)

> ➤ Memorandum brief in support of petition for writ of habeas corpus (§2241 savings clause)

> ➤ *Form* letter for request of §2254 *Form* petition

> ➤ Memorandum brief in support of petition for writ of habeas (§2254)

> ➤ Amendment to petition for writ of habeas corpus (§2254)

> ➤ Memorandum brief in support of amendment to petition for writ of habeas corpus (§2254)

> ➤ Motion for expansion of record

> ➤ Motion for an evidentiary hearing

> ➤ Motion for appointment of counsel

Title 28 United States Code, Section 2241 provides:

§2241.   Power to grant writ

(a)   Writ of habeas corpus may be granted by the Supreme Court, any justice thereof, the district courts and any circuit judge within their respective jurisdictions. The order of a circuit judge shall be entered in the records of the district court of the district wherein the restraint complained of is had.

(b)   The Supreme Court, any justice thereof, and any circuit judge may decline to entertain an application for a writ of habeas corpus and may transfer the application for hearing and determination to the district court having jurisdiction to entertain it.

(c)   The writ of habeas corpus shall not extend to a prisoner unless—
(1) He is in custody under or by color of the authority of the United States or is committed for trial before some court thereof; or
(2) He is in custody for an act done or omitted in pursuance of an Act of Congress, or an order, process, judgment or decree of a court or judge of the United States; or
(3) He is in custody in violation of the Constitution or laws or treaties of the United States; or
(4) He, being a citizen of a foreign state and domiciled therein is in custody for an act done or omitted under any alleged right, title, authority, privilege, protection, or exemption claimed under the commission, order or sanction of any foreign state, or under color thereof, the validity and effect of which depend upon the law of nations; or
(5) It is necessary to bring him into court to testify or for trial.

(d)   Where an application for a writ of habeas corpus is made by a person in custody under the judgment and sentence of a State court of a State which contains two or more Federal judicial districts, the application may be filed in the district court for the district wherein such person is in custody or in the district court for the district within which the State court was held which convicted and sentenced him and each of such district courts shall have concurrent jurisdiction to entertain the application. The district court for the district wherein such an application is filed in the exercise of its discretion and in furtherance of justice may transfer the application to the other district court for hearing and determination.

(e)(1) No court, justice, or judge shall have jurisdiction to hear or consider an application for a writ of habeas corpus filed by or on behalf of an alien detained by the United States who has been determined by the United States to have been properly detained as an enemy combatant or is awaiting such determination.
(2) Except as provided in paragraphs (2) and (3) of section 1005(e) of the Detainee Treatment Act of 2005 (10 U.S.C. 801 note), no court, justice, or judge shall have jurisdiction to hear or consider any other action against the United States or its agents relating to any aspect of the detention, transfer, treatment, trial, or conditions of confinement of an alien who is or was detained by the United States and has been determined by the United States to have been properly detained as an enemy combatant or is awaiting such determination.

(June 25, 1948, ch 646, 62 Stat. 964; May 24, 1949, ch 139, § 112, 63 Stat. 105; Sept. 19, 1966, P.L. 89-590, 80 Stat. 811; Dec. 30, 2005, P.L. 109-148, Div A. Title X, § 1005(e)(1), 119 Stat. 2742; Jan. 6, 2006, P.L. 109-163, Div A, Title XIV, § 1405(e)(1), 119 Stat. 3477; Oct. 17, 2006, P.L. 109-366, § 7(a), 120 Stat. 2635; Jan. 28, 2008, P.L. 110-181, Div A, Title X, Subtitle F, § 1063(f), 122 Stat. 323)

(C) any redetermination of an application for a writ of habeas corpus or related appeal following a remand by the court of appeals en banc or the Supreme Court for further proceedings, in which case the limitation period shall run from the date the remand is ordered.

(3) The time limitations under this section shall not be construed to entitle an applicant to a stay of execution, to which the applicant would otherwise not be entitled, for the purpose of litigating any application or appeal.

(4)(A) The failure of a court to meet or comply with a time limitation under this section shall not be a ground for granting relief from a judgment of conviction or sentence.

(B) The State may enforce a time limitation under this section by applying for a writ of mandamus to the Supreme Court.

(5) The Administrative Office of the United States Courts shall submit to Congress an annual report on the compliance by the courts of appeals with the time limitations under this section.

(Added April 24, 1996, P.L. 104-132, Title I, § 107(a), 110 Stat. 1224; March 9, 2006, P.L. 109-177, Title V, § 507(e), 120 Stat. 251)

Title 28 United States Code, Section 2242 provides:

§ 2242.   Application

Application for a writ of habeas corpus shall be in writing signed and verified by the person for whose relief it is intended or by someone acting in his behalf.

It shall allege the facts concerning the applicant's commitment or detention, the name of the person who has custody over him and by virtue of what claim or authority, if known.

It may be amended or supplemented as provided in the rules of procedure applicable to civil actions.

If addressed to the Supreme Court, a justice thereof or a circuit judge it shall state the reasons for not making application to the district court of the district in which the applicant is held.

(June 25, 1948, ch 646, 62 Stat. 965.)

Title 28 United States Code, Section 2243 provides:

§ 2243.   Issuance of writ; return; hearing; decision

A court, justice or judge entertaining an application for a writ of habeas corpus shall forthwith award the writ or issue an order directing the respondent to show cause why the writ should not be granted, unless it appears from the application that the applicant or person detained is not entitled thereto.

The writ, or order to show cause shall be directed to the person having custody of the person detained. It shall be returned within three days unless for good cause additional time, not exceeding twenty days, is allowed.

The person to whom the writ or order is directed shall make a return certifying the true cause of the detention.

When the writ or order is returned a day shall be set for hearing, not more than five days after the return unless for good cause additional time is allowed.

Unless the application for the writ and the return present only issues of law the person to whom the writ is directed shall be required to produce at the hearing the body of the person detained.

The applicant or the person detained may, under oath, deny any of the facts set forth in the return or allege any other material facts.

The return and all suggestions made against it may be amended, by leave of court, before or after being filed.

The court shall summarily hear and determine the facts, and dispose of the matter as law and justice require.

(June 25, 1948, ch 646, 62 Stat. 965.)

Title 28 United States Code, Section 2244 provides:

§ 2244.   Finality of determination

(a) No circuit or district judge shall be required to entertain an application for a writ of habeas corpus to inquire into the detention of a person pursuant to a judgment of a court of the United States if it appears that the legality of such detention has been determined by a judge or court of the United States on a prior application for a writ of habeas corpus, except as provided in section 2255.

(b)(1) A claim presented in a second or successive habeas corpus application under section 2254 that was presented in a prior application shall be dismissed.

(2) A claim presented in a second or successive habeas corpus application under section 2254 that was not presented in a prior application shall be dismissed unless—

(A) the applicant shows that the claim relies on a new rule of constitutional law, made retroactive to cases on collateral review by the Supreme Court, that was previously unavailable; or

(B)(i) the factual predicate for the claim could not have been discovered previously through the exercise of due diligence; and

(ii) the facts underlying the claim, if proven and viewed in light of the evidence as a whole, would be sufficient to establish by clear and convincing evidence that, but for constitutional error, no reasonable fact finder would have found the applicant guilty of the underlying offense.

(3)(A) Before a second or successive application permitted by this section is filed in the district court, the applicant shall move in the appropriate court of appeals for an order authorizing the district court to consider the application.

(B) A motion in the court of appeals for an order authorizing the district court to consider a second or successive application shall be determined by a three-judge panel of the court of appeals.

(C) The court of appeals may authorize the filing of a second or successive application only if it determines that the application makes a prima facie showing that the application satisfies the requirements of this subsection.

(D) The court of appeals shall grant or deny the authorization to file a second or successive application not later than 30 days after the filing of the motion.

(E) The grant or denial of an authorization by a court of appeals to file a second or successive application shall not be appealable and shall not be the subject of a petition for rehearing or for a writ of certiorari.

(4) A district court shall dismiss any claim presented in a second or successive application that the court of appeals has authorized to be filed unless the applicant shows that the claim satisfies the requirements of this section.

(c) In a habeas corpus proceeding brought in behalf of a person in custody pursuant to the judgment of a State court, a prior judgment of the Supreme Court of the United States on an appeal or review by a writ of certiorari at the instance of the prisoner of the decision of such State court, shall be conclusive as to all issues of fact or law with respect to an asserted denial of Federal right which constitutes ground for discharge in a habeas corpus proceeding, actually adjudicated by the Supreme Court therein, unless the applicant for the writ of habeas corpus shall plead and the court shall find the existence of a material and controlling fact which did not appear in the record of the proceeding in the Supreme Court and the court shall further find that the applicant for the writ of habeas corpus could not have caused such fact to appear in such record by the exercise of reasonable diligence.

(d)(1) A 1-year period of limitation shall apply to an application for a writ of habeas corpus by a person in custody pursuant of the judgment of a State court. The limitation period shall run from the latest of—

(A) the date on which the judgment became final by the conclusion of direct review or the expiration of the time for seeking such review;

(B) the date on which the impediment to filing an application created by State action in violation of the Constitution or laws of the United States is removed, if the applicant was prevented from filing by such State action;

(C) the date on which the constitutional right asserted was initially recognized by the Supreme Court, if the right has been newly recognized by the Supreme Court and made retroactively applicable to cases on collateral review; or

(D) the date on which the factual predicate of the claim or claims presented could have been discovered through the exercise of due diligence.

(2) The time during which a properly filed application for State post-conviction or other collateral review with respect to the pertinent judgment or claim is pending shall not be counted toward any period of limitation under this subsection.

(June 25, 1948, ch 646, 62 Stat. 965; Nov. 2, 1966, P.L. 89-711, § 1, 80 Stat. 1104; April 24, 1996, P.L. 104-132, Title I, §§ 101, 106, 110 Stat. 1217, 1220.)

Title 28 United States Code, Section 2245 provides:

§ 2245.　　　　Certificate of trial judge admissible in evidence

On the hearing of an application for a writ of habeas corpus to inquire into the legality of the detention of a person pursuant to a judgment the certificate of the judge who presided at the trial resulting in the judgment, setting forth the facts occurring at the trial, shall be admissible in evidence. Copies of the certificate shall be filed with the court in which the application is pending and in the court in which the trial took place.

(June 25, 1948, ch 646, 62 Stat. 965.)

Title 28 United States Code, Section 2246 provides:

§ 2246.　　　　Evidence; depositions; affidavits

On application for a writ of habeas corpus, evidence may be taken orally or by deposition, or, in the discretion of the judge, by affidavit. If affidavits are admitted any party shall have the right to propound written interrogatories to the affiants, or to file answering affidavits.

(June 25, 1948, ch 646, 62 Stat. 966.)

Title 28 United States Code, Section 2247 provides:

§ 2247.　　　　Documentary evidence

On application for a writ of habeas corpus documentary evidence, transcripts of proceedings upon arraignment, plea and sentence and a transcript of the oral testimony introduced on any previous similar application by or in behalf of the same petitioner, shall be admissible in evidence.

(June 25, 1948, ch 646, 62 Stat. 966.)

Title 28 United States Code, Section 2248 provides:

§ 2248.　　　　Return or answer; conclusiveness

The allegations of a return to the writ of habeas corpus or of an answer to an order to show cause in a habeas corpus proceeding, if not traversed, shall be accepted as true except to the extent that the judge finds from the evidence that they are not true.

(June 25, 1948, ch 646, 62 Stat. 966.)

Title 28 United States Code, Section 2249 provides:

§ 2249.   Certified copies of indictment, plea and judgment; duty of respondent

On application for a writ of habeas corpus to inquire into the detention of any person pursuant to a judgment of a court of the United States, the respondent shall promptly file with the court certified copies of the indictment, plea of petitioner and the judgment, or such of them as may be material to the questions raised, if the petitioner fails to attach them to his petition, and same shall be attached to the return to the writ, or to the answer to the order to show cause.

(June 25, 1948, ch 646, 62 Stat. 966.)

Title 28 United States Code, Section 2250 provides:

§ 2250.   Indigent petitioner entitled to documents without cost

If on any application for a writ of habeas corpus an order has been made permitting the petitioner to prosecute the application in forma pauperis, the clerk of any court of the United States shall furnish to the petitioner without cost certified copies of such documents or parts of the record on file in his office as may be required by order of the judge before whom the application is pending.

(June 25, 1948, ch 646, 62 Stat. 966.)

Title 28 United States Code, Section 2251 provides:

§ 2251.   Stay of State court proceedings

(a) **In general.**

(1) Pending matters. A justice or judge of the United States before whom a habeas corpus proceeding is pending, may, before final judgment or after final judgment of discharge, or pending appeal, stay any proceeding against the person detained in any State court or by or under the authority of any State for any matter involved in the habeas corpus proceeding.

(2) Matter not pending. For purposes of this section, a habeas corpus proceeding is not pending until the application is filed.

(3) Application for appointment of counsel. If a State prisoner sentenced to death applies for appointment of counsel pursuant to section 3599(a)(2) of title 18 in a court that would have jurisdiction to entertain a habeas corpus application regarding that sentence, that court may stay execution of the sentence of death, but such stay shall terminate not later than 90 days after counsel is appointed or the application for appointment of counsel is withdrawn or denied.

(b) **No further proceedings.** After the granting of such a stay, any such proceeding in any State court or by or under the authority of any State shall be void. If no stay is granted, any such proceeding shall be as valid as if no habeas corpus proceedings or appeal were pending.

(June 25, 1948, ch 646, 62 Stat. 966; March 9, 2006, P.L. 109-177, Title V, § 507(f), 120 Stat. 251.)

Title 28 United States Code, Section 2252 provides:

§ 2252.   Notice

Prior to the hearing of a habeas corpus proceeding in behalf of a person in custody of State officers or by virtue of State laws notice shall be served on the attorney general or other appropriate officer of such State as the justice or judge at the time of issuing the writ shall direct.

(June 25, 1948, ch 646, 62 Stat. 967.)

Title 28 United States Code, Section 2253 provides:

§ 2253.   Appeal

(a) In a habeas corpus proceeding or a proceeding under section 2255 before a district judge, the final order shall be subject to review, on appeal, by the court of appeals for the circuit in which the proceeding is held.

(b) There shall be no right of appeal from a final order in a proceeding to test the validity of a warrant to remove to another district or place for commitment or trial a person charged with a criminal offense against the United States, or to test the validity of such person's detection pending removal proceedings.

(c)(1) Unless a circuit justice or judge issues a certificate of appeaability, an appeal may not be taken to the court of appeals from—

> (A) the final order in a habeas corpus proceeding in which the detention complained of arises out of process issued by a State court; or
> (B) the final order in a proceeding under section 2255.

(2) A certificate of appealability may issue under paragraph (1) only if the applicant has made a substantial showing of the denial of a constitutional right.

(3) The certificate of appealability under paragraph (1) shall indicate which specific issue or issues satisfy the showing required by paragraph (2).

(June 25, 1948, ch 646, 62 Stat. 967; May 24, 1949, ch 139, § 113, 63 Stat. 105; Oct. 31, 1951, ch 655, § 52, 65 Stat. 727; April 24, 1996, P.L. 104-132, Title I, § 102, 110 Stat. 1217.)

Title 28 United States Code, Section 2254 provides:

§ 2254.   State custody; remedies in Federal courts

(a) The Supreme Court, a Justice thereof, a circuit judge, or a district court shall entertain an application for a writ of habeas corpus in behalf of a person in custody pursuant to the judgment of a State court only on the ground that he is in custody in violation of the Constitution or laws or treaties of the United States.

(b) (1) An application for a writ of habeas corpus on behalf of a person in custody pursuant to the judgment of a State court shall not be granted unless it appears that—
    (A) the applicant has exhausted the remedies available in the courts of the State; or
    (B) (i) there is an absence of available State corrective process; or
        (ii) circumstances exist that render such process ineffective to protect the rights of the applicant.
    (2) An application for a writ of habeas corpus may be denied on the merits, notwithstanding the failure of the applicant to exhaust the remedies available in the courts of the State.
    (3) A State shall not be deemed to have waived the exhaustion requirement or be estopped from reliance upon the requirement unless the State, through counsel, expressly waives the requirement.

(c) An applicant shall not be deemed to have exhausted the remedies available in the courts of the State, within the meaning of this section, if he has the right under the law of the State to raise, by any available procedure, the question presented.

(d) An application for a writ of habeas corpus on behalf of a person in custody pursuant to the judgment of a State court shall not be granted with respect to any claim that was adjudicated on the merits in State court proceedings unless the adjudication of the claim—
    (1) resulted in a decision that was contrary to, or involved an unreasonable application of, clearly established Federal law, as determined by the Supreme Court of the United States; or
    (2) resulted in a decision that was based on an unreasonable determination of the facts in light of the evidence presented in the State court proceeding.

(e)(1) In a proceeding instituted by an application for a writ of habeas corpus by a person in custody pursuant to the judgment of a State court, a determination of a factual issue made by a State court shall be presumed to be correct. The applicant shall have the burden of rebutting the presumption of correctness by clear and convincing evidence.
    (2) If the applicant has failed to develop the factual basis of a claim in State court proceedings, the court shall not hold an evidentiary hearing on the claim unless the applicant shows that—
    (A) the claim relies on—
        (i) a new rule of constitutional law, made retroactive to cases on collateral review by the Supreme Court, that was previously unavailable; or
        (ii) a factual predicate that could not have been previously discovered through the exercise of due diligence; and
    (B) the facts underlying the claim would be sufficient to establish by clear and convincing evidence that but for constitutional error, no reasonable fact finder would have found the application guilty of the underlying offense.

(f) If the applicant challenges the sufficiency of the evidence adduced in such State court proceeding to support the State court's determination of a factual issue made therein, the applicant, if able, shall produce that part of the record pertinent to a determination of the sufficiency of the evidence to support such determination. If the applicant, because of indigency or other reason is unable to produce such part of the record, then the State shall produce such part of the record and the Federal court shall direct the State to do so by order directed to an appropriate State official. If the State cannot provide such pertinent part of the record, then the court shall determine under the existing facts and circumstances what weight shall be given to the State court's factual determination.

(g) A copy of the official records of the State court, duly certified by the clerk of such court to be a true and correct copy of a finding, judicial opinion, or other reliable written indicia showing such a factual determination by the State court shall be admissible in the Federal court proceeding.

(h) Except as provided in section 408 of the Controlled Substance Acts [21 USCS § 848], in all proceedings brought under this section, and any subsequent proceedings on review, the court may appoint counsel for an applicant who is or becomes financially unable to afford counsel, except as provided by a rule promulgated by the Supreme Court pursuant to statutory authority. Appointment of counsel under this section shall be governed by section 3006A of title 18.

(i) The ineffectiveness or incompetence of counsel during Federal or State collateral post-conviction proceedings shall not be a ground for relief in a proceeding arising under section 2254.

(June 25, 1948, ch 646, 62 Stat. 967; Nov. 2, 1966, P.L. 89-711, § 2, 80 Stat. 1105; April 24, 1996, P.L. 104-132, Title I, § 104, 110 Stat. 1218.)

Rules governing 28 U.S.C. §2254 proceedings in the United States District Courts

Rule 1.   Scope

(a) **Cases involving a petition under 28 U.S.C. § 2254.** These rules govern a petition for a writ of habeas corpus filed in a United States district court under 28 U.S.C. § 2254 by:

    (1) a person in custody under a state-court judgment who seeks a determination that the custody violates the Constitution, laws, or treaties of the United States; and

    (2) a person in custody under a state-court or federal-court judgment who seeks a determination that future custody under a state-court judgment would violate the Constitution, laws, or treaties of the United States.

(b) **Other cases.** The district court may apply any or all of these rules to a habeas corpus petition not covered by Rule 1(a).

    (As amended Dec. 1, 2004.)

Rule 2.   The Petition

(a) **Current custody; naming the respondent.** If the petitioner is currently in custody under a state-court judgment, the petition must name as respondent the state officer who has custody.

(b) **Future custody; naming the respondents and specifying the judgment.** If the petitioner is not yet in custody—but may be subject to future custody—under the state-court judgment being contested, the petition must name as respondents both the officer who has current custody and the attorney general of the state where the judgment was entered. The petition must ask for relief from the state-court judgment being contested.

(c) **Form.** The petition must

    (1) specify all the grounds of relief available to the petitioner;

    (2) state the facts supporting each ground;

    (3) state the relief requested;

    (4) be printed, typewritten, or legibly handwritten; and

    (5) be signed under penalty of perjury by the petitioner or by a person authorized to sign it for the petitioner under 28 U.S.C. § 2242.

(d) **Standard form.** The petition must substantially follow either the form appended to these rules or a form prescribed by a local district-court rule. The clerk must make forms available to petitioners without charge.

(e) **Separate petitions for judgments of separate courts.** A petitioner who seeks relief from judgments of more than one state court must file a separate petition covering the judgment or judgments of each court.

    (As amended Sept. 28, 1976, P.L. 94-426, § 2(1), (2), 90 Stat. 1334; eff. Aug. 1, 1982; Dec. 1, 2004.)

Rule 3.   Filing the Petition; Inmate Filing

(a) **Where to file; copies; filing fee.** An original and two copies of the petition must be filed with the clerk and must be accompanied by:

    (1) the applicable filing fee, or

(2) a motion for leave to proceed in forma pauperis, the affidavit required by 28 U.S.C. § 1915, and a certificate from the warden or other appropriate officer of the place of confinement showing the amount of money or securities that the petitioner has in any account in the institution.

(b) **Filing.** The clerk must file the petition and enter it on the docket.

(c) **Time to file.** The time for filing a petition is governed by 28 U.S.C. § 2244(d).

(d) **Inmate filing.** A paper filed by an inmate confined in an institution is timely if deposited in the institution's internal mailing system on or before the last day for filing. If an institution has a system designed for legal mail, the inmate must use that system to receive the benefit of this rule. Timely filing may be shown by a declaration in compliance with 28 U.S.C. § 1746 or by a notarized statement, either of which must set forth the date of deposit and state that first-class postage has been prepaid.

(As amended Dec. 1, 2004.)

Rule 4. Preliminary Review; Serving the Petition and Order

The clerk must promptly forward the petition to a judge under the court's assignment procedure, and the judge must promptly examine it. If it plainly appears from the petition and any attached exhibits that the petitioner is not entitled to relief in the district court, the judge must dismiss the petition and direct the clerk to notify the petitioner. If the petition is not dismissed, the judge must order the respondent to file an answer, motion, or other response within a fixed time, or to take other action the judge may order. In every case, the clerk must serve a copy of the petition and any order on the respondent and on the attorney general or other appropriate officer of the state involved.

(As amended Dec. 1, 2004.)

Rule 5. The Answer and the Reply

(a) **When required.** The respondent is not required to answer the petition unless a judge so orders.

(b) **Contents: addressing the allegations; stating a bar.** The answer must address the allegations in the petition. In addition, it must state whether any claim in the petition is barred by a failure to exhaust state remedies, a procedural bar, non-retroactivity, or a statute of limitations.

(c) **Contents: transcripts.** The answer must also indicate what transcripts (of pretrial, trial, sentencing, or post-conviction proceedings) are available, when they can be furnished, and what proceedings have been recorded but not transcribed. The respondent must attach to the answer parts of the transcript that the respondent considers relevant. The judge may order that the respondent furnish other parts of existing transcripts or that parts of untranscribed recordings be transcribed and furnished. If a transcript cannot be obtained, the respondent may submit a narrative summary of the evidence.

(d) **Contents: briefs on appeal and opinions.** The respondent must also file with the answer a copy of:

(1) any brief that the petitioner submitted in an appellate court contesting the conviction or sentence, or contesting an adverse judgment or order in a post-conviction proceeding;

(2) any brief that the prosecution submitted in an appellate court relating to the conviction or sentence; and

(3) the opinions and dispositive orders of the appellate court relating to the conviction or the sentence.

(e) **Reply.** The petitioner may submit a reply to the respondent's answer or other pleading within a time fixed by the judge.

(As amended Dec. 1, 2004.)

Rule 6.   Discovery

(a) **Leave of court required.** A judge may, for good cause, authorize a party to conduct discovery under the Federal Rules of Civil Procedure and may limit the extent of discovery. If necessary for effective discovery, the judge must appoint an attorney for a petitioner who qualifies to have counsel appointed under 18 U.S.C. § 3006A.

(b) **Requesting discovery.** A party requesting discovery must provide reasons for the request. The request must also include any proposed interrogatories and requests for admission, and must specify any requested documents.

(c) **Deposition expenses.** If the respondent is granted leave to take a deposition, the judge may require the respondent to pay the travel expenses, subsistence expenses, and fees of the petitioner's attorney to attend the deposition.

(As amended Dec. 1, 2004.)

Rule 7.   Expanding the record

(a) **In general.** If the petition is not dismissed, the judge may direct the parties to expand the record by submitting additional materials relating to the petition. The judge may require that these materials be authenticated.

(b) **Types of materials.** The materials that may be required include letters predating the filing of the petition, documents, exhibits, and answers under oath to written interrogatories propounded by the judge. Affidavits may also be submitted and considered as part of the record.

(c) **Review by the opposing party.** The judge must give the party against whom the additional materials are offered an opportunity to admit or deny their correctness.

(As amended Dec. 1, 2004.)

Rule 8. Evidentiary Hearing

(a) **Determining whether to hold a hearing.** If the petition is not dismissed, the judge must review the answer, any transcripts and records of state-court proceedings, and any materials submitted under Rule 7 to determine whether an evidentiary hearing is warranted.

(b) **Reference to a magistrate judge.** A judge may, under 28 U.S.C. § 636(b), refer the petition to a magistrate judge to conduct hearings and to file proposed findings of fact and recommendations for disposition. When they are filed, the clerk must promptly serve copies of the proposed findings and recommendations on all parties. Within 14 days after being served, a party may file objections as provided by local court rule. The judge must determine de novo any proposed finding or recommendation to which objection is made. The judge may accept, reject, or modify any proposed finding or recommendation.

(c) **Appointing counsel; time of hearing.** If an evidentiary hearing is warranted, the judge must appoint an attorney to represent a petitioner who qualifies to have counsel appointed under 18 U.S.C. § 3006A. The judge must conduct the hearing as soon as practicable after giving the attorneys adequate time to investigate and prepare. These rules do not limit the appointment of counsel under § 3006A at any stage of the proceeding.

(As amended Sept. 28, 1976, P.L. 94-426, § 2(5), (8), 90 Stat. 1334; Oct. 21, 1976, P.L. 94-577, § 2(a)(1), (b)(1), 90 Stat. 2730, 2731; Dec. 1, 2004; Dec. 1, 2009.)

Rule 9. Second or Successive Petitions

Before presenting a second or successive petition, the petitioner must obtain an order from the appropriate court of appeals authorizing the district court to consider the petition as required by 28 U.S.C. § 2244(b)(3) and (4).

(As amended Sept. 28, 1976, P.L. 94-426, § 2(7), (8), 90 Stat. 1335; Dec. 1, 2004.)

Rule 10. Powers of a Magistrate Judge

A magistrate judge may perform the duties of a district judge under these rules, as authorized under 28 U.S.C. § 636.

(As amended Sept. 28, 1976, P.L. 94-426, § 2(11), 90 Stat. 1335; eff. Aug. 1, 1979; Dec. 1, 2004.)

Rule 11. Certificate of Appealability; Time to Appeal

(a) **Certificate of appealability.** The district court must issue or deny a certificate of appealability when it enters a final order adverse to the applicant. Before entering the final order, the court may direct the parties to submit arguments on whether a certificate should issue. If the court issues a certificate, the court must state the specific issue or issues that satisfy the showing required by 28 U.S.C. § 2253(c)(2). If the court denies a certificate, the parties may not appeal the denial but may seek a certificate from the court of appeals under Federal Rule of Appellate Procedure 22. A motion to reconsider a denial does not extend the time to appeal.

(b) **Time to appeal.** Federal Rule of Appellate Procedure 4(a) governs the time to appeal an order entered under these rules. A timely notice of appeal must be filed even if the district court issues a certificate of appealability. (As amended Dec. 1, 2009).

Rule 12   Applicability of the Federal Rules of Civil Procedure and the Federal Rules of Criminal Procedure

The Federal Rules of Civil Procedure and the Federal Rules of Criminal Procedure, to the extent that they are not inconsistent with any statutory provisions or these rules, may be applied to a proceeding under these rules.

(As amended Dec. 1, 2004.)

Form Letter No. 1

[Your Name & Prison Number]
[Institution]
[Your Address]
[Town, State & Zip Code]

[Date]

Office of the Clerk
Attn: [Clerk's Name]_____
Address_____
Town, State & Zip Code____

Re: **28 U.S.C. §2241 <u>Form Applications</u>**
        Petition for a Writ of Habeas Corpus

Dear Clerk:

At this time, I am requesting a **28 U.S.C. §2241 <u>Form</u> Application for a Writ of Habeas Corpus** that is used in this district to be forwarded to me by your office. I have enclosed a self-addressed stamped envelope for the return of the **28 U.S.C. §2241 Form Application**.

Thank you.

Sincerely,

_____
[Your Name]

CC:
    p/file.

Certified Mail No _____

FORMS TO BE USED BY FEDERAL PRISONERS IN FILLING A PETITION FOR WRIT OF HABEAS CORPUS UNDER 28§2241

IN THE UNITED STATES DISTRICT COURT
_____ DISTRICT OF _____
-_____ DIVISION

_____
PETITIONER.

_____

_____

_____
(Address or place of confinement and prison number. Full name which you were convicted under).

VS.

_____
RESPONDENT.

_____

_____

_____
(Name of Warden or other authorized person having custody of petitioner)

PLEASE COMPLETE THE FOLLOWING: (check appropriate number)

This Petition concerns:

1. a. _____ a conviction.
    b. _____ a sentence.
    c. _____ jail or prison conditions.
    d. _____ prison discipline.
    e. _____ a parole problem
    f.   _____ other.

2.   Place of detention_____

3.   Name and location of court which imposed sentence_____

_____

4.   The indictment number or numbers (if known) upon which, and the offense or

offenses for which, sentence was imposed:

(a) _____

(b) _____

(c) _____

5.   The date upon which sentence was imposed and the terms of the sentence:

(a) _____

(b) _____

(c) _____

6.   Check whether a finding of guilty was made:

(a) After a plea of guilty _____

(b) After a plea of not guilty _____

(c) After a plea of nolo contendere _____

7.   If you were found guilty after a plea of not guilty, check whether that finding was

made by:

(a) a jury _____

(b) a judge without a jury _____

8.   Did you appeal from the judgement of conviction or the imposition of sentence?

(   ) Yes   (   ) No

9.   If you did appeal, give the following information for each appeal:

a. (1) Name of court _____

(2) Result _____

a. (Continued)

   (3) Date of result _____

   (4) Citation or number of opinion _____

   (5) Grounds raised (list each) _____

      (a) _____

      (b) _____

      (c) _____

      (d) _____

b. (1) Name of Court _____

   (2) Result _____

   (3) Date of result _____

   (4) Citation or number of opinion _____

   (5) Grounds raised (list each)

      (a) _____

      (b) _____

      (c) _____

      (d) _____

CAUTION: ***If you are attacking a sentence imposed under a federal judgement, you must first file a direct appeal or motion under 28 U.S.C. §2255 in the federal court which entered the judgement.***

10. State **CONCISELY** every ground on which you claim that you are being held unlawfully. Summarize briefly the facts supporting each ground. If necessary attach a SINGLE page only behind this page.

CAUTION: ***If you fail to set forth all grounds in this petition, you may be barred from presenting additional grounds at a later date.***

179

PAGE 4

10.   Continued

   (a) Ground One _____

   _____

   Supporting <u>FACTS</u> (Tell your story <u>BRIEFLY</u> without citing cases or law).

   CAUTION: ***You must state <u>facts not conclusions</u> in support of your grounds. A***
   rule of thumb to follow is—who did exactly what to violate your
   rights at what time or place.

   _____

   _____

   _____

   _____

   _____

   _____

   _____

   _____

   _____

   (b) Ground Two _____

   _____

   Supporting <u>FACTS</u> (Tell your story <u>BRIEFLY</u> without citing cases or law).

   _____

   _____

   _____

   _____

   _____

   _____

   _____

10.   Continued

(c) Ground Three _____

_____

Supporting <u>FACTS</u> (Tell your story <u>BRIEFLY</u> without citing cases or law).

_____

_____

_____

_____

_____

_____

_____

(d) Ground Four _____

_____

Supporting <u>FACTS</u> (Tell your story <u>BRIEFLY</u> without citing cases or law).

_____

_____

_____

_____

_____

_____

_____

11.   Have you filed previous petitions for habeas corpus, motions under §2255 of Title
       28 United States Code, or any other applications, petitions or motions with respect
       to this conviction?

                                  (   ) Yes   (   ) No

PAGE 6

12. If your answer to question number 11 was "yes," give the following information:

(a) (1) Name of Court _____

(2) Nature of proceeding _____

(3) Grounds raised _____

_____

_____

_____

(4) Result _____

(5) Date of Result _____

(6) Citation or number of any written opinion or order entered pursuant to each disposition.

_____

(b) (1) Name of Court _____

(2) Nature of proceeding _____

(3) Grounds raised _____

_____

_____

_____

(4) Result _____

(5) Date of Result _____

(6) Citation or number of any written opinion or order entered pursuant to each disposition.

_____

13.   If you did not file a motion under §2255 of Title 28, United States Code, or if you filed such a motion and it was denied, state why your remedy by way of such motion is inadequate or ineffective to test the legality of your detention:

_____

_____

_____

_____

_____

_____

_____

14.   Are you presently represented by counsel? Yes ( )   No ( )

If so, name, address and telephone number _____

_____

Case name and Court _____

_____

15.   If you are seeking to proceed in forma pauperis, have you completed the declaration setting forth the required information? ( ) Yes   ( ) No

WHEREFORE, Petitioner prays that the court grant Petitioner's relief to which he may be entitled in this proceeding.

Signed this _____ day of _____, 20 ____.

_____

Signature of Petitioner

IN THE UNITED STATES DISTRICT COURT
FOR THE _____ DISTRICT OF _____

_____,

Petitioner,

VS.   **Civil Action No. _____**

_____, **Warden**
FEDERAL BUREAU OF PRISONS, and
UNITED STATES ATTORNEY GENRAL,

Respondent.

MEMORANDUM BRIEF IN SUPPORT OF PETITION
FOR WRIT OF HABEAS CORPUS

TO THE HONORABLE JUDGE OF SAID COURT:

COMES NOW_____, the petitioner, pro se, and respectfully moves files this memorandum brief in support of his petition for writ of habeas corpus pursuant to **28 U.S.C. §2241**. Petitioner moves the Court to issue a writ of habeas corpus directing the respondent to recalculate Petitioner's sentence. In support thereof, Petitioner will show the Court as follows:

STATEMENT OF JURISDICTION

Jurisdiction is invoked pursuant to **28 U.S.C. §2241** to entertain a petition for writ of habeas corpus. See **Barden v. Keohane, 921 F.2d 476 (3rd Cir. 1991); Braden v. 30th Judicial Circuit Court of Kentucky, 410 U.S. 484, 488-89, 93 S.Ct. 1123, 1126, 35 L.Ed.2d 443 (1973)**.

_____ § _____

STATEMENT OF THE CASE

[Insert the statement of the case]

STATEMENT OF THE FACTS

[Insert a statement of facts in support of the claims]

A more precise set of facts are set forth throughout this memorandum brief.

ADMINISTRATIVE REMEDIES

On _____ ____, 20___, Petitioner filed a **Informal Resolution** with, _____, an Inmate Systems Manager Technician at FCI _____, _____, seeking nunc pro tunc designation of the _____ Department Corrections Institution as a federal facility in order to credit his federal sentence with time served in the state institution. Alternatively, Petitioner sought credit for the pretrial detention time, which the federal judgment recommended by stating: "1. DEFENDANT TO RECEIVE CREDIT FOR TIME SERVED AS APPLICABLE BY STATUTE." Id. at page 2. As of this date, the Informal Resolution has not been answered.

On _____ ____, 20___, the Petitioner filed a BP-9 Administrative Remedy. See Exhibit "___" a copy of said Administrative Remedy. This BP-9 Administrative Remedy was denied. See Exhibit "___" a copy of the denial.

On _____ ____, 20___, the Petitioner filed his BP-10 Administrative Remedy. See Exhibit "D" a copy of the BP-10 Administrative Remedy. This BP-10 Administrative Remedy was denied. See Exhibit "___" a copy of the denial.

On _____ ____, 2008, the Petitioner filed his BP-11 Administrative Remedy. See Exhibit "F" a copy of the BP-11 Administrative Remedy. This BP-11 Administrative Remedy was denied. See Exhibit "___" a copy of the denial.

———————— § ————————

ISSUES

(A) THE BUREAU OF PRISONS ERRED BY FAILING TO ENTERTAIN PETITIONER'S REQUEST FOR A NUNC PRO TUNC DESIGNATION OF THE _____ DEPARTMENT OF CORRECTIONS AS A FEDERAL FACILITY IN ORDER TO CREDIT PETITIONER'S FEDERAL SENTENCE WITH PRETRIAL DETENTION TIME SERVED AS RECOMMENDED BY THE SENTENCING JUDGE

(B) THE BUREAU ERRED IN REFUSING TO RECOGNIZE ITS AUTHORITY TO MAKE SUCH DESIGNATION

(C) THE BUREAU ERRED IN REFUSING TO DESIGNATE PETITIONER'S STATE PRISON AS A PLACE OF CONFINEMENT FOR SERVICE OF HIS FEDERAL SENTENCE

(D) THE BUREAU ERRED FAILING TO TREAT PETITIONER FAIRLY AND IMPARTIALLY AS THEY HAVE OTHER PRISONERS

ARGUMENTS AND AUTHORITIES

First, Petitioner argues that: the Bureau erred by failing to entertain his request for a nunc pro tunc designation of the _____ Department of Corrections as a federal facility in order to credit his federal sentence with pretrial detention time served as recommended by the sentencing judge. Second, the Bureau erred in refusing to recognize its authority to make such designation. Third, the Bureau erred in refusing to designate the _____ Department of Corrections as a place of confinement for service of his federal sentence. Fourth, the Bureau erred by failing to treat petitioner fairly and impartially as mandated by **28 CFR §542.12 (2006)**.

Petitioner's administrative remedies sought a nunc pro tunc designation of his state prison facility as a place of confinement for his federal sentence in order to gain credit for time served in the state custody towards his federal sentence. Alternatively, Petitioner sought credit for the pretrial detention time served, which the federal sentencing judgment recommended _____ by _____ stating: _____. Id. at page ___. **See Exhibit "B through G"** a copy of the administrative remedies and their responses attached hereto and made part of this petition by reference herein.

Statutory Authority

18 United States Code, Section 3621(b) provides:

The Bureau of Prisons shall designate the place of the prisoner's imprisonment. The Bureau may designate any available penal or correctional facility that meets the minimum standards of health and habitability established by the Bureau, whether maintained by the Federal Government or otherwise and whether within or without the judicial district in which the person was convicted, that the Bureau determines to be appropriate and suitable, considering—

    (1)   the resources of the facility contemplated;

    (2)   the nature and circumstances of the offense;

    (3)   the history and characteristics of the prisoner;

    (4)   any statement by the court that imposed the [federal[sentence-

    (A)   concerning the purposes for which the sentence to imprisonment was determined to be warranted; or

    (B)   recommending a type of penal or correctional facility as appropriate; and

    (5)   any pertinent policy statement issued by the Sentencing Commission pursuant to section 994(a)(2) of title 28.

The Bureau may at any time, having regard for the same matters, direct the transfer of a prisoner from one penal or correctional facility to another. **See 18 U.S.C. §3621(b)**. **See also <u>Barden</u>, 921 F.2d at 482**.

The Bureau's failure to even to consider Petitioner's claim for relief from possible mistake or inadvertence in failing to designate the state prison as a place of federal confinement carries a serious potential for a miscarriage of justice. **See Barden, 921 F.2d at 479**. Accordingly, the Bureau's error is fundamental and can be corrected through habeas. **See Murray v. Carrier, 477 U.S. 478, 495, 196 S.Ct. 2639, 2649, 91 L.Ed.2d 397 (1986)** (habeas available to avoid potentially serious miscarriage of justice).

Petitioner is entitled to have the Bureau consider his claim and decide it by exercising the statutory discretion it failed to recognize is available to it. **See Farmworker Justice Fund, Inc. v. Brock, 811 F.2d 613, 619-23 (D.C. Cir. 1987)** (agency refusal to issue field worker sanitation standard as required by statute is abuse of discretion through inaction). The Bureau must at least consider Petitioner's case in accord with the broad statutory authority it has to make such **nunc pro tunc** designations, authority it openly recognizes in general but denies with respect to Petitioner's case. See **Barden, 921 F.2d at 481**.

Program Statement 5160.05 (1/16/2003)

The Federal Bureau of Prisons Program Statement 5160.05, Designation of State Institution for the Service of Federal Sentence, is attached hereto and made part of this petition by reference herein. **See Exhibit "H"**. The Bureau's own Program Statement regarding designation of state institutions for concurrent service of federal and state sentences recognizes both the Bureau's authority to make this type of designation and its obligation pursuant to **Barden v. Keohane** to consider [the] inmate requests for designation. **See McCarthy v. Doe, 146 F.3d 118, 123 fn. 3 (2nd Cir. 1998); P.S. 5160.05**.

P.S. 5160.05 authorizes the Bureau to consider the Sentencing Judge's intent; the Sentencing Court's recommendation, and at least six other exceptions to the general rule. **See Exhibit "H"**.

In this case, the sentencing court on _____ ___, 20___, ordered that the defendant is hereby committed to the custody of the United States Bureau of Prisons to be imprisoned for a term of: _____. The Court then made the following recommendations to the Bureau of Prisons: _____. The Court then imposed a $_____ special assessment fee to be paid immediately. Petitioner paid the $_____ special assessment fee immediately as ordered by the Court through his attorney.

Fair and Impartial Treatment

Under the statute and the BOP's regulations, Petitioner is entitled to "fair treatment" on his application for **nunc pro tunc** designation of the state facility as a place of confinement for his federal sentence. **See 28 C.F.R. §542.12 (2006)** ("[Inmates] . . . have the right to expect that as a human being [they] will be treated respectfully, impartially and fairly by all personnel."). See also **Barden, 921 F.2d at 483**.

The Bureau has wide discretion to designate the place of confinement for purposes of serving federal sentences of imprisonment. The Bureau's regulations require "fair treatment" of petitioner's application. Petitioner is not fairly treated when the

Bureau refuses to consider his request and denies having discretion that Congress afforded it. **See Barden, 921 F.2d at 483.**

Special Assessment Fee

Petitioner argues that his sentence commenced immediately when he paid his special assessment fee because a special assessment fee constitutes punishment. See **United States v. Smith, 818 F.2d 687, 690 (9th Cir. 1987). See also United States v. Bass, 310 F.3d 321, 330 (5th Cir. 2001).**

The aforementioned facts, arguments and authorities stand for the proposition that the Bureau erred failing to entertain Petitioner's application for a nunc pro tunc designation of the _____ Department of Corrections as a federal facility in order to credit petitioner's federal sentence with pretrial detention time served as recommended by the judge. Further, that the Bureau erred in failing to recognize it had authority to grant such a request and its refusal to grant such designation was an abuse of discretion. **See Barden, supra.**

_____ § _____

CONCLUSION

Petitioner, _____, has been deprived of basic fundamental rights guaranteed by the Fifth Amendment Due Process Clause of the United States Constitution and seeks to restore those rights in this Court. The Bureau of Prisons deprived Petitioner of his statutory rights to have the Bureau consider his application for nunc pro tunc designation of the _____ Department of Correction as a federal facility in order that time served there can be credited towards his federal sentence. Petitioner moves this Court for an order directing the Bureau of Prisons to fully and carefully consider his application for nunc pro tunc designation.

Respectfully submitted on this ____ day of _____ 200___.

_____

PRO SE REPRESENTATION

IN THE UNITED STATES DISTRICT COURT
FOR THE _____ DISTRICT OF _____
_____ DIVISION

_____,

Petitioner,

VS.   Civil No. _____

_____, **Warden**

FEDERAL BUREAU OF PRISONS, and
UNITED STATES ATTORNEY GENRAL,

Respondent.

PETITION FOR WRIT OF HABEAS CORPUS

TO THE HONORABLE JUDGE OF SAID COURT:

COMES NOW_____, the petitioner, pro se, and respectfully moves this Honorable Court pursuant to **28 U.S.C. §2241** to issue a writ of habeas corpus directing the Bureau of Prisons to recalculate petitioner's term of imprisonment. In support thereof, Petitioner will show this Court as follows:

I.
STATEMENT OF JURISDICTION

Jurisdiction is invoked pursuant to **28 U.S.C. §2241** to entertain a petition for writ of habeas corpus. See **Barden v. Keohane, 921 F.2d 476 (3rd Cir. 1991); Braden v. 30th Judicial Circuit Court of Kentucky, 410 U.S. 484, 488-89, 93 S.Ct. 1123, 1126, 35 L.Ed.2d 443 (1973).**

II.
STATEMENT OF CASE

On _____ ___, 20___, Petitioner was arrested and subsequently, charged with _____; and _____. On _____ ___, 20___, a federal grand jury for the _____ District of _____, indicted Petitioner on the above charges. On that same date, Federal authorities lodged a detainer against Petitioner for the instant charges, which prevented him from posting a state bond. On that same date, a federal warrant was issued for Mr. _____ arrest. See (Docket Sheet). Because of the federal detainer Mr. _____ was prevented from making bond so he conceded to a probation violation to resolve a state's revocation of probation charge.

On _____ ___, 20___, a federal writ of habeas corpus ad Prosequendum was issued.

On _____ ___, 20___, Petitioner was arraigned on the instant charges in federal court. See (Doc. No. _____).

On _____ ___, 20___, Petitioner plead guilty in federal court to Count One _____; and _____.

On _____ ___, 20___, Petitioner appeared before the Honorable Judge _____, for sentencing. During sentencing defense counsel _____ argued that the court should order that the federal sentence should be ordered to be served concurrently with the State revocation of probation proceeding under USSG §5G1.3(2). Counsel _____ advised the Court that Mr. _____ had been incarcerated on these charges since _____ ___, 20___. (ST pp. ____).

The Court at sentencing stated:

> THE COURT: I have listened to the defendant, defendant's counsel, and counsel for the government. I've also listened to the witnesses called by the defendant. I've reviewed the presentence investigation report in this case. I've also considered the factors set forth in 18 United States Code, Section 3553(a).
>
> Pursuant to the Sentencing Reform Act of 1984, IT IS THE JUDGMENT OF THE COURT that the defendant _____ _____ _____ is herby committed to the custody of the Bureau of Prisons to be imposed for a term of ___ months as to each of Counts ___ and ___, to be served concurrently. This sentence shall be served concurrently to the **revoked state parole term the defendant is presently serving.** (ST pp. ___).

III.
SENTENCE MONITORING COMPUTATION DATA

The original calculation by the Bureau of Prisons through a nunc pro tunc designation awarded Mr. _____ jail credits from _____ ___, 20___, through _____ ___, 20___. A total of ___ days jail credits. **See Exhibit "A"** (Sentence Monitoring Computation Data). This Sentence Monitoring Computation Data dated _____ ___, 20___, was certified on _____ by Desg/Sentence Computation CTR.

IV.
ADMINISTRATIVE REMEDIES

Petitioner has exhausted his administrative remedies through the Bureau of Prison seeking his jail credit from _____ ___, 20___, through his sentencing dated _____ ___, 20___. **See Exhibit "B"** (Administration Remedies).

The Bureau of Prisons **(BOP)** initially credited Petitioner's sentence with jail credits from _____ ___, 20___, through _____ ___, 20___, through a nunc pro tunc designation. **See Exhibit "A" (Sentence Monitoring Computation Data)**, certified on _____.

In retaliation, for Mr. _____ processing his administrative remedy seeking jail credits from _____ ___, 20___, through _____ ___, 20___, the BOP retaliated and took the previously awarded jail credits from _____ ___, 20___, through _____ ___, 20___,. **See Exhibit "C" (Sentence Monitoring Computation Data)**, dated _____.

_____ § _____

STATEMENT OF THE FACTS

On _____ ___, 20___, Mr. _____ was arrested by federal authorities and subsequently turned over to the State of _____. The federal authorities lodged a detainer against Mr. _____, with the State of _____ which prevented the State from releasing him.

The Bureau of Prisons initially granted a nunc pro tunc designating the _____ Department of Corrections as a federal facility, and awarded Mr. _____ credit for time spent in pretrial detention from _____ ___, 20___, through _____ ___, 20___. **See Exhibit "A" (Sentence Monitoring Computation Data)**, certified on _____. Alternatively, the Bureau awarded Mr. _____ pretrial detention credits from _____ ___, 20___, through _____ ___, 20___, because the United States lodged a detainer on Mr. _____ on the date of his arrest which prevented his release from state custody.

The Bureau of Prisons retaliated against Mr. _____ for seeking additional pretrial detention credits from _____ ___, 20___, through _____ ___, 20___. **See Exhibit "B"** Administrative Remedies. The proof that the Bureau retaliated against Mr. _____ lies in the Bureau's removal of the _____ days pretrial detention credits previously awarded. **See Exhibit "C".**

ISSUE I

The Bureau Erred By Failing To Comply With Procedure Set Forth By Congress And Its Own Regulation

The BOP erred by failing to comply with the procedure outlined in its own Program Statement 5160.05 (1/16/2005), and **18 U.S.C. §3621(b)(1)-(5)**, to consider Mr. _____ request for a nunc pro tunc designation of the _____ Department of Corrections as a Federal facility in order to credit his federal sentence with pretrial detention time served as recommended by the sentencing court. **See Barden, 921 F.2d at 481**. The BOP failed to comply with the Sentencing Court's intent to award jail credits and its recommendation to run Mr. _____ federal sentence concurrently with his state sentence.

191

18 U.S.C. §3621(b) provides: The Bureau of Prisons shall designate the place of the prisoner's imprisonment. The Bureau may designate any available penal or correctional facility that meets the minimum standards of health and habitability by the Federal Government or otherwise and whether, within or without the judicial district in which the person was convicted, considering—(4) any statement by the court that imposed the [federal] sentence—(A) concerning the purposes for which the sentence to imprisonment was determined to be warranted; or (B) recommending a type of penal or correctional facility as appropriate; . . . Id. at **18 U.S.C. §3621(b)(4)(A)&(B)**.

The Federal Bureau of Prisons Program Statement 5160.05 Designation of State Institution for the Service of the Federal Sentence. See www.bop.gov/PS5160.05. The Bureau's own Program Statement regarding designation of state institutions for concurrent service of federal and state sentence recognizes both the Bureau's authority to make this type of designation and its obligation pursuant to **Barden v. Keohane** to consider [the] inmate requests for designation. **See McCarthy v. Doe, 146 F.3d 118, 123 fn.3 (2nd Cir. 1998)**, and PS 5160.05.

PS 5160.05 authorizes the Bureau to consider the Sentencing Judge's intent; the Sentencing Court's recommendation, and at least six other exception to the general rule. In this case, the sentencing court intent was to award jail credits to Mr. _____ for pretrial detention time served and as stated by the Court at sentencing: "This sentence shall be served concurrently to the revoked state parole term the defendant is presently serving." **(ST pp. 8-9)**.

The National Administrative Remedy No. _____ Part B-Response states: "A nunc pro tunc designation was determined at the time your sentence was computed, dated _____ ___, 20___." Id. See **Exhibit "___"**. On _____ ___, 20___, the BOP initially computed Petitioner's sentence. The BOP did a nunc pro tunc designation and awarded Mr. _____ credit for pretrial detention time from _____ ___, 20___, through _____ ___, 20___. See Exhibit "A". Therefore, according to PS 5160.05 the Bureau wrote the Sentencing Judge a letter and requested the Court's opinion whether the court wanted to award Mr. _____ with time spent in pretrial detention from _____ ___, 20___, through _____ ___, 20___. Apparently, the Sentencing Court recommended that Mr. _____ receive jail credits for pretrial detention from _____ ___, 20___, through _____ ___, 20___, because the BOP awarded such credits. **See Exhibit "A"**.

Mr. _____ filed his administrative Remedy seeking additional time from _____ ___, 20___, through _____ ___, 20___. See **Exhibit "B"**. The BOP by its own admission had already awarded Mr. _____ a nunc pro tunc designation and credited towards his federal sentence the pretrial detention time from _____ ___, 20___, through _____ ___, 20___, acted in a vindictive manner and took the time that it had awarded by the sentencing recommendation and the Bureau. **See Exhibit "C"** Sentence Monitoring Computation Data, dated _____.

Petitioner is entitled to have the BOP consider his claims and decide it by exercising its statutory discretion that it failed to recognize is available to it under **18 U.S.C. §3621(b)(1)-(5)**. **See Farmworker Justice Fund, Inc. v. Brock, 811 F.2d 613,**

619-23 (D.C. Cir. 1987)(agency refusal to issue field worker sanitation standard as required by statute is abuse of discretion through inaction). The Bureau must at least consider Petitioner's case in accord with the broad statutory authority it openly recognizes in general, but denies with respect to Petitioner's case. **See Barden, 921 F.2d at 481**. The BOP erred failing to comply with its own procedures outlined in PS 5160.05 and **18 U.S.C. §3621(b)(1)-(5)**.

The Bureau's failure to even consider Petitioner's claim for relief because of possible mistake or in advertence in failing to designate the state prison as a place of federal confinement carries a serious potential for a miscarriage of justice. **See Barden, 921 F.2d at 479**. Accordingly, the Bureau's error is fundamental and can be corrected through habeas. **See Murray v. Carrier, 477 U.S. 478, 495, 106 S.Ct. 2639, 2649, 91 L.Ed.2d 397 (1986)** (habeas available to avoid potentially serious miscarriage of justice). The BOP failure to comply with its statutory authority on Mr. _____'s case constitutes error and warrants relief. **See Barden, 921 F.2d at 481**.

Mr. _____ moves this Court to direct the Respondents to show proof of its compliance with its statutory authority.

———————— § ————————

ISSUE II

The Bureau Erred Removing Mr. _____'s Previously Awarded **Willis** and **Kayfez** Pretrial Detention Credits Because A Federal Detainer Prevented Him From Making Bail On the State Case

The BOP erred by removing Mr. _____'s **Willis** and **Kayfez** pretrial detention credits from _____ ___, 20___, through _____ ___, 20___, because Mr. _____ filed his Administrative Remedy seeking additional pretrial credits. First, federal authorities lodged a detainer against Mr. _____ on _____ ___, 20___, which prevented Mr. _____ from posting bail. A second detainer was lodged after the grand jury return its indictment on _____ ___, 20___, which also prevent Mr. _____ from posting bond. Therefore, Mr. _____ is entitled to all his pretrial detention time to be credited towards his federal sentence. **See United States v. Harris, 876 F.2d 1502, 1506-07 (11th Cir. 1989)** (time in state jail credited to federal sentence because defendant held on request of federal officials); **Kayfez v. Gasele, 993 F.2d 1288, 1289-90 (7th Cir. 1993)** (defendant entitled to credit against federal sentence for all presentence incarceration even though time had already been credited against concurrent state sentence because crediting only against state sentence would not reduce period of actual imprisonment).

In **United States v. Haney, 711 F.2d 113, 114-115 (8th Cir. 1993)(per curiam)**, the court found that the defendant was entitled to credit for time served in state custody because denial of release on bail due to outstanding federal detainer. The government has the burden of proving that pretrial state confinement not the result of federal detainer. **Haney, 711 F.2d at 114-115**. A federal prisoner is entitled to credit towards his federal sentence for time spent in presentence custody, where a federal detainer was responsible for his confinement by state authorities because state officials relied on detainer warrant in refusing to release him on bail on state charges. **See Davis v. Attorney General, 425 F.2d 238 (5th Cir. 1970)**. Mr. _____ is entitled to an evidentiary hearing where federal detainer prevented him from making bond on state charges to determine whether he was entitled to credit for time spent on his state charges which were run concurrently with his federal sentence. **See Willis v. United States, 438 F.2d 923, 925 (5th Cir. 1971)**.

Mr. _____ moves for this Court to grant him all of his pretrial detention time from _____ ___, 20___, the date the federal detainer was lodged against him forward. Alternatively, direct the Respondent to produce a copy of all records and detainers filed by federal authorities on this matter and for an evidentiary hearing.

_____ § _____

ISSUE III

Denial Of Fair And Impartial Treatment

The BOP erred by treating Mr. _____ unfairly and acting in a vindictive manner because he sought additional pretrial detention credits through Administrative Remedy process, in violation of the First and Fifth Amendments of the United States Constitution. Under the statute and BOP regulation, Mr. _____ is entitled to "fair treatment" on his application for nunc pro tunc designation of the state facility as a place of confinement for his federal sentence. See **28 CFR §542.12 (2006)**("[Inmate] . . . has the right to except that as a human being [they] will be treated respectfully, impartially and fairly by all personnel."). **See also Barden, 921 F.2d at 483**.

The Bureau has wide discretion to designate the place of confinement for purposes of serving federal sentence of imprisonment. Once the Bureau made its decision on _____ ___, 20___, and granted Mr. _____ pretrial detention credits from _____ ___, 20___, through _____ ___, 20___, it unfairly took said pretrial detention credits through Administrative remedy process. The Bureau's regulations require "fair treatment" of Petitioner's application. Petitioner has not been treated fairly when the Bureau refuses to consider his request and denies having discretion that Congress afforded it. **See Barden, 921 F.2d at 483**. Mr. _____ maintains that the Bureau's action by taken his previously awarded pretrial detention credits _____ ___, 20___, through _____ ___, 20___, because he filed his administrative remedy seeking additional pretrial detention credits constitutes unfair treatment, in violation of the First and Fifth Amendments of the United States Constitution.

─────────── § ───────────

CONCLUSION

WHEREFORE based on the above, _____ _____ _____,
respectfully moves this Honorable Court to issue a writ of habeas corpus directing the
respondents to award him all pretrial detention credits from _____ ___, 20___,
forward towards his federal sentence to comply with the Sentencing Court's
recommendation and intent. Additionally, award Petitioner all pretrial detention credits
from the date that a federal detainer was lodged against him forward.

Respectfully submitted on this ___ day of _____ 2009.

_____

PRO SE REPRESENTATION

IN THE UNITED STATES DISTRICT COURT
FOR THE _____ DISTRICT OF _____
_____ DIVISION

_____,

Petitioner,

VS.   Civil Action No. _____

_____, Warden
_____, United States
Attorney General,

Respondent.

MEMORANDUM BRIEF IN SUPPORT OF PETITION FOR
WRIT OF HABEAS CORPUS PURSUANT TO 28 U.S.C.
§2241 SAVINGS CLAUSE PROVISION

TO THE HONORABLE JUDGE OF SAID COURT:

COMES NOW_____, the Petitioner, pro se, and respectfully files this Memorandum brief in support of petition for a writ of habeas corpus pursuant to **28 U.S.C. §§2241 and 2243** directing the Respondents to release petitioner from federal custody immediately. In support thereof, Petitioner will show this Court as follows:

<u>STATEMENT OF JURISDICTION</u>

Jurisdiction is invoked pursuant to **28 U.S.C. §§2241** and **§2255** savings clause. See **<u>Wofford v. Scott</u>, 177 F.3d 1236, 1244 (11th Cir. 1999); <u>Sawyer v. Holder</u>, 326 F.3d 1363, 1365 (11th Cir.), cert. denied, 540 U.S. 900 (2003)**. In this case, **28 U.S.C. §2255** provides an inadequate or ineffective remedy to test the legality of Mr. _____ detention. See **<u>Wofford</u>, 177 F.3d at 1244**, "The savings clause of §2255 applies to a claim when: 1) that claim is based upon a retroactively applicable Supreme Court decision; 2) the holding of that Supreme Court decisions establishes that the prisoner was convicted of a nonexistent offense; and, 3) circuit law squarely foreclosed such a claim at the time it otherwise should have been raised in the petitioner's trial, appeal, or first §2255 motion." Id. Mr. _____ invokes the savings clause provision to obtain relief based on the substantive change in law by the Supreme Court in **<u>Begay v. United States</u>, 128 S.Ct. 1581, 1583, 170 L.Ed.2d 490 (2008)**. **<u>Chambers v. United States</u> 555 U.S. _____, 129 S.Ct. 687, 691-93, 172 Led.2d 484 (2009)**.

_____ § _____

STATEMENT OF THE FACTS

1. Mr. _____ proceeded to trial in the United States District Court for the _____ District of _____ (_____ Division), and was convicted for possession of ammunition by a convicted felon in violation of **18 U.S.C. §922(g)(1), 924(e)** (Case Number _____).

2. At sentencing the district court concluded that Mr. _____ prior convictions for the following offenses made him an Armed Career Criminal: (1) a 1967 conviction for armed robbery; (2) a 1986 conviction for attempted homicide; and a 1987 conviction for escape, in violation of Fla Law Ch. 944.40. Defense counsel objected to the use of the escape charge claiming that it was not a violent felony, but conceded that **United States v. Gay, 251 F.3d 950 (11th Cir. 2001)**, held otherwise.

3. On _____ ___, 20___, the United States District Court for the _____ District of _____, sentenced Mr. _____ as an Armed Career Criminal to ____ months imprisonment to be followed by _____ (__) years supervised release.

4. Mr. _____ appealed, claiming that the District Court erred 1) denying his motion to suppress and 2) by enhancing his sentence based on his prior convictions that were not proven to the jury beyond a reasonable doubt. The Eleventh circuit affirmed.

5. On _____ ___, 20___, Mr. _____ filed a **28 U.S.C. §2255** motion in the district court of conviction (case Number _____). In this motion, Mr. _____ argued that: 1) the district court erred by sentencing him as an armed Career Criminal; 2) counsel was ineffective for failing to object to the same; 3) the district court constructively amended his indictment; 4) counsel was ineffective for failing to object to the same; 5) counsel was ineffective during pretrial stage for failing to advise him to admit guilty so he could get a sentence reduction for acceptance of responsibility. The district court denied Mr. _____ §2255 motion.

6. Mr. _____ filed an appeal and sought a Certificate of Appealability from the _____ Circuit which was denied.

7. Mr. _____ prior conviction for escape, in violation of Florida Law ch. 944.40 no longer constitutes a "violent felony" in light of the new interpretation of **18 U.S.C. §924(e)(B)(ii)**, by the Supreme Court in **Begay**. Mr. _____is actually innocent of being an Armed Career Criminal and was convicted and sentenced of a non-existent offense in light of **Begay**.

A more precise set of facts are set forth throughout this memorandum brief.

———— § ————

A. "Violent Felony" Under the ACCA

Mr. _____ conviction of being a felon in possession of ammunition under **18 U.S.C. §922(g)(1)** would ordinarily subject to him to a term of imprisonment not to exceed ten years. **18 U.S.C. §924(a)(2)**. In Mr. _____ case, the United States charged him by indictment of being a felon in possession of a firearm with three "violent felonies" predicate offenses in order to convict him of violating **18 U.S.C. §924(e)(2)(B)(ii)**, which provides, where a felon violates §922(g)(1) "and has three previous convictions . . . for a violent felony . . . such person shall be imprisoned not less than fifteen years," and not more than life. **See United States v. Brame, 997 F.2d 1426, 1428 (11th Cir. 1993)**. Therefore, the question of what constitutes a violent felony can make all the difference. **See Begay v. United States, 128 S.Ct. 1581, 1583, 170 L.Ed.2d 490 (2008)** ("[The ACCA] imposes a more stringent 15-year mandatory minimum sentence on [such] an offender who has three prior convictions 'for a violent felony or a serious drug offense.' " **(quoting 18 U.S.C. §924(e)(1)))**.

Section 924(e)(2)(B) of the ACCA defines a "violent felony" as:

> any crime punishable by imprisonment for a term exceeding one year . . . that-
>
> (i) has as an element the use, attempted use, or threatened use of physical force against the person of another; or
>
> (ii) is burglary, arson, or extortion, involves use of explosives, **or otherwise involves conduct that presents a serious potential risk of physical injury to another . . .**

18 U.S.C.§924(e)(2)(B) (emphasis added).

The Supreme Court has, on three separate occasions, instructed lower courts on **its** <u>interpretation</u> of the residual clause. **See Chambers v. United States, 555 U.S. ___, 129 S.Ct. 687, 691-93, 172 L.Ed.2d 484 (2009); Begay, 128 S.Ct. at 1586-88 (2008); James v. United States, 550 U.S. 192, 127 S.Ct. 1586, 1597, 167 L.Ed.2d 532 (2007)**. In each case, the Supreme Court determined whether a state crime was a "violent felony" under the ACCA. Therefore, we recount the Supreme Court's recent foray into determining whether a state crime involved "conduct that presents a serious potential risk of physical injury to another" within the meaning of the ACCA.

B. Categorical Approach

Before assessing the riskiness of a crime under the ACCA, a court first identify exactly what the crime at issue is. **United States v. Harrison, 558 F.3d 1280, 1284 (11th Cir. 2009)**. In **James**, the Supreme Court instructed that lower courts should employ a "categorical approach" to focus its analyses. **127 S.Ct. at 1593-94**. That is, courts should "look only to the fact of conviction and the statutory definition of the prior offense." **Id. at 1594. (quoting Taylor v. United States, 495 U.S. 575, 602, 110 S.Ct. 2143, 2160, 109 L.Ed.2d 607 (1990))**. Generally speaking, courts should not consider the "particular facts disclosed by the record of conviction." **Id. (quotation marks omitted)**. Such an approach requires looking to the "elements of the offense . . . without inquiring into the specific conduct of this particular offender." **Id. (emphasis omitted)**. Therefore, we look to the way the crime is "generally committed"—not by examining the particular facts in a defendant's case or by focusing on extreme situations. **Chambers, 129 S.Ct. at 690**. It is the "ordinary case" or the "generic sense" of the state crime that counts. **Begay, 128 S.Ct. at 1584** ("In determining whether [a] crime is a violent felony, we consider the offense generically, that is to say, we examine it in terms of how the law defines the offense and not in terms of how an individual offender might have committed it on a particular occasion."); **James, 127 S.Ct. at 1597** ("[T]he proper inquiry is whether the conduct encompassed by the elements of the offense, in the ordinary case, presents a serious potential risk of injury to another). The Supreme Court has warned that "[t]his categorical approach requires courts to choose the right category. And sometimes the choice is not obvious." **Chambers, 129 S.Ct. at 690**.

C. **Begay**: Similar in Kind, as Well as Risk

The Supreme Court in **Begay v. United States, 128 S.Ct. 1581, 1583, 170 L.Ed.2d 490 (2008)**, interpreted the meaning of the Armed Career Crimnal Act residual clause of **18 U.S.C. §924(e)(2)(B)(ii)**, adding the requirement that, to quantify as a "violent felony," the crime must be "roughly similar, in kind as well as in degree of risk posed." Id. at 1585. Simply put, "the provision's listed examples-burglary, arson, extortion, or crimes involving the use of explosives-illustrate the kinds of crimes that fall within the statute's scope." Id. at 1584-85. "Their presence indicates that the statute covers only **similar** crimes, rather than **every** crime that 'presents a serious potential risk of physical injury to another.' " Id. at 1585 (quoting §924(e)(2)(B)(ii)).

The **Begay** Court reasoned that "purposeful, violent, and aggressive conduct" is the type that "makes [it] more likely that an offender, later possessing a gun, will use that gun deliberately to harm a victim." Id. "Crimes committed in such a purposeful, violent, and aggressive manner are potentially more dangerous when firearms are involved." Id. (quotation marks and citation omitted). "And such crimes are characteristics of the statute." Id. The **Begay** Court concluded that DUIs are not "purposeful, violent, and aggressive." Id. They are strict liability crimes with no intent requirement. Id. at 1586-87. A prior DUI conviction does not "show an increased likelihood that the offender is the kind of person who might deliberately point [a] gun and pull the trigger." Id. at 1587. "We have no reason to believe that congress intended a 15-year mandatory prison term where that increased likelihood does not exist." Id. A DUI "is simply too unlike the provision's listed examples for us to believe that Congress intended the provision to cover it." Id. at 1584. Therefore, the **Begay** Court concluded that felony DUI does not qualify as a "violent felony" under the ACCA. Id.

James and **Begay**, taken together, establish a three-step inquiry for determining whether a crime falls under the ACCA's residual clause. First, what is the relevant category of crime, determined by looking to how the crime is ordinarily committed? Second, does that crime pose a "serious potential risk of physical injury" that is similar in degree to the risks posed by the enumerated crimes? Third, is that crime similar in kind to the enumerated crimes? **See Harrison, 558 F.3d at 1287**.

D. Fla Stat. 944.40 Escapes; penalty. Any prisoner confined in any prison, jail, road camp, or other, penal institution, state, county, or municipal, working upon the public roads, or being transported to or from a place of confinement who escapes or attempts to escape from such confinement shall be guilty of a felony of the second degree, punishable as provided in s. 775.082, s. 775.083, or s. 775.084. The punishment of imprisonment imposed under this section shall run consecutive to any former sentence imposed upon any prisoner.

E. **Begay and Chambers** Applies to Fla. Statute 944.40

Applying **Begay and Chambers** to Mr. _____ prior conviction for escape under Fla. Statute 944.40 establishes that said crime is not a "violent felony." **See United States v. Lowery, 2009 U.s. Dist. LEXIS 16299 (M.D. Ala. March 3, 2009)** (Defendant's prior conviction for third degree escape, pursuant to Ala. Code §13A-10-33, was not a violent felony with the meaning of the ACCA in light of **Begay**. There were no statutory elements upon which a §13A-10-33 conviction could rest that necessarily involved the kinds of conduct covered by **18 U.S.C.S. §924(e)(2)(B)(ii)'s** residual clause). The exact same scenario applies in Mr. _____ case, pursuant to Fla. Statute 944.40. **See also United States v. Harrison, 558 F.3d 1280, 1292 fn 21 (11th Cir. 2009)** (Based on **Gay**, this Court subsequently held that a conviction under Florida's escape statute-including a failure to return to a halfway house—is a violent felony under §924(e)(2)(B) of the ACCA. **United States v. Taylor, 489 F.3d 1112, 1113-14 (11th Cir. 2007)**. The Supreme Court has vacated **Taylor** for reconsideration in light of **Chambers**. **See Taylor v. United States, 129 S.Ct. 990 (2009)**.

Mr. _____ escape occurred when he was transported to the hospital. He was left alone in the waiting room and he walked off. **See Fla. Stat. 944.40**. When assessing risk, this Court examines the crime as "generally committed," see **Chambers, 129 S.Ct. at 690**, and settle on the appropriate crime by looking to the "elements of the offense" under Florida law, **James, 127 S.Ct. at 1594**. After **Chambers,** courts must examine the particular form of escape at issue on its own merits. **Chambers** has already spawned a reconsideration of circuit precedent involving escape crimes. **See United States v. Oaks, 554 F.3d 1087, 1088 (6th Cir. 2009)** (remanding for determination of whether defendant's felony conviction for knowingly escaping from the custody of the sheriff's department "qualifies as 'violent'" because the appellate court was "unable to determine whether, at the time of his escape, [defendant] was held in 'secure custody,' 'law enforcement custody,' or 'nonsecure custody,'" and noting **Chamber's** consideration of "empirical evidence of how often different types of 'escapes' led to injury"); **United States v. Pearson, 553 F.3d 1183, 1185-86 (8th Cir. 2009)** (stating **"Chambers** overrules this circuit's precedent that all escapes—including failures to return or report to custody—are crimes of violence, but leaves intact our precedent holding that escape from custody is a crime of violence," and remanding for determination of whether the defendant's prior conviction was a crime of violence). **See Harrison, 558 F.3d at 1298-99 (11th Cir.)**

In accordance with Florida Statute 944.40, Mr. _____ walk away from the waiting room in the hospital did not constitute a "violent felony" in light of **Begay** and **Chambers**. **See Harrison, 558 F.3d at 1298-99**.

F. The Savings Clause Provision

The savings clause of §2255 applies to a claim when: (1) that claim is based upon a retroactively applicable Supreme Court decision; (2) the holding of that Supreme Court decisions establishes that the prisoner was convicted of a nonexistent offense; and, (3) circuit law squarely foreclosed such a claim at the time it otherwise should have been raised in petitioner's trial, appeal, or first §2255 motion." **Wofford v. Scott, 177 F.3d 1236, 1244 (11th Cir. 1999).**

F1. Retroactively Applicable Supreme Court Decision

The Supreme Court in **Begay v. United States**, 553 U.S. ___, 128 S.Ct. 1581, 170 L.Ed.2d 490 (2008), established a new standard for determining whether a prior conviction is a "violent felony" under the ACCA. The **Begay** Court interpreted the list of enumerated crimes in the first clause of **§924(e)(2)(B)(i)** as having a limiting effect on the second clause of **§924(e)(2)(B)(ii). Id. at 1584-1585.** The **Begay** Court concluded that the second clause did not cover all crimes that involved a "serious potential risk of physical injury to another," but only those crimes that were "roughly similar, in kind as well as in degree of risk posed" to burglary, arson, extortion, or crimes involving use of explosives. **Id. at 1585.** The Court also noted that all of these enumerated crimes "typically involve purposeful, violent, and aggressive conduct." **Id. at 1586 (quotations omitted).**

In **United States v. Leonard, 2009 U.S. App. LEXIS 15957 (2009)**, the Court held that **Begay** applied retroactively to cases on collateral review. "To determine if defendant can seek relief based on the rule announced in **Begay** through a §2255 motion, the Court must consider whether **Teague v. Lane, 489 U.S. 288, 109 S.Ct. 1060, 103 L.Ed.2d 334 (1989)**, applies and, if so, whether defendant can rely on **Begay** as a basis for relief in collateral proceedings. In **Teague**, the Supreme Court held that new rules of criminal procedure are generally inapplicable to cases on collateral review. **Id. at 305-06.** The Supreme Court has subsequently clarified that a "new rule applies retroactively in collateral proceedings only if (1) the rule is substantive or (2) the rule is a 'watershed rul[e] of criminal procedure implicating the fundamental fairness and accuracy of the criminal proceedings." **Whorton v. Bockting, 549 U.S. 406, 127 S.Ct. 1173, 1180, 167 L.Ed.2d 1 (2007).** An example of a new substantive rule was created in **Bailey v. United States, 516 U.S. 501, 133 L.Ed.2d 472 (1995)**, when the Supreme Court held that the "use" element of **18 U.S.C. §924(c)(1)** required the government to prove "active employment of the firearm" rather than mere possession. **Id. at 144.** In **Bousley v. United States, 523 U.S. 614, 118 S.Ct. 1604, 140 L.Ed2d 828 (1998)**, the Supreme Court determined that **Bailey** announced a new substantive rule and **Teague** did not prevent the defendant from raising a claim based on **Bailey** in collateral proceedings. **Bousley, 523 U.S. at 619-20** ("[B]ecause **Teague** by its terms applies only to procedural rules, we think it is inapplicable to the situation in which this Court decides the meaning of criminal statute enacted by Congress"). The Supreme Court has not recognized any new rule of criminal procedure as a watershed rule since **Teague** was decided. **Whorton, 127 S.Ct. at 1181-82.**

In **Leonard**, "[t]he government concedes that **Begay** announced a new substantive rule and defendant's claim is not subject to the restriction of **Teague**. A rule is procedural if it "merely raise[s] the possibility that someone convicted with use of the invalidated procedure might have been acquitted otherwise," while a substantive rule "narrows the scope of a criminal statute by interpreting its terms ... [or] place[s] particular conduct or persons covered by the statute beyond the State's power to punish." **Schriro v. Summerlin, 542 U.S. 348, 351-52, 124 S.Ct. 2519, 159 L.Ed.2d 442 (2004).** In **Begay**, the Supreme Court construed that **ACCA** and found that DUI did not fall within the statutory definition of violent felony. **Begay. 128 S.Ct. at 1588.** Therefore, a DUI conviction may not be used to enhance a defendant's sentence under ACCA and a defendant who was classified as an armed career offender based, in part, on a DUI conviction may have been improperly sentence. **Begay** did not craft a new sentencing procedure but, instead, limited the types of crimes that may [be] treated as predicate offenses under the ACCA. A new rule is substantive if it limits the reach of federal criminal statute and creates a risk that a person has been punished for "an act that the law does not make criminal" or, in this case, that a person's sentence has been increased based on conduct outside the scope of the federal statute used to enhance the person's sentence. **See Bousley, 523 U.S. at 620-21.** The Court finds that **Begay** announced a new substantive rule, rather that a procedural rule, because **Begay** limits the authority of a court to increase a defendant's punishment for certain types of conduct. Therefore, **Teague** is inapplicable and defendant may rely on **Begay** to challenge his sentence in a §2255 motion." **Id. See Leonard, 2009 U.S. Dist. LEXIS 15957** (holding that **Begay** applies retroactively on collateral review). **See also United States v. Radabaugh, 268 Fed. App. 748, 2008 U.S. App LEXIS 5087 (10th Cir. 2008).**

G. Section 2255 Is Ineffective & Inadequate Remedy

Mr. _____ has previously filed one §2255 motion. Section 2255 permits second or successive motions only if the motion contains:

> (1) newly discovered evidence that, if proven and viewed in light of the evidence as a whole, would be sufficient to establish by clear and convincing evidence that no reasonable factfinder would have found the movant guilty of the offense; or

> (2) a new rule of constitutional law, made retroactive to cases on collateral review by the Supreme Court, that was previously unavailable.

28 U.S.C. §2255 (2000).

And, as subsection (2) speaks only to intervening Supreme Court decisions based on constitutional grounds, the provision does not provide any avenue through which a petitioner could rely on an intervening Court decision based on the substantive reach of a federal statute. **See Lorentsen v. Hood, 223 F.3d 950, 953 (9th Cir. 2000).** The inadequacy or inefficacy of the remedy will therefore permit a federal prisoner to file a write of habeas corpus under provisions such as §2241. **See Reyes-Requena, 243 F.3d at 901-903 fn 19, 29-29.**

Section 2255 is inadequate and ineffective to test the legality of a conviction when: (1) at the time of the conviction, settled law of the circuit or the Supreme Court established the legality of the conviction; (2) subsequent to the prisoner's direct appeal and first §2255 motion, the substantive law change such that the conduct of which the prisoner was convicted is deemed not to be criminal; and (3) the prisoner cannot satisfy the gatekeeping provisions of §2255 because the new rule is not one of constitutional law. See **In re Jones, 226 F.3d 328, 333-34 (4th Cir. 2000)**. "A federal prisoner should be permitted to seek habeas corpus relief only if he had no reasonable opportunity to obtain earlier judicial correction of a fundamental defect in his conviction or sentence because the law changed after his first 2255 motion." **In re Davenport, 147 F.3d 605, 611 (7th Cir. 1998)**.

"A [federal] prisoner barred by res judicata would seem as a consequence to have an 'inadequate or ineffective' remedy under §2255, and thus, be entitled to proceed in federal habeas corpus." See **In re Hanserd, 123 F.3d 922, 930 (6th Cir. 1997)**. Section 2255's savings clause is available for "a prisoner who had no earlier opportunity to challenge his conviction for a crime that an intervening change in substantive law may negate." **See In re Dorsainvil, 119 F.3d 245, 251 (3rd Cir. 1997)**.

In Mr. _____ case, Section 2255 for a second or successive motion does not provide an avenue through which a petitioner could rely on for the intervening **Begay** decision of the Supreme Court based on the substantive reach of a federal statute. Thus, §2255 provides an inadequate or ineffective remedy. See **Jones, 226 F.3d at 333-34; Hanserd, 123 F.3d at 930; Dorsainvil, 119 F.3d at 251; Sustache-Rivera v. U.S., 221 8, 16 (1st Cir. 2000); Wofford, 177 F.3d at 1244;** and **Reyes-Requena, 243 F.3d at 902-903**.

—————— § ——————

CONCLUSION

WHEREFORE, based on the above, _____, urges this Honorable Court to issue a writ of habeas corpus directing the respondents to release him from federal custody. Alternatively, appoint counsel and schedule this case for an evidentiary hearing.

Respectfully submitted on this ___ day of _____, 2009.

———————————————————
PRO SE REPRESENTATION

Form Letter No. 2

[Your Name & Prison Number]
[Your Institution]
[Your Address]
[Town, State & Zip Code]

[Date]

Clerk of the Court
United States District Court
Address
Town, State & Zip Code

Re: Form Petition Under 28 U.S.C. §2254 for a Writ of Habeas Corpus.
        Petition for Relief Form a Conviction or Sentence By a Person in State Custody

Dear Clerk:

At this time, I am requesting a **form** Petition Under 28 U.S.C. §2254 for a Writ of Habeas Corpus. Petition for Relief From a Conviction or Sentence By a Person in State Custody. The Law Library here at the _____ Correctional Institution does not have the necessary §2254 Form Petition. Therefore, I am requesting a §2254 Form Petition from your office because I have an upcoming deadline.

Your assistance on this matter is greatly appreciated. Thank you.

Sincerely,

_____
[Your Name]

CC:

    p/file.

IN THE UNITED STATES DISTRICT COURT
FOR THE _____ DISTRICT OF _____
_____ DIVISION

_____,

Petitioner,

VS.   **Civil No.** _____

_____,

Respondents.

MEMORANDUM BRIEF IN SUPPORT OF PETITION FOR WRIT OF HABEAS CORPUS PURSUANT TO 28 U.S.C. §2254

TO THE HONORABLE JUDGE OF SAID COURT:

COMES NOW_____, the Petitioner, pro se, and respectfully files this Memorandum brief in support of petition for writ of habeas corpus pursuant to 28 U.S.C. §2254, directing the respondent to release him from custody. This §2254 petition is timely filed under §2244(d)(1)(A).

I.
PRELIMINARY STATEMENT

[Insert a preliminary statement briefly describing your constitutional and procedural claims].

II.
STATEMENT OF THE CASE

[Set forth briefly the proceedings below. Include the State habeas proceedings showing that you exhausted your claims below].

III.
STATEMENT OF THE FACTS

[Set forth facts in support of your constitutional and procedural claims].

IV.
STANDARD OF REVIEW

Under the 1996 AEDPA, the _____ Court's ruling denying petitioner's constitutional claims are reviewable under **28 U.S.C. §2254(d)(1)&(2)**, where a federal court may grant relief if the state court's adjudication of the claim is: (1) resulted in a decision that was contrary to, or involved an unreasonable application of, clearly established Federal law, as determined by the Supreme Court of the United States; or (2) resulted in a decision that was based on an unreasonable determination of the facts in light of the evidence presented in the State court proceeding. **See, e.g., <u>Bell v. Cone</u>, 535**

U.S. 685, 122 S.Ct. 1843, 152 L.Ed.2d 914 (2002). A State court's merit determination is "contrary to" the United States Supreme Court clearly established law if it applies a rule "different from the governing law set forth in Supreme Court cases," or if it "confronts a set of facts that are materially indistinguishable from a decision of the Supreme Court and nevertheless arrives at a result different from Supreme Court precedent." **See also Price v. Vincent, 538 U.S. 634, 123 S.Ct. 1848, 1853, 155 L.Ed.2d 877 (2003)**. Under the "unreasonable application" clause, a federal habeas court may grant the writ if the state court identifies the correct governing legal principle from the court's decisions but unreasonably applies that legal principle to the facts of the prisoner's case. **See William v. Taylor, 529 U.S. 420, 120 S.Ct. 1495, 1522-1523, 146 L.Ed.2d 435 (2000)**.

V.
INEFFECTIVE ASSISTANCE OF COUNSEL

The Sixth Amendment of the United States Constitution guarantees the right to effective assistance of counsel in criminal prosecutions. **See McMann v. Richardson, 397 U.S. 759, 711 n. 14 (1970)** (6th Amendment right to counsel is right to effective assistance of counsel). The Sixth Amendment right to effective assistance of counsel is made applicable to the State's through the Fourteenth Amendment. **See Gideon v. Wainwright, 372 U.S. 335, 9 L.Ed.2d 799, 83 S.Ct. 792 (1963)**. Claims of ineffective assistance of counsel are reviewable under a two-prong test set forth by the Supreme Court in **Strickland v. Washington, 466 U.S. 687-688, 104 S.Ct. 2052, 2064-74, 80 L.Ed.2d 674 (1984)**. To succeed on any claim of ineffective assistance of counsel, the defendant must show: (1) that his attorney's representation fell below an objective standard of reasonableness; and (2) that counsel's deficient performance prejudiced the defendant.

A. [State Your Ineffective Assistance of Counsel Proposition]

Assert facts supported by the record or affidavits showing how your counsel's performance fell below an objective standard of reasonableness for counsel in a criminal case and cite case law supporting your claim.

Blend the facts with case law showing the validity of your claim.

Present facts showing how the outcome of the proceedings would have been different, absent counsel's unprofessional errors and omissions. Then meet the standards set forth in §2254(d)(1) or §2254(d)(2).

B. [State Your Ineffective Assistance of Counsel Proposition]

Assert facts supported by the record or affidavits showing how your counsel's performance fell below an objective standard of reasonableness for counsel in a criminal case and cite case law supporting your claim.

Blend the facts with case law showing the validity of your claim.

Present facts showing how the outcome of the proceedings would have been different, absent counsel's unprofessional errors and omissions. Then meet the standards set forth in §2254(d)(1) or (2).

C. [State Your Ineffective Assistance of Counsel Proposition]

Assert facts supported by the record or affidavits showing how your counsel's performance fell below an objective standard of reasonableness for counsel in a criminal case and cite case law supporting your claim.

Blend the facts with case law showing the validity of your claim.

Present facts showing how the outcome of the proceedings would have been different, absent counsel's unprofessional errors and omissions. Then meet the standards set forth in §2254(d)(1) or (2).

D. [State Your Constitutional Claim]

Assert facts supported by the record or affidavits relevant to your constitutional claim and cite case law supporting your claim.

Blend the facts with case law showing the validity of your claim. Then establish how your constitutional claim is not procedural barred for failure to raise the claim at trial and on appeal.

Present facts showing how the outcome of the proceedings would have been different, absent your constitutional claim. Then meet the standards set forth in §2254(d)(1) or (2).

WHEREFORE, based on the above, _____ _____, the petitioner, respectfully moves to: _____ _____. Alternatively, appoint counsel and conduct an evidentiary hearing to resolve the factual disputes.

Respectfully submitted on this _____ day of _____ 20 ___.

_____

PRO SE REPRESENTATION

IN THE UNITED STATES DISTRICT COURT
FOR THE _____ DISTRICT OF _____
_____ DIVISION

_____,

Petitioner,

VS.   Civil No. _____

_____,

Respondents.

AMENDMENT TO PETITION FOR WRIT OF
HABEAS CORPUS PURSUANT TO 28 U.S.C. §2254

COMES NOW_____, the Petitioner, pro se, and respectfully files this Amendment to his 28 U.S.C. §2254 petition for writ of habeas corpus, pursuant to Federal Rules of Civil Procedure, Rule 15(a). This amended §2254 petition is timely. The Respondent has not filed a responsive pleading. Petitioner will show this Court as follows:

1.   Insert facts relevant to your amended claim.

2.   Insert facts relevant to your amended claim.

3.   Insert facts relevant to your amended claim.

4.   Insert facts relevant to your amended claim.

WHEREFORE, based on the above, _____, the petitioner, respectfully moves this Court to: _____. Alternatively, appoint counsel and conduct an evidentiary hearing to resolve the factual disputes.

A memorandum brief in support of this Amendment to petition for writ of habeas corpus pursuant to 28 U.S.C. §2254 is attached hereto and made part of this amendment by reference herein.

Respectfully submitted on this ___ day of _____ 20 ___.

_____
PRO SE REPRESENTATION

IN THE UNITED STATES DISTRICT COURT
FOR THE _____ DISTRICT OF _____
_____ DIVISION

_____,

Petitioner,

VS.   **Civil No. _____**

_____,

Respondents.

MEMORANDUM BRIEF IN SUPPORT OF AMENDMENT TO PETITION
FOR WRIT OF HABEAS CORPUS PURSUANT TO 28 U.S.C. §2254

COMES NOW_____, the Petitioner, pro se, and respectfully files this Memorandum brief in support of the Amendment to his 28 U.S.C. §2254 petition for writ of habeas corpus, pursuant to Federal Rules of Civil Procedure, Rule 15(a). See **Mayle v. Felix, 125 S.Ct. 2562, 2569 (2005)** ("Before a responsive pleading is served, pleadings may be amended once as a 'matter of course,' i.e., without leave."). This amended §2254 motion is timely filed under §2244(d)(1)(A). See **Jimenez v. Quarterman, 555 U.S. ___, 129 S.Ct. ___, 172 L.Ed.2d 475 (2009)**. The Respondent has not filed a responsive pleading.

I.
STATEMENT OF THE FACTS

The facts stated in ¶¶___ through ___ in the Amendment to the petition for writ of habeas corpus pursuant 28 U.S.C. §2254 are hereby adopted herein.

II.
INEFFECTIVE ASSISTANCE OF COUNSEL

A. [State Your Ineffective Assistance of Counsel Proposition]

Assert facts supported by the record or affidavits showing how your counsel's performance fell below an objective standard of reasonableness for counsel in a criminal case and cite case law supporting your claim.

Then blend the facts with case law showing the validity of your claim.

Assert facts showing how the outcome of the proceedings would have been different, absent counsel's unprofessional errors and omissions.

B. [State Your Ineffective Assistance of Counsel Proposition]

Assert facts supported by the record or affidavits showing how your counsel's performance fell below an objective standard of reasonableness for counsel in a criminal case and cite case law supporting your claim.

Then blend the facts with case law showing the validity of your claim.

Assert facts showing how the outcome of the proceedings would have been different, absent counsel's unprofessional errors and omissions.

C. [State Your Ineffective Assistance of Counsel Proposition]

Assert facts supported by the record or affidavits showing how your counsel's performance fell below an objective standard of reasonableness for counsel in a criminal case and cite case law supporting your claim.

Then blend the facts with case law showing the validity of your claim.

Assert facts showing how the outcome of the proceedings would have been different, absent counsel's unprofessional errors and omissions.

D. [State Your Constitutional Claim]

Assert facts supported by the record or affidavits relevant to your constitutional claim and cite case law supporting your claim.

Then blend your facts with case law showing the validity of your claim. Then establish how your constitutional claim is not procedurally barred for failure to raise the claim at trial and on appeal.

Assert facts showing how the outcome of the proceedings would have been different, absent your constitutional claim.

WHEREFORE based on the above, _____, the petitioner, respectfully moves this to: _____. Alternatively, appoint counsel and conduct an evidentiary hearing to resolve the factual disputes.

Respectfully submitted on this ___ day of _____ 20 ___.

_____
PRO SE REPRESENTATION

IN THE UNITED STATES DISTRICT COURT
FOR THE _____ DISTRICT OF _____
_____ DIVISION

_____

_____,

Petitioner,

VS.   Crim. No. _____

_____,   Civil No. _____

Respondent.

_____

MOTION FOR EXPANSION OF RECORD

_____

TO THE HONORABLE JUDGE _____:

    COMES NOW _____, the Petitioner, pro se, and respectfully files this motion for expansion of the record pursuant to **Rule 7(b)** governing **28 U.S.C. §2254** proceedings.

    Petitioner moves for expansion of the record to include all Exhibits and Affidavits attached to his §2254 petition and Memorandum Brief. The Exhibits and Affidavits have been served on the opposing party and should be included within the record in accordance with Rule 7(b), which provides: **"Rule 7(b) Types of Materials.** The materials that may be required include letters predating the filing of the petition, documents, exhibits, and answers under oath to written interrogatories propounded by the judge. Affidavits may also be submitted and considered as part of the record." **Id.**

    WHEREFORE based on the above, _____, the Petitioner urges this Honorable Court to grant this motion for expansion of the record.

    Respectfully submitted on this ___ day of _____, 201__.

_____
PRO SE REPRESENTATION

IN THE UNITED STATES DISTRICT COURT
FOR THE _____ DISTRICT OF _____
_____ DIVISION

_____

_____,

Petitioner,

VS.   Civil. No. _____

_____,   Criminal No. _____

Respondents.

_____

MOTION FOR EVIDENTIARY HEARING
_____

      COMES NOW _____, the Petitioner, pro se, and respectfully moves this Honorable Court for evidentiary hearing pursuant to **Rule 8**, governing **28 U.S.C. §2254** proceedings. Petitioner filed his §2254 petition and move for discovery material, the respondent filed a response and moved for an evidentiary hearing. In light of Rules 6 and 8 governing §2254 proceedings, this Court should appoint counsel to represent petitioner, and schedule this case for a hearing.

      WHEREFORE, premises considered, _____,the petitioner, respectfully moves for appointment of counsel to represent his 28 U.S.C. §2254 petition for writ of habeas corpus.

      Respectfully submitted on this ___ day of _____, 201__.

_____
PRO SE REPRESENTATION

IN THE UNITED STATES DISTRICT COURT
FOR THE _____ DISTRICT OF _____
_____ DIVISION

_____

_____,

Petitioner,

VS.   Civil. No. _____

_____,   Criminal No. _____

Respondents.

_____

MOTION FOR APPOINTMENT OF COUNSEL

_____

    COMES NOW _____, the Petitioner, pro se, and respectfully moves this Honorable Court for appointment of counsel to represent his 28 U.S.C. §2254 petition for writ of habeas corpus, pursuant to 18 U.S.C. §3006A. Petitioner filed his §2254 petition and move for discovery material, the respondent filed a response and moved for an evidentiary hearing. In light of Rules 6 and 8 governing §2254 proceedings, this Court should appoint counsel to represent petitioner.

    WHEREFORE, premises considered, _____,the petitioner, respectfully moves for appointment of counsel to represent his 28 U.S.C. §2254 petition for writ of habeas corpus.

    Respectfully submitted on this ___ day of _____, 201__.

_____

PRO SE REPRESENTATION

213

Chapter VI
Federal Prisoners Motion to Vacate, Set-Aside Or Correct Sentence

❑ 28 U.S.C. §2255. Rules governing §2255 proceedings

- ➢ *Form* letter requesting §2255 Form motion

- ➢ Motion to vacate, set-aside or correct sentence

- ➢ Memorandum brief in support of motion to vacate, set-aside or correct sentence (several sample briefs) and (§2255 guilty plea [skeleton]) and a (§2255 trial [skeleton]) memorandums

- ➢ *Sample* Affidavit

- ➢ Amendment to Motion to vacate, set-aside or correct 28 U..C. §2255 (with memorandum brief)

- ➢ Motion for appointment of counsel

- ➢ Motion for an extension of time to file a reply to government's response

- ➢ Reply to United States' answer to Movant's 28 U.S.C. §2255 motion

- ➢ Motion for temporary stay of the proceedings

- ➢ Motion for discovery and production of documents pursuant to Rule 6 (with memorandum brief)

- ➢ Interrogatories for defense counsel

- ➢ Interrogatories for assistant United States Attorney

- ➢ Motion for expansion of record

- ➢ Motion for evidentiary hearing (with memorandum brief)

- ➢ Motion for an enlargement of time to file objections to the magistrate judge's report & recommendation

- ➢ Petitioner's objections to report of magistrate judge

- ➢ Movant's objections to the magistrate judge's report and recommendation

- ➢ Motion for production of evidentiary hearing transcripts at government's expense

- ➢ Notice of appeal

- ➢ *Form* letter requesting an in forma pauperis application

- ➢ Motion for leave to proceed on appeal in forma pauperis (with affidavit)

Title 28 United States Code, Section 2255 provides:

§ 2255.   Federal custody; remedies on motion attacking sentence

(a) A prisoner in custody under sentence of a court established by Act of Congress claiming the right to be released upon the ground that the sentence was imposed in violation of the Constitution or laws of the United States, or that the court was without jurisdiction to impose such sentence, or that the sentence was in excess of the maximum authorized by law, or is otherwise subject to collateral attack, may move the court which imposed the sentence to vacate, set aside or correct the sentence.

(b) Unless the motion and the files and records of the case conclusively show that the prisoner is entitled to no relief, the court shall cause notice thereof to be served upon the United States attorney, grant a prompt hearing thereon, determine the issues and make findings of fact and conclusions of law with respect thereto. If the court finds that the judgment was rendered without jurisdiction, or that the sentence imposed was not authorized by law or otherwise open to collateral attack, or that there has been such a denial or infringement of the constitutional rights of the prisoner as to render the judgment vulnerable to collateral attack, the court shall vacate and set the judgment aside and shall discharge the prisoner or resentence him or grant a new trial or correct the sentence as may appear appropriate.

(c) A court may entertain and determine such motion without requiring the production of the prisoner at the hearing.

(d) An appeal may be taken to the court of appeals from the order entered on the motion as from the final judgment on application for a writ of habeas corpus.

(e) An application for a writ of habeas corpus in behalf of a prisoner who is authorized to apply for relief by motion pursuant to this section, shall not be entertained if it appears that the applicant has failed to apply for relief, by motion, to the court which sentenced him, or that such court has denied him relief, unless it also appears that the remedy by motion is inadequate or ineffective to test the legality of his detention.

(f) A 1-year period of limitation shall apply to a motion under this section. The limitation period shall run from the latest of—

> (1) the date on which the judgment of conviction becomes final;

> (2) the date on which the impediment to making a motion created by governmental action in violation of the Constitution or laws of the United States is removed, if the movant was prevented from making a motion by such governmental action;

> (3) the date on which the right asserted was initially recognized by the Supreme Court, if that right has been newly recognized by the Supreme Court and made retroactively applicable to cases on collateral review; or

(4) the date on which the facts supporting the claim or claims presented could have been discovered through the exercise of due diligence.

(g) Except as provided in section 408 of the Controlled Substances Act, in all proceedings brought under this section, and any subsequent proceedings on review, the court may appoint counsel, except as provided by a rule promulgated by the Supreme Court pursuant to statutory authority. Appointment of counsel under this section shall be governed by section· 3006A of title 18.

(h) A second or successive motion must be certified as provided in section 2244 by a panel of the appropriate court of appeals to contain—

(1) newly discovered evidence that, if proven and viewed in light of the evidence as a whole, would be sufficient to establish by clear and convincing evidence that no reasonable fact finder would have found the movant guilty of the offense; or

(2) a new rule of constitutional law, made retroactive to cases on collateral review by the Supreme Court, that was previously unavailable.

(June 25,1948, ch 646,62 Stat. 967; May 24,1949, ch 139, § 114, 63 Stat. 105; April 24,1996, P. L. 104-132, Title I, § 105,110 Stat. 1220; Jan. 7, 2008, P. L. 110-177, Title V, § 511,121 Stat. 2545.)

Rules governing 28 U.S.C. §2255 proceedings in the United States District Courts

Rule 1.	Scope
Rule 2.	The Motion
Rule 3.	Filing the Motion; Inmate Filing
Rule 4.	Preliminary Review
Rule 5.	The Answer and the Reply
Rule 6.	Discovery
Rule 7.	Expanding the Record
Rule 8.	Evidentiary Hearing
Rule 9.	Second or Successive Motions
Rule 10.	Powers of a Magistrate Judge
Rule 11.	Certificate of Appealability; Time of Appeal
Rule 12.	Applicability of the Federal Rules of Civil Procedure and the Federal Rules of Criminal Procedure

Rule 1.   Scope

These rules govern a motion filed in a United States district court under 28 U.S.C. § 2255 by:

(a) a person in custody under a judgment of that court who seeks a determination that:

(1) the judgment violates the Constitution or laws of the United States;

(2) the court lacked jurisdiction to enter the judgment;

(3) the sentence exceeded the maximum allowed by law; or

(4) the judgment or sentence is otherwise subject to collateral review; and

(b) a person in custody under a judgment of a state court or another federal court, and subject to future custody under a judgment of the district court, who seeks a determination that:

> (1) future custody under a judgment of the district court would violate the Constitution or laws of the United States;
>
> (2) the district court lacked jurisdiction to enter the judgment;
>
> (3) the district court's sentence exceeded the maximum allowed by law; or
>
> (4) the district court's judgment or sentence is otherwise subject to collateral review.

(As amended Dec. 1, 2004.)

Rule 2.   The Motion

(a) **Applying for relief.** The application must be in the form of a motion to vacate, set aside, or correct the sentence.

(b) **Form.** The motion must:

> (1) specify all the grounds for relief available to the moving party;
>
> (2) state the facts supporting each ground;
>
> (3) state the relief requested;
>
> (4) be printed, typewritten, or legibly handwritten; and
>
> (5) be signed under penalty of perjury by the movant or by a person authorized to sign it for the movant.

(c) **Standard form.** The motion must substantially follow either the form appended to these rules or a form prescribed by a local district-court rule. The clerk must make forms available to moving parties without charge.

(d) **Separate motions for separate judgments.** A moving party who seeks relief from more than one judgment must file a separate motion covering each judgment.

(As amended Sept. 28,1976, P.L. 94-426, § 2(3), (4), 90 Stat. 1334; eff. Aug. 1, 1982; Dec. 1,2004.)

Rule 3.   Filing the Motion; Inmate Filing

(a) **Where to file; copies.** An original and two copies of the motion must be filed with the clerk.

(b) **Filing and service.** The clerk must file the motion and enter it on the-criminal docket of the case in which the challenged judgment was entered. The clerk must then deliver or serve a copy of the motion on the United States attorney in that district, together with a notice of its filing.

(c) **Time to file.** The time for filing a motion is governed by 28 U.S.c. § 2255 para. 6.

(d) **Inmate filing.** A paper filed by an inmate confined in an institution is timely if deposited in the institution's internal mailing system on or before the last day for filing. If an institution has a system designed for legal mail, the inmate must use that system to receive the benefit of this rule. Timely filing may be shown by a declaration in compliance with 28 U.S.C. § 1746 or by a notarized statement, either of which must set forth the date of deposit and state that first-class postage has been prepaid.

(As amended Dec. 1,2004.)

Rule 4.   Preliminary Review

(a) **Referral to a judge.** The clerk must promptly forward the motion to the judge who conducted the trial and imposed sentence or, if the judge who imposed sentence was not the trial judge, to the judge who conducted the proceedings being challenged. If the appropriate judge is not available, the clerk must forward the motion to a judge under the court's assignment procedure.

(b) **Initial consideration by the judge.** The judge who receives the motion must promptly examine it. If it plainly appears from the motion, any attached exhibits, and the record of prior proceedings that the moving party is not entitled to relief, the judge must dismiss the motion and direct the clerk to notify the moving party. If the motion is not dismissed, the judge must order the United States attorney to file an answer, motion, or other response within a fixed time, or to take other action the judge may order.

(As amended Dec. 1, 2004.)

Rule 5.   The Answer and the Reply

(a) **When required.** The respondent is not required to answer the motion unless a judge so orders.

(b) **Contents.** The answer must address the allegations in the motion. In addition, it must state whether the moving party has used any other federal remedies, including any prior post-conviction motions under these rules or any previous rules, and whether the moving party received an evidentiary hearing.

(c) **Records of prior proceedings.** If the answer refers to briefs or transcripts of the prior proceedings that are not available in the court's records, the judge must order the government to furnish them within a reasonable time that will not unduly delay the proceedings.

(d) **Reply.** The moving party may submit a reply to the respondent's answer or other pleading within a time fixed by the judge.

(As amended Dec. 1, 2004.)

Rule 6.   Discovery

(a) **Leave of court required.** A judge may, for good cause, authorize a party to conduct discovery under the Federal Rules of Criminal Procedure or Civil Procedure, or in accordance with the practices and principles of law. If necessary for effective discovery, the judge must appoint an attorney for a moving party who qualifies to have counsel appointed under 18 U.S.C. § 3006A.

(b) **Requesting discovery.** A party requesting discovery must provide reasons for the request. The request must also include any proposed interrogatories and requests for admission, and must specify any requested documents.

(c) **Deposition expenses.** If the government is granted leave to take a deposition, the judge may require the government to pay the travel expenses, subsistence expenses, and fees of the moving party's attorney to attend the deposition.
(As amended Dec. 1, 2004.)

Rule 7. Expanding the Record

(a) **In general.** If the motion is not dismissed, the judge may direct the parties to expand the record by submitting additional materials relating to the motion. The judge may require that these materials be authenticated.

(b) **Types of materials.** The materials that may be required include letters predating the filing of the motion, documents, exhibits, and answers under oath to written interrogatories propounded by the judge. Affidavits also may be submitted and considered as part of the record.

(c) **Review by the opposing party.** The judge must give the party against whom the additional materials are offered an opportunity to admit or deny their correctness.
(As amended Dec. 1, 2004.)

Rule 8 Evidentiary Hearing

(a) **Determining Whether to Hold a Hearing.** If the motion is not dismissed, the judge must review the answer, any transcripts and records of prior proceedings, and any materials submitted under Rule 7 to determine whether an evidentiary hearing is warranted.

(b) **Reference to a Magistrate Judge.** A judge may, under 28 U.S.C. §636(b), refer the motion to a magistrate judge to conduct hearings and to file proposed findings of fact and recommendations for disposition. When they are filed, the clerk must promptly serve copies of the proposed findings and recommendations on all parties. Within 14 days after being served, a party may file objections as provided by local court rule. The judge must determine de novo any proposed finding or recommendation to which objection is made. The judge may accept, reject, or modify any proposed finding or recommendation.

(c) **Appointing Counsel; Time of Hearing.** If an evidentiary hearing is warranted, the judge must appoint an attorney to represent a moving party who qualifies to have counsel appointed under 18 U.S.C. §3006A. The judge must conduct the hearing as soon as practicable after giving the attorneys adequate time to investigate and prepare. These rules do not limit the appointment of counsel under §3006A at any stage of the proceeding.

(d) **Producing a Statement.** Federal Rule of Criminal Procedure 26.2(a)-(d) and (f) applies at a hearing under this rule. If a party does not comply with a Rule 26.2(a) order to produce a witness's statement, the court must not consider that witness's testimony.
(As amended Dec. 1, 2009)

Rule 9.   Second or Successive Motions

Before presenting a second or successive motion, the moving party must obtain an order from the appropriate court of appeals authorizing the district court to consider the motion, as required by 28 U.S.C. § 2255, para. 8.

(As amended Sept. 28, 1976, P.L. 94-426. § 2(9), (10). 90 Stat. 1335; Dec. 1, 2004.)

Rule 10.   Powers of a Magistrate Judge

A magistrate judge may perform the duties of a district judge under these rules, as authorized by 28 U.S.C. §636.

(As amended Dec. 1, 2004).

Rule 11.   Certificate of Appealability; Time of Appeal

(a) **Certificate of Appealability.** The district court must issue or deny a certificate of appealability when it enters a final order adverse to the applicant. Before entering a final order, the court may direct the parties to submit arguments on whether a certificate should issue. If the court issues a certificate, the court must state the specific issue or issues that satisfy the showing required by 28 U.S.C. §2253(c)(2). If the court denies a certificate, a party may not appeal the denial but may seek a certificate from the court of appeals under Federal Rule of Appellate Procedure 22. A motion to reconsider a denial does not extend the time to appeal.

(b) **Time to Appeal.** Federal Rule of Appellate Procedure 4(a) governs the time to appeal an order entered under these rules. A timely notice of appeal **must be filed even** if the district court issues a certificate of appealability. These rules do not extend the time to appeal the original judgment of conviction. **(Emphasis added).**

(As amended Dec.1, 2009).

Rule 12.   Applicability of the Federal Rules of Civil Procedure and the Federal Rules of Criminal Procedure

The Federal Rules of Civil Procedure and the Federal Rules of Criminal Procedure, to the extent that they are not inconsistent with any statutory provisions or these rules; may be applied to a proceeding under these rules.

(As amended Dec. 1, 2009).

Form Letter No. 1

[Your Name & Prison Number]
[Institution]
[Your Address]
[Town, State & Zip Code]

[Date]

Office of the Clerk
Attn: [Clerk's Name]_____
Address_____
Town, State & Zip Code____

Re: 28 U.S.C. §2255 Form Motion

Dear Clerk:

At this time, I am requesting a **28 U.S.C. §2255 <u>Form</u> Motion to vacate, set aside or correct sentence** that is used in this district to be forwarded to me by your office. I have enclosed a self-addressed stamped envelope for the return of the **28 U.S.C. §2255 Motion**.

Thank you.

Sincerely,

_____
[Your Name]

CC:
    p/file.

Certified Mail No. _____

Motion to Vacate, Set Aside, or Correct a Sentence
By a Person in Federal Custody

(Motion Under 28 U.S.C. § 2255)

Instructions

1. To use this form, you must be a person who is serving a sentence under a judgment against you in a federal court. You are asking for relief from the conviction or the sentence. This form is your motion for relief.

2. You must file the form in the United States district court that entered the judgment that you are challenging. If you want to challenge a federal judgment that imposed a sentence to be served in the future, you should file the motion in the federal court that entered that judgment.

3. Make sure the form is typed or neatly written.

4. You must tell the truth and sign the form. If you make a false statement of a material fact, you may be prosecuted for perjury.

5. Answer all the questions. You do not need to cite law. You may submit additional pages if necessary. If you do not fill out the form properly, you will be asked to submit additional or correct information. If you want to submit a brief or arguments, you must submit them in a separate memorandum.

6. If you cannot pay for the costs of this motion (such as costs for an attorney or transcripts), you may ask to proceed *in forma pauperis* (as a poor person). To do that, you must fill out the last page of this form. Also, you must submit a certificate signed by an officer at the institution where you are confined showing the amount of money that the institution is holding for you.

7. In this motion, you may challenge the judgment entered by only one court. If you want to challenge a judgment entered by a different judge or division (either in the same district or in a different district), you must file a separate motion.

8. When you have completed the form, send the original and two copies to the Clerk of the United States District Court at this address:

    Clerk, United States District Court for _____
    Address
    City, State Zip Code

9. <u>CAUTION:</u> **You must include in this motion <u>all</u> the grounds for relief from the conviction or sentence that you challenge. And you must state the facts that support each ground. If you fail to set forth all the grounds in this motion, you may be barred from presenting additional grounds at a later date.**

10. <u>CAPITAL CASES:</u> **If you are under a sentence of death, you are entitled to the assistance of counsel and should request the appointment of counsel.**

MOTION UNDER 28 U.S.C. § 2255 TO VACATE, SET ASIDE, OR CORRECT SENTENCE BY A PERSON IN FEDERAL CUSTODY

United States District Court	District
Name (under which you were convicted):	Docket or Case No.:
Place of Confinement:	Prisoner No.:
UNITED STATES OF AMERICA	Movant (include name under which you were convicted)
v.	

MOTION

1. (a) Name and location of court that entered the judgment of conviction you are challenging:

(b) Criminal docket or case number (if you know):

2. (a) Date of the judgment of conviction (if you know):

(b) Date of sentencing:

3. Length of sentence:

4. Nature of crime (all counts):

5. (a) What was your plea? (Check one)

   (1) Not guilty ❏   (2) Guilty ❏   (3) Nolo contendere (no contest) ❏

(b) If you entered a guilty plea to one count or indictment, and a not guilty plea to another count or indictment, what did you plead guilty to and what did you plead not guilty to?

6. If you went to trial, what kind of trial did you have? (Check one)   Jury ❏   Judge only ❏

7. Did you testify at a pretrial hearing, trial, or post-trial hearing?   Yes ❏   No ❏

8. Did you appeal from the judgment of conviction?   Yes ❏   No ❏

9. If you did appeal, answer the following:

   (a) Name of court:

   (b) Docket or case number (if you know):

   (c) Result:

   (d) Date of result (if you know):

   (e) Citation to the case (if you know):

   (f) Grounds raised:

   (g) Did you file a petition for certiorari in the United States Supreme Court?   Yes ❏   No ❏

     If "Yes," answer the following:

     (1) Docket or case number (if you know):

     (2) Result:

     (3) Date of result (if you know):

     (4) Citation to the case (if you know):

     (5) Grounds raised:

10. Other than the direct appeals listed above, have you previously filed any other motions, petitions, or applications concerning this judgment of conviction in any court?

   Yes ❏   No ❏

11. If your answer to Question 10 was "Yes," give the following information:

   (a) (1) Name of court:

      (2) Docket or case number (if you know):

      (3) Date of filing (if you know):

(4) Nature of the proceeding:

(5) Grounds raised:

(6) Did you receive a hearing where evidence was given on your motion, petition, or application?   Yes ❏ No ❏

(7) Result:

(8) Date of result (if you know):

(b) If you filed any second motion, petition, or application, give the same information:

(1) Name of court:

(2) Docket or case number (if you know):

(3) Date of filing (if you know):

(4) Nature of the proceeding:

(5) Grounds raised:

(6) Did you receive a hearing where evidence was given on your motion, petition, or application?   Yes ❏   No ❏

(7) Result:

(8) Date of result (if you know):

(c) Did you appeal to a federal appellate court having jurisdiction over the action taken on your motion, petition, or application?

(1) First petition: Yes ❏   No ❏

(2) Second petition: Yes ❏   No ❏

(d) If you did not appeal from the action on any motion, petition, or application, explain briefly why you did not:

12. For this motion, state every ground on which you claim that you are being held in violation of the Constitution, laws, or treaties of the United States. Attach additional pages if you have more than four grounds. State the <u>facts</u> supporting each ground.

GROUND ONE:

(a) Supporting facts (Do not argue or cite law. Just state the specific facts that support your claim.):

(b) **Direct Appeal of Ground One:**

    (1) If you appealed from the judgment of conviction, did you raise this issue?

        Yes ❏   No ❏

    (2) If you did not raise this issue in your direct appeal, explain why:

(c) **Post-Conviction Proceedings:**

    (1) Did you raise this issue in any post-conviction motion, petition, or application?

        Yes ❏ No ❏

    (2) If your answer to Question (c)(1) is "Yes," state:

Type of motion or petition:

Name and location of the court where the motion or petition was filed:

Docket or case number (if you know):

Date of the court's decision:

Result (attach a copy of the court's opinion or order, if available):

(3) Did you receive a hearing on your motion, petition, or application?

    Yes ❑   No ❑

(4) Did you appeal from the denial of your motion, petition, or application?

    Yes ❑   No ❑

(5) If your answer to Question (c)(4) is "Yes," did you raise this issue in the appeal?

    Yes ❑   No ❑

(6) If your answer to Question (c)(4) is "Yes," state:

Name and location of the court where the appeal was filed:

Docket or case number (if you know):

Date of the court's decision:

Result (attach a copy of the court's opinion or order, if available):

(7) If your answer to Question (c)(4) or Question (c)(5) is "No," explain why you did not appeal or raise this issue:

GROUND TWO:

(a) Supporting facts (Do not argue or cite law. Just state the specific facts that support your claim.):

(b) **Direct Appeal of Ground Two:**

    (1) If you appealed from the judgment of conviction, did you raise this issue?

    Yes ❏   No ❏

    (2) If you did not raise this issue in your direct appeal, explain why:

(c) **Post-Conviction Proceedings:**

    (1) Did you raise this issue in any post-conviction motion, petition, or application?

    Yes ❏   No ❏

    (2) If your answer to Question (c)(1) is "Yes," state:

    Type of motion or petition:

    Name and location of the court where the motion or petition was filed:

    Docket or case number (if you know):

    Date of the court's decision:

    Result (attach a copy of the court's opinion or order, if available):

    (3) Did you receive a hearing on your motion, petition, or application?

    Yes ❏   No ❏

    (4) Did you appeal from the denial of your motion, petition, or application?

    Yes ❏   No ❏

    (5) If your answer to Question (c)(4) is "Yes," did you raise this issue in the appeal?

    Yes ❏   No ❏

    (6) If your answer to Question (c)(4) is "Yes," state:

    Name and location of the court where the appeal was filed:

    Docket or case number (if you know):

    Date of the court's decision:

    Result (attach a copy of the court's opinion or order, if available):

(7) If your answer to Question (c)(4) or Question (c)(5) is "No," explain why you did not appeal or raise this issue:

GROUND THREE:

(a) Supporting facts (Do not argue or cite law. Just state the specific facts that support your claim.):

(b) **Direct Appeal of Ground Three:**

    (1) If you appealed from the judgment of conviction, did you raise this issue?

        Yes ❑   No ❑

    (2) If you did not raise this issue in your direct appeal, explain why:

(c) **Post-Conviction Proceedings:**

    (1) Did you raise this issue in any post-conviction motion, petition, or application?

        Yes ❑   No ❑

    (2) If your answer to Question (c)(1) is "Yes," state:

Type of motion or petition:

Name and location of the court where the motion or petition was filed:

Docket or case number (if you know):

Date of the court's decision:

Result (attach a copy of the court's opinion or order, if available):

(3) Did you receive a hearing on your motion, petition, or application?

Yes ❏   No ❏

(4) Did you appeal from the denial of your motion, petition, or application?

Yes ❏   No ❏

(5) If your answer to Question (c)(4) is "Yes," did you raise this issue in the appeal?

Yes ❏   No ❏

(6) If your answer to Question (c)(4) is "Yes," state:

Name and location of the court where the appeal was filed:

Docket or case number (if you know):

Date of the court's decision:

Result (attach a copy of the court's opinion or order, if available):

(7) If your answer to Question (c)(4) or Question (c)(5) is "No," explain why you did not appeal or raise this issue:

GROUND FOUR:

(a) Supporting facts (Do not argue or cite law. Just state the specific facts that support your claim.):

(b) **Direct Appeal of Ground Four:**

(1) If you appealed from the judgment of conviction, did you raise this issue?

Yes ❑ No ❑

(2) If you did not raise this issue in your direct appeal, explain why:

(c) **Post-Conviction Proceedings:**

(1) Did you raise this issue in any post-conviction motion, petition, or application?

Yes ❑ No ❑

(2) If your answer to Question (c)(1) is "Yes," state:

Type of motion or petition:

Name and location of the court where the motion or petition was filed:

Docket or case number (if you know):

Date of the court's decision:

Result (attach a copy of the court's opinion or order, if available):

(3) Did you receive a hearing on your motion, petition, or application?

Yes ❑ No ❑

(4) Did you appeal from the denial of your motion, petition, or application?

Yes ❑ No ❑

(5) If your answer to Question (c)(4) is "Yes," did you raise this issue in the appeal?

Yes ❑ No ❑

(6) If your answer to Question (c)(4) is "Yes," state:

Name and location of the court where the appeal was filed:

Docket or case number (if you know):

Date of the court's decision:

Result (attach a copy of the court's opinion or order, if available):

(7) If your answer to Question (c)(4) or Question (c)(5) is "No," explain why you did not appeal or raise this issue:

13. Is there any ground in this motion that you have <u>not</u> previously presented in some federal court? If so, which ground or grounds have not been presented, and state your reasons for not presenting them:

14. Do you have any motion, petition, or appeal <u>now pending</u> (filed and not decided yet) in any court for the judgment you are challenging?   Yes ❑   No ❑
If "Yes," state the name and location of the court, the docket or case number, the type of proceeding, and the issues raised.

15. Give the name and address, if known, of each attorney who represented you in the following stages of the judgment you are challenging:
(a) At preliminary hearing:

(b) At arraignment and plea:

(c) At trial:

(d) At sentencing:

(e) On appeal:

(f) In any post-conviction proceeding:

(g) On appeal from any ruling against you in a post-conviction proceeding:

16. Were you sentenced on more than one count of an indictment, or on more than one indictment, in the same court and at the same time?   Yes ❑ No ❑

17. Do you have any future sentence to serve after you complete the sentence for the judgment that you are challenging?   Yes ❑ No ❑

    (a) If so, give name and location of court that imposed the other sentence you will serve in the future:

    (b) Give the date the other sentence was imposed:

    (c) Give the length of the other sentence:

    (d) Have you filed, or do you plan to file, any motion, petition, or application that challenges the judgment or sentence to be served in the future?   Yes ❑   No ❑

18. TIMELINESS OF MOTION: If your judgment of conviction became final over one year ago, you must explain why the one-year statute of limitations as contained in 28 U.S.C. § 2255 does not bar your motion.*

---

* The Antiterrorism and Effective Death Penalty Act of 1996 ("AEDPA") as contained in 28 U.S.C. § 2255, paragraph 6, provides in part that:

A one-year period of limitation shall apply to a motion under this section. The limitation period shall run from the latest of —

(1) the date on which the judgment of conviction became final;

(2) the date on which the impediment to making a motion created by governmental action in violation of the Constitution or laws of the United States is removed, if the movant was prevented from making such a motion by such governmental action;

(3) the date on which the right asserted was initially recognized by the Supreme Court, if that right has been newly recognized by the Supreme Court and made retroactively applicable to cases on collateral review; or

(4) the date on which the facts supporting the claim or claims presented could have been discovered through the exercise of due diligence.

Therefore, movant asks that the Court grant the following relief:

or any other relief to which movant may be entitled.

_____

Signature of Attorney (if any)

I declare (or certify, verify, or state) under penalty of perjury that the foregoing is true and correct and that this Motion under 28 U.S.C. § 2255 was placed in the prison mailing system on _____ (month, date, year).

Executed (signed) on _____ (date).

_____

Signature of Movant

If the person signing is not movant, state relationship to movant and explain why movant is not signing this motion.

235

IN THE UNITED STATES DISTRICT COURT
FOR THE _____ DISTRICT OF _____
_____ DIVISION

_____,

Petitioner,

VS.   Civil No. _____

UNITED STATES OF AMERICA

Respondent.

MEMORANDUM BRIEF IN SUPPORT OF MOTION TO VACATE, SET ASIDE, OR CORRECT SENTENCE, PURSUANT TO 28 U.S.C. §2255

TO THE HONORABLE JUDGE _____:

COMES NOW_____, the petitioner, pro se, and respectfully files this memorandum brief in support of his motion to vacate, set aside, or correct sentence, pursuant to **28 U.S.C. §2255**, imposed by this Court on _____ ___, 20___ proceedings. Petitioner is presently incarcerated at the Federal Correctional Institution, _____, _____. In support thereof, Petitioner states as follows:

STATEMENT OF THE FACTS

1. On _____ ___, 20___, during sentencing this Court informed Petitioner that he had a right to appeal and has ten (10) days to file notice of appeal. Petitioner informed this Court on the record at sentencing that he understood his appellate rights and that he wanted to appeal his conviction and sentence. This Court informed Petitioner that defense counsel _____ would file the necessary paperwork for the appeal.

2. Petitioner advised defense counsel after sentencing that he wanted to talk to him concerning the appeal. Defense counsel _____ advised Petitioner that he would come over to the jail and talk with him concerning the appeal.

3. Petitioner called defense counsel _____ office on numerous occasions and left several messages with his secretary concerning his appeal. Defense counsel _____ avoided Petitioner's phone calls and never answered his messages. **See Exhibit "A"** Petitioner _____ affidavit.

4. Petitioner's family called counsel _____ office on numerous occasions to find out about the status of his appeal and were never able to talk with counsel personally, but they left messages with counsel's secretary. As of this date, defense counsel has not wrote Petitioner nor consulted with him concerning his appeal. **See Exhibit "A"** Petitioner's affidavit. Petitioner wrote a letter to the Clerk of this Court and requested a copy of the last page of the Criminal Docket Sheet so he could verify

whether defense counsel filed his requested notice of appeal. **See Exhibit "B"** A copy of Petitioner's Letter to the Clerk's Office.

5. On _____ ___, 20___, the Clerk of this Court mailed Petitioner a copy of the-Criminal Docket Entry Sheet which shows that counsel never filed Petitioner's requested notice of appeal. **See Exhibit "C"**.

A more precise set of facts are set forth throughout this Memorandum Brief.

§§§

ISSUE I

THE SENTENCE IS UNCONSTITUTIONAL BECAUSE PETITIONER DID NOT RECEIVE EFFECTIVE ASSISTANCE OF COUNSEL AS GUARANTEED BY THE SIXTH AMENDMENT OF THE UNITED STATES CONSTITUTION

Claims of ineffective assistance of counsel are governed by the Supreme Court's decision in **Strickland v. Washington**, **466 U.S. 668, 687-88, 694, 104 S.Ct. 2052, 2064-65, 2068, 80 L.Ed.2d 674 (1984)**. To succeed on any claim of ineffective assistance of counsel, a defendant must show that: (1) the attorney's representation fell below an objective standard of reasonableness, and (2) there is a reasonable probability that except for the attorney's unprofessional errors, the result of the proceedings would have been different. **United States v. King**, **917 F.2d 181, 183 (5th Cir. 1990) (citing Strickland, supra)**.

In this case, defense counsel _____ committed several unprofessional errors and omissions that amounted to performance below an objective standard of reasonableness for counsel in a criminal case. Petitioner asserts that counsel committed the following errors and omissions:

Counsel was constitutionally ineffective for failing to perfect Petitioner's requested notice of appeal and failing to consult with Petitioner after sentencing concerning the appeal

Petitioner asserts that defense counsel _____ provided constitutionally ineffective assistance of counsel for: (1) failing to file Petitioner's requested notice of appeal; and (2) failing to consult with Petitioner after sentencing concerning the appeal. **See Gomez-Diaz v. United States**, **433 F.3d 788, 792 (11th Cir. 2005)**. Petitioner attaches hereto his affidavit detailing the facts related to this claim. **See Exhibit "A"** Petitioner's affidavit. Petitioner contends that such unprofessional errors and omissions by counsel constitutes ineffective assistance of counsel. **See Roe v. Flores-Ortega**, **528 U.S. 470, 120 S.Ct. 1029, 145 L.Ed.2d 985 (2000)**.

The Supreme Court in **Flores-Ortega** reaffirmed the well-settled rule that an attorney who fails to file an appeal on behalf of a client who specifically requests it acts in a professional unreasonable manner per se. **Id. at 477, 120 S.Ct. at 1035 (citing Rodriguez v. United States**, **395 U.S. 327, 89 S.Ct. 1715, 23 L.Ed.2d 340 (1969))**. The **Flores-Ortego** Court went on to hold that, even if a client has not made a specific request of his attorney to file an appeal, a court must inquire whether the attorney consulted with the client regarding the advantages and disadvantages of appealing and made a reasonable effort to determine the client's wishes. **id. at 478, 120 S.Ct. at 1035**. If so, the attorney has only acted unreasonably if he has ignored the client's wishes to appeal the case. **Id**. If not, the court must further inquire whether the attorney had the affirmative duty to consult. **Id**. An attorney has this duty when either (1) any rational defendant would want to appeal, or (2) his particular client reasonably demonstrated an interest in appealing. **Id. at 480, 120 S.Ct. at 1036**. Petitioner advised this Court at sentencing that he wanted to appeal. This Court informed Petitioner that counsel _____ would file the necessary paper work for the appeal. Counsel _____ ignored Petitioner's request to appeal. Petitioner has meet the criteria of **Flores-Ortega, supra**.

As to the second prong of the **Strickland**, test, the **Flores-Ortega** court held that the failure to file an appeal that the defendant wanted filed denies the defendant his constitutional right to counsel at a critical stage. **Id. at 483, 120 S.Ct. at 1038**. In such cases, prejudice is presumed because rather than being denied the opportunity for a fair proceedings, the defendant is denied the opportunity for a proceeding at all. **Id. (citing Smith v. Robbins, 528 U.S. 259, 286, 120 S.Ct. 746, 765, 145 L.Ed.2d 756 (2000); Penson v. Ohio, 488 U.S. 75, 88-89, 109 S.Ct. 346, 354, 102 L.Ed.2d 300 (1988); United States v. Cronic, 466 U.S. 648, 659, 104 S.Ct. 2039, 2047, 80 L.Ed.2d 657 (1984)); Gomez-Diaz v. United States, 433 F.3d 788, 792 (11th Cir. 2005)**. Accordingly, to satisfy the prejudice prong of the Strickland test, a defendant who shows that his attorney has ignored his wishes and failed to appeal his case need only demonstrate that, but for the attorney deficient performance, he would have appealed. **Flores-Ortega, 528 U.S. at 484, 120 S.Ct. at 1038**. Petitioner is in entitled to an out-of-time appeal regardless of whether he can identify any arguably meritorious ground for his appeal. **See Gomez-Diaz, 433 F.3d at 793**.

Flores-Ortega requires an attorney to consult with his client and to make a reasonable effort to determine his clients wishes in reference to appeal his case. The evidence in this case establishes that Petitioner advised this Court at sentencing that he wanted to appeal. This Court informed Petitioner that defense counsel _____ would file the necessary paperwork to process the appeal and counsel _____ ignored petitioner's request to appeal. **See Sentencing Transcript**. Additionally, this Court's attention is referred to Petitioner's affidavit detailing the facts related to this claim. This Court must grant an out-of-time appeal or conduct an evidentiary hearing to resolve the factual disputes. **See Gomes-Diaz, 433 F.3d at 794**.

§§§

238

CONCLUSION

WHEREFORE based on the above, _____, the petitioner, moves this Honorable Court to **VACATE** the sentence and judgment. Appoint new counsel for appellate purposes and reimpose sentence affording petitioner an opportunity to file a timely notice of appeal through appointed counsel.

Respectfully submitted on this _____ day of _____ 20___.

_____
PRO SE REPRESENTATION

CERTIFICATE OF SERVICE

I HEREBY CERTIFY that a true and correct copy of this foregoing instrument has been mailed postage prepaid on this _____ day of _____ 20___, to the Assistant United States Attorney, _____, _____ _____, _____, _____.

Executed under penalty of perjury pursuant to 28 U.S.C. §1746, on this ____ day of _____ 20___.

_____

IN THE UNITED STATES DISTRICT COURT
FOR THE _____ DISTRICT OF _____
_____ DIVISION

_____

_____,

VS.   **Civil No.** _____

UNITED STATES OF AMERICA

_____

AFFIDAVIT OF _____

_____

I, _____, depose and state that the following facts are true and correct under penalty of perjury to wit:

1. I, _____, state that on _____ __, 20___, during sentencing that this Court informed me that I had a right to appeal and had ten (10) days to file notice of appeal. I, _____, state that I informed this Court on the record at sentencing that I understood my appellate rights and that I wanted to appeal my conviction and sentence. This Court informed me that defense counsel _____ would file the necessary paperwork for the appeal.

2. I, _____, state that I advised defense counsel _____ after sentencing that I wanted to talk to him concerning the appeal. Defense counsel _____ advised me that he would come over to the jail and talk with me concerning the appeal.

3. I, _____, stated that I called defense counsel _____ office on numerous occasions and left several messages with his secretary concerning my appeal. Defense counsel _____ avoided my phone calls and never answered my messages.

4. I, _____, state that my mother _____ called counsel _____ office on numerous occasions to find out about the status of my appeal and were never able to talk with counsel personally, but she left messages with counsel's secretary. As of this date, defense counsel has not wrote me, nor consulted with me concerning my appeal.

5. I, _____, state that I wrote a letter to the Clerk of this Court and requested a copy of the last page of the Criminal Docket Sheet so that I could verify that defense counsel filed my requested notice of appeal.

6. I, _____, state that on _____ __, 20___, the Clerk of this Court mailed me a copy of the Criminal Docket Entry Sheet which shows that counsel never filed my requested notice of appeal.

I, _____, declare under penalty of perjury pursuant to 28 U.S.C. §1746, that the above stated facts are true and correct.

Executed on this _____ __, 20___.

_____

IN THE UNITED STATES DISTRICT COURT
FOR THE _____ DISTRICT OF _____
_____ DIVISION

UNITED STATES OF AMERICA,

      Respondent,

VS.

      Civil No. _____

      Criminal No. _____

_____

      Movant.

MEMORANDUM BRIEF IN SUPPORT OF MOTION TO VACATE, SET ASIDE, OR CORRECT SENTENCE, PURSUANT TO 28 U.S.C. §2255

TO THE HONORABLE JUDGE _____:

    COMES NOW _____, the Movant, pro se, and respectfully files this Memorandum brief in support of his to **28 U.S.C. §2255** motion to vacate, set aside or correct the sentence imposed by this Court on _____ __, 20___.

    In support thereof, Movant states as follows:

I.
STATEMENT OF THE CASE

    On _____ __, 20___, a federal grand jury returned a two count indictment charging Movant with possession of cocaine base (Count One), and distribution of cocaine base (Count Two), in violation of 21 U.S.C. §841 (a)(1).

    On _____ __, 20___, Movant appeared before this Honorable Court with counsel _____ and entered a guilty plea to count two with an agreement that the United States would move to dismiss count one at sentencing. This Court accepted Movant's guilty plea and ordered a Presentence Investigation to be prepared by the Probation Department.

    On _____ __, 20___, this Court sentenced Movant to a term of two hundred and forty (240) months imprisonment and a five (5) year term of supervised release, and a $100 special assessment fee.

    On _____ __, 20___, a timely notice of appeal was filed. Appellant counsel _____ then filed an **Anders v. California, 386 U.S. 738, 18 L.Ed.2d 493, 87 S.Ct. 1396 (1967),** brief requesting to withdraw as counsel.

    On _____ __, 20___, the United States Court of Appeals for the _____ Circuit granted counsel's motion and dismissed the appeal. This §2255 motion follows.

II.
STATEMENT OF THE FACTS

1. The Presentence Report (PSR) at paragraph 21 held Movant accountable for four (4) grams of cocaine base that Movant sold to an undercover officer. The PSR determined that four (4) grams of cocaine base provides a Base Offense Level 24. **See PSR at ¶¶29 and 31**. A three (3) level reduction for acceptance of responsibility was applied which resulted in an adjusted Base Offense Level **21**. See PSR at ¶22. A Level 21 with a Criminal History Category III provides a sentencing range of 46 to 57 months imprisonment. **See U.S.S.G. §§2D1.1(c)(8)**, and **3E1.1** at ¶¶21, 22, 29, 31 of the PSR. See also Sentencing Table.

2. The PSR at paragraphs 29 and 31 used two simple possession of cocaine prior convictions to classify Movant as a Career Offender.

3. Defense counsel _____ failed to object to the PSR use of the two simple possession of cocaine prior convictions as predicate offenses to place Movant into the Career Offender enhancement provision.

4. The PSR at paragraphs 35 and 37 recommended that Movant not receive a three level reduction for acceptance of responsibility because of Movant's classification of a Career Offender.

5. Defense counsel _____ failed to object to the PSR recommendation to deny Movant a downward adjustment for acceptance of responsibility because of Movant's classification of a Career Offender.

6. The PSR found that Movant's statutory maximum sentence was twenty years and his base offense level was Level 32 with a Criminal History Category VI because of the Career Offender classification. **See U.S.S.G. §4B1.1(b)**. The PSR recommended a sentencing 210 to 262 months imprisonment. This Court imposed a 240 month term of imprisonment.

A more precise set of facts are set forth throughout this memorandum brief.

§§§

ISSUE

THE CONVICTION AND SENTENCE ARE UNCONSTITUTIONAL BECAUSE MOVANT DID NOT RECEIVE EFFECTIVE ASSISTANCE OF COUNSEL AS GUARANTEED BY THE SIXTH AMENDMENT OF THE UNITED STATES CONSTITUTION

Claims of ineffective assistance of counsel are governed by the two prong test set forth in **Strickland v. Washington, 466 U.S. 668, 687-88, 694, 104 S.Ct. 2052, 2064-65, 2068, 80 L.Ed.2d 674 (1984)**. To succeed on any claim of ineffective assistance of counsel, a defendant must show that: (1) the attorney's representation fell below an objective standard of reasonableness, and (2) there is a reasonable probability that except for the attorney's unprofessional errors, the result of the proceedings would have been different. **United States v. King, 917 F.2d 181, 183 (5th Cir. 1990) (citing Strickland, supra)**. The Supreme Court has found that "any amount of actual jail time has Sixth Amendment significance" and prejudicial under **Strickland**. **See Glover v. United**

States, 531 U.S. 198, 203, 121 S.Ct. 696, 148 L.Ed.2d 602 (2001); **United States v. Chase,** 499 F.3d 1061, 1068 (9th Cir. 2007); **Alaniz v. United States,** 351 F.3d 365, 368 (8th Cir. 2003).

In this case, defense counsel committed several unprofessional errors and omissions that amounted to performance below an objective standard of reasonableness for counsel in a criminal case. Movant asserts that counsel committed the following errors and omissions as grounds for relief:

A. Counsel was ineffective for failing to challenge the use of the two simple possession of cocaine prior convictions as non-qualifying predicate offenses for Career Offender enhancement provision under USSG §4B1.2(b)

Movant argues that defense counsel was ineffective for failing to object and challenge the use of two non-qualifying predicate offenses for simple possession of cocaine convictions as crimes of violence under **U.S.S.G. §4B1.2(b)**. See **United States v. Kissick, 69 F.3d 1048 (10th Cir. 1995)**. Under USSG §4B1.1, a defendant is classified as a career offender if: (1) he is at least 18 years old at the time of the instant offense; (2) the instant offense is a felony that is either a "crime of violence" or a "controlled substance offense"; or a "controlled substance offense"; and (3) he has at least two prior felony convictions for either a "crime of violence" or a "controlled substance offense."

USSG §4B1.2 defines the terms "crime of violence" and "controlled substance offense." At the time of Mr. _____'s sentencing, USSG §4B1.2(b) defined: The term "controlled substance offense" means an offense federal or state law, punishable by imprisonment for a term exceeding one year, that prohibits the manufacture, import, distribution, or dispensing of a controlled substance (or a counterfeit substance). **See USSG §4B1.2(b) (2002).**

Mr. _____ maintains that the mere possession of cocaine does not constitute a "controlled substance offense" under the definitions of USSG §4B1.2(b). **See Kissick, 69 F.3d at 1053-1054; United States v. Neal, 27 F.3d 90, 94 (4th Cir. 1994); United States v. McNeil, 415 F.3d 273, 278 (2nd Cir. 2005); United States v. Hernandez, 218 F.3d 272, 274 (3rd Cir. 2000).**

Had counsel objected to the PSR use of the two simple possession of cocaine prior convictions as non-qualifying predicate offenses, Mr. _____'s sentence would not have been increased under the Career Offender provision. **See Kissick, Neal, McNeil,** and **Hernandez**, all supra. Mr. _____'s sentencing range would have been 46 to 57 months as opposed to the 240 months he received as a result of counsel's errors. Thus, prejudice has been shown under **Strickland. See Glover v. United States,** 531 U.S. 198, 203, 121 S.Ct. 696, 148 L.Ed.2d 602 (2001); **United States v. Chase,** 499 F.3d 1061, 1068 (9th Cir. 2007); **Alaniz v. United States,** 351 F.3d 365, 368 (8th Cir. 2003) (concluding that an error increasing a defendant's sentence by as little as six months can be prejudicial within the meaning of **Strickland**). In the present case, Mr. _____ sentence was increased from 46 months to 240 months.

§§§

243

B. **Counsel was ineffective for failing to object to the PSR improperly declining to award Movant a three level decrease for acceptance of responsibility because he was classified as a career offender.**

Movant argues that defense counsel's performance fell below an objective standard of reasonableness where counsel failed to object to the PSR improperly declining to award Movant a three (3) level downward adjustment for acceptance of responsibility because he was classified as a Career Offender. **See United States v. Ford, 918 F.2d 1343, 1350 (1990). See also USSG §4B1.1(b) which provides: "*If an adjustment from §3E1.1 (Acceptance of Responsibility) applies, decrease the offense level by the number of levels corresponding to that adjustment." Id,**

Had counsel objected to the PSR not recommending that Movant's Base Offense Level **32** be reduced to a **Level 29** for acceptance of responsibility Movant's base offense level would have been reduced to Level **29**. A Level 29 with a Criminal History Category VI provides a sentencing range of **151 to 188** months. A **151** months sentence is significantly less harsh than the **240** month sentence that Movant received. Thus, prejudice under **Strickland** has been shown. **See Ford, 918 F.2d at 1350; Chase, 499 F.3d at 1068; Alaniz, 351 F.3d at 368.**

§§§

CONCLUSION

WHEREFORE based on the above, _____, urges this Honorable Court to reduce his sentence to **46** months. Alternatively, appoint counsel and conduct an evidentiary hearing.

Respectfully submitted on this _____ day of _____, 20___.

_____
PRO SE REPRESENTATION

IN THE UNITED STATES DISTRICT COURT
FOR THE _____ DISTRICT OF _____
_____ DIVISION

UNITED STATES OF AMERICA,

Respondent,

VS.   Civil No. _____

Movant.

AMENDMENT TO 28 U.S.C. §2255 MOTION TO VACATE, SET ASIDE OR CORRECT SENTENCE

COMES NOW _____, the Movant, pro se, and respectfully files this Amendment to his 28 U.S.C. §2255 Motion to vacate, set aside or correct sentence, pursuant to Federal Rules of Civil Procedure, Rule 15(a). This amended §2255 motion is timely filed under §2255(f)(1). Movant will show this Court as follows:

1.   Movant filed a detailed §2255 motion concerning defense counsel _____ ineffectiveness claims related to sentencing.

2.   On _____ __, 20___, this Court issued a show cause order directing the United States to respond to Movant's §2255 motion, and to address whether Movant's claims were barred by the plea agreement waiver of the right to appeal and collateral attack his conviction or sentence. The Court's order afforded Movant thirty (30) days to file his reply to the United States' response to the waiver.

3.   Movant amends his §2255 motion because this Court invoked the "plea agreement waiver of the right to appeal and collateral attack pursuant to 28 U.S.C. §2255," and moves to withdraw his guilty plea. Movant's guilty plea was induced based on faulty and erroneously legal advice by counsel _____ and the waiver of the right to appeal and collateral attack his conviction or sentence pursuant to 28 U.S.C. §2255 was not voluntary or intelligently entered.

4.   Counsel _____ induced Movant's guilty plea based on the fact that whatever sentence received on Count 2 for conspiring to possess a firearm during the commission of a drug trafficking offense pursuant to 18 U.S.C. §924(o), would be run concurrently with the sentence on count one, the drug conspiracy offense. At no time, during the guilty plea colloquy did this Court or the United States advise Movant that count two carried a mandatory consecutive sentence. Additionally, the plea agreement did not mention that count two, the §924(o) charge, carried a mandatory consecutive sentence.

5.   The Plea Agreement did not call for an upward departure based on the Career Offender provision of the Guidelines. This Court enhancement Movant's sentence based on its finding that Movant was a career offender pursuant to **USSG §4B1.1**, by using a prior conviction for simple possession of cocaine.

6. Paragraph ¶7 of the plea agreement states in pertinent part: "The defendant may appeal only (a) a sentence imposed above the statutory maximum; or (b) an upward departure from the Sentencing Guidelines which had not been requested by the United States, as set forth in 18 U.S.C. §3742(b). Additionally, the defendant is aware that 28 U.S.C. §2255, affords the right to contest or 'collateral attack' a conviction or sentence after the conviction or sentence has become final. The defendant waives the right to contest his/her conviction or sentence by means of any post-conviction proceeding." Id. Movant understood the plea agreement to afford him an opportunity to challenge any upward departure from the Guidelines.

7.   _____ did not know that he was waiving his right to effective assistance of counsel at sentencing by entering into the plea agreement. The plea agreement waiver of the right to appeal or collateral attack his conviction or sentence was not knowingly or voluntary entered and must be set aside.

8.   After receiving a copy of the Presentence Report prior to sentencing, Movant directed defense counsel _____ to file a motion to withdraw his guilty plea because the plea was induced based on faulty and erroneous legal advice. Defense counsel lied to Movant by advising him that it was to late to file a motion to withdraw his guilty plea. Counsel knew that if Movant filed a motion to withdraw his guilty plea that he would be forced to defend himself against a valid claim of ineffective assistance of counsel and possible bar complaint because of his faulty and erroneous legal advice and sentence inducements to get Movant to plead guilty. In order to prevent Movant from filing a motion to withdraw his guilty plea exposing his own ineffectiveness of counsel he lied to Movant.

9.   The United States has not filed there reply/answer to Movant's §2255 motion and will not be prejudiced by this amendment.

A Memorandum Brief is attached hereto and made part of this §2255 Amendment by reference herein.

WHEREFORE based on the above, _____, respectfully moves to set aside his guilty plea and afford him an opportunity to plead a new. Alternatively, appoint counsel and conduct an evidentiary hearing to resolve the factual disputes.

Respectfully submitted on this _____ day of _____, 20___.

                                        _____
                                        PRO SE REPRESENTATION

IN THE UNITED STATES DISTRICT COURT
FOR THE _____ DISTRICT OF _____
_____ DIVISION

UNITED STATES OF AMERICA,

        Respondent,

VS.   **Civil No. _____**

_____

        Movant.

MEMORANDUM BRIEF IN SUPPORT OF AMENDMENT TO 28 U.S.C. §2255 MOTION TO VACATE, SET ASIDE OR CORRECT SENTENCE

    COMES NOW _____, the Movant, pro se, and respectfully files this Memorandum brief in support of Amendment to his 28 U.S.C. §2255 Motion to vacate, set aside or correct sentence, pursuant to Federal Rules of Civil Procedure, Rule 15(a). See **Mayle v. Felix, 125 S.Ct. 2562, 2569 (2005)** ("Before a responsive pleading is served, pleadings may be amended once as a 'matter of course,' i.e., without leave."). This amended §2255 motion is timely filed under §2255(f)(1). See **Clay v. United States, 537 U.S. 522, 155 L.Ed.2d 88, 123 S.Ct. 1072 (2003)**. The United States has not filed a responsive pleading.

I.
STATEMENT OF THE FACTS

    The facts stated in ¶¶1 through 8 in the Amendment to 28 U.S.C. §2255 Motion to vacate, set aside or correct sentence are hereby adopted herein.

II.
INEFFECTIVE ASSISTANCE OF COUNSEL

    A. Counsel provided constitutionally ineffective because he induced Movant's guilty plea based on faulty and erroneously legal advice that: (1) Movant would be sentence to a base offense level 26, which would be reduced three levels to a level 23 for acceptance of responsibility, with Criminal History Category III, that provides a sentencing range 57 to 71 months; (2) Movant's sentence on counts one and two would be run concurrently; and (3) Movant could appeal any upward departure by the Court. This erroneous and faulty legal advice rendered the guilty plea and the waiver of the right to appeal and collateral attack the conviction or sentence pursuant to 28 U.S.C. §2255 motion, not voluntary or intelligently enter. See **Tollet v. Henderson, 411 U.S. 258, 93 S.Ct. 1602, 36 L.Ed.2d 235 (1973)** (A criminal defendant can only attack the voluntary and intelligent character of guilty plea based on the advice of counsel); **United States v.**

Rumery, 698 F.2d 764, 766 (5th Cir. 1983) (counsel induced defendant's guilty plea based on erroneous advice which renders the guilty plea involuntary and unintelligently entered and constitutes ineffective assistance of counsel). To enter a knowing and voluntary guilty plea, the defendant must have a full understanding of what the plea connotes and of its consequences." See **Boykin v. Alabama, 395 U.S. 238, 244, 89 S.Ct. 1709, 23 L.Ed.2d 274 (1969)**. To determine validity of an appeal/collateral review waiver, this Court conducts a two-step inquiry, asking (1) whether the waiver was knowing and voluntary and (2) whether under the plain language of the plea agreement, the waiver applies to the circumstances at issue. See **United States v. Bond, 414 F.3d 542, 544 (5th Cir. 2005),**

Movant addresses counsel's faulty and erroneous legal advise as stated in ¶¶ (1) through (3) above separately: Counsel provided faulty and erroneous legal advice to Movant that by pleading guilty:

(1) Movant would be sentenced based on an adjusted base offense level 23, with a Criminal History III which provides a sentencing range of 57 to 71 months; where as if Movant proceeded to trial he would receive 240 months. Such unprofessional legal advice by counsel constitutes ineffective assistance and renders the guilty plea involuntary and unintelligently entered. See **United States v. Colon-Torres, 382 F.3d 76, 87 (1st Cir. 2004)**. Counsel's failure to learn the facts and familiarize himself with the law (Sentencing Guidelines) in relation to the plea constitutes ineffective assistance and renders the guilty plea invalid. See **Scott v. Wainwright, 698 F.2d 427, 429-30 (11th Cir. 1983); Herring v. Estelle, 491 F.2d 125, 127-128 (5th Cir. 1974); United States v. Espinoza, 866 F.2d 1067, 1069 (9th Cir. 1988)** (counsel's promise that defendant would receive a specific sentence to induce guilty plea required an evidentiary hearing to resolve claim of ineffectiveness of counsel). See also **Ostrander v. Green, 46 F.3d 347 (4th Cir. 1995); Craver v. Procunier, 756 F.2d 1212, 1214 (5th Cir. 1985)**. Movant was erroneously sentenced to 240 months as a career offender for two prior convictions for simple possession of cocaine and because of counsel lack of understanding of the Guidelines he failed to object to the use of the two prior convictions for simple possession, which did not qualify as predicate offenses under **USSG §4B1.1** See **United States v. Horney, 333 F.3d 1185, 1187-88 (10th Cir. 2003); United States v. Kissick, 69 F.3d 1048, 1050-51 (10th Cir. 1995).**

A defendant who pleads guilty in reliance on his or her attorney's "gross mischaracterization of the likely outcome" of his or her case may be entitled to withdraw the plea on ineffective assistance of counsel. **Iaea v. Sunn, 800 F.2d 864, 865 (9th Cir. 1994)**. Had Movant been accurately advised of his potential sentence under the Guidelines he would not have pled guilty, but would have proceeded to trial to preserve his rights. In the context of §2255 challenges brought by federal prisoners, that waivers cannot bar ineffective assistance of counsel claims associated with the negotiations of plea agreements. See **United States v. White, 307 F.3d 336, 341 (5th Cir. 2002)** ("[A] waiver of appeal may not be enforced against a section 2255 petitioner who claims that ineffective assistance of counsel rendered that waiver unknowing or involuntary."); **United States v. Cockerham, 237 F.3d 1179, 1187 (10th Cir. 2001)** (We hold that a plea agreement waiver of post-conviction rights does not waive the right to bring a §2255 petition based on ineffective assistance of counsel claims challenging the validity of the plea or the waiver.").

Had it not been for counsel's faulty and erroneous legal advice, Movant would have proceeded to trial and preserved his rights to challenge the application of the career offender provision. Thus, the plea was not voluntary or intelligently enter as a result of ineffective assistance of counsel. Prejudice has been shown. See **Hill v. Lockhart, 474 U.S. 52, 59, 88 L.Ed 2d 203, 106 S.Ct. 366 (1985)**.

(2)   Movant's sentence on counts one and two would be run concurrently. Such unprofessional legal advice by counsel constitutes ineffective assistance and renders the guilty plea on the 18 U.S.C. §924(o), charge not voluntary or intelligently entered. See **Fowler-Cornwell v. United States, 159 F.Supp.2d 291, 294-295 (ND W. Va. 2001)** (Defense counsel was ineffective in failing to advise Fowler-Cornwell that consecutive sentences were required on drug and firearm offenses rendering the guilty plea involuntary and unintelligently entered); **United States v. Stubbs, 279 F.3d 402, 412 (6th Cir. 2002)** (The waiver of appeal in plea agreement was invalid where defendant's guilty plea was not voluntary or intelligently entered. Neither the defendant, his counsel, nor the district court was aware that defendant was not subject to a mandatory consecutive minimum 60-month sentence under 18 U.S.C. §924(o), and there is no evidence that defendant was aware of the true nature of the crime charged, and the statutory consequences of his guilty plea. Thus, rendering the guilty plea not voluntary or intelligently entered). The exact same scenario applies to Mr. _____ case his guilty plea was not voluntary or intelligently entered as a result of counsel ineffective assistance.

(3)   The Plea Agreement did not call for an upward departure based on the Career Offender provision of the Guidelines. This Court enhancement of Movant's sentence based on its finding that Movant was a career offender pursuant to **USSG §4B1.1**, by using a prior conviction for simple possession of cocaine. A finding by the Court that Movant was a career offender is an upward departure. See **United States v. Breckenridge, 93 F.3d 132, 135 (4th Cir. 1996)**. The plea agreement does not preclude claims raised in this Amended §2255 motion. See **United States v. Bond, 414 F.3d 542, 544 (5th Cir. 2005)**.

Paragraph ¶7 of the plea agreement states in pertinent part: "The defendant may appeal only (a) a sentence imposed above the statutory maximum; or (b) an upward department from the Sentencing Guidelines which had not been requested by the United States, as set forth in 18 U.S.C. §3742(b). Additionally, the defendant is aware that 28 U.S.C. §2255, affords the right to contest or 'collateral attack' a conviction or sentence after the conviction or sentence has become final. The defendant waives the right to contest his/her conviction or sentence by means of any post-conviction proceeding." Id. Movant understood the plea agreement to afford him an opportunity to challenge any upward departure from the Guidelines. See **Bond, 414 F.3d at 544**.

B.   Movant did not know that he was waiving his right to effective assistance of counsel at sentencing by entering into the plea agreement. See **Johnson v. Zebst, 304 U.S. 458 (1938)**. The plea agreement waiver of the right to appeal or collateral attack his conviction or sentence was not knowingly or voluntary entered and must be set aside.

See **Bond**, 414 F.3d at 544; **United States v. Henderson**, 72 F.3d 463, 465 (5th Cir. 1995).

      C.   Defense counsel deprived Movant of effective assistance because he represented conflicting interest. After receiving a copy of the Presentence Report prior to sentencing, Movant directed defense counsel to file a motion to withdraw his guilty because the plea was induced based on faulty and erroneous legal advice. Defense counsel lied to Movant by advising him that it was too late to file a motion to withdraw his guilty plea. See **United States v. Segarra-Rivera**, 473 F.3d 381, 383 (1st Cir. 2007). Counsel knew that if Movant filed a motion to withdraw his guilty plea that he would be forced to defend himself against a valid claim of ineffective assistance of counsel and possible bar complaint because of his faulty and erroneous legal advice and sentence inducements to get Movant to plead guilty. See **Segarra-Rivera**, 473 F.3d at **383**; **United States v. Colon-Torres**, 382 F.3d 76, 89 (1st Cir. 2004). In order to prevent Movant from filing a motion to withdraw his guilty plea exposing his own ineffectiveness of counsel he lied to Movant. See **Segarra-Rivera, supra**. The guilty plea was not knowingly and voluntary entered as a result of ineffective assistance of counsel and must be set aside. **Segarra-Rivera, supra**.

      WHEREFORE based on the above, _____, respectfully moves to set aside his guilty plea and afford him an opportunity to plead a new. Alternatively, appoint counsel and conduct an evidentiary hearing to resolve the factual disputes.

      Respectfully submitted on this _____ day of _____, 20___.

_____

PRO SE REPRESENTATION

IN THE UNITED STATES DISTRICT COURT
FOR THE _____ DISTRICT OF _____
_____ DIVISION

UNITED STATES OF AMERICA,

        Respondent,

VS.   **Civil No. _____**

_____

        Movant.

MOTION FOR APPOINTMENT OF COUNSEL

       COMES NOW _____, the Movant, pro se, and respectfully moves this Honorable Court for appointment of counsel pursuant to 18 U.S.C. §3006A, to represent Movant in the 28 U.S.C. §2255 proceedings.

       Movant filed a detailed §2255 motion and moved for an evidentiary hearing. The United States filed its reply brief and conceded that an evidentiary hearing should be conducted to resolve factual disputes. Movant sought discovery material from both the United States and prior defense counsel _____.

       In light of Rules 6 and 8 governing §2255 proceedings, this Court should appoint counsel to represent Movant.

       WHEREFORE, based on the above, _____,urges this Court to grant this motion and appoint counsel.

       Respectfully submitted on this _____ day of _____, 20___.

                                  _____
                                   PRO SE REPRESENTATION

IN THE UNITED STATES DISTRICT COURT
FOR THE _____ DISTRICT OF _____
_____ DIVISION

UNITED STATES OF AMERICA,

        Respondent,

VS.   **Civil Action No. _____**

                                                 Case No. _____

_____

        Petitioner-Movant.

MEMORANDUMN BRIEF IN SUPPORT OF MOTION TO VACATE, SET ASIDE OR CORRECT SENTENCE PURSUANT TO TITLE 28 UNITED STATES CODE, SECTION 2255

TO THE HONORABLE JUDGE_____:

    COMES NOW _____ _____, the petitioner, pro se, and respectfully moves this Honorable Court pursuant to **Title 28 United States Code, Section 2255**, to: vacate, set aside or correct sentence imposed by this Court on the ____ day of _____ 200___. Petitioner is presently incarcerated at the Federal Correctional Institution, _____, _____.

STATEMENT OF THE FACTS

    [State the facts relevant to your constitutional claims and support the facts with affidavits].

<u>**ISSUE I**</u>

THE CONVICTION IS UNCONSTITUTIONAL BECAUSE PETITIONER DID NOT RECEIVE EFFECTIVE ASSISTANCE OF COUNSEL AS GUARANTEED BY THE FIFTH AND SIXTH AMENDMENTS OF THE UNITED STATES CONSTITUTION

Claims of ineffective assistance of counsel in criminal cases are evaluated under a two-prong test set forth in **<u>Strickland v. Washington</u>, 466 U.S. 668, 687-88, 694, 104 S.Ct. 2052, 2064-74, 80 L.Ed.2d 674 (1984)**, and its progeny. "To succeed on any claim of ineffective assistance of counsel, a defendant must show that: (1) the attorney's representation fell below an objective standard of reasonableness, and (2) there is a reasonable probability that except for the attorney's unprofessional errors, the results of the proceeding would have been different." **<u>Vines v. United States</u>, 28 F.3d 1123, 1127 (11th Cir. 1994) (citing <u>Strickland</u>, supra.)**. In the plea bargaining context, a petitioner seeking to establish ineffective assistance of counsel must demonstrate that: (1) counsel's advice and performance fell below an objective standard of reasonableness; and (2) the petitioner would not have pleaded guilty and would have insisted on going to trial in the absence of his attorney's errors. **<u>Hill v. Lockhart</u>, 474 U.S. 52, 58-59, 106 S.Ct. 366,370-71, 88 L.Ed.2d 203 (1985)**.

In **<u>Hill</u> 474 U.S. at 59** the Court explained that: In many guilty plea cases, the "prejudice" inquiry would closely resemble the inquiry engaged in by courts reviewing ineffective assistance challenges to convictions obtained through a trial. For example, where the alleged error of counsel is a failure to investigate or discover potentially exculpatory evidence, the determination whether the error "prejudiced" the defendant by causing him to plead guilty rather than go to trial will depend on the likelihood that discovery of the evidence would have led counsel to change his recommendation as to the plea. This assessment, in turn, will depend in large part on a prediction whether the evidence likely would have changed the outcome of a trial. Similarly, where the alleged error of counsel is a failure to advise the defendant of a potential affirmative defense to the crime charged, the resolution of the "prejudice" inquiry will depend largely on whether the affirmative defense likely would have succeeded at trial. Id.

In this case, trial counsel committed several errors and omissions which amounted to performance at a level below the acceptable objective standard of reasonableness for defense counsel in a criminal case. Petitioner asserts the following errors and omissions as grounds for relief:

A.   [State Your Ineffective Assistance of Counsel Proposition]

Assert facts supported by the record or affidavits showing how counsel's legal advice to you to plead guilty fell below an objective standard of reasonableness for counsel in a criminal case. Then cite case law supporting your claim that counsel's advice was deficient and rendered the guilty plea not voluntary and intelligently entered.

Blend your facts with supporting case law showing the validity of your claim.

Assert facts showing why you would not have plead guilty, had it not been for counsel's legal advice that you would have proceeded to trial. In other words show how the outcome of the plea proceeding would have been different, had it not been for counsel's advice to plead guilty.

§§§

B.   [State Your Ineffective Assistance of Counsel Proposition]

Assert facts supported by the record or affidavits showing how counsel's advice to you to plead guilty fell below an objective standard of reasonableness for counsel in a criminal case. Then cite case law supporting that counsel's performance was deficient.

Blend your facts with supporting case law showing the validity of your claim.

Assert facts and show how that had it not been for counsel's erroneous legal advice you would not have plead guilty, but would have proceeded to trial. In other words, show how the outcome of the plea proceedings would have been different, had it not been for counsel's legal advice.

§§§

CONCLUSION

WHEREFORE, based on the above, _____ urges this Court to set aside his guilty plea and afford him an opportunity to plead a new. Alternatively, schedule this case for an evidentiary hearing to resolve the factual disputes and appoint counsel.

Respectfully submitted on this _____ day of _____, 20___.

_____
PRO SE REPRESENTATION

254

IN THE UNITED STATES DISTRICT COURT
FOR THE _____ DISTRICT OF _____
_____ DIVISION

UNITED STATES OF AMERICA,

      Respondent,

VS.
                                 Civil Action No. _____

                                   Case No. _____

_____

      Petitioner-Movant.

MEMORANDUM BRIEF IN SUPPORT OF MOTION TO VACATE, SET ASIDE OR CORRECT SENTENCE PURSUANT TO TITLE 28 UNITED STATES CODE, SECTION 2255

TO THE HONORABLE JUDGE _____:

      COMES NOW _____, the petitioner, pro se, and respectfully moves this Honorable Court pursuant to **Title 28 United States Code, Section 2255**, to: vacate, set aside or correct sentence imposed by this Court on the ____ day of _____ 200___. Petitioner is presently incarcerated at the Federal Correctional Institution, _____, _____.

STATEMENT OF THE FACTS

      [State the facts relevant to your constitutional claims and support the facts with affidavits].

<u>ISSUE I</u>

THE CONVICTION IS UNCONSTITUTIONAL BECAUSE PETITIONER DID NOT RECEIVE EFFECTIVE ASSISTANCE OF COUNSEL AS GUARANTEED BY THE CONSTITUTION

Legal Standard

Claims of ineffective assistance of counsel in criminal cases are evaluated under a two-prong test set forth in **Strickland v. Washington, 466 U.S. 668, 687-88, 694, 104 S.Ct. 2052, 2064-74, 80 L.Ed.2d 674 (1984)**, and its progeny. "To succeed on any claim of ineffective assistance of counsel, a defendant must show that: (1) the attorney's representation fell below an objective standard of reasonableness, and (2) there is a reasonable probability that except for the attorney's unprofessional errors, the results of the proceeding would have been different." **Vines v. United States, 28 F.3d 1123, 1127 (11th Cir. 1994) (citing Strickland, supra.).**

In this case, trial counsel committed several errors and omissions which amounted to performance at a level below the acceptable objective standard of reasonableness for defense counsel in a criminal case. Petitioner asserts the following errors and omissions as grounds for relief:

A.   [State Your Ineffective Assistance of Counsel Proposition]

Assert facts supported by the record or affidavits showing how counsel's performance fell below an objective standard of reasonableness for counsel in a criminal case. Then cite case law supporting your claim that counsel's performance was deficient.

Blend your facts with supporting case law showing the validity of your claim.

Assert facts and show how the result of the proceeding would have been different, absent counsel's unprofessional errors and omissions. In other words, show how the outcome of the proceedings would have been different, had it not been for counsel's errors or omissions.

§§§

B.   [State Your Ineffective Assistance of Counsel Proposition]

Assert facts supported by the record or affidavits showing how counsel's performance fell below an objective standard of reasonableness for counsel in a criminal case. Then cite case law supporting that counsel's performance was deficient.

Blend your facts with supporting case law showing the validity of your claim.

Assert facts and show how the result of the proceeding would have been different, absent counsel's unprofessional errors and omissions. In other words, show how the outcome of the proceedings would have been different, had it not been for counsel's errors or omissions.

§§§

C. [State Your Ineffective Assistance of Counsel Proposition]

Assert facts supported by the record or affidavits showing how counsel's performance fell below an objective standard of reasonableness for counsel in a criminal case. Then cite case law supporting that counsel's performance was deficient.

Blend your facts with supporting case law showing the validity of your claim.

Assert facts and show how the result of the proceeding would have been different, absent counsel's unprofessional errors and omissions. In other words, show how the outcome of the proceedings would have been different, had it not been for counsel's errors or omissions.

§§§

CONCLUSION

WHEREFORE, based on the above, _____ urges this Court to vacate the conviction and sentence and grant a new trial based on claims raised in Issue A and B. Alternatively, schedule this case for an evidentiary hearing to resolve the factual disputes and appoint counsel. Petitioner moves to be resentenced based on the claim raised in Issue C to the low end of the guideline range of _____ months.

Respectfully submitted on this _____ day of _____, 20___.

_____
PRO SE REPRESENTATION

IN THE UNITED STATES DISTRICT COURT
FOR THE _____ DISTRICT OF _____
_____ DIVISION

_____,

Movant,

VS.   Case No. _____

UNITED STATES OF AMERICA

Respondent.

MOTION FOR AN EXTENSION OF TIME TO FILE A REPLY TO THE GOVERNMENT'S RESPONSE TO MOVANT'S 28 U.S.C. §2255 MOTION

COMES NOW _____, the Movant, pro se and respectfully moves this Honorable Court for an extension of time to file a reply to the government's response to Movant's 28 U.S.C. §2255 Motion. Movant will show this Court as follows:

1.   This is Movant's first request for an extension of time to file a reply to the United States' response to Movant's **§2255** motion.

2.   The United States sought and received an extension of time to file their response to Movant's **§2255** motion.

3.   Movant currently represents himself pro se. Movant has no training in the field of law and needs the additional time to respond to the United States' _____ page response.

4.   Movant works a regular full time job at the Federal Correctional Institution _____, _____, with limited access to the law library. Movant needs the additional time to read the case laws cited by the United States and to conduct his own research in order to properly prepare and file his reply.

5.   This motion is made in the interest of justice and not meant to delay the proceeding. The United States will not be prejudiced by a thirty (30) day delay.

WHEREFORE, based on the above, _____, urges this Honorable Court to grant him a thirty (30) day extension of time to file his reply to the United States' response to Movant's **28 U.S.C. §2255** motion.

Respectfully submitted on this _____ day of _____, 20___.

PRO SE REPRESENTATION

258

IN THE UNITED STATES DISTRICT COURT
FOR THE _____ DISTRICT OF _____
_____ DIVISION

UNITED STATES OF AMERICA,

         Respondent,

VS.

         Civil No. _____

         Criminal No. _____

_____

         Movant.

REPLY TO UNITED STATES' ANSWER TO MOVANT'S 28 U.S.C. §2255 MOTION TO VACATE, SET ASIDE OR CORRECT SENTENCE

TO THE HONORABLE JUDGE _____ :

    COMES NOW _____, the Movant, pro se, and respectfully files this Reply to the United States' Answer To Movant's 28 U.S.C. §2255 Motion, pursuant to Rule 5 governing §2255 proceedings. Movant stands firmly on all points raised in his initial §2255 motion and memorandum brief. This Reply will address only the points raised in the United States' Answer/Response that requires a reply.

    The United States contends that both of Movant's claims that: "Counsel was ineffective for failing to challenge the use of two simple possession of cocaine prior convictions as non-qualifying predicate offenses for Career Offender enhancement provisions under USSG §4B1.2(b);" and "Counsel was ineffective for failing to object to the PSR improperly declining to award Movant a three level decrease for acceptance of responsibility because he was classified as a career offender," are procedurally barred in light of **United States v. Frady, 456 U.S., 152, 167-168, 71 L.Ed.2d 816, 102 S.Ct. 1584 (1982)** (general rule that claims not raised on direct appeal may not be raised on collateral review unless the petitioner shows cause and prejudice).

    Contrary the United States' Response/Answer the United States Supreme Court in **Massaro v. United States, 538 U.S. 500, 155 L.Ed.2d 714, 720, 123 S.Ct. 1690 (2003)**, rejected the United States' proposition. The **Massaro** Court found that the **Frady** procedural-default rule is neither a statutory nor a constitutional requirement, but it is a doctrine adhered to by the courts to conserve judicial resources and to respect the law's important interest in the finality of judgments. We conclude that requiring a criminal defendant to bring ineffective-assistance of counsel claims on direct appeal does not promote these objectives. **Id. Massaro, 155 L.Ed.2d at 720.**

    The threat of default and resulting procedural bar has doubtless resulted in many claims being asserted on direct appeal only to protect the record. This, of counsel, unnecessarily burdens both parties and the court with a presentation and review leading only to dismissal for reassertion in a petition under 28 U.S.C. §2255. Thus, while ordinarily the procedural bar rule of **United states v. Frady, 456 U.S. 15, 71 L.Ed.2d 816, 102 S.Ct. 1584 (1982)**, applies to section 2255 proceedings. **See United States v. Allen, 16 F.3d 377 (10th Cir. 1994)**, we hold that it does not apply to ineffective assistance of counsel claims. **See United States v. DeRewal, 10 F.3d 100. 101 (3rd Cir. 1993), cert. denied, 128 L.Ed.2d 196, 114 S.Ct. 1544 (1994)**. A federal prisoner's failure to raise a claim of ineffective assistance of counsel on direct appeal does not bar review on 28 U.S.C. §2255 motion. **Massaro, 155 L.Ed.2d at 720-22.**

The United States did not address the merits of either of Movant's constitutional claims of ineffective assistance of counsel which amounts to conceding that the facts stated therein are true. **See Bland v. California Department of Corrections, 29 F.3d 1469, 1474 (1994)**. Additionally, Movant established cause for procedural default in his §2255 motion. Ineffective assistance of counsel is cause for procedural default. **See Murray v. Carrier, 477 U.S. 478, 496, 106, S.Ct. 2639, 2649-50, 91 L.Ed.2d 397 (1985)**. Movant established that he was prejudice by counsel's ineffectiveness as he received 240 months imprisonment as opposed to the 46 months he would have received, absent counsel's unprofessional errors and omissions. **See Glover v. United States, 531 U.S. 198, 148 L.Ed.2d 607, 611, 121 S.Ct. 696 (2001).**

WHEREFORE, based on the above, _____, the Movant's claims are not procedurally barred and this Court must address the merits of his constitutional claims of ineffective assistance of counsel and reduce his sentence to 46 months.

Respectfully submitted on this _____ day of _____, 20___.

_____

PRO SE REPRESENTATION

CERTIFICATE OF SERVICE

Form Letter No. 2

[Your Name & Prison Number]
[Institution]
[Your Address]
[Town, State & Zip Code]

[Date]

Honorable _____
U.S. District Judge
Address _____
Town, State & Zip Code _____

Re: United States v. _____
    Criminal No. _____

Dear Judge _____:

This letter is in reference to the above entitled action. I filed a motion to temporary stay the proceedings because I was in transit. I arrived at my new institution and at this time I request that the Court lift the temporary stay.

Thank you.

Sincerely,

_____
[Your Name]

CC:

Your prosecutor name
p/file.

261

[CAPTION]

MOTION TO TEMPORARY STAY THE PROCEEDINGS

TO THE HONORABLE JUDGE OF SAID COURT:

    COMES NOW _____, the petitioner, pro se, and respectfully moves this Honorable Court to temporary stay the proceeding. In support thereof, petitioner will show this Court as follows:

    1.   On _____ ___, 200___, the Petitioner was called to the FCI _____, _____, Receiving and Discharging and instructed by Prison Staff Officials to pack all of his personal property because he was being transferred to FCI _____, _____. Petitioner packed his personal property including all of his legal material and files and took them to receiving and discharging for transporting them to FCI _____.

    2.   Petitioner will probably be in transit between thirty to forty days and request that this Honorable Court temporary stay the proceeding while petitioner is in transit and until he notifies this Court that he has arrived at the new institution FCI _____.

    3.   Upon arriving at FCI _____, _____, the Petitioner will immediately notify this Court and request that the stay be lifted.

    4.   This motion is made in the interest of justice and not meant to delay the proceeding.

    WHEREFORE, based on the above, _____, the petitioner, urges this Honorable Court to **GRANT** this motion to temporary stay the proceeding.

    Respectfully submitted on this _____ day of _____, 20___.

Name   Prison Number
PRO SE REPRESENTATION
Address
Town, State and Zip Code

IN THE UNITED STATES DISTRICT COURT
FOR THE _____ DISTRICT OF _____
_____ DIVISION

UNITED STATES OF AMERICA,

         Respondent,

VS.

        Civil No. _____

        CR No. _____

_____

         Petitioner.

MOTION FOR DISCOVERY AND PRODUCTION OF DOCUMENTS PURSUANT TO RULE 6 GOVERNING 28 U.S.C. §2255 PROCEEDINGS

TO THE HONORABLE JUDGE _____:

    COMES NOW _____, the petitioner, pro se, and respectfully seeks leave from this Honorable Court to conduct discovery and production of documents pursuant to **Rule 6(a) & (b)** governing **28 U.S.C. §2255** proceedings. Petitioner will show this Court as follows:

    1.   Petitioner filed his §2255 motion with detailed facts concerning his claim that defense counsel _____ provided ineffective assistance of counsel because he failed to communicate the government's five (5) year plea offer to Petitioner. The United States files its response claiming that it never offered a five (5) year plea offer to petitioner.

    2.   Petitioner attached to the §2255 motion his affidavit detailing the facts concerning defense counsel _____ ineffectiveness related to his failure to communicate the government's five (5) year plea offer to petitioner. Additionally, Petitioner attached to his §2255 motion a letter from co-defendant _____'s counsel _____ an officer of this Court, which showed that the United States in fact made a five (5) years plea offer to Petitioner.

    3.   This motion seeks leave to conduct discovery, production of documents, and disclosure from the United States of all typed, written, or electronic versions of any and all e-mails, letters, memos, or any form of communications from the United States Attorney Office to counsel _____ concerning plea offers for Petitioner. Production and disclosure of these documents will prove Petitioner's claim that he was denied effective assistance of counsel, where counsel _____ failed to communicate the government's plea offer to him.

    4.   Counsel _____ refuses to disclose the case file to Petitioner or any correspondence from the United States Attorney's Office concerning a plea offer.

Petitioner has offered to pay for copying and shipping cost for the case file. See Exhibits "___" and "___." Petitioner seeks disclosure of the entire case file in counsel _____ possession because it will provide Petitioner with the necessary documentation which supports his claim of ineffective assistance of counsel.

     5.   Counsel _____ who represented co-defendant _____, claims in his letter to _____ that the United States offered Petitioner a five (5) year plea. **See Exhibit "___"** attached hereto. Counsel _____ claims that he received a copy of the United States letter concerning the five (5) year plea offer which had a deadline date for the pleas in this case. Because of counsel _____ statements in his letter Petitioner seeks to submit the attached proposed interrogatories and production documents. The documents being the letter/letters from the United States Attorney's Office concerning the plea offers in this case. Production of these documents and answers to the interrogatories will provide Petitioner with the necessary proof to support his claim of ineffective assistance of counsel.

     6.   Petitioner seeks to have defense counsel _____ answer the attached interrogatories concerning the plea offers made by the United States and production and disclosure of all written, typed, or electronic communications from the United States Attorney's Office to counsel _____ concerning plea offers to petitioner.

     7.   Good Cause is shown because production of the requested documents will establish the validity of petitioner's constitutional claim that defense counsel _____ provided ineffective assistance for failure to communicate the government's five (5) year plea offer to Petitioner.

     WHEREFORE, based on the above, _____, respectfully urges this Honorable Court for leave to conduct discovery and for production of documents pursuant to Rule 6(a) & (b) governing §2255 proceedings.

     A memorandum brief is attached hereto and made part of this motion by reference hereto.

     Respectfully submitted on this _____ day of _____, 20___.

                         _____
                                  PRO SE REPRESENTATION

                                CERTIFICATE OF SERVICE

IN THE UNITED STATES DISTRICT COURT
FOR THE _____ DISTRICT OF _____
_____ DIVISION

UNITED STATES OF AMERICA,

      Respondent,

VS.

Civil No. _____

CR No. _____

_____

      Petitioner.

MEMORANDUM BRIEF IN SUPPORT OF MOTION FOR DISCOVERY AND PRODUCTION OF DOCUMENTS PURSUANT TO RULE 6 GOVERNING 28 U.S.C. §2255

TO THE HONORABLE JUDGE _____ :

    COMES NOW _____, the petitioner, pro se, and respectfully files this memorandum brief in support of his motion for discovery and production of documents pursuant to **Rule 6(a) & (b)** governing **28 U.S.C. §2255** proceedings. In support thereof, Petitioner will show this Court as follows:

    Rule 6 of the Rules governing 28 U.S.C. §2254 and 2255 proceedings entitles litigants to request discovery process available under the Federal Rules of Civil Procedure, if good cause is shown and the court exercises its discretion allowing discovery. Federal Rules of Civil Procedure, Rule 26(a) through 36 provides a wide range of discovery devices available which includes but not limited to: depositions, production of documents or other physical materials, physical and mental examinations, request for admissions and interrogatories, permission to enter upon land or other property for inspection or other purposes. The Court may appoint counsel for indigent prisoners if necessary for effective utilization of discovery. See, **18 U.S.C. §3006A(g)**.

    Good cause for discovery exists under Rule 6(a) governing Section §§2254 and 2255 cases ("Habeas Rule") where specific allegations before the court showed reason to believe that the petitioner may, if the facts are fully developed be able to demonstrate that he is entitled to relief. **See <u>Harris v. Nelson</u>, 394 U.S. 286, 89 S.Ct. 1082, 22 L.Ed.2d 281 (1969); <u>Bracy v. Gramley</u>, 520 U.S. 899, 117 S.Ct. 1793, 138 L.Ed.2d 97 (1998); <u>Payne v. Bell</u>, 89 F.Supp.2d 967 (W.D. Tenn. 2000).**

    Petitioner attached to the §2255 motion his affidavit detailing the facts concerning defense counsel _____ ineffectiveness related to his failure to communicate the government's five (5) year plea offer to petitioner. Additionally, Petitioner attached to his §2255 motion a letter from co-defendant _____ counsel _____ an officer of this Court, which showed that the United States in fact made a five (5) years plea offer to petitioner. Such unprofessional errors and omissions by counsel

_____ constitutes ineffective assistance of counsel and warrants an evidentiary hearing to resolve the factual dispute. See **Valentine v. United States, 488 F.3d 325, 332-333 (6th Cir. 2007); Griffin v. United States, 330 F.3d 733, 739 (6th Cir. 2003)**.

This motion seeks leave to conduct discovery, production of documents, and disclosure from the United States of all typed, written, or electronic versions of any and all e-mails, letters, memos, or any form of communications from the United States Attorney Office to counsel _____ concerning plea offers for petitioner. Production and disclosure of these documents will prove petitioner's claim that he was denied effective assistance of counsel where counsel _____ failed to communicate the government's plea offer to him. See **United States ex rel. Caruso v. Zelinsky, 689 F.2d 435 (3rd Cir. 1982)** (The defendant alleged that his counsel had failed to communicate to him a plea offer. The **Caruso** Court held that "[t]he decision to reject a plea bargain offer . . . is a decision for the accused to make . . . a failure of counsel to advise his client of a plea bargain . . . constitute[s] a gross deviation from accepted professional standards"). The exact same scenario applies to Mr. _____.

Counsel _____ refused to disclose the case file to petitioner or any correspondence from the United States Attorney's Office concerning a plea offer. Petitioner has offered to pay for copying and shipping cost for the case file. See Exhibits "___" and "___." Petitioner seeks disclosure of the entire case file in counsel _____ possession because it will provide petitioner with the necessary documentation which supports his claim of ineffective assistance of counsel. Both the law and the American Bar Association recognize that counsel has a duty not to impede Petitioner's attempt to challenge his conviction and/or sentence. See, **ABA Standards for Criminal Justice, Defense Functions Standards and Commentary** ("the resounding message is that defense attorneys, because of their intimate knowledge of the trial proceedings and their possession of unique information regarding possible post-conviction claims, have an obligation to cooperate with their client's attempt to challenge their convictions."); **Maxwell v. Florida, 479 U.S. 972, 93 L.Ed.2d 418, 107 S.Ct. 474 (1986)** ("The right to effective assistance fully encompasses the client's right to obtain from trial counsel the work files generated during and pertinent to that client's defense. It further entitles the client to utilize materials contained in these files in any proceeding at which the adequacy of trail counsel's representation may be challenged"); **Spivey v. Zant, 683 F.2d 881, 885 (5th Cir. 1982)** (Habeas corpus petitioner is entitled to former trial attorneys file and the work-product doctrine does not apply to situation in which the client seeks access to documents or other tangible things created during course of attorney's representation).

Counsel _____ who represented co-defendant _____ claims in his letter to _____ that the United States offered Petitioner a five (5) year plea. **See Exhibit "___"** attached hereto. Counsel _____ claims that he received a copy of the United States letter concerning the five (5) year plea offer which had a deadline date for the pleas in this case. Because of counsel _____ statements in his letter, Petitioner seeks to submit the attached proposed interrogatories and production documents. The documents being the letter/letters from the United States Attorney's Office concerning the plea offers in this case. Production of these documents and answers to the interrogatories will provide Petitioner with the necessary proof to support his claim of ineffective assistance of counsel. **See <u>Valentine</u>, 488 F.3d at 332-333**.

Petitioner seeks to have defense counsel _____ answer the attached interrogatories concerning the plea offers made by the United States and production and disclosure of all written, typed, or electronic communications from the United States Attorney's Office to counsel _____ concerning plea offers to petitioner.

Good Cause is shown because production of the requested documents will establish the validity of Petitioner's constitutional claim that defense counsel _____ provided ineffective assistance for failure to communicate the government's five (5) year plea offer to Petitioner. **See <u>Valentine</u>, 488 F.3d at 332-333**.

WHEREFORE, based on the above, _____, respectfully urges this Honorable Court for leave to conduct discovery and for production of documents pursuant to Rule 6(a) & (b) governing §2255 proceedings.

Respectfully submitted on this _____ day of _____, 20___.

_____
PRO SE REPRESENTATION

<u>CERTIFICATE OF SERVICE</u>

IN THE UNITED STATES DISTRICT COURT
FOR THE _____ DISTRICT OF _____
_____ DIVISION

_____

_____

VS.   **Civil No.** _____
                                         Criminal No. _____

_____

_____

FIRST SET OF INTERROGATORIES FOR _____

_____

_____, hereby, presents this first set of interrogatories to _____, pursuant to Federal Rules of Civil Procedure, Rule 33, to be answered separately in writing and under oath within thirty (30) days. A place for your answer is provided below each interrogatory. If additional space is needed for your answer use additional paper.

Each of the interrogatories inclusive deemed to be a continuing interrogatory pursuant to Federal Rule Civil Procedure, Rule 26(e). _____ requests that _____, amend or supplement answers to these interrogatories promptly and fully if at a later date, _____, obtains additional facts or obtains or makes assumptions or reaches conclusions that are different from those set forth in the answer to these interrogatories.

INTERROGATORY NO. 1: Mr. _____, you're a licensed attorney who practices in the State of _____ and represented _____ in the United States District Court for the _____ District of _____.

ANSWER NO. 1:

INTERROGATORY NO. 2: Did anybody from the United States Attorney's Office for the _____ District of _____ make a plea offer for your client _____?

ANSWER NO. 2:

INTERROGATORY NO. 3: Mr. _____, do you as a standard practice file in your client's case files all corresponding letters, memos, emails, or written communications from the opposing party attempting to settle the case against your client?

ANSWER NO. 3:

INTERROGATORY NO. 4: Mr. _____, isn't it true that a representative of the United States Attorney's Office for the _____ District of _____, made to you or your office a plea offer for _____-?

ANSWER NO. 4:

INTERROGATORY NO. 5: Mr. _____, isn't it true that you never presented the United States' five (5) year cooperation plea offer to _____?

ANSWER NO. 5:

INTERROGATORY NO. 6: Mr. _____, isn't it true that _____ paid the funds for you to represent _____?

ANSWER NO. 6:

INTERROGATORY NO. 7: Mr. _____, isn't it true that you represent _____ in a drug case in State Court?

ANSWER NO. 7:

INTERROGATORY NO. 8: Mr. _____, isn't it true that the reason that you did not present the United States' plea offer to _____ is to protect your other client _____?

ANSWER NO. 8:

INTERROGATORY NO. 9: Mr. _____, isn't it true that _____ has requested to purchase a copy of the case file pertaining to his case in your possession on numerous occasions?

ANSWER NO. 9:

Date: _____

_____

_____

IN THE UNITED STATES DISTRICT COURT
FOR THE _____ DISTRICT OF _____
_____ DIVISION

_____

_____

VS.   Civil No. _____
                                                 Criminal No. _____

_____

_____

FIRST SET OF INTERROGATORIES FOR _____

_____

_____, hereby, presents this first set of interrogatories to _____, pursuant to Federal Rules of Civil Procedure, Rule 33, to be answered separately in writing and under oath within thirty (30) days. A place for your answer is provided below each interrogatory. If additional space is needed for your answer use additional paper.

Each of the interrogatories inclusive deemed to be a continuing interrogatory pursuant to Federal Rule Civil Procedure, Rule 26(e). _____ requests that _____, amend or supplement answers to these interrogatories promptly and fully if at a later date, _____, obtains additional facts or obtains or makes assumptions or reaches conclusions that are different from those set forth in the answer to these interrogatories.

INTERROGATORY NO. 1: Mr. _____, did you represent the United States of America in <u>United States v.</u>_____, Criminal No. _____, in the United States District Court for the _____ District of _____?

ANSWER NO. 1:

INTERROGATORY NO. 2: Did you or anybody else from the United States Attorney's Office for the _____ District of _____ make a plea offer for defendant _____?

ANSWER NO. 2:

INTERROGATORY NO. 3: Mr. _____, as a representative of the United States Attorney's Office for the _____ District of _____, did you present the plea offer for defendant _____ in writing to his counsel _____?

ANSWER NO. 3:

INTERROGATORY NO. 4:   Mr. _____ did defense counsel _____ advise you that defendant _____ refused to accept the United States plea offer?

ANSWER NO. 4:

Date: _____

_____

_____

IN THE UNITED STATES DISTRICT COURT
FOR THE _____ DISTRICT OF _____
_____ DIVISION

UNITED STATES OF AMERICA,

VS.

          Criminal No. _____

          Civil No. _____

_____,

Movant.

MOTION FOR EXPANSION OF RECORD

TO THE HONORABLE JUDGE _____:

    COMES NOW _____, the Movant, pro se, and respectfully files this motion for expansion of the record pursuant to **Rule 7(b)** governing **28 U.S.C. §2255** proceedings.

    Movant moves for expansion of the record to include all Exhibits and Affidavits attached to his §2255 motion and Memorandum Brief. The Exhibits and Affidavits have been served on the opposing party and should be included within the record in accordance with Rule 7 governing §2255 proceedings.

    WHEREFORE, based on the above, _____, the Movant urges this Honorable Court to grant this motion for expansion of record.

    Respectfully submitted on this _____ day of _____, 20___.

_____
PRO SE REPRESENTATION

IN THE UNITED STATES DISTRICT COURT
FOR THE _____ DISTRICT OF _____
_____ DIVISION

_____

_____,

Petitioner,

VS.   Civil No. _____

UNITED STATES OF AMERICA,

Respondent.

_____

MOTION FOR AN EVIDENTIARY HEARING ON
28 U.S.C. §2255 MOTION

_____

TO THE HONORABLE JUDGE _____ :

    COMES NOW _____, the petitioner, pro se, and respectfully moves this Honorable Court for an evidentiary hearing pursuant to **Rule 8**, governing **28 U.S.C. §2255** proceedings. Petitioner _____ will show this Court as follows:

    1.   Petitioner filed his §2255 motion with detailed facts concerning defense counsel _____ inducement for petitioner's guilty plea.

    2.   Petitioner attached to his §2255 motion his affidavit detailing the facts that defense counsel _____ inducement used to induce his guilty plea. Additionally, petitioner filed with his §2255 motion an affidavit of _____ who heard and witnessed defense counsel _____'s inducements.

    3.   The United States obtained an affidavit from defense counsel _____ concerning his inducement to Petitioner.

    4.   This court is faced with conflicting affidavits based on disputed factual issues in this §2255 proceedings.

    WHEREFORE, based on the above _____, the petitioner requests an evidentiary hearing to resolve the disputed facts.

    A memorandum brief is attached hereto and made part of this motion by reference herein.

    Respectfully submitted on this _____ day of _____, 20___.

_____
PRO SE REPRESENTATION

IN THE UNITED STATES DISTRICT COURT
FOR THE _____ DISTRICT OF _____
_____ DIVISION

_____

_____,

Petitioner,

VS.   **Civil No.** _____

UNITED STATES OF AMERICA,

Respondent.

_____

MEMORANDUM BRIEF IN SUPPORT OF MOTION FOR AN
EVIDENTIARY HEARING ON 28 U.S.C. §2255 MOTION

_____

    COMES NOW _____, the petitioner, pro se, and respectfully files this memorandum brief in support of his motion for an evidentiary hearing, pursuant to **Rule 8**, governing **28 U.S.C. §2255** proceedings.

    This court is faced with conflicting affidavits based on disputed factual issues in this §2255 proceedings. Contested factual issues may not be decided on the basis of affidavits alone unless the affidavits are supported by other evidence in the record. **United States v. Hughes, 635 F.2d 449, 451 (5th Cir. 1981)**. When facts are at issue in a §2255 proceeding, a hearing is required if: (1) the record, as supplemented by the trial judge's personal knowledge or recollection, does not conclusively negate the facts alleged in support of the claim for §2255 relief; and (2) the movant would be entitled to post-conviction relief as a legal matter if his factual allegations are true. **Friedman v. United States, 558 F.2d 1010, 1015 (5th Cir. 1979); see United States v. Briggs, 939 F.2d 222, 228 (5th Cir. 1991)**.

    Petitioner _____ has identified factual disputes with respect to his ineffective assistance of counsel claims that cannot be decided on the basis of these affidavits alone. See **Hughes, 635 F.2d at 451**. Therefore, the motions, files, and records in this case do not show conclusively that _____ is not entitled to any relief on his claims of ineffective assistance of trial counsel. **See §2255. See also Fontaine v. United States, 411, U.S. 213, 36 L.Ed., 2d 169, 93 S.Ct. 1461 (1973)**.

    WHEREFORE, based on the facts detailed in the §2255 and its supporting affidavits _____, the Petitioner, urges this Court to schedule the case for an evidentiary hearing to resolve the disputed facts.

    Respectfully submitted on this _____ day of _____, 20___.

_____
Name   Prison Number
PRO SE REPRESENTATION
Address
Town, State and Zip Code

IN THE UNITED STATES DISTRICT COURT
FOR THE _____ DISTRICT OF _____
_____ DIVISION

UNITED STATES OF AMERICA,

VS.   Case No. _____

_____

MOTION FOR AN ENLARGEMENT OF TIME TO FILE OBJECTIONS TO THE MAGISTRATE JUDGE'S REPORT AND RECOMMENDATION

COMES NOW _____, the movant, pro se, and respectfully moves this Honorable Court for an enlargement of time to file objections to the United States' Magistrate Judge's Report and Recommendation related to his 28 U.S.C. §2255 motion. In support thereof, Movant states:

1.   Movant currently represents himself, pro se, and is not trained in the field of law with limited access to the prison law library.

2.   Movant works a regular full time job at the prison and goes to school half a day five days a week. Therefore, Movant's access to the prison law library is very limited. Movant needs an additional _____ (___) days to properly research, prepare and file his objections to the Magistrate's Report and Recommendation.

3.   The Magistrate's Report and Recommendation only authorized Movant ten (10) days to file his objections to the Report. Movant request an additional _____ days to file his objections.

4.   This motion is made in the interest of justice and not meant to delay the proceedings.

WHEREFORE based on the above, _____, urges this Honorable Court to grant this motion and afford him an additional _____ (___) days to file objections to the Magistrate's Report and Recommendation.

Respectfully submitted on this _____ day of _____, 20___.

_____
PRO SE REPRESENTATION

IN THE UNITED STATES DISTRICT COURT
FOR THE _____ DISTRICT OF _____
_____ DIVISION

_____,

Petitioner,

VS.

Civil No. _____

Crim. No. _____

UNITED STATES OF AMERICA,

Respondent.

PETITIONER'S OBJECTIONS TO REPORT OF MAGISTRATE JUDGE

TO THE HONORABLE JUDGE _____ :

COMES NOW _____, the petitioner, pro se, respectfully files his objection to the Report of Magistrate Judge, recommending to deny petitioner's 28 U.S.C. §2255 motion without conducting an evidentiary hearing or resolve factual disputes. Petitioner makes the following objections to wit:

OBJECTIONS NO. 1: Petitioner objects to the Report of the Magistrate Judge (hereinafter "RMJ"), mischaracterization his constitutional claims by the RMJ re-phrasing his claim and then addressing only part of the claim or an entirely different claim than raised by Petitioner.

OBJECTION NO. 2: Petitioner objections to the RMJ misstatement on the Procedural History of the case. The RMJ incorrect concludes that Mr. _____ was charged with conspiracy to possession with intent to distribute over five (5) grams of cocaine and possession with intent to distribute over 5 grams of cocaine and possession with intent to distribute over 5 grams of cocaine. Contrary to the RMJ findings, Petitioner was charged with a quantity of over five (5) kilograms, not five grams. See Indictment (Doc. No. 4). The jury returned a verdict on the lesser included of 5 grams. See Verdict (Doc. No. ___U).

OBJECTION NO. 3: Petitioner objects to the RMJ findings based on the facts set forth in the Presentence Report and the _____ Circuit Appellate Opinion and the government's response to petitioner's §2255. Petitioner asserted facts throughout his §2255 motion, which would have changed the outcome of the trial, and those facts warrant relief under Section 2255. See 2255 MB at pp. 2-45; Mr. _____ affidavit Exhibit "A" _____ affidavit; Exhibit "B"; and Exhibit "D" _____, which shows that Petitioner worked a full day on the dated of the alleged crime. The RMJ fails to address the facts set forth in Mr. _____'s §2255 MB, which if true, warrant relief under §2255 and requires this Court to conduct an evidentiary haring to resolve the factual dispute. **See Holmes v. United States, 876 F.2d 1545, 1547 (11th Cir. 1989); United States v. Miller, 760 F.2d 1116 (11th Cir. 1985).**

OBJECTION NO. 4: Petitioner objects to the RMJ addressing claims **not** raised in Petitioner's §2255 motion, in reference to <u>Claims 1 and 3</u>, on page 6 of the RMJ. Petitioner's claim (1) is: Counsel was constitutionally ineffective for failing to **present Mr. _____'s <u>defense</u>** through cross-examination of government witnesses _____, _____, and _____ and then **call defense** witness _____ "(Emphasis added). Id. at MB at p. 7. Petitioner's claim (3) is: Counsel was constitutionally ineffective for failing to investigate impeachment evidence, subpoena impeachment witnesses, use prior inconsistent statements, and to impeach government witnesses _____ and _____ during cross-examination." See §2255 MB at pages 18-23. The RMJ does not address the claims raised by Mr. _____, which is a violation of **Clisby v. Jones, 960 F.2d 925, 935-936 (11th Cir. 1992) (en banc).** Instead of addressing these claims the RMJ states what occurred at trial which does not address the claim and facts before the Court in the §2255 pleadings.

OBJECTION NO. 5: The RMJ re-phrased Petitioner's initial claim which is: "Counsel was constitutionally ineffective for failing to present Mr. _____ <u>defense</u> through cross-examination of government witness is _____, _____, and _____ and then call defense witness _____ _____. See pages 7-14 of the §2255 MB. Compare to page 2 of the RMJ. Instead of addressing Mr. _____ claim the RMJ tells what occurred at trial. This type of action by the RMJ violates **Clisby v. Jones, 960 F.2d 925, 935-936 (11th Cir. 1992).**

OBJECTION No. 6: Petitioner objects to the RMJ at p. 7 fn. 2, findings of fact based solely on counsel _____ affidavit, where the Court is faced with conflicting affidavits Mr. _____, and Mr. _____, versus trial counsel _____'s affidavit on material facts. Contested factual issues may not be decided on the basis of affidavits alone unless the affidavits are supported by other evidence in the record. See **United States v. Hughes, 635, F.2d 449, 451 (5th Cir. 1981).** When facts are at issue in a §2255 proceeding, a hearing is required if: (1) the record, as supplemented by the trial judge's personal knowledge or recollection, does not conclusively negate the facts alleged in support of the claim for §2255 relief; and (2) the movant would be entitled to post-conviction relief as a legal matter if his factual allegations are true. See **Friedman v. United States, 588 F.2d 1010, 1015 (5th Cir. 1979); United States v. Briggs, 939 F.2d 222, 228 (5th Cir. 1991).** The RMJ relies on counsel _____'s affidavit and fails to address the facts stated in Mr. _____'s and Mr. _____'s affidavit.

OBJECTION NO. 7: Petitioner objects to the RMJ findings and conclusion in reference to Claim 2 at pages 7 & 8. Contrary to the RMJ findings Petitioner's requested witnesses were **not** alibi witnesses, rather they were material witnesses whose testimony would have created a reasonable doubt respecting petitioner's guilt based on the prosecution's theory of the case. Because his witnesses would have put Petitioner arriving back at <u>work</u>, at approximately the same time the arrests were made on his <u>alleged</u> co-defendants which created a reasonable doubt that Petitioner did not go to the robbery scene. Instead, the jury would have heard testimony that Petitioner arrived back at work at the time the arrests were being made. Once again, this Court is faced with conflicting affidavits, which warrants an evidentiary hearing. See **Hughes, 635 F.2d at**

277

451; **Friedman**, 588 F.2d at 1015. The RMJ findings is based on a misapplication of the law and facts and address a separate issue than what was raised.

OBJECTION NO. 8: Petitioner objects to the RMJ findings and conclusion in reference to Claims 4 and 5 at page 8. The RMJ at p. 8, <u>fails</u> to address counsel's failure to use the cell phone records to impeach the credibility of _____ and _____ raised throughout the claim. **See §2255 MB at pp. 24-27.** Nor does counsel _____ explain any strategic decision not to use the cell phone records to impeach the co-defendant _____ and _____'s credibility.

OBJECTION NO. 9: Petitioner objects to the RMJ findings and conclusion concerning Claim 6. As Petitioner, clearly explained how CI _____ testimony would have supported Mr. _____ defense, and disputed the government's theory of the case and warrants an evidentiary hearing.

OBJECTION NO. 10: Petitioner objects to the RMJ findings and conclusions related to Claim 7. The RMJ findings **<u>fails</u> entirely** to address his claim that counsel was ineffective for failing to object to the <u>incorrectly scored</u> Career Offender provision because it used the incorrect <u>statutory maximum sentence</u> to determine the Career Offender provision. Such failure constitutes reversible error in light of **Clisby v. Jones, 960 F.2d 925, 935-936 (11th Cir. 1992) (en banc).** Petitioner's sentence should be reduced to 210 months to relieve the prejudice. **See United States v. Garcia, 405 F.3d 1260, 1275-76 (11th Cir. 2005).**

OBJECTION NO. 11: Petitioner objects to the RMJ findings and recommendation on Claim 8, the imposition of consecutive sentence in accordance to Congressional mandate 18 U.S.C. §3584(a) (**except that the terms may not run consecutively for an attempt and for another offense that was sole objective of the attempt**), which clearly fits this case. The RMJ incorrect concludes that the Sentencing Guidelines trumps statute, which is an incorrect application of the law.

OBJECTION NO. 12: Petitioner objects to the RMJ's incorrect findings and conclusion of law on Claim 9, that a guilty verdict on conspiracy (elements is an agreement) constitutes the necessary elements for an enhancement under USSG §2D1.1(b)(1).

OBJECTION NO. 13: Petitioner objects the RMJ findings and conclusion of law on Claim 10 as being based on an incorrect finding of fact resulting in an incorrect conclusion of law.

OBJECTION NO. 14: Petitioner objects to the Conclusion of the RMJ based on the foregoing reasons stated herein, and respectfully moves this Court to reject the RMJ findings and recommendation and remand for an evidentiary hearing before a new magistrate judge.

Respectfully submitted on this _____ day of _____, 20___.

_____
Your Name   Prison Number
PRO SE REPRESENTATION
Address
Town, State and Zip Code

CERTIFICATE OF SERVICE

I HEREBY CERTIFY that a true and correct copy of this foregoing instrument has been mailed first class postage prepaid on this _____ day of _____ 20___, to the Assistant United States Attorney, _____, _____ _____, _____, _____.

Executed under penalty of perjury pursuant to 28 U.S.C. §1746, on this ____ day of _____ 20___.

_____
Name

IN THE UNITED STATES DISTRICT COURT
FOR THE _____ DISTRICT OF _____
_____ DIVISION

UNITED STATES OF AMERICA,

     Respondent,

VS.

             Civil No. _____

             Criminal No. _____

_____,

     Movant.

MOVANT'S OBJECTIONS TO THE MAGISTRATE JUDGE'S REPORT AND RECOMMENDATION

TO THE HONORABLE JUDGE _____:

    COMES NOW _____, the Movant, pro se, respectfully files his Objections to the Magistrate Judge's Report and Recommendation ("R&R") to Movant's 28 U.S.C. §2255 Motion. Movant objects to the R&R legal conclusion to wit:

    OBJECTIONS 1: The R&R at page ___ makes the legal conclusion that Movant's claims of ineffective assistance of counsel are procedurally barred because he did not raise the claims on direct appeal citing **United States v. Frady**, **456 U.S. 152, 167-168, 71 L.Ed.2d 816, 102 S.Ct. 1584 (1982)**. Contrary to the "R&R" legal conclusion the Supreme Court in **Massaro v. United States**, **538 U.S. 500, 155 L.Ed.2d 714, 123 S.Ct. 1690 (2003)**, rejected the R&R legal conclusion. **See also United States v. Allen**, **16 F.3d 377 (10th Cir. 1994)**; **United States v. DeRewal**, **10 F.3d 100, 101 (3rd Cir. 1994)**. A federal prisoner's failure to raise a claim of ineffective assistance of counsel on direct appeal does not bar review on 28 U.S.C. §2255 motion. **Massaro, 155 L.Ed.2d at 720-22**. The R&R should be overruled.

    OBJECTIONS 2: The R&R concludes that Movant did not show prejudice under **Strickland v. Washington**, **466 U.S. 668, 80 L.Ed.2d 674, 104 S.Ct. 2052 (1984)**, based on his claim that counsel failed to object to two simple possessions of cocaine convictions that were used to place him into a career Offender sentence enhancement provision under the Guidelines. Contrary to the R&R, Movant showed that he would have received a sentence under the Sentencing Guidelines range of **46 to 57** months, instead of the **240** months he received as a result of counsel's unprofessional errors and omissions. Thus, prejudice is shown. **See Glover v. United States**, **531 U.S. 198, 203, 121 S.Ct. 696, 148 L.Ed.2d 602 (2001)**; **United States v. Chase**, **499 F.3d 1061, 1068 (9th Cir. 2007)**; **Alaniz v. United States**, **351 F.3d 365, 368 (8th Cir. 2003)** (concluding that an error increasing a defendant's sentence by as little as six months can be prejudicial within the meaning of **Strickland**). Mr. _____ has shown prejudice because his sentence was increased from **46** months to **240** months as a result of counsel's errors. **See <u>Glover</u>, supra**.

  WHEREFORE, based on the above _____, this Court should overrule the "R&R" and grant Movant's §2255 motion and reduce his sentence to 46 months.

  Respectfully submitted on this _____ day of _____, 20___.

_____

Name   Prison Number
PRO SE REPRESENTATION
Address
Town, State and Zip Code

IN THE UNITED STATES DISTRICT COURT
FOR THE _____ DISTRICT OF _____
_____ DIVISION

_____

_____ ,

Movant,

VS.   Case No. _____

UNITED STATES OF AMERICA,

Respondent.

_____

MOTION FOR PRODUCTION OF EVIDENTIARY HEARING TRANSCRIPT AT GOVERNMENT'S EXPENSE

_____

TO THE HONORABLE JUDGE _____ :

COMES NOW _____ , the movant, pro se and respectfully moves this Honorable Court, pursuant to **18 U.S.C. §3006(a)** for production of evidentiary hearing transcripts at the government's expense. In support thereof, Movant states the following:

1.   This Court ordered an evidentiary hearing to resolve factual disputes on a claim in Movant's 28 U.S.C. §2255 motion, and appointed counsel _____ to represent Movant.

2.   On _____ ___, 200___, this Court conducted an evidentiary hearing to resolve factual disputes related to Movant's §2255 claims. In order to properly prepare a Motion For Certificate Of Appealability, it is necessary that Movant have an opportunity to review the evidentiary hearing transcript.

3.   Appointed counsel _____ , advised Movant that he ordered the evidentiary hearing transcript. However, a review of the docket entry sheets reveals that the evidentiary hearing transcript have not been ordered.

4.   The evidentiary hearing transcript is necessary in the preparation of the appeal and motion for certificate of appealability to show that Movant's constitutional claims are debatable among jurist of reason.

5.   This Court recently found Movant to be of the in forma pauperis status when it appointed counsel. Movant's status has not changed.

WHEREFORE, based on the above, _____ , urges this Court to grant this motion and order the production of the evidentiary hearing transcript at the government's expense.

Respectfully submitted on this _____ **day of** _____ , 20___ .

_____

PRO SE REPRESENTATION

IN THE UNITED STATES DISTRICT COURT
FOR THE _____ DISTRICT OF _____
_____ DIVISION

VS.   Case No. _____

NOTICE OF APPEAL

Notice is hereby given that, _____, the petitioner, pro se, hereby

appeals to the United States Court of Appeals for the _____ Circuit from the

final judgment denying his _____, and all pleadings related thereto,

entered for record in the above action on the _____ day of _____, 200___.

RESPECTFULLY SUBMITTED

_____

Name   Prison Number
PRO SE REPRESENTATION
Address
Town, State and Zip Code

Form Letter No. 3

[Your Name & Prison Number]
[Institution]
[Your Address]
[Town, State & Zip Code]

[Date]

Office of the Clerk
Attn: [Clerk's Name]_____
Address_____
Town, State & Zip Code____

Re: _____ v. _____,
        Docket No. _____

Dear Clerk:

    At this time, I am requesting a **Application To Proceed In Forma Pauperis, Supporting Documentation and Order Form** from your office. I have enclosed a self-addressed stamped envelope for the return of the **Application To Proceed In Forma Pauperis Form**.

    Thank you.

Sincerely,

_____
[Your Name]

CC:
    p/file.

Certified Mail No. _____

Affidavit Accompanying Motion for
Permission to Appeal In Forma Pauperis

United States District Court for the _____ District of _____

v.

District Court No._____

Affidavit in Support of Motion	Instructions
I swear or affirm under penalty of perjury that, because of my poverty, I cannot prepay the docket fees of my appeal or post a bond for them. I believe I am entitled to redress. I swear or affirm under penalty of perjury under United States laws that my answers on this form are true and correct. (28 U.S.C. § 1746; 18 U.S.C § 1621.)	Complete all questions in this application and then sign it. Do not leave any blanks: if the answer to a question is "0," "none," or "not applicable (N/A)," write in that response. If you need more space to answer a question or to explain your answer, attach a separate sheet of paper identified with your name, your case's docket number, and the question number.
Signed: _____	Date: _____

My issues on appeal are:

1. For both you and your spouse estimate the average amount of money received from each of the following sources during the past 12 months. Adjust any amount that was received weekly, biweekly, quarterly, semiannually, or annually to show the monthly rate. Use gross amounts, that is, amounts before any deductions for taxes or otherwise.

Income source	Average monthly amount during the past 12 months		Amount expected next month	
	You	Spouse	You	Spouse
Employment	$_____	$_____	$_____	$_____
Self-employment	$_____	$_____	$_____	$_____
Income from real property (such as rental income)	$_____	$_____	$_____	$_____
Interest and dividends	$_____	$_____	$_____	$_____
Gifts	$_____	$_____	$_____	$_____
Alimony	$_____	$_____	$_____	$_____
Child support	$_____	$_____	$_____	$_____
Retirement (such as social security, pensions, annuities, insurance)	$_____	$_____	$_____	$_____
Disability (such as social security, insurance payments)	$_____	$_____	$_____	$_____
Unemployment payments	$_____	$_____	$_____	$_____
Public-assistance (such as welfare)	$_____	$_____	$_____	$_____
Other (specify): _____	$_____	$_____	$_____	$_____
Total monthly income:	$_____	$_____	$_____	$_____

2. List your employment history, most recent employer first. (Gross monthly pay is before taxes or other deductions.)

Employer	Address	Dates of employment	Gross monthly pay
_____	_____	_____	_____
_____	_____	_____	_____
_____	_____	_____	_____

3. List your spouse's employment history, most recent employer first. (Gross monthly pay is before taxes or other deductions.)

Employer	Address	Dates of employment	Gross monthly pay
_____	_____	_____	_____
_____	_____	_____	_____
_____	_____	_____	_____

4. How much cash do you and your spouse have? $_____
   Below, state any money you or your spouse have in bank accounts or in any other financial institution.

Financial institution	Type of account	Amount you have	Amount your spouse has
_____	_____	$_____	$_____
_____	_____	$_____	$_____
_____	_____	$_____	$_____

If you are a prisoner, you must attach a statement certified by the appropriate institutional officer showing all receipts, expenditures, and balances during the last six months in your institutional accounts. If you have multiple accounts, perhaps because you have been in multiple institutions, attach one certified statement of each account.

5. List the assets, and their values, which you own or your spouse owns. Do not list clothing and ordinary household furnishings.

Home
(Value)

Other real estate
(Value)

Motor vehicle #1
(Value)

Make & year: _____

Model: _____

Registration #: _____

Motor vehicle #2
(Value)

Make & year: _____

Model: _____

Registration #: _____

Other assets
(Value)

Other assets
(Value)

6. State every person, business, or organization owing you or your spouse money, and the amount owed.

Person owing you or your spouse money	Amount owed to you	Amount owed to your spouse
_____	_____	_____
_____	_____	_____
_____	_____	_____

286

7. State the persons who rely on you or your spouse for support.

Name	Relationship	Age
_____	_____	_____
_____	_____	_____
_____	_____	_____

8. Estimate the average monthly expenses of you and your family. Show separately the amounts paid by your spouse. Adjust any payments that are made weekly, biweekly, quarterly, semiannually, or annually to show the monthly rate.

	You	Your Spouse
Rent or home-mortgage payment (include lot rented for mobile home)	$_____	$_____
Are real-estate taxes included? ☐Yes ☐No		
Is property insurance included? ☐Yes ☐No		
Utilities (electricity, heating fuel, water, sewer, and telephone)	$_____	$_____
Home maintenance (repairs and upkeep)	$_____	$_____
Food	$_____	$_____
Clothing	$_____	$_____
Laundry and dry-cleaning	$_____	$_____
Medical and dental expenses	$_____	$_____
Transportation (not including motor vehicle payments)	$_____	$_____
Recreation, entertainment, newspapers, magazines, etc.	$_____	$_____
Insurance (not deducted from wages or included in mortgage payments)	$_____	$_____
Homeowner's or renter's	$_____	$_____
Life	$_____	$_____
Health	$_____	$_____
Motor Vehicle	$_____	$_____
Other: _____	$_____	$_____
Taxes (not deducted from wages or included in mortgage payments) (specify): _____	$_____	$_____
Installment payments	$_____	$_____
Motor Vehicle	$_____	$_____
Credit card (name): _____	$_____	$_____
Department store (name): _____	$_____	$_____
Other: _____	$_____	$_____
Alimony, maintenance, and support paid to others	$_____	$_____
Regular expenses for operation of business, profession, or farm (attach detailed statement)	$_____	$_____
Other (specify): _____	$_____	$_____
Total monthly expenses:	$_____	$_____

287

9. *Do you expect any major changes to your monthly income or expenses or in your assets or liabilities during the next 12 months?*
   ☐Yes ☐No   If yes, describe on an attached sheet.

10. *Have you paid — or will you be paying — an attorney any money for services in connection with this case, including the completion of this form?* ☐Yes ☐No

    If yes, how much? $_____

    If yes, state the attorney's name, address, and telephone number:

    _____

    _____

    _____

11. *Have you paid — or will you be paying — anyone other than an attorney (such as a paralegal or a typist) any money for services in connection with this case, including the completion of this form?*
    ☐Yes ☐No

    If yes, how much? $_____

    If yes, state the person's name, address, and telephone number:

    _____

    _____

    _____

12. *Provide any other information that will help explain why you cannot pay the docket fees for your appeal.*

13. *State the address of your legal residence.*

    _____

    _____

    Your daytime phone number: (____) _____

    Your age: _____ Your years of schooling: _____

    Your social security number: _____

IN THE UNITED STATES DISTRICT COURT
FOR THE _____ DISTRICT OF _____
_____ DIVISION

VS.   Case No. _____

MOTION FOR LEAVE TO PROCEED ON
APPEAL IN FORMA PAUPERIS

TO THE HONORABLE JUDGE OF SAID COURT:

      COMES NOW _____, the petitioner, pro se and respectfully moves this Honorable Court for leave to proceed on appeal through in forma pauperis status from the judgment entered on the _____ day of _____, 200__, for record denying Petitioner's _____ motion without prepayment of costs, fees or giving security therefore.

      An affidavit in support of this motion to proceed on appeal in forma pauperis is attached hereto and made part of this motion by reference herein.

Respectfully submitted

_____

Name   Prison Number
PRO SE REPRESENTATION
Address
Town, State and Zip Code

IN THE UNITED STATES DISTRICT COURT
FOR THE _____ DISTRICT OF _____
_____ DIVISION

_____

_____,

Movant-Petitioner,

VS.   Civil No. _____

UNITED STATES OF AMERICA,

Respondent.

_____

MOTION FOR ISSUANCE OF CERTIFICATE OF APPEALABILITY

_____

TO THE HONORABLE JUDGE _____:

    COMES NOW _____, the movant-petitioner, pro se, and respectfully moves this Honorable Court pursuant to **28 U.S.C. §2253(c)(2)** to issue a Certificate of Appealability ("COA") authorizing Mr. _____ to appeal the denial of his **28 U.S.C. §2255** motion to vacate, set aside correct sentence. **See <u>Slack v. McDaniel</u>, 529 U.S. 473, 484, 120 S.Ct. 1595, 146 L.Ed.2d 542 (2000); <u>Miller-El v. Cockrell</u>, 537 U.S. 322, 123 S.Ct. 1029, 1039, 154 L.Ed.2d 931 (2003).**

I.
<u>STATEMENT OF JURISDICTION</u>

    Jurisdiction to issue a COA is invoked pursuant **28 U.S.C. §§2253(c)(2); and 2255.**

II.
<u>STATEMENT OF THE CASE</u>

[A statement of the case can be drafted from the docket entry sheet].

III.
<u>STATEMENT OF THE FACTS</u>

[Present a clear statement of facts that support your procedural and constitutional claims].

A. Legal Standard for Certificate of Appealability

    In **<u>Henry v. Cockrell</u>, 327 F.3d 429, 431 (5th Cir. 2003)**, the Fifth Circuit explained that: Under the Antiterrorism and Effective Death Penalty Act (AEDPA), a petitioner must obtain a certificate of appealability (COA) before he can appeal the district court decision. **28 U.S.C. §2253(c)(1)**. A COA will be granted only if the petitioner makes "a substantial showing of the denial of a constitutional right." **28 U.S.C. §2253(c)(2)**. In order to make a substantial showing, a petitioner must demonstrate that a "reasonable jurists would find the district court's assessment of the constitutional claim debatable or wrong." **<u>Slack v. McDaniel</u>, 529 U.S. 473, 484, 120 S.Ct. 1595, 146**

L.Ed.2d 542 (2000). When the district court has denied a claim on procedural grounds, then the petitioner must demonstrate that a "jurists of reason would find it debatable whether the district court was correct in its procedural ruling." **id**. As the Supreme made clear in its decision in **Miller-El v. Cockrell, 537 U.S. 322, 123 S.Ct. 1029, 1039, 154 L.Ed.2d 931 (2003)**, a COA is "jurisdictional prerequisite," and "until a COA has been issued, the federal courts of appeals lacks jurisdiction to rule on the merits of appeals from habeas petitioners." When considering a request for a COA, "[t]he question is the debatability of the underlying constitutional claim, not the resolution of that debate." **id. at 1042**.

With this overview of the legal standard for issuance of a COA, Mr. _____ will proceed with his constitutional claims and show how they're debatable among jurists of reason.

§§§

ISSUE I

[State the procedural error committed by the Court]

[Make a substantial showing that the district court committed a procedural error in your case. Then demonstrate that your claim is debatable among jurists of reason and request that a COA be issued. A jurists of reason is a court decision that's in compliance with your claim or shows that a court could have resolved your claim in a different manner].

ISSUE II

[State your constitutional proposition]

[Make a substantial showing that your claim is of constitutional magnitude. Then demonstrate that your claim is debatable among jurists of reason and request that a COA be issued. A jurists of reason is a court decision that's in compliance with your claim or shows that a court could have resolved your claim in a different manner].

ISSUE III

[State your constitutional proposition]

[Make a substantial showing that your claim is of constitutional magnitude. Then demonstrate that your claim is debatable among jurists of reason and request that a COA be issued. A jurists of reason is a court decision that's in compliance with your claim or shows that a court could have resolved your claim in a different manner].

CONCLUSION

WHEREFORE, based on the above, _____, urges this Honorable Court issue a certificate of appealability authorizing Mr. _____ to appeal the district court's denial of his constitutional and procedural claims presented herein. Alternatively, grant the COA and remand for further proceedings.

Respectfully submitted on this _____ **day of** _____ **20___** .

_____
Name   Prison Number
PRO SE REPRESENTATION
Address
Town, State and Zip Code

<u>CERTIFICATE OF SERVICE</u>

    I HEREBY CERTIFY that a true and correct copy of this foregoing instrument has been mailed postage prepaid on this _____ day of _____ 20___, to the Assistant United States Attorney, _____, P.O. Box _____ _____, _____, _____ .

_____
Name

Chapter VII
Special Habeas Corpus
Procedures In Capital Cases

❑ Death Penalty Cases

➢ 28 U.S.C. §2261. Prisoners in State custody subject to capital sentence; appointment of counsel; requirement of rule of court or statute; procedures for appointment.

➢ 28 U.S.C. §2262. Mandatory stay of execution; duration; limits on stays of execution; successive petitions.

➢ 28 U.S.C. §2263. Filing of habeas corpus application; time requirements; tolling rules.

➢ 28 U.S.C. §2264. Scope of Federal review; district court adjudications.

➢ 28 U.S.C. §2265. Certification and judicial review.

➢ 28 U.S.C. §2266. Limitations period for determining application and motions.

➢ Motion for mandatory appointment of counsel for death sentence petitioner on petition for writ of habeas corpus (§2254)

➢ Motion for mandatory appointment of counsel for death sentence movant to file and represent him on A motion to vacate, set-aside or correct sentence (§2255)

SPECIAL HABEAS CORPUS PROCEDURES IN CAPITAL CASES

Section 2261. Prisoners in State custody subject to capital sentence; appoint of counsel; requirement of rule of court or statute; procedures for appointment.

Section 2262. Mandatory stay of execution; duration; limits on stays of execution; successive petitions.

Section 2263. Filing of habeas corpus application; time requirements; tolling rules.

Section 2264. Scope of Federal review; district court adjudications.

Section 2265. Certification and judicial review.

Section 2266. Limitation periods for determining application and motions.

Title 28 United States Code, Section 2261 provides:

§2261. Prisoners in State custody subject to capital sentence; appointment of counsel; requirement of rule of court or statute; procedures for appointment.

(a) This chapter shall apply to cases arising under section 2254 brought by prisoners in State custody who are subject to a capital sentence. It shall apply only if the provisions of subsections (b) and (c) are satisfied.

(b) **Counsel.** This chapter is applicable if—
(1) the Attorney General of the United States certifies that a State has established a mechanism for providing counsel in post-conviction proceedings as provided in section 2265; and
(2) counsel was appointed pursuant to that mechanism, petitioner validly waived counsel, petitioner retained counsel, or petitioner was found not to be indigent.

(c) Any mechanism for the appointment, compensation, and reimbursement of counsel as provided in subsection (b) must offer counsel to all State prisoners under capital sentence and must provide for the entry of an order by a court of record—
(1) appointing one or more counsels to represent the prisoner upon a finding that the prisoner is indigent and accepted the offer or is unable competently to decide whether or accept or reject the offer;
(2) finding, after a hearing if necessary, that the prisoner rejected the offer of counsel and made the decision with an understanding of its legal consequences; or
(3) denying the appointment of counsel upon a finding that the prisoner is not indigent.

(d) No counsel appointed pursuant to subsections (b) and (c) to represent a State prisoner under capital sentence shall have previously represented the prisoner at trial in the case for which the appointment is made unless the prisoner and counsel expressly request continued representation.

(c) The ineffectiveness or incompetence of counsel during State or Federal post-conviction proceedings in a capital case shall not be a ground for relief in a proceeding arising under section 2254. This limitation shall not preclude the appointment of different counsel, on the court's own motion or at the request of the prisoner, at any phase of State or Federal post-conviction proceedings on the basis of the ineffectivensss or incompetence of counsel in such proceedings.

(Added April 24, 1996, P.L. 104-132, Title I, § 107(a), 110 Stat. 1221; March 9, 2006, P.L. 109-177, Title V, §507(a), (b), 120 Stat. 250.)

Title 28 United States Code, Section 2262 provides:

§2262. Mandatory stay of execution; duration; limits on stays of execution; successive petitions.

(a) Upon the entry in the appropriate State court of record of an order under section 2261(c), a warrant or order setting an execution date for a State prisoner shall be stayed upon application to any court that would have jurisdiction over any proceedings filed under section 2254. The application shall recite that the State has invoked the post-conviction review procedures of this chapter [28 USCS §§2261 et seq.] and that the scheduled execution is subject to stay.

(b) A stay of execution granted pursuant to subjection (a) shall expire if—
(1) a State prisoner fails to file a habeas corpus application under section 2254 within the time required in section 2263;
(2) before a court of competent jurisdiction, in the presence of counsel, unless the prisoner has competently and knowingly waived such counsel, and after having been advised of the consequences, a State prisoner under capital sentence waives the right to pursue habeas corpus review under section 2254; or
(3) a State prisoner files a habeas corpus petition under section 2254 within the time required by section 2263 and fails to make a substantial showing of the denial of a Federal right or is denied relief in the district court or at any subsequent stage of review.

(c) If one of the conditions in subsection (b) has occurred, no Federal court thereafter shall have the authority to enter a stay of execution in the case, unless the court of appeals approves the filing of a second or successive application under section 2244(b).

(Added April 24, 1996, P.L. 104-132, Title I, § 107(a), 110 Stat. 1221.)

Title 28 United States Code, Section 2263 provides:

§2263. Filing of habeas corpus application; time requirements; tolling rules

(a) Any application under this chapter for habeas corpus relief under section 2254 must be filed in the appropriate district court not later than 180 days after final State court affirmance of the conviction and sentence on direct review or the expiration of the time for seeking such review.

(b) The time requirements established by subsection (a) shall be tolled—

(1) from the date that a petition for certiorari is filed in the Supreme Court until the date of final disposition of the petition if a State prisoner files the petition to secure review by the Supreme Court of the affirmance of a capital sentence on direct review by the court of last resort of the State or other final State court decision on direct review;

(2) from the date on which the first petition for post-conviction review or other collateral relief is filed until the final State court disposition of such petition; and

(3) during an additional period not to exceed 30 days, if—

(A) a motion for an extension of time is filed in the Federal district court that would have jurisdiction over the case upon the filing of a habeas corpus application under section 2254; and

(B) a showing of good cause is made for the failure to file the habeas corpus application within the time period established by this section.

(Added April 24, 1996, P.L. 104-132, Title I, § 107(a), 110 Stat. 1223.)

Title 28 United States Code, Section 2264 provides:

§2264. Scope of Federal review; district court adjudications

(a) Whenever a State prisoner under capital sentence files a petition for habeas corpus relief to which this chapter applies, the district court shall only consider a claim or claims that have been raised and decided on the merits in the State courts, unless the failure to raise the claim properly is—

(1) the result of State action in violation of the Constitution or laws of the United States;

(2) the result of the Supreme Court's recognition of a new Federal right that is made retroactively applicable; or

(3) based on a factual predicate that could not have been discovered through the exercise of due diligence in time to present the claim for State or Federal post-conviction review.

(b) Following review subject to subsections (a), (d), and (e) of section 2254, the court shall rule on the claims properly before it.

(Added April 24, 1996, P.L. 104-132, Title I, § 107(a), 110 Stat. 1223.)

Title 28 United States Code, Section 2265 provides:

§2265. Certification and judicial review

(a) **Certification.**
    (1) In general. If requested by an appropriate State official, the Attorney General of the United States shall determine—
        (A) whether the State has established a mechanism for the appointment, compensation, and payment of reasonable litigation expenses of competent counsel in State post-conviction proceedings brought by indigent prisoners who have been sentenced to death;
        (B) the date on which the mechanism described in subparagraph (A) was established; and
        (C) whether the State provides standards of competency for the appointment of counsel in proceedings described in subparagraph (A).
    (2) Effective date. The date the mechanism described in paragraph (1)(A) was established shall be the effective date of the certification under this subsection.
    (3) Only express requirements. There are no requirements for certification or for application of this chapter other than those expressly stated in this chapter.

(b) **Regulations.** The Attorney General shall promulgate regulations to implement the certification procedure under subsection (a).

(c) **Review of certification.**
    (1) In general. The determination by the Attorney General regarding whether to certify a State under this section is subject to review exclusively as provided under chapter 158 of this title.
    (2) Venue. The Court of Appeals for the District of Columbia Circuit shall have exclusive jurisdiction over matters under paragraph (1), subject to review by the Supreme Court under section 2350 of this title.
    (3) Standard of review. The determination by the Attorney General regarding whether to certify a State under this section shall be subject to de novo review.

(Added March 9, 3006, P.L. 109-177, Title V, § 507(c)(1), 120 Stat. 250.)

Title 28 United States Code, Section 2266 provides:

§2266. Limitation periods for determining applications and motions

(a) The adjudication of any application under section 2254 that is subject to this chapter, and the adjudication of any motion under section 2255 by a person under sentence of death, shall be given priority by the district court and by the court of appeals over all noncapital matters.

(b)(1)(A) A district court shall render a final determination and enter a final judgment on any application for a writ of habeas corpus brought under this chapter in a capital case not later than 450 days after the date on which the application is filed, or 60 days after the date on which the case is submitted for decision, whichever is earlier.

(B) A district court shall afford the parties at least 120 days in which to complete all actions, including the preparation of all pleadings and briefs, and if necessary, a hearing, prior to the submission of the case for decision.

(C)(i) A district court may delay for not more than one additional 30-day period beyond the period specified in subparagraph (A), the rendering of a determination of an application for a writ of habeas corpus if the court issues a written order making a finding, and stating the reasons for the finding, that the ends of justice that would be served by allowing the delay outweigh the best interests of the public and the applicant in a speedy disposition of the application.

(ii) The factors, among others, that a court shall consider in determining whether a delay in the disposition of an application is warranted are as follows:

(I) Whether the failure to allow the delay would be likely to result in a miscarriage of justice.

(II) Whether the case is so unusual or so complex, due to the number of defendants, the nature of the prosecution, or the existence of novel questions of fact or law, that it is unreasonable to expect adequate briefing within the time limitations established by subparagraph (A).

(III) Whether the failure to allow a delay in a case that, taken as a whole, is not so unusual or so complex as described in sub clause (II), but would otherwise deny the applicant reasonable time to obtain counsel, would unreasonably deny the applicant or the government continuity of counsel, or would deny counsel for the applicant or the government the reasonable time necessary for effective preparation, taking into account the exercise of due diligence.

(iii) No delay in disposition shall be permissible because of general congestion of the court's calendar.

(iv) The court shall transmit a copy of any order issued under clause (i) to the Director of the Administrative Office of the United States Courts for inclusion in the report under paragraph (5).

(2) The time limitations under paragraph (1) shall apply to—

(A) an initial application for a writ of habeas corpus;

(B) any second or successive application for a writ of habeas corpus; and

(C) any redetermination of an application for a writ of habeas corpus following a remand by the court of appeals or the Supreme Court for further proceedings, in which case the limitation period shall run from the date the remand is ordered.

(3) (A) The time limitations under this section shall not be construed to entitle an applicant to a stay of execution, to which the applicant would otherwise not be entitled, for the purpose of litigating any application or appeal.

(B) No amendment to an application for a writ of habeas corpus under this chapter shall be permitted after the filing of the answer to the application, except on the grounds specified in section 2244(b).

(4) (A) The failure of a court to meet or comply with a time limitation under this section shall not be a ground for granting relief from a judgment of conviction or sentence.

(B) The State may enforce a time limitation under this section by petitioning for a writ of mandamus to the court of appeals. The court of appeals shall act on the petition for a writ of mandamus not later than 30 days after the filing of the petition.

(5)(A) The Administrative Office of the United States Courts shall submit to Congress an annual report on the compliance by the district courts with the time limitations under this section.

(B) The report described in subparagraph (A) shall include copies of the orders submitted by the district courts under paragraph (1)(B)(iv).

(c)(1)(A) A court of appeals shall hear and render a final determination of any appeal of an order granting or denying, in whole or in part, an application brought under this chapter in a capital case not later than 120 days after the date on which the reply brief is filed, or if no reply brief is filed, not later than 120 days after the date on which the answering brief is filed.

(B)(i) A court of appeals shall decide whether to grant a petition for rehearing or other request for rehearing en banc not later than 30 days after the date on which the petition for rehearing is filed unless a responsive pleading is required, in which case the court shall decide whether to grant the petition not later than 30 days after the date on which the responsive pleading is filed.

(ii) If a petition for rehearing or rehearing en banc is granted, the court of appeals shall hear and render a final determination of the appeal not later than 120 days after the date on which the order granting rehearing or rehearing en banc is entered.

(2) The time limitations under paragraph (1) shall apply to—

(A) an initial application for a writ of habeas corpus;

(B) any second or successive application for a writ of habeas corpus; and

(C) any redetermination of an application for a writ of habeas corpus or related appeal following a remand by the court of appeals en banc or the Supreme Court for further proceedings, in which case the limitation period shall run from the date the remand is ordered.

(3) The time limitations under this section shall not be construed to entitle an applicant to a stay of execution, to which the applicant would otherwise not be entitled, for the purpose of litigating any application or appeal.

(4) (A) The failure of a court to meet or comply with a time limitation under this section shall not be a ground for granting relief from a judgment of conviction or sentence.

(B) The State may enforce a time limitation under this section by applying for a writ of mandamus to the Supreme Court.

(5) The Administrative Office of the United States Courts shall submit to Congress an annual report on the compliance by the courts of appeals with the time limitations under this section.

(Added April 24, 1996, P.L. 104-132, Title I, § 107(a), 110 Stat. 1224; March 9, 2006, P.L. 109-177, Title V, § 507(e), 120 Stat. 251.)

IN THE UNITED STATES DISTRICT COURT
FOR THE _____ DISTRICT OF _____
_____ DIVISION

_____

_____,

Petitioner,

VS.   Civil No. _____

Criminal No. _____

_____,

Respondent.

_____

MOTION FOR MANDATORY APPOINTMENT OF COUNSEL TO REPRESENT DEATH SENTENCE PETITIONER ON PETITION FOR WRIT OF HABEAS CORPUS PURSANT TO 28 U.S.C. §2254

_____

COMES NOW _____, the petitioner, pro se, and respectfully moves this Honorable Court for mandatory appointment of counsel to represent death sentence petitioner on a 28 U.S.C. §2254 petition for writ of habeas corpus, pursuant to 18 U.S.C. §3599(a)(2). Petitioner moves for death penalty qualified counsel to consult with, file, and represent Petitioner on a petition for writ of habeas corpus to challenge the constitutionality of petitioner's trial and sentence proceeding.

WHEREFORE premises considered, _____, the petitioner, respectfully moves for mandatory appointment of qualified counsel to represent death sentence prisoner on his 28 U.S.C. §2254 petition for writ of habeas corpus.

Respectfully submitted on this ____ day of _____ 20 _____.

PRO SE REPRESENTATION

300

IN THE UNITED STATES DISTRICT COURT
FOR THE _____ DISTRICT OF _____
_____ DIVISION

UNITED STATES OF AMERICA,

        Respondent,

VS.

Civil No. _____

Criminal No. _____

_____

        Movant.

MOTION FOR MANDATORY APPOINTMENT OF COUNSEL FOR DEATH SENTENCE MOVANT TO FILE AND REPRESENT HIM ON A MOTION TO VACATE, SET ASIDE OR CORRECT SENTENCE

TO THE HONORABLE JUDGE _____:

    COMES NOW _____, the Movant, pro se, and respectfully moves this Honorable Court for mandatory appointment of qualified counsel pursuant to **Title 18 U.S.C. §3599(a)(2)**, to consult with, file, and represent Movant _____ who has been sentenced to death on a motion to vacate, set aside or correct sentence, pursuant to **28 U.S.C. §2255**, challenging the constitutionality of trial counsel's performance and various other constitutional claims.

    WHEREFORE, based on the above, _____, respectfully moves for mandatory appointment of qualified counsel to represent death sentence prisoner on a **28 U.S.C. §2255** motion, pursuant to **18 U.S.C. §3599(a)(2)**.

    Respectfully submitted on this _____ day of _____, 20___.

_____

Name   Prison Number

PRO SE REPRESENTATION

Address

Town, State and Zip Code

Chapter VIII
Appellate Proceedings

❑   Appellate Proceedings

❑   Read the Rules of Appellate Procedure

> ➤   Notice of appeal

> ➤   Motion for leave to proceed on appeal in forma pauperis

> ➤   Motion for an enlargement of time to file a motion for certificate of appealability.

> ➤   Motion for order of designation of record on appeal

> ➤   Statement of evidence under Rule 10(c) of the appellate procedure when transcript is unavailable

> ➤   Motion for issuance of certificate of appealability

> ➤   Motion to be loaned/furnished a copy of the record on appeal

> ➤   Certificate of interested persons and corporate disclosure

> ➤   Motion for an enlargement of time to file appellant's opening brief

> ➤   Motion for extension of time to file petition for rehearing

> ➤   Motion for permission to file oversized brief

> ➤   Motion for leave to file and out-of-time appeal

> ➤   Appellant's opening brief (with cover letter)

> ➤   Certificate of compliance

> ➤   Motion to stay mandate

> ➤   Motion for reconsideration of entry of dismissal

> ➤   Motion for leave to file an out-of-time pro se appellant's reply brief

> ➤   Motion to recall mandate or amend judgment

> ➤   Motion to recall mandate and amend judgment

> ➤   *Form* letter requesting application for successive §2255 motion

> ➤   Application for leave to file a second or successive motion to vacate, set-aside or correct sentence

READ THE RULES OF APPELLATE PROCEDURE

Federal Appeals are governed by the Federal Rules of Appellate Procedure. State appeals are generally governed by that specific State's Rules of Appellate Procedure or applicable statutes. Therefore, it is a must, to read the Rules of Appellate Procedure when you're appealing a case. Here are a few reasons why it's necessary to read the Federal Rules of Appellate Procedure when you're appealing any district court decision by a federal court:

1.   Time limits for filing a "Notice Of Appeal" from an adverse decision in the federal courts are governed by Rule 4.

2.   Release in a criminal Case are governed by Rule 9.

3.   The Appellant is responsible for ordering the Record on Appeal. See Rule 10.

4.   Rule 11 governs Forwarding the Record.

5.   Rule 21 governs petition for writ of mandamus.

6.   Rule 22 governs "Certificate of Appealability" in habeas cases.

7.   Rule 24 governs Proceedings in Forma Pauperis.

8.   Rule 26 governs Computing and Extending Time.

9.   Rule 26.1 Corporate Disclosure.

10.   Rule 27 Motions.

11.   Rule 28 governs Appellant and Appellee Brief's, contents, size, length and Certificate of Compliance.

12.   Rule 32. Form of Briefs, Appendices, and Other Papers. This includes size of page, line spacing, text and signature, etc.

13.   Rule 34. Oral Argument.

14.   Rule 35. Petition For Hearing or Rehearing En Banc.

15.   Rule 40 governs Petition For Panel Rehearing.

16.   Rule 41 governs Mandates.

The Federal Rules of Appellate Procedure are easy to read and will guide you through the appellate process. As a general rule, the Federal Rules of Appellate Procedure has an APPENDIX OF FORMS at the end of the rules which will assist you in preparing various documents.

IN THE UNITED STATES DISTRICT COURT
FOR THE _____ DISTRICT OF _____
_____ DIVISION

_____

VS.   Case No. _____

_____

NOTICE OF APPEAL

_____

Notice is hereby given that, _____, the petitioner, pro se, hereby

appeals to the _____ Court of Appeals for the _____ Circuit from

the final judgment denying his _____, and all pleadings related thereto,

entered for record in the above action on the ____ day of _____, 200___.

RESPECTFULY SUBMITTED

_____
Name   Prison Number
PRO SE REPRESENTATION
Address
Town, State and Zip Code

IN THE UNITED STATES COURT OF APPEALS
FOR THE _____ CIRCUIT

UNITED STATES OF AMERICA,

VS.   **App. No. _____**

_____

Petitioner-Appellant.

MOTION FOR LEAVE TO PROCEED ON
APPEAL IN FORMA PAUPERIS

      COMES NOW_____, the petitioner, pro se, and respectfully moves this Honorable Court for leave to proceed on appeal through in forma pauperis from the judgment entered on ____ day of _____, 20___, denying petitioner's 28 U.S.C. §2255 motion, and motion for certificate of appealabiity, without prepayment of costs and fees and without giving security therefore. Mr. _____ filed a motion for leave to proceed on appeal through in forma pauperis in the District Court, but that court **failed to rule** on Mr. _____'s motion. Mr. _____ received a letter from the Clerk of the United States Court of Appeals for the _____ Circuit advising Mr. _____ that if he did not pay the $_____ filing and docketing fee within ( ) days that his appeal would be dismissed or alternatively he could file a motion for leave to proceed on appeal in forma pauperis. This motion follows.

      Mr. _____ states that because of his poverty he is unable to pay the costs of said proceeding or to give security therefore. The issues Mr. _____ desires to raise on appeal will entitle him to a reversal of the judgment below based on the following grounds:

[State Your Grounds For Relief]

      An affidavit in Support of this Motion to proceed on appeal in forma pauperis is attached hereto and made part of this motion by reference herein. Additionally, Mr. _____ has attached a certified copy of his inmate trust fund account for the past six months.

      Respectfully submitted on this _____ day of _____, 20_____.

_____
PRO SE REPRESENTATION

**IN THE
UNITED STATES COURT OF APPEALS
FOR THE _____ CIRCUIT
App. No. _____**

_____

_____,
Appellant-Petitioner,
VS.
UNITED STATES OF AMERICA,
Respondent-Appellee.

_____

**On Appeal from the United States District Court
For the _____ District of _____
_____Division
USDC Nos. _____**

_____

**MOTION FOR AN ENLARGEMENT OF TIME TO FILE
A MOTION FOR CERTIFICATE OF APPEALABILITY**

_____

TO THE HONORABLE JUDGES OF THE _____ CIRCUIT:

COMES NOW _____, the petitioner, pro se and respectfully moves this Honorable Court for an enlargement of time (30 days) pursuant to Federal Rules of Appellate Procedure, Rule 26(b), to file his motion for certificate of appealability. Petitioner will show this Honorable Court as follows:

1. This is the petitioner's first request for an enlargement of time to file his Motion For Certificate Of Appealability.

2. Petitioner currently represents himself pro se. Petitioner has no training in the field of law and needs the additional time to properly prepare and file his Motion for Certificate of Appealability.

3. Petitioner works at regular full time job at the Federal Correctional Institution _____, _____, with limited access to the law library. Petitioner needs the additional time to conduct his own research in order to properly prepare his motion.

4. Petitioner's current deadline for filing his Motion For Certificate Of Appealability is set for _____ ___, 20___. Petitioner requests an enlargement of time until _____ ___, 20___ to file his motion for certificate of appealability.

5. This motion is made in the interest of justice and not meant to delay the proceeding. The United States will not be prejudiced by a thirty (30) day delay.

WHEREFORE, based on the above, _____, urges this Honorable Court to grant him a thirty (30) day enlargement of time (to _____ ___, 20___) to file his Certificate of Appealability.

Respectfully submitted on this _____ day of _____ 20___.

_____
Name   Prison Number
PRO SE REPRESENTATION
Address
Town, State and Zip Code

[Your Name & Prison Number]
[Institution]
[Your Address]
[Town, State & Zip Code]

[Date]

UNITED STATES COURT OF APPEALS
FOR THE _____ CIRCUIT
OFFICE OF THE CLERK
Address _____
Town, State & Zip Code _____

Re: Appeal Number:
Case Style:
District Court Number:

Dear Clerk:

    Please find enclosed the original and four copies of my: MOTION FOR PERMISSION TO APPEAL IN FORMA PAUPERIS for filing with the Court. Additionally, enclosed is a self-addressed stamped envelope for the return of the fourth copy dated stamped.

    Thank you for your time.

                        Sincerely,

                        _____

                        [Your Name]

CC:
       _____, AUSA,
       p/file.

IN THE
UNITED STATES COURT OF APPEALS
FOR THE _____ CIRCUIT
App. No. _____

_____

_____,
Appellant-Petitioner,
VS.

_____,
Respondent-Appellee.

_____

On Appeal from the United States District Court
For the _____ District of _____
_____Division

_____

MOTION FOR PERMISSION TO APPEAL IN FORMA PAUPERIS

_____

TO THE HONORABLE JUDGES OF THE _____ CIRCUIT:

COMES NOW _____, the petitioner-appellant, pro se, and respectfully moves this Honorable Court for leave to proceed on appeal through in forma pauperis status from the judgment entered for record on _____ ____, 20___, denying Petitioner's 28 U.S.C. §2255 motion to vacate, set aside or correct sentence, without prepayment of costs, fees or giving security therefore.

An Affidavit Accompanying Motion For Permission to Appeal In Forma Pauperis.

Respectfully submitted on this _____ day of _____ 20___.

_____
Name   Prison Number
PRO SE REPRESENTATION
Your Address
Town, State, & Zip Code

309

IN THE UNITED STATES DISTRICT COURT
FOR THE _____ DISTRICT OF _____
_____ DIVISION

_____,

Petitioner,

VS.   **Civil No. _____**

UNITED STATES OF AMERICA

Respondent.

MOTION FOR ORDER OF DESIGNATION OF RECORD ON APPEAL

TO THE HONORABLE JUDGE OF SAID COURT:

COMES NOW_____, the petitioner, pro se, and respectfully moves this Court, pursuant to Federal Rules of Appellate Procedure, Rule 10(b)(1), for an order designating the record on appeal to include the following documents on file in the United States District Court Clerk's Office to wit:

1.   The trial transcripts from _____ ____, 20___, through _____ ____, 20___, which were previously transcribed for appellate purposes and should be on file in the Clerk's Office.

2.   The Presentence Report, Objections to the PSR, and the sentencing transcript dated _____ ____, 20___, which were previously transcribed for direct appeal and should be on file in the Clerk's Office.

3.   The jury verdict.

4.   All pleadings related to the 28 U.S.C. §2255 motion to vacate, set aside or correct sentence and the entire file in the Clerk's office related to this case.

WHEREFORE, based on above, _____, urges this Court to grant this motion and order the above documents to be designated as the record on appeal.

Respectfully submitted on this _____ ____, 20___,

_____
PRO SE REPRESENTATION

<u>CERTIFICATE OF SERVICE</u>

I HEREBY CERTIFY that a true and correct copy of this foregoing instrument has been mailed postage prepaid on this ____ day of _____ ____, 20___, to the: _____ _____ _____ _____.

Executed under penalty of perjury on this _____ ____, 20___,

_____

IN THE UNITED STATES DISTRICT COURT
FOR THE _____ DISTRICT OF _____
_____ DIVISION

_____,

Petitioner,

VS.   Civil No. _____

UNITED STATES OF AMERICA

Respondent.

ORDER OF DESIGNATION OF RECORD ON APPEAL

Came before the Court for consideration petitioner, _____'s motion for order of designation of record on appeal, pursuant to the Federal Rules Appellate Procedure, Rule 10(b)(1), for an order designating the record on appeal. This Court after careful review finds that the motion should be granted.

The Clerk shall prepare and file as the record on appeal the following documents: (1) The trial transcripts from _____ ____, 20___, through _____ ____, 20___; (2) The Presentence Report and Objections to the PSR; (3) the sentencing transcript dated _____ ____, 20___; (4) The jury verdict; and (4) all pleadings related to the 28 U.S.C. §2255 motion to vacate, set aside or correct sentence in the Clerk's office related to this case.

IT IS HEREBY ORDERED that the above listed documents are designated as the record on appeal.

Thus, done on this _____ day of _____ 20___.

_____
Presiding Judge

IN THE UNITED STATES DISTRICT COURT
FOR THE _____ DISTRICT OF _____
_____ DIVISION

UNITED STATES OF AMERICA,

      Respondent.

VS.   **Crim. No. _____**

_____

      Defendant.

STATEMENT OF EVIDENCE UNDER RULE 10(c) OF THE
APPELLATE PROCEDURE WHEN A TRANSCRIPT IS UNAVAILABLE

      COMES NOW_____, the defendant, pro se, and respectfully files this "Statement of Evidence Under Rule 10(c) of the Appellate Procedure When A Transcript Is Unavailable," as required by Rule 10(c) of the Federal Rules of Appellate Procedure.

<u>**STATEMENT OF EVIDENCE**</u>

1.

2.

3.

      The United States has ten (10) days to object to the above statement of evidence under Fed. R. App. P. 10(c). Alternatively, the United States can agree to the Statement of Evidence by signing below.

      Respectfully submitted on this ___ day of _____ 20 ___.

PRO SE REPRESENTATION

<u>AGREEMENT</u>

The United States agrees to the above, "Statement of Evidence" by signing here:

_____
United States Attorney

<u>CERTIFICATE OF SERVICE</u>

**IN THE UNITED STATES COURT OF APPEALS
FOR THE _____ CIRCUIT**
App. No.

_____,
Appellant-Movant,
VS.
UNITED STATES OF AMERICA,
Appellee-Respondent.

**On Appeal from the United States District Court
For the _____ District of _____
Criminal No. _____
Judge _____, Presiding**

MOTION FOR ISSUANCE OF CERTIFICATE OF APPEALABILITY

TO THE HONORABLE JUDGES OF THE _____ CIRCUIT:

COMES NOW _____, the movant-appellant, pro se, and respectfully moves this Honorable Court pursuant to **28 U.S.C. §2253(c)(2)** to issue a Certificate of Appealability ("COA") authorizing Mr. _____ to appeal the denial of his **28 U.S.C. §2255** motion to vacate, set aside or correct sentence. **See Slack v. McDaniel, 529 U.S. 473, 484, 120 S.Ct. 1595, 146 L.Ed.2d 542 (2000); Miller-El v. Cockrell, 537 U.S. 322, 123 S.Ct. 1029, 1039, 154 L.Ed.2d 931 (2003).**

I.
STATEMENT OF JURISDICTION

Jurisdiction to issue a COA is invoked pursuant **28 U.S.C. §§1291, 2253(c)(2); and 2255.**

II.
STATEMENT OF THE CASE

[A statement of the case can be drafted from the docket entry sheet].

III.
STATEMENT OF THE FACTS

[Present a clear statement of facts that support your procedural and constitutional claims].

313

A. Legal Standard for Certificate of Appealability

In **Henry v. Cockrell, 327 F.3d 429, 431 (5th Cir. 2003)**, the Fifth Circuit explained that: Under the Antiterrorism and Effective Death Penalty Act (AEDPA), a petitioner must obtain a certificate of appealability (COA) before he can appeal the district court decision. **28 U.S.C. §2253(c)(1)**. A COA will be granted only if the petitioner makes "a substantial showing of the denial of a constitutional right." **28 U.S.C. §2253(c)(2)**. In order to make a substantial showing, a petitioner must demonstrate that a "reasonable jurists would find the district court's assessment of the constitutional claim debatable or wrong." **Slack v. McDaniel, 529 U.S. 473, 484, 120 S.Ct. 1595, 146 L.Ed.2d 542 (2000)**. When the district court has denied a claim on procedural grounds, then the petitioner must demonstrate that a "jurists of reason would find it debatable whether the district court was correct in its procedural ruling." **id**. As the Supreme made clear in its decision in **Miller-El v. Cockrell, 537 U.S. 322, 123 S.Ct. 1029, 1039, 154 L.Ed.2d 931 (2003)**, a COA is "jurisdictional prerequisite," and "until a COA has been issued, the federal courts of appeals lacks jurisdiction to rule on the merits of appeals from habeas petitioners." When considering a request for a COA, "[t]he question is the debatability of the underlying constitutional claim, not the resolution of that debate." **id. at 1042**.

With this overview of the legal standard for issuance of a COA, Mr. _____ will proceed with his constitutional claims and show how they're debatable among jurists of reason.

§§§

ISSUE I

[State the procedure error committed by the Court]

[Make a substantial showing that the district court committed a procedural error in your case. Then demonstrate that your claim is debatable among jurists of reason and request that a COA be issued. A jurists of reason is a court decision that's in compliance with your claim or shows that a court could have resolved your claim in a different manner].

ISSUE II

[State your constitutional proposition]

[Make a substantial showing that your claim is of constitutional magnitude. Then demonstrate that your claim is debatable among jurists of reason and request that a COA be issued. A jurists of reason is a court decision that's in compliance with your claim or shows that a court could have resolved your claim in a different manner].

ISSUE III

[State your constitutional proposition]

[Make a substantial showing that your claim is of constitutional magnitude. Then demonstrate that your claim is debatable among jurists of reason and request that a COA be issued. A jurists of reason is a court decision that's in compliance with your claim or shows that a court could have resolved your claim in a different manner].

CONCLUSION

WHEREFORE, based on the above, _____, urges this Honorable Court issue a certificate of appealability authorizing Mr. _____ to appeal the district court's denial of his constitutional and procedural claims presented herein. Alternatively, grant the COA and remand for further proceedings.

Respectfully submitted on this _____ day of _____ 20___.

_____
Name   Prison Number
PRO SE REPRESENTATION
Address
Town, State and Zip Code

CERTIFICATE OF SERVICE

I HEREBY CERTIFY that a true and correct copy of this foregoing instrument has been mailed postage prepaid on this _____ day of _____ 20___, to the Assistant United States Attorney, _____, P.O. Box _____ _____, _____, _____.

_____
Name

IN THE
UNITED STATES COURT OF APPEALS
FOR THE _____ CIRCUIT

_____

App. No. _____

_____

Appellant-Petitioner,

VS.

_____,

Respondent-Appellee.

_____

MOTION TO BE LOANED/FURNISHED A COPY
OF THE RECORD ON APPEAL

_____

TO THE HONORABLE JUDGES OF THE _____ **CIRCUIT:**

    COMES NOW _____, the Appellant, pro se, and respectfully moves this Honorable Court to be loaned/furnished a copy of the record on appeal. Apellant will show this Court as follows:

    1.   The Appellant requests to be loaned/furnished a copy of the record on appeal for briefing purposes only.

    2.   Appellant needs the record in order to adequately prepare his Appellant's Opening Brief and refer this Court's attention to specific locations in the record that support his arguments, in accordance with Rule 28 (a)(9)(A) (appellant's contentions and the reason for them, with citations to the authorities and parts of the record on which the appellant relies"). The record supports Appellant's arguments. However, without a copy of the record it is impossible for the Apellant to tie the record to his arguments.

    3.   Appellant will return the record upon completing his Appellant's Opening Brief.

    4.   This motion is made in the interest of justice and not meant to delay the proceedings.

    WHEREFORE, based on the above, _____, urges this Honorable Court to grant this motion and loan/furnish him a copy of the record on appeal.

    Respectfully submitted on this _____ day of _____ 20 ___.

_____
PRO SE REPRESENTATION

Form Letter No. 2

[Your Name & Prison Number]
[Institution]
[Your Address]
[Town, State & Zip Code]

[Date]

UNITED STATES COURT OF APPEALS
FOR THE _____ CIRCUIT
OFFICE OF THE CLERK
Address _____
Town, State & Zip Code ____

Re: _____ v. _____ ,
    App. No. _____

Dear Clerk:

Please find enclosed the original and three copies of my: CERTIFICATE OF INTERESTED PERSONS AND CORPORATE DISCLOSURE, for filing with the Court.

Your assistance on this matter is greatly appreciated. Thank you for your time.

Sincerely,

_____
[Your Name]

CC:
    p/file.

IN THE
UNITED STATES COURT OF APPEALS
FOR THE _____ CIRCUIT

_____

No. _____

_____

_____

Appellant-Petitioner,

VS.

UNITED STATES OF AMERICA,

Appellee-Respondent.

On Appeal from the United States District Court
For the _____ District of _____
District Court Nos. _____

CERTIFICATE OF INTERESTED PERSONS AND CORPORATE DISCLOSURE

The undersigned Petitioner, pro se, of record certifies that the following listed persons and entities have an interest in the outcome of this case. These representations are made in order that the judges of this court may evaluate possible disqualifications of recusal.

Honorable _____
United States District Judge
_____, pro se
Appellant-Petitioner

United States Of America, and its
counsel _____

Respectfully submitted on this ____ day of _____ 20 ___.

_____

IN THE
UNITED STATES COURT OF APPEALS
FOR THE _____ CIRCUIT

_____

App. No. _____

_____

_____

Appellant-Petitioner,

VS.

_____,

Respondent-Appellee.

**MOTION FOR AN ENLARGEMENT OF TIME
TO FILE APPELLANT'S OPENING BRIEF**

TO THE HONORABLE JUDGES OF THE _____ CIRCUIT:
  COMES NOW _____, the Appellant, pro se, and respectfully moves this Honorable Court for a thirty (30) day enlargement of time pursuant to Federal Rules of Appellate Procedure, Rule 26(b), to file Appellant's Opening Brief. Appellant will show this Court as follows:

  1. This is appellant's first request for an enlargement of time to file Appellant's Opening Brief.

  2. Appellant currently represents himself pro se. He has had no training in the field of law and needs the additional time to properly prepare and file his motion for certificate of appealability.

  3. Appellant works a full time job at the _____ Correctional Institution, _____, _____, and he has limited access to the law library. Appellant needs the additional time to conduct his own research and to properly prepare his motion for certificate of appealability.

  4. This motion is made in the interest of justice and is not meant to delay the proceeding. The _____ will not be prejudiced by the delay.

  WHEREFORE, based on the above, _____, urges this Honorable Court to grant him a thirty (30) day enlargement of time to file his Appellant's Opening Brief.

  Respectfully submitted on this ___ day of _____ 20 ___.

_____
PRO SE REPRESENTATION

319

IN THE
UNITED STATES COURT OF APPEALS
FOR THE _____ CIRCUIT

_____

App. No. _____

_____

_____

Appellant-Defendant,

VS.

_____,

Appellee-Respondent.

**MOTION FOR EXTENSION OF TIME TO FILE PETITION
FOR REHEARING AND REHEARING EN BANC**

TO THE HONORABLE JUDGES OF THE _____ **CIRCUIT:**
    COMES NOW _____, the Appellant, pro se, and respectfully moves this Court pursuant to Federal Rules of Appellate Procedure, Rule 26(b) and 27 for an order extending the time to file a Petition for Rehearing; rehearing en banc, or a certiorari, from the current date of _____ ___, 20____, for a period of thirty (30) days, to _____ ___, 20____, because of the following reasons:

    1.   The Appellant received a copy of this Court decision in the above entitled action on _____ ___, 20____.

    2.   The Appellant had been in the local hospital from _____ ___, 20____, through _____ ___, 20____, for _____ and all of his legal material was packed away by Staff and just returned to Appellant on _____ ___, 20____.

    3.   The delay in Appellant receiving a copy of this Court's decision and being hospitalized for _____ is and was beyond the Appellant's control.

    4.   This motion is made in the interest of justice and not meant to delay the proceedings.

    WHEREFORE based on the above, _____, urges this Honorable Court to grant an order extending the time by thirty (30) days to file a Petition for rehearing; rehearing en banc, or a certiorari.

    Respectfully submitted on this _____ day of _____ 20 ___.

_____
PRO SE REPRESENTATION

**IN THE
UNITED STATES COURT OF APPEALS
FOR THE _____ CIRCUIT**

_____

App. No. _____

_____

Appellant,

VS.

_____

Appellee.

On Appeal from the United States District Court
For the _____ District of _____
_____ Division
USDC No. _____

MOTION FOR PERMISSION TO FILE OVERSIZED BRIEF

TO THE HONORABLE JUDGES OF THE _____ CIRCUIT:

      COMES NOW _____, the appellant, pro se, and respectfully moves this Honorable Court for an order granting him permission to file oversized brief pursuant to Federal Rules of Appellate Procedure, Rule 32(7), which exceeds the page limit set by Rule 32(7), by ____ additional pages. Appellant will show this Court as follows:

      1.   Appellant's proceeding pro se and has had no training in the field of law and needs the additional ____ pages to properly litigate his claims. Fed. R. App. P. 32(7)(A) provides that: "A principal brief may not exceed 30 pages, ..." Appellant requests this Court to issue an order granting him permission to file a <u>33</u> page brief which includes the: "Statement of Jurisdiction, Statement of the Case, Statement of the Facts, Statement of Issues, Summary of Arguments, Arguments, Conclusion, Certificate of Service and Certificate of Compliance," and all other essential elements as required by Fed. R. App. P. 28.

      2.   The complexity of the facts and issues involved in this appeal warrant granting Appellant permission to file an oversized brief. One issue is a first impression in this Court which involves a split among other circuit court of appeals and the oversized brief addresses each circuit court's holding.

321

3.   The remaining issues deal with the savings clause provision of 28 U.S.C. §2255(e), which have never been addressed by the court. Under the discrete facts and circumstances it would be unfair and unreasonable not to grant the Appellant permission to file an oversized Appellant's Brief.

4.   Appellant makes this motion in the interest of justice and not meant to delay the proceedings.

WHEREFORE based on the above, _____, prays that this Honorable Court grants this motion and issues an order given him permission to file a ____ page brief.

Respectfully submitted on this ____ day of _____, 20___.

_____
PRO SE REPRESENTATION

<u>CERTIFICATE OF SERVICE</u>

I HEREBY CERTIFY that a true and correct copy of this foregoing instrument has been mailed with first class postage affixed thereto on this ____ day of _____, 20__, by hand delivering the same to Mail Room Staff for processing through the internal legal mail system correctly addressed to:

Executed on this ____ day of _____, 20___.

_____

IN THE
UNITED STATES COURT OF APPEALS
FOR THE _____ CIRCUIT

_____

App. No. _____

_____

Appellant,

VS.

_____

Appellee.

On Appeal from the United States District Court
For the _____ District of _____
_____ Division
USDC No. _____

MOTION FOR LEAVE TO FILE AN OUT-OF-TIME APPEAL

TO THE HONORABLE JUDGES OF THE _____ CIRCUIT:

COMES NOW _____, the appellant, pro se, and respectfully moves this Honorable Court for leave to file out-of-time the appellant's brief attached hereto, which was due on the ___ day of _____, 20___, pursuant to Federal Rules of Appellate Procedure, Rule 26(b). Appellant will show this Court as follows:

1.   The _____ brief was scheduled to be filed on ___ day of _____, 20___.

2.   Appellate Rule 26(b) allows this court to extend the time beyond the scheduled filing deadline.

3.   For reasons completely beyond _____ control, it was impossible to file the brief timely. Timely filing became impossible on the ___ day of _____, 20___, the date that _____ Correctional Institution _____, _____, was placed in locked status and no movement by prisoner's was allowed throughout the institution. See Exhibit "___" Memorandum from _____ Correctional Institution showing the institution was on lock down status until the ___ day of _____, 20___.

4.   _____ was not able to complete his typing, copying and mailing of the attached brief until this date because of the locked down status.

5. _____ makes this motion in the interest of justice and not meant to delay the proceedings.

WHEREFORE based on the above, _____, prays that this Honorable Court grants this motion and allows him to file the out-of-time brief attached hereto.

Respectfully submitted on this ____ day of _____, 20___.

_____
PRO SE REPRESENTATION

<u>CERTIFICATE OF SERVICE</u>

I HEREBY CERTIFY that a true and correct copy of this foregoing instrument has been mailed with first class postage affixed thereto on this ____ day of _____, 20__, by hand delivering the same to Mail Room Staff for processing through the internal legal mail system correctly addressed to:

Executed on this ____ day of _____, 20___.

_____

Form Letter No. 3

[Your Name & Prison Number]
[Institution]
[Your Address]
[Town, State & Zip Code]

[Date]

Office of the Clerk
United States Court of Appeals
Address_____
Town, State & Zip Code_____

Re: _____ v. _____,
     App. No. _____

Dear Clerk:

Please find enclosed the original and three copies of my: "Appellant's Opening Brief, and a Motion For Permission To Proceed on Appeal In Forma Pauperis" for filing with the Court.

Your assistance on this matter is greatly appreciated. Thank you.

Sincerely,

_____
[Your Name]

CC:
     p/file.

IN THE

UNITED STATES COURT OF APPEALS

FOR THE _____ CIRCUIT

_____

App. No. _____

_____

_____Name_____

Petitioner-Appellant,

VS.

_____Respondent's Name___

_____,

Respondent-Appellee.

On Appeal from the United States District Court
For the _____ District of _____
_____ Division
USSD No. _____

APPELLANT'S OPENING BRIEF

Name
PRO SE REPRESENTATION
Address
Town, State, Zip Code

IN THE

UNITED STATES COURT OF APPEALS

FOR THE _____ CIRCUIT

_____

App. No. _____

_____

_____Name_____

Petitioner-Appellant,

VS.

_____Respondent's Name, Warden, and
_____, Attorney General,

Respondent-Appellee.

On Appeal from the United States District Court
For the _____ District of _____
_____ Division
USSD No. _____

APPELLANT'S OPENING BRIEF

Name
PRO SE REPRESENTATION
Address
Town, State, Zip Code

_____ v. _____

App. No. _____

USDC No. _____

CERTIFICATE OF INTERESTED PERSONS AND CORPORATE DISCLOSURE

The Appellant, _____, pro se, certifies that to his knowledge only the below listed persons or entities have an interest in the outcome of these proceedings. These representations are made so that the Judges of this Court may evaluate the possible disqualification or recusals.

_____, Appellant, pro se,
Address
Town, State & Zip Code

Opposing Party
Address
Town, State & Zip Code

Honorable Judge _____
Address

Town, State & Zip Code

_____
Name

STATEMENT REGARDING ORAL ARGUMENT

This case presents a first impression dealing with the savings clause of 28 U.S.C. §2255e, and may require additional briefing and appointment of counsel. Oral argument may benefit this Court during its decisional making process.

TABLE OF CONTENTS

TABLE OF AUTHORITIES

TABLE OF AUTHORITIES

UNITED STATES CODE
18 U.S.C. §922(g)(1)
18 U.S.C. §924€
28 U.S.C. §1291
28 U.S.C. §2241
28 U.S.C. §2255€

Fifth Amendment Due Process Clause

IN THE

UNITED STATES COURT OF APPEALS

FOR THE _____ CIRCUIT

_____

App. No. _____

_____

Petitioner-Appellant,

VS.

_____

_____,

Respondent-Appellee.

APELLANT'S OPENING BRIEF

TO THE HONORABLE JUDGES OF THE _____ CIRCUIT:

      COMES NOW _____, the Appellant, pro se, and respectfully files this Appellant's Opening Brief seeking reversal of the district court's judgment entered below. The Appellant (hereinafter "_____") will show this Court as follows:

I.
STATEMENT OF JURISDICTION

      Jurisdiction of this Court is invoked pursuant to **28 U.S.C. §§1291, 2241, 2243** and **2255(e)**. The district court had jurisdiction to entertain a petition for writ of habeas corpus pursuant to **28 U.S.C. §2241**.

II.
STATEMENT OF THE CASE

    A. Course of the proceedings below:

      On _____ ___, 20___, _____ filed a petition for writ of habeas corpus pursuant to 28 U.S.C. §2241 in the United States District Court for the _____ District of _____, _____ Division, challenging the legality of his detention. (Dkt. No. 1-2). _____ argued that in the wake of **Begay**, and **Chambers**, his prior conviction for escape does not qualify as a violent felony under the Armed Career Criminal Act. (Doc. 1-2 at 8-10). _____ argued that 28 U.S.C. §2255 provides an "inadequate and ineffective" remedy (Dkt. No. 1 at 13-14). _____ argued that **Begay** and **Chambers** were retroactive Supreme Court decisions because they decided a meaning of a criminal statute enacted by Congress. (Dkt. No. 1-2 at 8-13).

On _____ ___, 20___, the district court issued a show cause order directing the respondent to show cause, in writing why _____'s writ should not be granted within twenty (20) days of the date of service. (Dkt. No. 3).

On _____ ___, 20___, the Assistant United States Attorney _____, representing the respondent filed a motion to dismiss.

On or about _____ ___, 20___, _____ filed a reply in opposition to the respondent's motion to dismiss.

On _____ ___, 20___, the United States Magistrate Judge issued a report and recommendation to deny _____'s §2241 habeas petition. (Dkt. No. 13).

On or about _____ ___, 20___, _____ filed "objections to (the) report and recommendation." (Dkt. No. 15).

On _____ ___, 20___, the district court issued an opinion addressing _____ objections to the Magistrate Judge's report and recommendation. On that same date, the Court issued a final judgment denying _____ §2241 habeas petition.

On _____ ___, 20___, _____ filed a notice of appeal and a motion for permission to appeal in forma pauperis.

On _____ ___, 20___, the district court issued an order denying _____'s motion to proceed on appeal through in forma pauperis.

This appeal follows.

III.
STATEMENT OF THE FACTS

1. _____ was charged with possession of a firearm and ammunition by a convicted felon in the _____ District of Florida, _____ Division, in violation of 18 U.S.C. §922(g)(1) and 924(e) (Case No. _____). _____ proceeded to trial and was convicted for possession of ammunition by a convicted felon, in violation of 18 U.S.C. §§922(g)(1) and 924(e).

2. At sentencing the district court concluded that _____ prior conviction for: (1) a 1967 conviction for armed robbery; (2) a 1986 conviction for attempted homicide; and (3) a 1987 conviction for escape required the court to sentence _____ under the Armed Career Criminal Act. Defense counsel objected to the use of the escape, in violation of Fla Law Ch. 944.10 claiming that it was a walk away and not a crime of violence, but conceded that **United States v. Gay, 251 F.3d 950 (11th Cir. 2001)**, held otherwise.

3.   On September 25, 2003, the United States District Court for the Middle District of Florida, sentenced _____ to 235 months imprisonment to be followed by five (5) years supervised release under the Armed Career Criminal Act.

4.   _____ appealed claiming that the district court erred (1) denying his motion to suppress and (2) by enhancing his sentence based on his prior convictions that were not proven to the jury beyond a reasonable doubt. The Eleventh Circuit affirmed the conviction and sentence.

5.   On March 21, 2005, _____ filed a 28 U.S.C. §2255 motion in the district court of conviction (Case Number3:05cv249-J-25HTS). In his motion, _____ argue that: (1) the district court erred by sentencing him as an Armed Career Criminal; (2) counsel was ineffective for failing to object to the same; (3) the district court constructively amended the indictment; (4) counsel was ineffective for failing to object to the same; (5) counsel was ineffective during pretrial stage for failing to advise him to admit guilty so he could get a sentence reduction for acceptance of responsibility. The district court denied _____'s§2255 motion.

6.   _____ filed a timely notice of appeal and sought a certificate of appealability from the Eleventh Circuit which was denied.

7.   _____ filed his §2241 habeas petition asserting that his prior conviction for escape, in violation of Florida Law Ch. 944.40, no longer constitutes a "violent felony" in light of the new interpretation of 18 U.S.C. §924(e)(2)(B)(ii), by the Supreme Court in **Begay** and **Chambers**. _____ is actually innocent of being an Armed Career Criminal in light of **Begay** and **Chambers** and he was sentenced to the ACCA based on a nonexistent predicate offense.

8.   _____ conviction of being a felon in possession of ammunition under 18 U.S.C. §922(g)(1)—would ordinarily subject him to a term of imprisonment not to exceed ten (10) years. 18 U.S.C. §924(a)(2).

9.   The Magistrate Judge Report and Recommendation recommended that _____'s §2241 habeas petition be dismissed because he could not satisfy the second prong of **Wofford**.

10.   _____ filed numerous objections to the Magistrate Judge's Report and Recommendation.

11.   On April 8, 2010, the district court issued an opinion addressing _____ objections to the Magistrate Judge's Report and Recommendation. The district court concluded that "_____ clearly meets the first and third Prongs of **Wofford** requirements: _____ (and _____) applies retroactively, and Circuit precedent precluded Mr._____ argument at the time of his original section 2255 motion (which must be brought within one year of conviction)." The district court found that "_____ objects to the Magistrate Judge's use and interpretation of **Wofford**, the Magistrate Judge's conclusion that Mr. _____ failed to show that section 2255 is an ineffective or inadequate remedy, the Magistrate Judge's Report insofar as it constitutes an unconstitutional suspension of the writ of habeas corpus, and the Magistrate conclusion that **Wofford** applies to his claims. All of these objections surround the Magistrate Judge's interpretation of **Wofford**." The district court concluded

that _____ could not show the second prong of **Wofford**: "(2) the holding of that Supreme Court decision establishes the petitioner was convicted for a nonexistent offense."

§

STATEMENT OF THE ISSUES

1.   Whether the district court erred denying _____'s §2241 habeas petition based on the second prong of **Wofford** where _____ was sentenced under the Armed Career Criminal Act based on a nonexistent predicate offense, in light of the retroactively applicable Supreme Court decisions **Begay** and **Chambers**? Yes.

2.   Whether the **Wofford** savings clause extends to sentencing claims under the Armed Career Criminal Act based on a nonexistent predicate offense, in light of the retroactively applicable Supreme Court decision **Chambers**? Yes.

3.   Whether the district court erred denying _____'s habeas corpus petition without conducting an evidentiary hearing to afford _____ an opportunity to prove he is actually innocent of the ACCA? Yes.

§

SUMMARY OF THE ARGUMENTS

First, _____ argues that the district court erred relying on the second prong of **Wofford** to deny his habeas petition because he meets the criteria for the second prong. _____ argues a due process violation because his sentence exceeds the statutory maximum as he was sentenced under the Armed Career Criminal Act based on a nonexistence predicate offense, in light of the retroactively applicable Supreme Court decisions **Begay** and **Chambers**. The district court's failure to allow _____ to proceed through the savings clause constitutes a suspension of the writ, in violation of the Constitution.

Second, _____ argues that **Wofford** savings clause extends to sentencing claims under the Armed Career Criminal Act based on a nonexistent predicate offense, in light of the retroactively applicable Supreme Court decision **Chambers**.

Third, the district court abused its discretion denying _____ habeas petition without conducting an evidentiary hearing to afford him an opportunity to prove that he is actually innocent of the Armed Career Criminal Act because he was sentenced based on a nonexistent predicate offense, in light of the retroactively applicable Supreme Court decisions **Begay** and **Chambers**.

§

The district court erred denying _____ §2241 habeas petition based on the second prong of **Wofford** where _____ was sentenced under the Armed Career Criminal Act based on a nonexistent predicate offense in light of the retroactive applicable Supreme Court decisions **Begay** and **Chambers**

Standard of Review

The availability of habeas corpus relief under 28 U.S.C. §2241 savings clause presents a question of law this Court reviews de novo. **Darby v. Hawk-Sawyer**, 405 F.3d 942, 943 (11th Cir. 2005).

ARGUMENTS AND AUTHORITIES

The district court committed reversible error denying _____'s §2241 habeas petition based on the second prong of **Wofford** where _____ was sentenced to 235 months under the Armed Career Criminal Act enhancement provision based upon a nonexistent predicate offense, in light of the retroactively applicable Supreme Court decision. See **Wofford v. Scott**, 177 F.3d 1236, 1244-45 (11th Cir. 1999).[2] _____ is currently in custody, in violation of the Constitution or laws of the United States which is cognizable under habeas petition pursuant to **28 U.S.C. §2241(c)(3)**.

Unlike **Wofford**, _____ is relying on a retroactively applicable Supreme Court decision, **Chambers v. United States**, 129 S.Ct. 687, 172 L.Ed.2d 484 (2009); **Begay v. United States**, 128 S.Ct. 1581, 1583, 170 L.Ed.2d 490 (2008); **United States v. Shipp, Jr.**, 589 F.3d 1084, 1089-90 (10th Cir. 2009) (**Chambers** which involved a substantive rule of statutory interpretation applied retroactively habeas petitioner).

While discussing its second prong the **Wofford** Court stated: **"We need not decide whether** the savings clause **extends** to **sentencing claims** in those circumstances, or what a 'fundamental defect' in a sentence might be. It is enough to hold, as we do, that only sentencing claims that may conceivably be covered by the savings clause are those based upon a retroactively applicable Supreme Court decision overturning circuit precedent." **Wofford, 177 F.3d at 1244-45**.

---

[2] The **Wofford** Court adopted the Seventh Circuit's approach on the savings clause. The Court stated: "We think the Seventh Circuit's **[In re] Davenport]**, 147 F.3d 605, 611 (7th Cir. 1998)] approach is better reasoned than those of the other circuits, and its rule has the advantage of being specific. We adopt it as it comports with the following holding: The savings clause of §2255 applies to a claim when: (1) that claim is based upon a retroactively applicable Supreme Court decision; (2) the holding of that Supreme Court decision establishes the petitioner was convicted for a nonexistent offense; and, (3) circuit law squarely foreclosed such a claim at the time it other should have been raised in the petitioner's trial, appeal, or first §2255 motion." **Wofford, 177 F.3d at 1244**.

Under the discrete circumstance and facts of _____ case, the savings clause is applicable. See **Goldman v. Winn, 565 F.Supp.2d 200, 213 (D. Mass. 2008). Superintendent, Great Meadow Corr. Facility, 219 F.3d 162, 171 (2ⁿᵈ Cir. 2000); United States v. Mikalajunas, 186 F.3d 490, 495 (4ᵗʰ Cir. 1999); Haley v. Cockrell, 306 F.3d 257, 265 (5ᵗʰ Cir. 2002).**

The Circuits that have determined that the actual innocence exception may be extended to noncapital sentencing cases reasoning that the Supreme Court stated that the purpose of the rule is grounded in equitable discretion of habeas courts to see that federal constitutional errors do not result in the incarceration of innocent persons. See **Haley, 306 F.3d at 265 (quoting Herrera v. Collins, 506 U.S. 390, 404, 113 S.Ct. 853, 122 L.Ed.2d 203 (1992)).** It appears, that Eleventh Circuit has not addressed this issue. However, Judge Lazzara in the Middle District in **George v. United States, 2009 U.S. Dist. LEXIS 44788 (M.D. Fla. 2009)**, held that the actual innocence exception applies to noncapital sentencing cases. See also **Frederick v. United States, 2009 U.S. DIst. LEXIS 72701 (S.D. Fla. 2009)**.

_____ proved that Section 2255(h) provided an "Ineffective and Inadequate remedy" to challenge the legality of his detention based upon a retroactively applicable Supreme Court decision based on the substantive reach of a federal criminal statute. See **Lorentsen v. Hood, 223 F.3d 950, 953 (9ᵗʰ Cir. 2000); Reyes-Requena v. United States, 243 F.3d 893, 901-903 fn. 19, 20-29 (5ᵗʰ Cir. 2001); In re Jones, 226 F.3d 328, 333-34 (4ᵗʰ Cir. 2000); Wofford, 177 F.3d at 1244.** See also **§2241 M.B. at pp. 13-14.**

In **Triestman v. United States, 124 F.3d 361, 377 (2ⁿᵈ Cir. 1997)**, the Second Circuit devised its savings clause test based on whether failure to permit a remedy would "raise serious constitutional questions." **Triestman, 124 F.3d at 377.** Whenever a judge believes "justice would seem to demand a forum for the prisoner's claim in so pressing a fashion as to cast doubt on the constitutionality of the law that would bar the §2255 petition," the prisoner would be permitted access to habeas corpus writs. See id. at **378.** _____ case raises serious constitutional questions which should open the §2241 savings clause for relief. See **Triestman and Goldman, both supra**.

Failure to grant relief in _____ case results in the suspension of the writ, in violation of the United States Constitution Article I, Section 9 Clause 2 ("The Privilege of the Writ of Habeas Corpus shall not be suspended, unless when in Cases of Rebellion or Invasion the public Safety may require it."); **United States v. Hayman, 342 U.S. 205, 223, 72 S.Ct. 263, 96 L.Ed. 232 (1952).**

The aforementioned facts, arguments and authorities stand for the proposition that **Wofford** second prong was met where _____ was sentenced under the ACCA based upon a nonexistent predicate offense, in light of the retroactively applicable Supreme Court decisions in **Begay** and **Chambers**. _____ is actually innocent of being a ACCA and habeas relief should be granted under the savings clause. See, **e.g., Wofford, Triestman** and **Goldman, both supra.**

In 1993 **Goldman** was sentenced as a Career Offender under **USSG §4B1.1**, because of two qualifying prior convictions. One predicate offense was a 1977 conviction in the Massachusetts Superior Court for a kidnapping. In 2001 the court vacated the kidnapping conviction. **Goldman, 565 F.Supp.2d at 202-03**. The **Goldman** court allowed the petitioner to proceed under section 2241 when the petitioner was able to demonstrate that he was actually innocent of one of the prior convictions (kidnapping) underlying the Career Offender enhancement. Id. **at 228**. _____ is actually innocent of the Armed Career Criminal Act enhancement provision based upon a retroactively applicable Supreme Court decisions. **Chambers v. United States, 129 S.Ct. 687, 172 L.Ed.2d 484 (2009)**; and **Begay**, supra.

_____ presented a Fifth Amendment Due Process sentencing claim based upon a retroactively applicable Supreme Court decision **Begay** and **Chambers** which overturned Eleventh Circuit precedent. See, e.g., **United States v. Gay, 251 F.3d 950 (11th Cir. 2001); United States v. Harrison, 558 F.3d 1280, 1284 (11th Cir. 2009); United States v. Skipp Jr., 589 F.3d 1084, 1089-90 (10th Cir. 2009)** (**Chambers** which involved a substantive rule of statutory interpretation applied retroactively habeas petitioner).

Construing Mr. _____'s pro se pleadings liberally he is raising a due process challenge to the length of his sentence which exceeds the statutory maximum authorized by law based upon a retroactively applicable Supreme Court decision. Since **In re Winship, 397 U.S. 358, 90 S.Ct. 1068, 25 L.Ed.2d 368 (1970)**, the Supreme Court has "made clear beyond a peradventure that **Winship's** due process [ ] protections extend, to some degree, to determinations that [go] not to a defendant's guilt or innocence, but simply to the length of his sentence." **Apprendi v. New Jersey, 530 U.S. 466, 481, 120 S.Ct. 2348, 147 L.Ed.2d 435 (2000)**. Indeed, "due process requires [ ] that the sentence for the crime of conviction not exceed the statutory maximum." **United States v. Grier, 475 F.3d 556, 573 (3d Cir. 2007)**.

_____ offense of conviction of being a felon in possession of ammunition under **18 U.S.C. §922(g)(1)** carries a maximum statutory penalty of ten years. See **18 U.S.C. §924(a)(2)**. See **Shipp, 589 F.3d at 1088**. Under the ACCA, defendants qualifying as "armed career criminals" are subject to a mandatory minimum prison term of fifteen years to life. See **§924(e)(1)**; **Chambers, 129 S.Ct. at 689**. Relying in part on Mr. _____'s prior escape conviction, the sentencing court concluded that Mr. _____'s three prior violent felonies made him an armed career criminal. As such, Mr. _____ was sentenced to 235 months' imprisonment, nine (9) years and seven (7) months over the statutory maximum for the offense of conviction. See **§924(a)(2)**. The legal errors in _____'s case are fundamental and have resulted in a complete miscarriage of justice by causing _____ to be sentenced to an extra nine years and seven months for the Armed Career Criminal enhancement which he is actually innocent of based upon a retroactively applicable Supreme Court decision. **Chambers, supra.**

_____ is actually innocent of being an "Armed Career Criminal" and his sentence exceeds the statutory maximum ten (10) years which he has served and is currently being restrained of his liberty, in violation of Fifth Amendment Due Process Clause of the United States Constitution. See **Shipp, 589 F.3d at 1088; Spence v.**

———— § ————

ISSUE II

The <u>Wofford</u> savings clause extends to sentencing claims under the Armed Career Criminal Act based on a nonexistent predicate offenses in light of the retroactively applicable Supreme Court decision <u>Chambers</u>

<u>Standard of Review</u>

The availability of habeas corpus relief under 28 U.S.C. §2241 savings clause presents a question of law this Court reviews de novo. **Darby v. Hawk-Sawyer, 405 F.3d 942, 943 (11th Cir. 2005).**

<u>ARGUMENTS AND AUTHORITIES</u>

In the wake of the **Bailey v. United States, 516 U.S. 137, 133 L.Ed.2d 472, 116 S.Ct. 501 (1995)**, era the Eleventh Circuit in **Wofford** adopted its savings clause test from the Seventh Circuit, **In re Davenport, 147 F.3d 605, 611 (7th Cir. 1998)**. See **Wofford, 177 F.3d at 1244.** During the **Bailey** era court's addressed the applicability of the savings clause to federal prisoners challenging the legality of his detention, in light of **Bailey** which went directly to challenging the conviction not sentence.

This case presents a first impression and requires this Court to extend its **Wofford** decision to a sentencing claim based upon a retroactively applicable Supreme Court decision **Chambers**, which establishes that _____ has been sentenced under the ACCA based on a nonexistent predicate offense. See **United States v. Shipp, Jr., 589 F.3d at 1089-90 (10th Cir. 2009).**

_____ argues that the district court erred where it reached the erroneous conclusion of law that the savings clause did not provide relief for a sentencing claim based upon a retroactive applicable Supreme Court decision that establishes that _____ was sentenced as a Armed Career Criminal based upon a nonexistent predicate offense, in light of a retroactively applicable Supreme Court decision **Begay** and **Chambers**. See **Wofford v. Scott, 177 F.3d 1236, 1244-45 (11th Cir. 1999)** ("It is enough to hold, as we do, that the only sentencing claims that may conceivable be covered by the savings clause are those based upon a retroactively applicable Supreme Court decision overturning circuit precedent"); **Flint v. Jordan, 514 F.3d 1165, 1168 (11th Cir. 2008)** ("We need not address whether any of **Wofford's** other requirement are met, nor do we decide whether the savings clause could ever apply to a sentencing claim. See id. at 1245 ('It is enough to hold, as we do, that the only sentencing claims that may conceivably be covered by the savings clause are those based upon a retroactively applicable Supreme Court decision overturning circuit precedent").

Wofford applies to sentencing claims which establishes _____ was sentenced as a Armed Career Criminal based upon a nonexistent predicate offense, in light of the retroactively applicable Supreme Court decisions **Begay**, and **Chambers, supra**. This Court should reverse the judgment below and remand for further proceedings.

_____ § _____

ISSUE III

The district court erred denying _____ habeas corpus petition without conducting an evidentiary hearing to afford _____ an opportunity to prove he is actually innocent of the ACCA?

Standard of Review

This Court reviews issues of law related to the denial of a habeas relief under §2241 de novo. **Royal v. Tombone, 141 F.3d 596, 599 (5th Cir. 1998)**. This Court reviews the district court decision not to conduct an evidentiary hearing for abuse of discretion. **United States v. Massey, 89 F.3d 1433, 1443 (11th Cir. 1996)**. This Court also reviews pro se brief liberally. **Johnson v. Quarterman, 479 F.3d 358, 359 (5th Cir. 2007)**.

ARGUMENTS AND AUTHORITIES

The Supreme Court in **Bouseley v. United States, 523 U.S. 614, 140 L.Ed.2d 828, 118 S.Ct. 1604 (1998)**, found that the accused will be entitled to a hearing on the merits of his claim contesting the validity of his conviction to permit him to attempt to make a showing of actual innocence to relieve his procedural default. See **Jones v. United States, 153 F.3d 1305 (11th Cir. 1998)**.

In **Jones**, the defendant pleaded guilty to using and carrying a firearm during and in relation to a drug trafficking offense. Jones filed a 28 U.S.C. §2255 motion contending that the evidence did not support the conviction and that his plea was not voluntary after the Supreme Court's ruling in **Bailey** the district court denied the §2255 motion without conducting an evidentiary hearing. Jones appealed claiming that the Supreme Court's decision in **Bouseley, 118 S.Ct. 1604, 140 L.Ed.2d 828 (1998)**, required the case to be remanded for a hearing to determine whether Jones is actually innocent of the **18 U.S.C. §924(c)(1)**, charge and therefore can establish cause for procedural bar. The Eleventh Circuit remanded for a hearing. See **Jones, 153 F.3d at 1305**.

_____ maintains that the exact same scenario applies to his case and that this Court should vacate and remand for a hearing. See **Jones** and **Bouseley, supra**.

_____ § _____

341

CONCLUSION

WHEREFORE, based on the above foregoing facts, arguments and authorities, _____ prays that this Honorable Court **REVERSES** the judgment below and remands with instructions to entertain the merits of his petition for writ of habeas corpus.

Respectfully submitted on this _____ day of _____ 20 ____.

_____
PRO SE REPRESENTATION

CERTIFICATE OF SERVICE

I HEREBY CERTIFY that a true and correct copy of this foregoing instrument has been deposited in Federal Correctional Institution _____, _____, prison internal legal mailing system with first class postage affixed thereto on this _____ day of _____ 20 ____, correctly addressed to: the Assistant United States Attorney, _____ _____ _____, _____, _____.

The undersigned hereby executed this certificate under penalty of perjury pursuant to 28 U.S.C. §1746.

_____

CERTIFICATE OF COMPLIANCE

This brief complies with the type-volume limitation of Fed. R. App. P. 32.7 because it contains _____ pages typed on an IBM Wheelwriter 3500 and is less than 30 pages.

Executed on this _____ day of June 2010.

_____

IN THE
UNITED STATES COURT OF APPEALS
FOR THE _____ CIRCUIT

_____

App. No. _____

_____

_____

Appellant-Defendant,

VS.

_____,

Appellee-Respondent.

MOTION TO STAY MANDATE

TO THE HONORABLE JUDGES OF THE _____ CIRCUIT:

    COMES NOW _____, the Appellant, pro se, and respectfully moves this Honorable Court pursuant to Federal Rules of Appellate Procedure, Rule 41(d), for an order staying this Court's mandate pending certiorari to Supreme Court of the United States. In support thereof, Appellant will show this Court as follows:

    1.   On _____ ___, 20____, this Court entered its judgment in the above entitled action, affirming the Appellant's conviction and sentence.

    2.   The Court's judgment was entered on the assumption that theft of a vehicle constitutes a crime of violence under USSG §4B.1, making the Appellant a Career Offender under the Guidelines.

    3.   The Appellant is now applying for a writ of certiorari to the Supreme Court of the United States, in light of its recent decisions in **Begay, James,** and **Chambers**, and seeks to stay the mandate for ninety (90) days to allow preparation of the petition for writ of certiorari.

    WHEREFORE based on the above, _____, the Appellant urges this Court to stay for ninety (90) days its mandate under Rule 41(b), Fed. R. App. P., for the preparation of the petition for writ of certiorari before the Supreme Court.

    Respectfully submitted on this ___ day of _____ 20 ___.

PRO SE REPRESENTATION

343

IN THE UNITED STATES COURT OF APPEALS
FOR THE _____ CIRCUIT

_____

No. _____

_____

_____,

Petitioner-Appellant,

VS.

UNITED STATES OF AMERICA,

Respondent.

Appeal from the United States District Court
for the _____ District of _____

MOTION FOR RECONSIDERATION OF ENTRY OF DISMISSAL

TO THE HONORABLE JUDGES OF THE _____ **CIRCUIT:**

COMES NOW _____, the appellant, pro se, and respectfully moves this Honorable Court for Reconsideration of entry of dismissal dated _____ ___, 20___, and have his _____ ___, 20___, motion for permission to appeal in forma pauperis considered timely filed in light of Eleventh Circuit Rule 42-1(b).

1.   On _____ ___, 20___, Mr. _____ filed a motion for permission to appeal in forma pauperis in the district court.

2.   On _____ ___, 20___, the Clerk of this Court mailed Mr. _____ a notice that he has to file his motion for leave to proceed on appeal as a pauper and a motion for certificate of appealability within thirty (30) days.

3.   On _____ ___, 20___, Mr. _____ filed with this Court a "Motion for an enlargement of time to file a motion for issuance of certificate of appealability."

4.   This Court granted Mr. _____ an enlargement of time until _____ ___, 20___, to file his motion for certificate of appealability.

5.   On _____ ___, 20___, the district court denied Mr. _____ motion for leave to appeal in forma pauperis.

6.   On _____ ___, 20____, Mr. _____ filed with this Court his "Motion for permission to appeal in forma pauperis."

7.   On _____ ___, 20____, the Clerk of this Court ENTRY OF DISMISSAL: Pursuant to the 11th Cir. R. 42-1(b), this appeal is DISMISSED for want of prosecution because the appellant _____failed to pay the filing and docketing fees to the district court within the time fixed by the rules, effective _____ ___, 20____. See Exhibit "A".

8.   Eleventh Circuit Rule 42-1(b), states in pertinent part: The clerk shall not dismiss an appeal during the pendency of a timely filed motion for an extension of time to. . ." Mr. _____' motion for permission to appeal in forma paueris was timely filed under 11th Circuit Rule 42-1(b).

WHEREFORE, based on the above, _____ prays that this Court reconsiders its ENTRY OF DISMISSAL and reinstates his appeal and orders that his _____ _____ 20____, motion for permission to appeal in forma pauperis be considered timely filed.

Respectfully submitted on this ____ day of _____ 20___.

_____

PRO SE REPRESENTATION

CERTIFICATE OF SERVICE

I HEREBY CERTIFY that a true and correct copy of this foregoing instrument has been mailed first class postage prepaid on this ____ day of _____ 20___, by depositing in the institutional legal mail addressed correctly to:

Executed under penalty of perjury on this ____ day of _____ 20 ____.

_____

IN THE
UNITED STATES COURT OF APPEALS
FOR THE _____ CIRCUIT

_____ * _____

App. No. _____

_____ * _____

UNITED STATES OF AMERICA,

Appellee,

VS.

_____

Movant-Appellant.

On Appeal from the denial of Appellant's 28 U.S.C. §2255
Motion to vacate in the United States District Court
for the _____ District of _____

MOTION FOR LEAVE TO FILE AN OUT-OF-TIME, PRO SE, APPELLANT'S REPLY BRIEF TO THE APPELLEE'S BRIEF

TO THE HONORABLE JUDGES OF THE _____ CIRCUIT:

COMES NOW _____, the appellant, pro se, and respectfully moves this Honorable Court for leave to file an out-of-time, pro se, Appellant's Reply Brief to the Appellee's brief. Appellant will show this Court as follows:

1.   This Court granted the Appellant a certificate of appealability and appointed attorney _____ to represent the Appellant.

2.   The Appellant requested attorney _____ to consult with him on important decisions; to keep the Appellant informed of important developments in the course of the appellate prosecution; to serve the Appellant with a copy of the Appellee's brief upon counsel receiving a copy; and to file a Reply Brief to the Appellee's brief unless the Untied States' concedes that reversal is warranted.

3.   The United States served counsel _____ its Appellee's brief in ___ 20___. Counsel _____ failed to send the Appellant _____ a copy of the Appellee's brief and he failed to file a reply to the Appellee's brief. After the appellant

346

made numerous requests by phone and letters to counsel _____ to send him a copy of the Appellee's brief on _____ ___, 20___, counsel _____ finally mailed the Appellant a copy of the Appellee's brief. See Exhibit "1" Counsel _____ letter with enclosed Appellee's brief dated _____ ___, 20___.

4.   The Appellee Brief erroneously claims that the Appellant has not shown prejudiced under *Strickland v. Washington*, **466 U.S. 668, 80 L.Ed.2d 674, 104 S.Ct. 2052 (1984)**. Contrary to the Appellee's allegations, the record supports that the Appellant was prejudiced under *Strickland*, **supra.**

5.   Appellant seeks the opportunity to file an out-of-time, pro se, Appellant's Reply Brief quickly (less than 10 pages) pointing out the prejudiced under *Strickland.* This is a matter of great importance and requires a reply brief addressing the prejudice.

6.   This motion is made in the interest of justice and not meant to delay the proceedings.

WHEREFORE, based on the above, _____, urges this Court to **GRANT** this motion and afford him an opportunity to file a pro se out-of-time Appellant's Reply Brief.

Respectfully submitted on this _____ day of _____, 20___.

_____
Name & Prison Number
PRO SE REPRESENTATION
Address
Town, State & Zip COde

CERTIFICATE OF SERVICE

I HEREBY CERTIFY that a true and correct copy of this foregoing instrument has been mailed with first class postage affixed thereto on this _____ day of _____, 20__, by hand delivering the same to Mail Room Staff at the _____ Correctional Institution, _____, _____, for processing through the internal legal mail system correctly addressed to:

Executed on this _____ day of _____, 20___.

_____
Name

IN THE
UNITED STATES COURT OF APPEALS
FOR THE _____ CIRCUIT

App. No. _____

UNITED STATES OF AMERICA,

Plaintiff-Appellee,

VS.

Defendant-Appellant.

On Appeal from the United States District Court
For the _____ District of _____
_____ Division
USDC No. _____

MOTION TO RECALL MANDATE OR AMEND JUDGMENT

TO THE HONORABLE JUDGES OF THE _____ CIRCUIT:

    COMES NOW _____, the appellant, pro se, and respectfully moves this Honorable Court to recall mandate and to amend judgment pursuant to this Court's Local Rule 41-1. The Appellant will show this Court as follows:

    1.   On _____ ___, 20___, the district court determined that _____ was a career offender and he had a base offense level 42 and a total offense level of 44 applied to _____ case. _____ sentencing guidelines range was a mandatory term of life imprisonment regardless of the applicable criminal history category. See USSG §5A1.1. Sentencing Table (Nov. 1991). The district court also determined that a criminal history category VI applied, based upon the career offender provisions of the sentencing guidelines USSG §4B1.1. The district court sentenced _____ to life imprisonment.

    2.   On direct appeal the United States' in its appellate brief stated: "The presently available evidence will not establish that the burglary conviction was for a burglary of a dwelling; thus, the career offender provision cannot be applicable. Therefore, the Amended Judgment should be corrected to reflect _____'s true criminal history category and the inapplicability of the career offender provisions." id. at Government's appellate brief, 1995 WL 17062328, at 46-47. **Excerpts attached at**

348

Exhibit A). The government concluded that _____'s Criminal History Category is IV not VI and should not be treated as a career offender. Nevertheless, the government urged this Court to affirm the conviction and sentence. _____'s conviction and sentence were affirmed without an opinion. See, *United States v.   , ___* *F.3d _____ (___th Cir. _____)*.

       3.   The district court subsequently reduced _____'s sentence pursuant to 18 U.S.C. §3582(c)(2) based on Amendment 505 to USSG §2D1.1(c).

       4.   If this Court had ruled on the issue relating to whether _____ is a career offender on direct appeal he would be entitled to a sentence reduction under 18 U.S.C. §3582(c)(2), Amendment 706 to USSG §2D1.1(c). Therefore, to prevent an injustice this Court should recall the mandate and amend its judgment that the career offender provision of USSG §4B1.1 is not applicable to _____. It is no longer harmless error to deny the claim without an opinion especially when all parties concede that _____ is not a career offender.

       5.   _____ had no standing to raise the claim in a §2255 motion because it would not have changed his sentence at that time. Nor does he have a standing to raise the claim in a 18 U.S.C. §3582(c)(2) motion because it's not cognizable. The only available remedy to Mr. _____ is through recall of mandate. Therefore, in the interest of justice this Court should recall its mandate and amend its judgement holding that _____ is not a "career offender" as conceded by the parties. See *Harris v. Sentry Title Co., Inc.*, **727 F.2d 1368 (5th Cir.), cert. denied, 104 S.Ct. 2679, 467 U.S. 1226, 81 L.Ed.2d 874 reh. denied, 738 F.2d 437 (5th Cir. 1984)**.

       WHEREFORE based on the above, _____, urges this Honorable Court to recall or amend its judgment addressing the claim that _____ is not a "career offender."

       Respectfully submitted on this ___ day of _____, 20___.

                 _____
                 Name
                 PRO SE REPRESENTATION
                 Address
                 Town, State & Zip code

CERTIFICATE OF SERVICE

       I HEREBY CERTIFY that a true and correct copy of this foregoing instrument has been mailed with first class postage affixed thereto on this ____ day of _____, 20__, by hand delivering the same to Mail Room Staff at the _____ Correctional Institution, _____, _____, for processing through the internal legal mail system correctly addressed to: _____ _____, Assistant United States Attorney, _____, Suite _____, _____, _____.

       Executed on this ____ day of _____, 20___.

                 _____
                 Name

CERTIFICATE OF INTERESTED PERSONS AND CORPORATE DISCLOSURE

The undersigned Appellant, pro se, of record certifies that the following listed persons and entities have an interest in the outcome of this case. These representations are made in order that the judges of this court may evaluate possible disqualifications of recusal.

Honorable Judge _____
United States District Judge
_____ District of _____

Assistant United States Attorney
_____, Appellant

Respectfully submitted on this ____ day of _____ 20 ___.

_____
Name

IN THE
UNITED STATES COURT OF APPEALS
FOR THE _____ CIRCUIT

_____

App. No. _____

_____

UNITED STATES OF AMERICA,

Plaintiff-Appellee,

VS.

_____

Defendant-Appellant.

On Appeal from the United States District Court
For the _____ District of _____
_____ Division
USDC No. _____

MOTION TO RECALL MANDATE AND AMEND JUDGMENT

TO THE HONORABLE JUDGES OF THE _____ CIRCUIT:

    COMES NOW _____, the appellant, pro se, and respectfully moves this Honorable Court to recall mandate and amend judgment pursuant to this Court's Local Rule 41-1. The Appellant will show this Court as follows:

    1.   The court appointed attorney _____ _____ to represent the Appellant on direct appeal. A timely appellant's brief was filed.

    2.   The Appellant wrote numerous letters to attorney _____ _____ and requested for him to keep him informed of all decisions made on his direct appeal. Attorney _____ refused to answer the Appellant's phone calls and letters.

    3.   On _____ ___, 20___, the Appellant wrote Mr. _____ a final letter and requested to know the status of his appeal. See Exhibit "A" attached hereto. Attorney _____ refused to answer this letter.

    4.   On _____ ___, 20___, the Appellant wrote to the Honorable _____, Clerk of the _____ Circuit, and requested a Final Order taken by the United States Court of Appeals for the _____ Circuit in the above styled and numbered cause. See Exhibit "B" attached hereto.

351

5.   On _____ ___, 20___, the Clerk's Office of this Court issued a MEMORANDUM REGARDING FEES, and enclosed a courtesy copy of this Court's _____ ____, 20___, opinion affirming the Appellant's conviction and sentence.

6.   Upon receiving the Clerk's package dated _____ ____, 20___, the Appellant learned that this Court issued its ruling on _____ ___, 20___, affirming his conviction and sentence. Appellant immediately tired to contact attorney _____ _____ to request him file a petition for rehearing and a petition for writ of certiorari to the Supreme Court. Attorney _____ refused to answer his phone calls or respond to him in any manner.

7.   The Appellant respectfully moves this Court to reopen his appeal and re-issue the opinion in his case to afford him a opportunity to file a timely petition for rehearing and a timely petition for writ of certiorari to the United States Supreme Court because his counsel _____ _____ failed in his duty, loyalty and obligations to serve him a time copy of this Court's opinion.

8.   This motion is made in the interest of justice and not meant to delay the proceedings.

WHEREFORE, based on the above, _____, urges this Honorable Court to recall mandate and amend its judgment to afford him an opportunity to file a timely petition for rehearing, and a petition for write of certiorari to the Supreme Court.

Respectfully submitted on this _____ day of _____, 20___.

_____
PRO SE REPRESENTATION

CERTIFICATE OF SERVICE

I HEREBY CERTIFY that a true and correct copy of this foregoing instrument has been mailed with first class postage affixed thereto on this _____ day of _____, 20__, by hand delivering the same to Mail Room Staff at the Federal Correctional Institution, _____, _____, for processing through the internal legal mail system correctly addressed to: _____ _____, Assistant United States Attorney, _____, Suite _____, _____, _____.

Executed on this _____ day of _____, 20___.

_____
Name

Form Letter No. 4

[Your Name & Prison Number]
[Institution]
[Your Address]
[Town, State & Zip Code]

[Date]

Office of the Clerk
United States Court of Appeals
_____ Circuit
Address_____
Town, State & Zip Code____

Re: Application For Leave To File A Second or Successive Motion To Vacate, Set Aside or Correct Sentence 28 U.S.C. §2255

Dear Clerk:

I am requesting an "Application For Leave To File A Second or Successive Motion to Vacate, Set Aside or Correct Sentence 28 U.S.C. §2255," that is required by your Court. I have enclosed a self-addressed stamped envelope for your convenience returning said application.

Your assistance on this matter is greatly appreciated. Thank you.

Sincerely,

_____
[Your Name]

CC:
    p/file.

Sample Motion

UNITED STATES COURT OF APPEALS
FOR THE _____ CIRCUIT

APPLICATION FOR LEAVE TO FILE A SECOND OR
SUCCESSIVE MOTION TO VACATE, SET ASIDE
OR CORRECT SENTENCE
28 U.S.C. § 2255
BY A PRISONER IN FEDERAL CUSTODY

_____
Name

_____

_____   _____
Place of Confinement   Prisoner Number

_____   _____

INSTRUCTIONS-READ CAREFULLY

(1)   This application must be legibly handwritten or typewritten and signed by the applicant under penalty of perjury. Any false statement of a material fact may serve as the basis for prosecution and conviction for perjury.

(2)   All questions must be answered concisely in the proper space on the form.

(3)   The Judicial Conference of the United States has adopted the 8 ½ x 11 inch paper size for use throughout the federal judiciary and directed the elimination of the use of legal size paper. All pleadings **must** be on 8 ½ x 11 inch paper; otherwise we cannot accept them.

(4)   All applicants seeking leave to file a second or successive petition are required to use this form, except in capital (death penalty) cases. In capital cases only, the use of this form is optional.

(5)   Additional pages are not permitted except with respect to additional grounds for relief and facts which you rely upon to support those grounds. You may submit separate petitions, motions, briefs, arguments, etc., that support your application.

(6)   In accordance with the "Anti-Terrorism and Effective Death Penalty Act of

1996," as codified at 28 U.S.C. § 2255(b), effective April 24, 1996, before leave to file a second or successive motion can be granted by the United States Court of Appeals, it is the applicant's burden to make a prima facie showing that he satisfies either of the two conditions stated below.

A second or successive motion must be certified as provided in [28 U.S.C.] section 2255 by a panel of the appropriate court of appeals to contain--

(1) newly discovered evidence that, if proven and viewed in light of the evidence as a whole, would be sufficient to establish by clear and convincing evidence that no reasonable factfinder would have found the movant guilty of the offense; or

(2) a new rule of constitutional law, made retroactive to cases on collateral review by the Supreme Court, that was previously unavailable.

(7)   When this application is fully completed, the original and four copies, *with proof of service on all parties through counsel,* must be mailed to:

Clerk of Court
United States Court of Appeals for the _____ **Circuit**

_____

_____

_____

(Rev. 11/02)

APPLICATION

1. (a)   State and division of the United States District Court which entered the judgment of conviction under attack:

    _____

    _____

    (b)   Case Number: _____

2. Date of judgment of conviction: _____

3. Length of sentence: _____   Sentencing Judge: _____

4. Nature of offense or offenses for which you were convicted: _____

    _____

    _____

    _____

5. Related to this conviction and sentence, have you ever filed a motion to vacate in any federal court?

    Yes ( )   No ( )   If "yes", how many times? _____

    (if more than one, complete 6 and 7 below as necessary)

    (a) Name of court: _____

    (b) Case number: _____

    (c) Nature of proceeding: _____

    _____

    _____

    (d) Grounds raised (list all grounds; use extra pages if necessary): _____

    _____

    _____

    _____

    _____

    _____

    _____

    (e) Did you receive an evidentiary hearing on your motion?   Yes ( )   No ( )

    (f) Result: _____

    _____

    (g) Date of result: _____

6. As to any second federal motion, give the same information:

    (a) Name of court: _____

    (b) Case number: _____

Page 3 of 7

356

(c) Nature of proceeding: _____

_____

_____

(d) Grounds raised (list all grounds; use extra pages if necessary): _____

_____

_____

_____

_____

_____

_____

_____

(e) Did you receive an evidentiary hearing on your motion?   Yes ( )   No ( )

(f) Result: _____

_____

_____

(g) Date of result: _____

7.   As to any third federal motion, give the same information:

(a) Name of court: _____

(b) Case number: _____

(c) Nature of proceeding: _____

_____

_____

(d) Grounds raised (list all grounds; use extra pages if necessary): _____

_____

_____

_____

_____

_____

_____

_____

(e) Did you receive an evidentiary hearing on your motion?   Yes ( )   No ( )

(f) Result: _____

_____

(g) Date of result: _____

8.   Did you appeal the result of any action taken on your federal motion? (Use extra pages to reflect additional petitions if necessary)

           (1) First motion   No ( ) Yes ( )   Appeal No. _____
           (2) Second motion   No ( ) Yes ( )   Appeal No. _____
           (3) Third motion   No ( ) Yes ( )   Appeal No. _____

9.   If you did not appeal from the adverse action on any motion, explain briefly why you did not: _____

_____
_____
_____
_____
_____
_____
_____

10. State concisely every ground on which you now claim that you are being held unlawfully. Summarize briefly the facts supporting each ground.

    (a)   Ground one: _____

               _____
               _____

               Supporting FACTS (tell your story briefly without citing cases or law):

               _____
               _____
               _____
               _____
               _____
               _____

               Was this claim raised in a prior motion?   Yes ( )   No ( )

               Does this claim rely on a "new rule of law?" Yes ( ) No ( )
               If "yes," state the new rule of law (give case name and citation):

               _____
               _____

               Does this claim rely on "newly discovered evidence?" Yes ( ) No ( )
               If "yes," briefly state the newly discovered evidence, and why it was not previously available to you: _____

               _____
               _____
               _____
               _____
               _____

(b) Ground two: _____

_____

Supporting FACTS (tell your story briefly without citing cases or law):

_____
_____
_____
_____
_____

Was this claim raised in a prior motion?   Yes ( )   No ( )

Does this claim rely on a "new rule of law?"   Yes ( )   No ( )
If "yes," state the new rule of law (give case name and citation):

_____
_____

Does this claim rely on "newly discovered evidence?"   Yes ( )   No ( )
If "yes," briefly state the newly discovered evidence, and why it was not
previously available to you: _____

_____
_____
_____
_____
_____

[Additional grounds may be asserted on additional pages if necessary]

11. Do you have any motion or appeal now pending in any court as to the judgment now
under attack?   Yes ( )   No ( )

If yes, name of court: _____   Case Number: _____

Wherefore, applicant prays that the United States Court of Appeals for the____Circuit grant an Order Authorizing the District Court to Consider Applicant's Second or Successive Motion to Vacate under 28 U.S.C. § 2255.

_____
Applicant's Signature

I declare under Penalty of Perjury that my answers to all the questions in this Application are true and correct.

Executed on _____
            [date]

_____
Applicant's Signature

Page 6 of 7

359

Proof of Service

Applicant must send a copy of this application and all attachments to the United States Attorney's office in the district in which you were convicted.

I certify that on _____, I mailed a copy of this Application and all
                [date]

attachments to _____

at the following address:

_____

_____

_____
Applicant's Signature

_____

Pursuant to Fed.R.App.P. 25(c), "If an inmate confined in an institution files a notice of appeal . . ., the notice of appeal is timely filed if it is deposited in the institution's internal mail system on or before the last day of filing. Timely filing may be shown by a notarized statement or declaration (in compliance with 28 U.S.C. § 1746) setting forth the date of deposit and stating that first-class postage has been prepaid."

Chapter IX
Supreme Court Proceedings

❑ Supreme Court Proceedings

➢ Read the Rules of the Supreme Court

➢ *Form* letter for guide for prospective indigent petitioners for writ of certiorari

➢ *Form* letter requesting counsel to file petition for writ of certiorari

➢ Motion for leave to proceed in forma pauperis (with affidavit)

➢ Petition for writ of certiorari

READ THE RULES OF THE SUPREME COURT

Petitions for writ of certiorari are governed by the Rules of the Supreme Court of the United States. State petitions for writ of certiorari to the State Supreme Court are governed by each State's Supreme Court Rules or applicable statutes. It's a must, to read the Rules of the Supreme Court when you're preparing a petition for writ of certiorari. Here are a few reasons why it's necessary to read the Rules of the Supreme Court when you're preparing a petition for writ of certiorari:

First, if the Clerk of the Supreme Court receives a petition for writ of certiorari that fails to comply with the Rules of the Supreme Court it may return the petition to the sender with instruction to correct the petition because it fails to comply with the rules.

Second, the rules give the applicable time limits involved for filing a petition for writ of certiorari. See Supreme Court Rule 13. The rules explain that review on a writ of certiorari is not a matter of right, but judicial discretion. A petition for writ of certiorari will be granted only for compelling reasons partially set forth in Rule 10(a), (b) & (c).

Third, the rules explain the contents required, procedures, briefs in opposition, reply briefs, proceedings In Forma Pauperis, number of copies, appendix, and everything else applicable to the construction of the petition for writ.

The Rules of the Supreme Court have been clearly laid out and will guide you through the Supreme Court proceedings if the litigant takes time to read them.

GUIDE FOR PROSPECTIVE INDIGENT PETITIONERS FOR WRITS OF CERTIORARI

Most prison law libraries have a "GUIDE FOR PROSPECTIVE INDIGENT PETITIONERS FOR WRITS OF CERTIORARI" for the Supreme Court of the United States which has a Form: "MOTION FOR LEAVE TO PROCEED IN FORMA PAUPERIS" with an "AFFIDAVIT OR DECLARATION IN SUPPORT OF MOTION FOR LEAVE TO PROCEED IN FORMA PAUPERIS" and a Form: "PETITION FOR WRIT OF CERTIORARI" which is a fill in the blank type of motion and petition. Ask the prison law library clerk for a petition for writ of certiorari forms or package. If the prison law library does not supply the form motion and petitions then write a letter to the Clerk of the Supreme Court of the United States or Clerk of the State Supreme Court whichever the case may be and request one. See **Form Letter No. 1.**

REQUEST COUNSEL TO FILE PETITION FOR WRIT OF CERTIORARI

If the court appointed counsel or you retained counsel which represented you in the Court of Appeals then you can always write that counsel a letter requesting him/her to file your petition for writ of certiorari. **See Form Letter No. 2.** Sometimes the attorney will do the petition for writ of certiorari for you.

Form Letter No. 1

[Your Name & Prison Number]
[Institution]
[Your Address]
[Town, State & Zip Code]

[Date]

Honorable William K. Suter, Clerk
Office of the Clerk
United States Supreme Court Bldg.
One First Street N.E.
Washington, D.C. 20543

Re: GUIDE FOR PROSPECTIVE INDIGENT PETITIONERS FOR WRITS OF
     CERTIORARI

Dear Mr. Suter:

At this time, I am requesting a "Guide For Prospective Indigent Petitioners For Write of Certiorari." The prison law library does not have a copy of the "guide" at this institution.. I have enclosed four (4) first class postage stamps for the return of the "Guide for Prospective Indigent Petitioners for Writs of Certiorari."

Your assistance on this matter is greatly appreciated. Thank you.

Sincerely,

_____

[Your Name]

CC:
    p/file.

Form Letter No.2

[Your Name & Prison Number]
[Institution]
[Your Address]
[Town, State & Zip Code]

[Date]

(Your Attorney's Name)
Attorney At Law
Address
Town, State & Zip Code

Re: _____ v._____
App. No. _____ (__th Cir. 20__)
REQUEST TO FILE PETITION FOR WRIT OF CERTIORARI

Dear Mr. _____:

This letter is in reference to the above entitled action which you represented me on direct appeal. On _____ ___, 20___, I received your letter and the _____ Circuit Court of Appeals decision affirming my conviction and sentence. Please file a "Petition For Writ of Certiorari" to the United States Supreme Court on my behalf seeking review of the _____ Circuit Court of Appeals decision affirming my conviction and sentence.

Your assistance on this matter is greatly appreciated. Thank you.

Sincerely,

_____
[Your Name]

CC:
    p/file.
Certified Mail No. _____

No. _____

IN THE

SUPREME COURT OF THE UNITED STATES

_____ § _____

_____, Petitioner,

VS.

_____, Respondent(s).

MOTION FOR LEAVE TO PROCEED IN FORMA PAUPERIS

The petitioner, _____, pro se, respectfully moves for leave to file the attached petition for writ of certiorari without prepayment of costs and to proceed **in forma pauperis**.

Petitioner has previously been granted leave to proceed **in forma pauperis** in the _____ _____ _____ _____.

Petitioner's affidavit or declaration in support of this motion is attached hereto.

Respectfully submitted on this ___ day of _____ 20___.

_____
Name & Prison Number
PRO SE REPRESENTATION
Address
Town, State & Zip Code

365

AFFIDAVIT OR DECLARATION
IN SUPPORT OF MOTION FOR LEAVE TO PROCEED *IN FORMA PAUPERIS*

I, _____, am the petitioner in the above-entitled case. In support of my motion to proceed *in forma pauperis*, I state that because of my poverty I am unable to pay the costs of this case or to give security therefor; and I believe I am entitled to redress.

1. For both you and your spouse estimate the average amount of money received from each of the following sources during the past 12 months. Adjust any amount that was received weekly, biweekly, quarterly, semiannually, or annually to show the monthly rate. Use gross amounts, that is, amounts before any deductions for taxes or otherwise.

Income source	Average monthly amount during the past 12 months		Amount expected next month	
	You	Spouse	You	Spouse
Employment	$_____	$_____	$_____	$_____
Self-employment	$_____	$_____	$_____	$_____
Income from real property (such as rental income)	$_____	$_____	$_____	$_____
Interest and dividends	$_____	$_____	$_____	$_____
Gifts	$_____	$_____	$_____	$_____
Alimony	$_____	$_____	$_____	$_____
Child Support	$_____	$_____	$_____	$_____
Retirement (such as social security, pensions, annuities, insurance)	$_____	$_____	$_____	$_____
Disability (such as social security, insurance payments)	$_____	$_____	$_____	$_____
Unemployment payments	$_____	$_____	$_____	$_____
Public-assistance (such as welfare)	$_____	$_____	$_____	$_____
Other (specify): _____	$_____	$_____	$_____	$_____
Total monthly income:	$_____	$_____	$_____	$_____

366

2. List your employment history for the past two years, most recent first. (Gross monthly pay is before taxes or other deductions.)

Employer	Address	Dates of Employment	Gross monthly pay
_____	_____	_____	$_____
_____	_____	_____	$_____
_____	_____	_____	$_____

3. List your spouse's employment history for the past two years, most recent employer first. (Gross monthly pay is before taxes or other deductions.)

Employer	Address	Dates of Employment	Gross monthly pay
_____	_____	_____	$_____
_____	_____	_____	$_____
_____	_____	_____	$_____

4. How much cash do you and your spouse have? $_____
Below, state any money you or your spouse have in bank accounts or in any other financial institution.

Financial institution	Type of account	Amount you have	Amount your spouse has
_____	_____	$_____	$_____
_____	_____	$_____	$_____
_____	_____	$_____	$_____

5. List the assets, and their values, which you own or your spouse owns. Do not list clothing and ordinary household furnishings.

☐ Home
   Value _____

☐ Other real estate
   Value _____

☐ Motor Vehicle #1
   Year, make & model _____
   Value _____

☐ Motor Vehicle #2
   Year, make & model _____
   Value _____

☐ Other assets
   Description _____
   Value _____

6. State every person, business, or organization owing you or your spouse money, and the amount owed.

Person owing you or your spouse money	Amount owed to you	Amount owed to your spouse
_____	$_____	$_____
_____	$_____	$_____
_____	$_____	$_____

7. State the persons who rely on you or your spouse for support.

Name	Relationship	Age
_____	_____	_____
_____	_____	_____
_____	_____	_____

8. Estimate the average monthly expenses of you and your family. Show separately the amounts paid by your spouse. Adjust any payments that are made weekly, biweekly, quarterly, or annually to show the monthly rate.

	You	Your spouse
Rent or home-mortgage payment (include lot rented for mobile home) Are real estate taxes included? ☐ Yes ☐ No Is property insurance included? ☐ Yes ☐ No	$_____	$_____
Utilities (electricity, heating fuel, water, sewer, and telephone)	$_____	$_____
Home maintenance (repairs and upkeep)	$_____	$_____
Food	$_____	$_____
Clothing	$_____	$_____
Laundry and dry-cleaning	$_____	$_____
Medical and dental expenses	$_____	$_____

	You	Your spouse
Transportation (not including motor vehicle payments)	$_____	$_____
Recreation, entertainment, newspapers, magazines, etc.	$_____	$_____
Insurance (not deducted from wages or included in mortgage payments)		
Homeowner's or renter's	$_____	$_____
Life	$_____	$_____
Health	$_____	$_____
Motor Vehicle	$_____	$_____
Other: _____	$_____	$_____
Taxes (not deducted from wages or included in mortgage payments)		
(specify): _____	$_____	$_____
Installment payments		
Motor Vehicle	$_____	$_____
Credit card(s)	$_____	$_____
Department store(s)	$_____	$_____
Other: _____	$_____	$_____
Alimony, maintenance, and support paid to others	$_____	$_____
Regular expenses for operation of business, profession, or farm (attach detailed statement)	$_____	$_____
Other (specify): _____	$_____	$_____
Total monthly expenses:	$_____	$_____

9. Do you expect any major changes to your monthly income or expenses or in your assets or liabilities during the next 12 months?

☐ Yes ☐ No If yes, describe on an attached sheet.

10. Have you paid – or will you be paying – an attorney any money for services in connection with this case, including the completion of this form? ☐ Yes ☐ No

If yes, how much? _____

If yes, state the attorney's name, address, and telephone number:

11. Have you paid—or will you be paying—anyone other than an attorney (such as a paralegal or a typist) any money for services in connection with this case, including the completion of this form?

☐ Yes ☐ No

If yes, how much? _____

If yes, state the person's name, address, and telephone number:

12. Provide any other information that will help explain why you cannot pay the costs of this case.

I declare under penalty of perjury that the foregoing is true and correct.

Executed on: _____ , 20____

_____

(Signature)

No. _____

_____

IN THE

SUPREME COURT OF THE UNITED STATES

OCTOBER TERM, 20___

_____ * _____

_____,

Petitioner,

VS.

UNITED STATES OF AMERICA

Respondent.

_____ * _____

On Petition for Writ of Certiorari
To the United States Court of Appeals
For the _____ Circuit

_____ * _____

PETITION FOR WRIT OF CERTIFICATE

_____ * _____

_____
PRO SE REPRESENTATION
REG. NO. _____
_____
_____

371

Was petitioner's guilty plea sustained in violation of due process warranting habeas relief where the district court failed to advise petitioner of the correct statutory maximum penalty and then imposed a sentence "greater" than its Rule 11 statutory maximum advisement?

Was counsel constitutionally ineffective because he misadvised petitioner of the statutory maximum sentence he faced was twenty (20) years; failed to object when the sentencing court imposed a sentence that exceeded the statutory maximum admonishments; and failed to raise the claim on direct appeal?

Did the courts below commit reversible err denying petitioner's §2255 motion without conducting an evidentiary hearing to resolve the factual disputes?

PARTIES TO THE PROCEEDINGS

Name_____ # _____, Petitioner,
Address
City, State & Zip code

Pro se representation for Petitioner

Attorney for Respondent,
United States,

_____

Solicitor General
Department of Justice
Washington, D.C. 20530

TABLE OF CONTENTS

INDEX OF AUTHORITIES

INDEX OF AUTHORITIES (CONTINUED)

JURISPRUNDENCE PAGE(S)

Petitioner, _____, prays that this Honorable Court will issue a writ of certiorari to review the judgment and opinion of the United States of Court of Appeals for the _____ Circuit, entered in the above proceeding on _____ ___, 20___.

_____ * _____

I.
CITATIONS OF OPINIONS AND ORDERS IN CASE

The original judgment of conviction of Petitioner in the United States District Court for the _____ District of _____ was not reported and is attached hereto as **Appendix "1"**.

The original judgment of conviction of Petitioner was appealed to the United States Court of Appeals for the _____ Circuit, which affirmed the conviction and sentence in an unpublished opinion attached hereto as **Appendix "2"**.

The report and recommendation of the United States Magistrate Judge for the _____ District of _____ on Petitioner's Section 2255 motion is unpublished and attached hereto as **Appendix "3"**.

The opinion and order of the United States District Court for the _____ District of _____ adopting the United States Magistrate Judge's report and recommendation is unpublished and attached hereto as **Appendix "4"**.

The opinion of the United States Court of Appeals for the _____ Circuit is unpublished and is attached hereto as **Appendix "5"**.

_____ * _____

II.
JURISDICTIONAL STATEMENT

The judgment of the United States Court of Appeals for the _____ Circuit was entered on _____ ___, 20___. The jurisdiction of this Court is invoked under 28 U.S.C. §1254(1).

_____ * _____

III.
CONSTITUTIONAL PROVISIONS AND STATUTES INVOLVED

1. The Fifth Amendment of the United States Constitution provides:

    "No person shall be . . . deprived of life, liberty, or property without due process of law; nor shall private property be taken for public use, without just compensation."

2. The Sixth Amendment of the United States Constitution provides:

    "In all criminal prosecutions, the accused shall enjoy the right to . . . be informed of the nature and cause of the accusation; . . . and to have the assistance of counsel for his defence."

3.   The statutes involved and under review are, Title 18, United States Code, Federal Rules of Criminal Procedure, Rule 11(c)(1), which states:

> (c) **ADVISE TO DEFENDANT.** Before accepting a plea of guilty or nolo contender, the court must address the defendant personally in open court and inform the defendant of, and determine that the defendant understands, the following:

> (1) the nature of the charge to which the plea is offered, the mandatory minimum penalty provided by law if any, and the maximum possible penalty provided by law, including the effect of any special parole or supervised release term, the fact that the court is required to consider any applicable sentencing guidelines but may depart from those guidelines under some circumstances, and, when applicable, that the court may also order the defendant to make restitution to any victim of the offense; and . . . Id.

4.   The statute under which Petitioner sought habeas corpus relief was 28 U.S.C. §2255 which states in pertinent part:

> **§2255 Federal custody; remedies on motion attacking sentence**

> A prisoner in custody under sentence of a court established by Act of Congress claiming the right to be released upon the ground that the sentence was imposed in violation of the Constitution or laws of the United States, or that the court was without jurisdiction to impose such sentence, or that the sentence was in excess of the maximum authorized by law, or is otherwise subject to collateral attack, may move the court which imposed the sentence to vacate, set aside or correct sentence.

> Unless the motion and the files and records of the case conclusively show that the prisoner is entitled to no relief, the court shall cause notice to be served upon the United States attorney, grant a prompt hearing thereon, determine the issues and make findings of fact and conclusions of law with respect thereto.   If the courts finds that the judgment was rendered without jurisdiction, or that the sentence imposed was not authorized by law or otherwise open

378

to collateral attack, or that there has been such a denial or infringement of the constitutional rights of the prisoner as to render the judgment vulnerable to collateral attack, the court shall vacate and set aside the judgment aside and shall discharge the prisoner or resentence him or grant a new trial or correct the sentence as may appear appropriate.

_____ * _____

IV.
STATEMENT OF THE CASE

On _____ ___, 20___, a federal grand jury for the _____ District of _____, _____ Division returned a seven count indictment charging _____ _____ and various other co-defendants with the offenses of conspiracy to manufacture phenyl acetone and amphetamine [Count One], manufacturing or attempting to manufacture phenyl acetone and amphetamine [Count Two], possession of a firearm by a convicted felon [Count four]. See **Title 21 United States Code, Section 846; 21 United States Code, Section 841(a)(1); 18 United States Code, Section 924(c), and 18 United States Code, Section 922(g)(1).**

On _____ ___, 20___, the day of trial, Petitioner announced _____ decision to plead guilty to count one the conspiracy to manufacture phenyl acetone and amphetamine charge, in exchange for an agreement that Petitioner would not receive more than a maximum term of twenty (20) years imprisonment and a fine of not more than one million dollars ($1,000,000.00), or both, and the government agreed to dismiss the remaining charges against Petitioner.

During the guilty plea colloquy as required by Rule 11(c)(1), the district court advised Petitioner that the maximum sentence _____ could receive was twenty (20) years imprisonment and a fine of not more than one million dollars ($1,000,000.00), or both. See Guilty Plea Transcript attached hereto as Appendix "__". The government presented a written plea agreement to the district court which specifically defined that Petitioner could not receive more than twenty (20) years imprisonment and up to a fine of one million dollars ($1,000,000.00), or both.

The district court never advised Petitioner that the sentence might include a period of supervised release. Nor did the district court explain to Petitioner the effect of supervised release. The plea agreement signed by Petitioner and all parties, and accepted by the district court did not mention the possibility of supervised release, but merely stated that the maximum sentence was twenty (20) years imprisonment and a fine of not more than one million dollars or both.

On _____ 19___, a hearing was conducted as a result of defense counsel's objections to the presentence report based on the quantity of drugs attributed to Petitioner. The Magistrate Judge issued a report and recommendation to deny Petitioner's objections to the presentence report.

On _____ ___, 20___, the district court assessed punishment at 235 months imprisonment and a five (5) year term of supervised release to follow the term of imprisonment, a $_____ special assessment. The total sentence imposed is twenty four (24) years and seven (7) months. See the district court's judgment attached hereto as Appendix "___". A timely notice of appeal was filed.

On _____ ___, 20___, Petitioner's co-defendant wrote appellate counsel _____ _____ a letter specifically requested counsel _____ to raise the claim on direct appeal that the district court erred by failure to advise Petitioner of the mandatory term of supervised release and imposed a sentence which exceeded the Rule 11(c)(1) statutory maximum advisement. See Appendix "___" the letter from _____ _____ to counsel _____.

On _____ ___, 20___, the United States Court of Appeals for the _____ Circuit affirmed petitioner's conviction and sentence in an unpublished opinion in ***United States v.*** _____, App. No. _____ (___th Cir. _____).

_____ * _____

V.

A. COURSE OF PROCEEDINGS IN THE SECTION 2255 CASE BEFORE THIS COURT.

On _____ ___, 20___, Petitioner filed a 28 U.S.C. §2255 motion to vacate, set aside or correct sentence challenging the constitutionality of the conviction, which asserted that: (1) The guilty plea was sustained in violation of due process because Petitioner did not knowingly, voluntarily and intelligently understand the consequences of the plea: (2) counsel was constitutionally ineffective for inducing Petitioner's guilty plea based on faulty and erroneous legal advice concerning the statutory maximum sentence; (3) counsel was constitutionally ineffective for failure to object to the district court imposing a sentence which exceeded the statutory maximum contained in the written plea agreement and the Rule 11(c)(1) colloquy; and (4) counsel was constitutionally ineffective for failure to raise the Rule 11(c)(1) violation on direct appeal. See Memorandum Brief in support of 28 U.S.C. §2255 motion to vacate, set aside or correct sentence.

On _____ ___, 20___, the district court issued a show cause order directing the United States to respond to Petitioner's §2255 motion within thirty (30) days. See Appendix "___".

On _____ ___, 20___, the United States filed a response to Petitioner's §2255 motion.

On _____ ___, 20___, Petitioner filed a traverse reply to the United States' response to Petitioner's §2255 motion.

On _____ ___, 20___, the district court appointed counsel _____ _____ to represent Petitioner during the §2255 proceedings.

On _____ ___, 20___, three years later the United States Magistrate Judge _____ _____ issued a Report and Recommendations to deny Petitioner's §2255 motion, which is attached hereto as Appendix "___".

On _____ ___, 20___, Petitioner filed timely objections to the Magistrte Judge's report and recommendation.

On _____ ___, 20___, the district court adopted the report and recommendation and issued a final judgment denying Petitioner's §2255 motion, which is attached hereto as Appendix "___".

A timely notice of appeal and a motion for issuance of certificate of appealability was filed which were subsequently denied by the district court.

On _____ ___, 20___, appointed counsel _____ _____ filed an Appelant's brief in the United States Court of Appeals for the _____ Circuit. Petitioner filed a motion for leave to file a pro se supplemental of appealability.

On _____ ___, 20___, , the United States Court of Appeals for the _____ Circuit delivered its opinion affirming the district court's denial of Petitioner's §2255 motion without evidentiary hearing to resolve the factual disputes.

_____ * _____

VI.
EXISTENCE OF JURISDICTION BELOW

Petitioner was indicted and convicted in the United States District Court for the District Court for the _____ District of _____, _____ Division, for conspiracy to manufacture phenylacetone and amphetamine, under 21 U.S.C. §§841(a)(1) and 846. A Section 2255 motion was appropriately made in the convicting court and subsequently denied. A timely appeal to the United States Court of Appeals for the Circuit was filed.

_____ * _____

VII.
REASONS FOR GRANTING THE WRIT

B. THE COURT OF APPEALS HAS DECIDED A FEDERAL QUESTION IN DIRECT CONFLICT WITH THE APPLICABLE DECISION OF THIS COURT.

1. The _____ Circuit Panel Opinion affirming the district court's denial of Petitioner's §2255 motion holding that, a Rule 11 violations is not cognizable in a §2255 proceeding because Petitioner did not establish "cause" for procedural default. Contrary to the _____ Circuit Court's holding, Petitioner received a sentence "greater" than the district court's Rule 11 statutory maximum admonishment and asserted in the §2255 motion that Petitioner would not have plead guilty had Petitioner been advised of the statutory maximum penalty provided by law. The guilty plea was sustained in violation of due process and in direct conflict with the applicable decisions of this Court and is cognizable in a §2255 motion, in light of this Court's precedence. This Court should exercise its supervisor powers over the lower courts and issue the writ.

2. The _____ Circuit Panel Opinion erred affirming the district court's denial of Petitioner's ineffective assistance of counsel claims because its decision is in direct conflict with this Court's decision in *Strickland*, *Hill* and *Evitts*, infra. The record reveals

that counsel signed a plea agreement which stated Petitioner faced a statutory maximum of twenty (20) years; failed to object when the sentencing court imposed a sentence that exceeded the Rule 11 statutory maximum admonishment; and then failed to raise the obvious Rule 11 (c)(1) violation on direct appeal. Petitioner asserted in the §2255 motion that he would not have plead guilty, absent counsel's erroneous and faulty legal advice concerning the statutory maximum penalty provided by law.

3.   The _____ Circuit Courts erred affirming the denial of Petitioner's §2255 motion where the district court failed to conduct an evidentiary hearing to resolve the factual disputes, which if true, warrants habeas relief and the record did not "conclusively show" that he could not establish facts warranting relief under §2255, which entitled Petitioner to a hearing.

Petitioner respectfully urges that all aspects of the Circuit Court decision are erroneous and at a variance with this Court's decisions as explained in the argument below.

————————— * —————————

VIII.
ARGUMENTS AMPLIFYING REASONS FOR WRIT

I. THE COURT OF APPEALS ERRED IN AFFIRMING THE CONVICTION ON THE BASIS THAT A RULE 11 (c) (1) VIOLATION WAS NOT COGNIZABLE IN A §2255 PROCEEDINGS AND PETITIONER FAILED TO SHOW CAUSE FOR PROCEDURAL DEFAULT

The guilty plea was sustained in violation of due process because Petitioner received a sentence "greater" than the Rule 11 (c)(1) statutory maximum admonishment, which is inconsistent with the rudimentary demands of fair procedure. See *United States v. Scott*, **625 F.2d 623, 625 (5th Cir. 1980)**. Petitioner's §2255 motion asserted that he would not have plead guilty had he been correctly advised of the statutory maximum penalty provided by law. The district court advised Petitioner that his maximum penalty was twenty (20) years imprisonment and a fine up to one million dollars ($1,000,000.00), or both. The district court imposed a nineteen (19) years and seven (7) month term of imprisonment and five (5) years supervised release. A total sentence of twenty-four (24) years and seven months. See Appendix "___" attached hereto.

Under the **"worse case"** scenario, Petitioner would serve his nineteen (19) years and seven (7) month term of imprisonment in full and commence the five (5) year term of supervised release and have the supervised release revoked on the last day of the supervision period and serve every day of the additional five (5) year prison following revocation. *United States v. Bachynsky*, **934 F.2d 1349, 1353 (5th Cir. 1991)**; *United States v. Hekiman*, **975 F.2d 1098, 1103 (5th Cir. 1992)**. Under this scenario, twenty nine (29) years, six (6) months and approximately thirty (30) days would pass from Petitioner's first day of imprisonment to his last.

Petitioner did not and could not have understood the consequences of his guilty plea, the plea itself was not voluntary or intelligently entered and was sustained in violation of the Fifth Amendment Due Process Clause of the United States Constitution. Due process requires that before the court accepts a plea of guilty the defendant be fully advised with respect to the nature of the charges and the maximum possible penalty for the offense. *Brady v. United States*, **397 U.S. 742, 25 L.Ed.2d 747, 90 S.Ct. 1463 (1970)**; *United States v. Wolak*, **510 F.2d 164 (6th Cir. 1975)**. Constitutional protection of due process mandate that an accused's guilty plea be voluntary and intelligent. **Boykin v. Alabama, 395 U.S. 238, 242, 89 S.Ct. 1709, 1711-12, 23 L.Ed.2d 274 (1969)**. Because a guilty plea waives the rights against self-incrimination, to trial by jury, and to confront one's accusers, its acceptance requires the "utmost solicitude of which courts are capable in canvassing the matter with the accused to make sure he has a full understanding of what the-plea connotes and of its consequences." Id. at 243-44, 89 S.Ct. at 1712.

"It is well settled that a plea of guilty is invalid as not being understandingly entered if the defendant does not know the maximum possible penalty for the offense." *Marvel v. United States*, **380 U.S. 262, 85 S.Ct. 953, 13 L.Ed.2d 960 (1965)**. Failure of trial court to assure itself with respect to ascertaining whether accused knew outer limits of penalty which he could suffer upon entering plea of guilty is inconsistent with due process. *Wade v. Wainwright*, **420 F.2d 898 (5th Cir. 1969)**. Due process requires that before the court accepts a plea of guilty it is necessary that the defendant be fully advised with respect to the nature of the charges and the maximum possible penalty for the offense. *United States v. Wolak*, **510 F. 2d 164 (6th Cir. 1975)** (Not only is a defendant to be informed of the maximum possible period of incarceration but he is to be made aware of other direct consequences of a guilty plea).

The _____ Circuit Court in affirming the denial of Petitioner's §2255 motion relied on this Court's decision in *United States v. Timmreck*, **441 U.S. 780, 60 L.Ed.2d 634, 99 S.Ct. 2085 (1979)**, which held that "a conviction based on a guilty plea is not subject to collateral attack under 28 U.S.C. §2255 solely on the basis that a formal violation of Rule 11 occurred, such a violation being neither constitutional nor jurisdictional especially where no claim could reasonably be made that any error resulted in a complete miscarriage of justice or in a proceeding inconsistent with the rudimentary demands of fair procedure." Id. The _____ Circuit erroneously relied on *Timmreck* to affirm the denial of petitioner's §2255 motion.

The *Timmreck* case is readily distinguished from Petitioner's case. Unlike *Timmreck* the Petitioner received a sentence that was "greater" than the district court Rule 11 statutory maximum advisement and the written plea agreement accepted by the district court which violates due process and constitutes a proceeding inconsistent with the rudimentary demands of fair procedure governed by Rule 11. See *Timmreck*, and *Scott*, both supra.

A conviction on a guilty plea tendered solely as a result of faulty advice is a miscarriage of justice. *United States v. Scott*, **625 F.2d 623, 625 (5th Cir. 1980)**. *Scott* alleged that he would not have tendered a guilty plea had the trial court he advised him of the potential six-year sentence under the Youth Corrections Act. The Fifth Circuit found that this allegation distinguishes Scott's pleading albeit slightly from those in *Timmreck*, where *Timmreck* never alleged that if he had been properly advised by the trial court he would not have pled guilty. 441 U.S. at 784, 99 S.Ct. at 2087. Scott's pleadings sufficiently alleged prejudice, which, if proved, would afford a basis for collateral attack. *Scott*, 625 F.2d at 625.

A miscarriage of justice excuses "cause" for procedural default. See ***Murray v. Carrier***, **477 U.S. 478,496, 106 S.Ct. 2639, 2649-50, 91 L.Ed.2d 397 (1985)** (habeas available to avoid miscarriage of justice); ***Swayer v. Collins***, **494 U.S. 108, 108 L.Ed.2d 93, 110 S.Ct. 974 (1990)**. Where defendant did not claim a mere technical violation of formal provision of Rule of Criminal Procedure but, rather, error committed was of constitutional magnitude, since waiver of defendant's constitutional rights was based on a promise that was unkept, and the actual consequences of pleading guilty were contrary to the consequences conveyed to the defendant by the district court prior to acceptance of the guilty plea, defendant could collateral attack conviction under statute to vacate the judgment of conviction and sentence. Rule 11, 18 U.S.C.A.; 28 U.S.C. §2255. See ***United States v. Mercer***, **510 F.2d 343 (7th Cir. 1982)**.

SAME CONSIDERATION COMPEL FINDING THAT PETITIONER'S CLAIM VIOLATES DUE PROCESS AND RESULTS IN A MISCARRIAGE OF JUSTICE EXCUSING "CAUSE" FOR PROCEDURAL DEFAULT

The very same consideration which compelled the Courts to conclude that ***Scott, Brady, Boykin, Marvel, Timmreck, Mercer*** and ***Murray***, all supra, that a guilty plea sustained in violation of due process was open for collateral attack and a miscarriage of justice excuses "cause" for procedural default applies to Petitioner.

*

II. THE COURT OF APPEALS ERRED BY DETERMINING THAT PETITIONER'S INEFFECTIVE ASSISTANCE OF COUNSEL CLAIMS DID NOT MEET THE STANDARDS SET FORTH BY THIS COURT IN *Strickland* AND *Hill*

Petitioner asserted in his §2255 motion as grounds for relief that: Counsel was constitutionally ineffective because counsel misadvised Petitioner that he faced a statutory maximum penalty of twenty (20) years imprisonment; failed to object when the sentencing court imposed a sentence that exceeded the statutory maximum admonishments; and failed to raise the Rule 11violation on direct appeal. Petitioner's §2255 motion asserted that he would not have pleaded guilty had he been correctly advised of the statutory maximum penalty provided by law, but instead would exercised his constitutional rights to a trial by jury. See ***Teague v. Scott***, **60 F. 3d 1167, 1171-72 (5th Cir. 1995)** (Failing to properly advise the defendant of the maximum sentence that he could receive falls below the objective standard required by Strickland. When the defendant lacks a' full understanding of the risks of going to trial, he is unable to make an intelligently choice of whether to accept a plea or take his chances in court).

Claims of ineffective assistance of counsel is governed by the two prong test set forth in ***Strickland v. Washington***, **466 U.S. 668,104 S.Ct. 2052, 2064,80 L.Ed.2d 674 (1984)**. In the plea bargaining context, a petitioner seeking to establish ineffective assistance of counsel must demonstrate that (1) counsel's advice and performance fell below an objective standard of reasonableness, and (2) the petitioner would not have pleaded guilty and would have insisted on going to trial in the absence of his attorney's errors. ***Hill v. Lockhart***, **474 U.S. 52, 58-59, 106 S.Ct. 366, 370-71, 88 L.Ed.2d 203**

(1985). In this case, the record reflects that counsel induced Petitioner's guilty plea with a specific maximum sentence of twenty (20) years. Relying substantially on *United States v. Timmreck*, **441 U.S. 780, 60 L.Ed.2d 634, 99 S.Ct. 2085 (1979)**, the district court denied relief without an evidentiary hearing, ruling that the claimed errors were not of sufficient magnitude to warrant collateral relief.

In *Timmreck*, the Supreme Court held that "formal" or "technical" violations of Federal Rules of Criminal Procedure 11 do not warrant collateral relief. See **Id. at 738-84**. In that case, the defendant had brought a §2255 motion based on the trial court's failure to advise him of a mandatory special parole term. Significantly, the defendant did "not argue that he was actually unaware of the special parole term or that, if he had been properly advised by the trial judge, he would not have pleaded guilty." **Id. at 784**. Thus, Timmreck's only claim was indeed a purely technical one: the trial judge failed to adhere ritualistically to the dictates of Rule 11 and dismissed this portion of his motion pursuant to *Timmreck*.

Petitioner argued on appeal that the deficiencies in the trial court's and defense counsel's misadvice concerning the statutory maximum penalty involved cannot be characterized as a mere technical or formal errors, but instead are of constitutional magnitude because he received a sentence which exceeded the statutory maximum advisement.

The written plea agreement signed by counsel, the Assistant United States Attorney, and the Petitioner was then ratified by the district court. The plea agreements states in pertinent part:

> "Defendant acknowledges that sentencing in this matter is totally within the discretion of the court, and she faces a maximum penalty of twenty (20) years imprisonment or a fine of not more than $1,000,000.00 or both on Count 1 ... *Maximum Penalty*: A fine of not more than $1,000,000.00 or imprisonment of not more than twenty (20) years or both." (Emphasis added).

The agreement further stated that the government would agree to dismiss the remaining charges pending against defendant. Counsel became a party to the twenty (20) year maximum sentence agreement when he placed his signature on the agreement and had it ratified by the Court.

The district court sentenced Petitioner to 235 month imprisonment (19 years and 7 month term of imprisonment) and a five (5) year term of supervised release to follow said term of imprisonment. The total sentence imposed by the district court was twenty-four (24) years and seven months. See Appendix "___" attached hereto.

This case involves affirmative misstatements of the maximum possible penalty provided by law by the district court and defense counsel. The district court then imposed a sentence which exceeded the Rule 11 statutory maximum advisement without objection from counsel constituting deficient performance. See *Pitts v. United States*, **763 F.2d 197, 201 (6th Cir. 1985)**; *Teague v. Scott*, **60 F.3d 1167, 1171-72**. Numerous cases have held that misunderstanding of this nature invalidate a guilty plea. See, e.g., *United States v.* **Rumery, 698 F.2d 764 (5th Cir. 1983)** (on appeal of denial of motion to withdraw plea, the court held that defendant was denied effective assistance of counsel because his maximum exposure was five years but court appointed attorney advised him of maximum possible exposure of thirty years); *United States v. Herrold*, **635 F.2d 213 (3rd Cir. 1980)** (per curiam) (on appeal of denial of motion to withdraw plea, court held that trial court's misadvice in telling defendant of maximum possible sentence of forty-five years invalidated the plea when twenty-five years was the maximum possible sentence); *United States v. Scott*, **625 F.2d 623, 625 (5th Cir. 1980)**(per curiam)(on collateral attack, court held that guilty plea is invalidated by the trial court's telling the defendant of a five year maximum exposure when he faced a possible six year maximum exposure); *Hammond v. United States*, **528 F.2d 15 (4th Cir. 1975)** (on collateral attack, guilty plea invalidated when court clerk and court appointed attorney misadvised defendant that total exposure was in excess of ninety years when total exposure was actually only fifty-five years).

Had counsel raised the Rule 11 claim on direct appeal Petitioner's conviction would have been reversed and sentence vacated and remanded to plead a new. See *United States v. Bounds*, **943 F.2d 541, 543 (5th Cir. 1991)**, where the court summarized the exact same issue: "The court erred in failing to advise Bounds in open court of the possibility of supervised release. We cannot examine this failure for harmless error because the total length of the imposed penalty, based on the periods of incarceration and supervised release is greater than the statutory maximum of which Bounds was advised. " The Fifth Circuit reversed Bounds' conviction, vacated his sentence and remanded for him to plead a new. The exact same scenario would have applied to Petitioner, absent counsel's unprofessional errors and omissions. Thus, prejudice has been shown. *Strickland*, **466 U.S. at 694, 80 L.Ed.2d at 698**.

Contrary to the _____ Circuit's opinion, Petitioner asserted that he would not have pleaded guilty had he been correctly advised of the statutory maximum penalty provided by law. Thus, establishing prejudice under *Strickland*. See *Hill v. Lockhart*, **477 U.S. at 58-59**. There exists more than a reasonable probability that absent counsel's unprofessional legal advice and omissions the results of the trial court and appellate court proceedings would have been different. See *Herrold*, *Scott*, *Hammond* and *Bounds*, all supra.

———————— * ————————

III. THE COURT OF APPEALS ERRED AFFIRMING THE DENIAL OF PETITIONER IS §2255 MOTION WHERE THE DISTRICT COURT FAILED TO CONDUCT AN EVIDENTIARY HEARING TO RESOLVE THE FACTUAL DISPUTES

Section 2255 provides that "[u]nless the motion and the files and records of the case conclusively show that the prisoner is entitled to no relief, the court shall . . . grant a prompt hearing thereon, determine the issues and make findings of fact and conclusions of law with respect thereto." **28 U. S.C. §2255 (2000)**. See, e.g., *Fontaine v. United States*, **411 U.S. 213, 215 (1973)**(reversing summary dismissal and remanding for hearing because "motion and the files and records of the case [did not] conclusively show that the petitioner is entitled to no relief"); **Sanders v. United States, 373 U.S. 1, 19-1 (1963)**.

Petitioner's §2255 petition alleged facts that, if proved, entitle the petitioner to relief. See **Hill v. Lockhart, 474 U.S. 52, 60 (1985)**; and **Blackledge v. Allison, 431 U.S. 63, 82-83 (1977)**. Petitioner asserted that he would not have pleaded guilty had he been correctly advised of the statutory maximum sentence penalty provided by law. Petitioner presented an affidavit detailing the facts concerning the statutory maximum penalty he was advised of by counsel which is supported by the record and stated under oath he would not have pleaded guilty had he known the correct statutory maximum penalty provided by law. Thus, petitioner was entitled to an evidentiary hearing. See, **United States v. Scott, 625 F.2d 623, 625 (5th Cir. 1980)**; **Pitts v. United States, 763 F.2d at 201; United States v. Birdwell, 887 F.2d 643, 645 (5th Cir. 1989)** (evidentiary hearing warranted if petition contains "specific factual allegations not directly contradicted in the record").

—————— * ——————

CONCLUSION

Petitioner, _____, has been deprived of basic fundamental rights guaranteed by the Fifth and Sixth Amendments of the United States Constitution and seeks relief in this Court to restore those rights. Based on the arguments and authorities presented herein, Petitioner's guilty plea was sustained in violation of due process and not voluntarily or intelligently entered because he did not understand the consequences of his plea. Petitioner was deprived of his right to effective assistance of counsel in the district court and appellate court. Petitioner prays this Court will issue a writ of certiorari and reverse the judgment of the _____ Circuit Court of Appeals.[3]

Respectfully submitted on this ____ day of _____ 20___.

————————————————
PRO SE REPRESENTATION

————————————
[3] If this Court elects not to address the issues presented in this petition at this time, it is requested that the writ issue and the matter be remanded to the _____ Circuit Court of Appeals for reconsideration in light of this Court's opinion in **Strickland, Hill, Timmereck, Fontaine** and **Sanders**, all supra.

No. _____

IN THE

SUPREME COURT OF THE UNITED STATES

_____ * _____

_____, Petitioner,

VS.

UNITED STATES OF AMERICA, Respondent

PROOF OF SERVICE

I, _____, do swear or declare that on this date, _____ ___, 20___, as required by Supreme Court Rule 29, I have served the enclosed MOTION FOR LEAVE TO PROCEED IN FORMA PAUPERIS; PETITION FOR WRIT OF CERTIORARI and Appendix on each party to the above proceeding on that party's counsel, and on every other person required to be served, by depositing an envelope containing the above documents in the United States mail properly addressed to each of them and with first-class postage prepared as follows: _____

_____

_____

Name_____
PRO SE REPRESENTATION
REG. NO. _____
Address
Town, State & Zip Code

Chapter X
Miscellaneous Motions and Letters

❑ Miscellaneous Motions and Letters

➢ Motion to expunge conviction (state)

➢ Verification for petition/motion

➢ Notice of change of address

➢ Motion to set aside order

➢ Motion for modification of term of imprisonment (with memorandum brief) (crack cocaine motion)

➢ Motion to compel United States to file a Rule 35(b) motion to reduce sentence (substantial assistance)

➢ Certificate of service

➢ Motion to correct typographic error in judgment

➢ Notary public statement

➢ Motion to set aside order and final judgment

➢ Motion for status report or hearing

➢ Motion for status conference

➢ Motion to enter guilty plea in absentia for time served on traffic tickets

➢ Motion for return of seized property (with memorandum brief)

➢ Petition for writ of mandamus

➢ Motion to terminate supervised release

MOTION TO EXPUNGE

TO THE HONORABLE JUDGE OF SAID COURT:

    COMES NOW _____, the defendant, pro se and respectfully moves this Honorable Court to issue an order expunging the conviction for _____ and _____. The Defendant will show this Court as follows:

    1.   On _____ ___, 20___, the Defendant at the age of ____ years old was arrested and charged with _____ by the _____ Police Department. The defendant bonded out of jail.

    2.   On _____ ___, 20___, the Defendant failed to appear for a court hearing and his bond was forfeited.

    3.   The Defendant was not adjudicated guilty of any of the charges which stemmed from the arrest or alleged criminal activities.

    4.   To the best of the Defendant's knowledge and belief, he is eligible to have his records sealed and expunged as requested in this motion.

    WHEREFORE, the defendant, _____, urges this Honorable Court to expunge the conviction on the _____ and _____ offenses and order the records to be sealed.

    Respectfully submitted on this ____ day of _____ 200___.

_____

PRO SE REPRESENTATION

VERIFICATION

    I, _____, hereby verify under penalty of perjury that I have read this document and the facts stated therein are true and correct to the best of my knowledge and memory. **See 28 U.S.C. §1746.** Executed on this ___ day of _____ 200____.

CERTIFICATE OF SERVICE

    I HEREBY CERTIFY that a true and correct copy of this foregoing instrument has been mailed with first class postage prepaid on this ___ day of August 2007, to _____, District Attorney, _____, _____, _____, by hand delivering a copy of the same to prison officials at _____, _____, for processing through the legal mail system. I hereby execute this certificate under penalty of perjury pursuant to **28 U.S.C. §1746.**

_____

VERIFICATION

    I, _____, hereby verify that I have read this motion and have personal knowledge that the facts stated herein are true and correct under penalty of perjury. **See 28 U.S.C. §1746**. Executed on this _____ day of April 2008.

                                    _____

[Caption]

NOTICE OF CHANGE OF ADDRESS TO COURT

COMES NOW _____, the petitioner, pro se, and respectfully files this Notice Of Change of Address to the Court. Petitioner's new and current address is:

Your Name & Prison Number
Institution
Address
Town, State & Zip Code

Petitioner request that this Court direct the Clerk to note his change of address for record.

WHEREFORE based on the above, _____, the petitioner request that this Court note his change of address as listed above for record.

Respectfully submitted on this ____ day of _____ 20___.

_____
Your Name   Prison Number
PRO SE REPRESENTATION
Address
Town, State and Zip Code

IN THE UNITED STATES DISTRICT COURT
FOR THE _____ DISTRICT OF _____
_____ DIVISION

_____
                    Petitioner,

VS.   CIVIL ACTION No.

_____ , Warden and
_____, Attorney General,
            Respondents.

MOTION TO SET ASIDE ORDER DATED _____

TO THE HONORABLE JUDGE _____:

    COMES NOW _____, the petitioner, pro se, and respectfully moves this Honorable Court to set aside the order issued by United States Magistrate Judge, _____ on _____ _____, ____, as being non-applicable to the current **28 U.S.C. §2241** habeas corpus proceedings. See **Anderson v. Singletary, 111 F.3d 801 (11ᵗʰ Cir. 1997)**. The Honorable Magistrate Judge _____ order requires Mr. _____ a habeas petitioner to fill out a "Prison Litigation Reform Prisoner Consent Form On Appeal." See attachment to order. This is not applicable in a habeas corpus proceedings.

    Filing fee requirements of Prison Litigation Reform Act do not apply to habeas corpus proceedings since habeas corpus proceedings are not "civil action" for purposes of amended §1915 requiring that prisoners bringing in forma pauperis civil actions pay all filing fees; Congress promulgated PLRA to curtail prisoner tort, civil rights and conditions litigation, not filing of habeas corpus petitions, as further indicated by contemporaneous passage of Antiterrorism and Effective Death Penalty Act imposing significant restrictions on filing successive habeas petitions. **Anderson v. Singletary, 111 F.3d 801 (11ᵗʰ Cir. 1997)**. See also **Naddi v. Hill, 106 F.3d 275 (9ᵗʰ Cir. 1997)**; and **Smith v. Angelone, 111 F.3d 1126 (4ᵗʰ Cir. 1997)**.

    WHEREFORE based on the above, _____, urges this Honorable Court to grant this motion and set aside the _____ ___, ____, order issued by Magistrate Judge _____.

    Respectfully submitted on this ____ day of _____ 20___.

_____
PRO SE REPRESENTATION

Form Letter No. 1

[Your Name & Prison Number]
[Correctional Institution]
[Your Address]
[Town, State & Zip Code]

[Date]

OFFICE OF THE CLERK
UNITED STATES DISTRICT COURT
U.S. COURTHOUSE
Address _____
Town, State & Zip Code

Re: United States v. _____
        Criminal No. _____

Dear Clerk:

In reference to the above entitled action, I am requesting to purchase a copy of the following CD digital sound recordings from your office concerning the following hearings:

Initial appearance as to _____ _____ held on _____ ___, 200__.
See Docket Entry Sheet Number ____ (Digital).

ARRAIGNMENT as to _____ _____ held on _____ ___, 200__.
See Docket Entry Sheet Number ____ (Digital).

CHANGE of plea hearing as to _____ _____ held on _____ ___, 200__. See Docket Entry Sheet Number ____ (Digital). And;

SENTENCING HEARING as to _____ _____ held on _____ ___, 200__. See Docket Entry Sheet Number ____.

For prompt payment for the above listed CD sound recordings please contact _____ at _____. Additionally, I have enclosed a self-addressed stamped envelope for your convenience.

Your speedy response will be greatly appreciated. Thank you.

Sincerely,

_____
Your Name

CC:
p/file

IN THE UNITED STATES DISTRICT COURT
FOR THE _____ DISTRICT OF _____

UNITED STATES OF AMERICA

VS.   Criminal No.

Defendant.

MOTION FOR MODIFICATION OF TERM OF IMPRISONMENT

TO THE HONORABLE JUDGE _____

    COMES NOW _____, the Defendant, pro se, and respectfully moves this Honorable Court, pursuant to **18 U.S.C. §3582(c)(2)** and **§1B1.10(c)** of the Sentencing Guidelines, to reduce his sentence based upon Amendments 706 and 711, which became effective for retroactive application on March 3, 2008, concerning weight equivalency of cocaine base "crack."

    In support thereof, the defendant states as follows:

    1.   On _____ ___, 20___, the Defendant was sentenced to a term of imprisonment of _____ months, by this Honorable Court on one count of conspiracy to possess with intent to distribute cocaine base in violation of **21 U.S.C. §841(a)**.

    2.   Pursuant to the Plea Agreement entered between the United States Attorney and the Defendant, the Presentence Report as adopted by this Honorable Court in the Judgment entered in this action, the quantity of cocaine base alleged to be involved in the Defendant's conspiracy was _____ grams.

    3.   Applying the applicable provisions of the guidelines as they existed on the date of the Defendant's sentencing, the _____ grams translated into a base offense level _____.

    4.   Amendments 706 and 711 of Section 2D1.1(c) of the Sentencing Guidelines changed the quantity of "cocaine base" and results in a two level reduction in the Defendant's base offense level. Amendments 706 and 711 were made retroactive by the Sentencing Commission pursuant to **U.S.S.G. §1B1.10(c)**, effective March 3, 2008.

    5.   When the Defendant's base offense level is recalculated under the Drug Quantity Table, as outlined in **§2D1.1** of the Sentencing Guidelines, the base offense level for conspiracy involving _____ grams of cocaine base is Level ____. Therefore, the Defendant is entitled to be resentenced under-the retroactively applied amendment 706 and 711.

6.   Factors for consideration under **§1B1.l0(c), Application Notes: l(B)(iii)** **Post-Sentencing Conduct** - The Court may consider post-sentencing conduct of the defendant that occurred after imposition of the original term of imprisonment in determining: (I) whether a reduction in the defendant's term of imprisonment is warranted; and (II) the extent of such reduction, but only within the limits described in subsection (b) [(1) **Determination of Reduction in Term of Imprisonment**]. The Defendant has attached hereto a copy of the Certificates/Accomplishments that he has received since sentencing. See **Exhibit "A"** attached hereto.

7.   After the appropriate adjustment is calculated, the Defendant's offense level for purposes of resentencing is Level _____ The Defendant's criminal history computation remains a Category _____ as computed in the Presentence Report.

8.   The appropriate guideline range for an Offense Level ____with a Criminal History Category _____ is ____to _____ months. The Defendant moves for the low end of the guideline range. The Defendant has demonstrated favorable post-sentencing conduct warranting the low end of the guideline range.

A memorandum brief in support of this motion is attached hereto and made part of this motion by reference herein.

WHEREFORE, based on the foregoing arguments and authorities, this Honorable Court is respectfully urged to reduce the Defendant's sentence to _____ months and enter an amended Judgment reflecting said change in the Defendant's sentence, alternatively reduce the Defendant's sentence to a term of imprisonment that this Honorable Court deems just and fair.

Respectfully submitted on this _____ day of _____ 20____.

_____

Name   Prison Number
PRO SE REPRESENTATION
Address
Town, State and Zip Code

IN THE UNITED STATES DISTRICT COURT
FOR THE _____ DISTRICT OF _____

UNITED STATES OF AMERICA

VS.   Criminal No.

_____ ,

Defendant.

MEMORANDUM BRIEF IN SUPPORT OF MOTION FOR MODIFICATION OF TERM OF IMPRISONMENT

TO THE HONORABLE JUDGE _____

The defendant, _____, pro se, respectfully files this memorandum brief in support of his motion pursuant to **18 U.S.C.(c)(2)** and **§1B1.10(c)** of the Sentencing Guidelines, to reduce his sentence based upon Amendments 706 and 711, which became effective for retroactive application on March 3, 2008, concerning weight equivalency and cocaine base "crack."

Title 18 United States Code, Section 3582(c)(2) provides:

(c) **Modification of an imposed term of imprisonment**. — The court may modify a term of imprisonment once it has been imposed except that—

(2)   In the case of a defendant who has been sentenced to a term of imprisonment based on a sentencing range that has subsequently been lowered by the Sentencing Commission pursuant to 28 U.S.C. §994(o), upon motion of the defendant or the Director of Bureau of Prisons, or on its own motion, the court may reduce the term of imprisonment, after considering the factors set forth in section 3553(a) to the extent that they are applicable policy statements issued by the Sentencing Commission.

U.S.S.G. §1B1.10(b)(1) provides:

(b)   **Determination of Reduction in Term of Imprisonment.—**

(1)   **In General.**— In determining whether, and to what extent, a reduction in the defendant's term of imprisonment under 18 U.S.C. §3582(c)(2) and this policy statement is warranted, the court shall determine the amended guideline

397

range that would have been applicable to the defendant if the amendment(s) to the guidelines listed in subsection (c) had been in effect at the time the defendant was sentenced. In making such determination, the court shall substitute only the amendments listed in subsection (c) for the corresponding guidelines provisions that were applied when the defendant was sentenced and shall leave all other guideline application decisions unaffected.

Amendments 706 and 711 were made retroactive by the United States Sentencing Commission effective—March 3, 2008. See **U.S.S.G. §1B1.10(c)** which provides:

(c)   **Covered Amendments.** — Amendments covered by this policy statement are listed in Appendix C as follows: 125, 130, 156, 176, 269, 329, 341, 371, 379, 380, 433, 454, 461, 844, 488, 490, 499, 505, 506, 516, 591, 599, 606, 657, 702, and 706 as amended by 711.

U.S.S.G. §1B1.10 Commentary, Application Notes, provide in pertinent part:

(A)   **Eligibility**. — Eligibility for consideration under 18 U.S.C. §3582(c)(2) is triggered only by an amendment listed in subsection (c) that lowers the applicable guideline range. Accordingly, a reduction in the defendant's term of imprisonment is not authorized under 18 U.S.C. §3582(c) and is not consistent with this policy statement if: (A) none of the amendments listed in subsection (c) is applicable to the defendant; or (B) an amendment listed in subsection (c) is applicable to the defendant but the amendment does not have the effect of lowering the defendant's applicable guideline range because of the operation of another guideline or statutory provision (e.g., a statutory mandatory minimum term of imprisonment).

(B)   **Factors for Consideration.** —

(iii)   **Post-Sentencing Conduct**. — The court may consider post-sentencing conduct of the defendant that occurred after imposition of the original term of imprisonment in determining: (I) whether a reduction in the defendant's term of imprisonment is warranted; and (II) the extent of such reduction, but only within the limits described in subsection (b). (March 3, 2008)

The Defendant, _____, has shown that: (1) Amendment 706 and 711 are applicable to his case; (2) Amendment 706 and 711 were made retroactive by the Sentencing Commission; and (3) that he has clearly demonstrated favorable post-sentencing conduct significant to warrant sentencing to the low end of the new guideline range. See **U.S.S.G. §§1B1.10(B)(iii) and 1B1.10(c)**.

Both the relevant federal statute and the Sentencing Guidelines provide that a court has the discretion to decide whether to apply, retroactively, an amended Guideline to reduce the length of incarceration. Under 18 U.S.C. §3582(c) (2), if a defendant was sentenced according to a sentencing range that has been lowered by the Sentencing Commission, a court may reduce the term of imprisonment if such a reduction is consistent with the applicable policy statements issued by the Sentencing Commission. See U.S.S.G. §lBl.l0; **United States v. Bravo, 203 F.3d 778 (11th Cir. 2000); United States v Brown, 104 F.3d 1254 (11th Cir. 1997)** (holding that court must consider relevant considerations set forth in the statute but is not required to make written findings on each factor); **United States v. Vautier, 144 F.3d 756 (11 Cir. 1998).**

When deciding whether to reduce a defendant's sentence under §3582(c)(2) the court should consider the factors set forth in 18 U.S.C. §3553(a). Though it is not required to make specific findings regarding each of the factors enumerated in §3553(a), the court should tailor it comments to show that the sentence imposed is appropriate in light of these factors. The court should also consider the sentence it would have imposed had the [A]mendment been in effect at the time the defendant was sentenced. **United States v. Vautier, supra; United States v. Carter, 110 F.3d 759 (11th Cir. 1997); United States v. Eggersdorf, 126 F.3d 1318 (11th Cir. 1997)** (a district court does not err by failing to articulate specifically the applicability, if any, of each of §3553 (a) factors, as long as the record demonstrates that the pertinent factors were taken into account). The district court, not the appellate court, should be the initial forum to decide whether to reduce a sentence in this circumstance. **United States v. Vazquez, 53 F.3d 1216 (11th Cir. 1995).**

Whether to reduce a sentence because of a change in the Guidelines is governed by §lBl.l0 (a) , which states that retroactive application of a new Guideline to an already-sentenced defendant is only appropriate when the specific Amendment is listed in §lBl.l0(c) as one which should be applied to the defendants who have already been sentenced. **United States v. Rodriquez-Diaz, 19 F.3d 1340 (11th Cir. 1994).**

WHEREFORE, based on the foregoing arguments and authorities, _____, urges this Honorable Court to **GRANT** this motion and reduce his sentence to _____ months imprisonment.

Respectfully submitted on this _____ day of March 2008/

_____

Name   Prison Number
PRO SE REPRESENTATION
Address
Town, State and Zip Code

CERTIFICATE OF SERVICE

I HEREBY CERTIFY that a true and correct copy of this foregoing instrument has been mailed with first class postage prepaid on this _____ day of _____ 2008, to the parties listed below, by hand delivering a copy of the same to prison officials at the Federal Correctional Institution _____, _____ mailroom for mailing through the internal legal mail system.

I hereby execute this certificate under penalty of perjury as being true and correct pursuant to 28 U.S.C. §1746.

_____
Name

IN THE UNITED STATES DISTRICT COURT
FOR THE _____ DISTRICT OF _____

_____

_____

UNITED STATES OF AMERICA

VS.   Criminal No.

_____ ,

           Defendant.

_____

ORDER AND JUDGMENT

_____

    After carefully review of the defendant, _____'s Motion For Modification of Term of Imprisonment, based a **Amendments 706** and **711** of Section 2D1.1(c) of the United States Sentencing Guidelines, which were made retroactively by the Sentencing Commission pursuant to **U.S.S.G. §1B1.10(c)(March 3, 2008),** this Court finds that the motion should be **GRANTED**.

    IT IS HEREBY; ORDERED AND JUDGMENT entered that _____'s term of imprisonment is reduced to _____ months. The Clerk of this Court shall amended the Judgment to reflect the reduction.

    Thus, done on this _____ day of _____, 2008.

_____

UNITED STATES DISTRICT JUDGE

IN THE UNITED STATES DISTRICT COURT
FOR THE _____ DISTRICT OF _____
_____ DIVISION

UNITED STATES OF AMERICA

VS.   Criminal No.

_____ ,

                Defendant.

MOTION TO COMPEL THE UNITED STATES TO FILE A
RULE 35(b) MOTION TO REDUCE SENTENCE

TO THE HONORABLE JUDGE _____

COMES NOW _____, the defendant, pro se, and respectfully moves this Honorable Court to compel the United States to file a Rule 35(b) motion to reduce the Defendant's sentence. In support thereof, the Defendant states:

1.   On _____, ___, 200___, the Defendant was arrested. The Defendant agreed to cooperate with the government and in late _____ 200____ Special Agents _____ and _____ debriefed the defendant. The Defendant provided a full and detailed information concerning the criminal activity of _____, and _____.

2.   In ___ 2000 ___ _____ and _____ were both arrested based on the information the Defendant provided during his debriefing. Approximately, one (1) year later _____ was arrested.

3.   On _____, ___, 200___, the defendant entered into a written plea agreement which required his cooperation and provided that the government would file a USSG §5K1.1 or a Rule 35(b) motion, if the Defendant provided substantial assistance to the United States.

4.   On _____, ___, 200___, during the defendant's sentencing the Assistant United States Attorney, _____ _____, advised this Court that the defendant has cooperated with the Government and qualifies for a downward departure pursuant to USSG §5K1.1, and that the defendant may be a witness in that case. This Court then asked the Assistant United States Attorney, _____ _____, what he wanted the Court to do because the Court was going to go ahead and grant the downward departure. The Assistant United States Attorney, Mr. _____, stated that he didn't mind the Defendant getting the downward departure now. Judge _____ _____, then called the Assistant United States Attorney, Mr. _____, and defense counsel _____

_____ both to the bench. Judge _____ informed defense counsel _____ to explain to the Defendant, that they are going to wait until the other case is resolved, and then give the Defendant his downward departure under Rule 35(b), because he might have to testify against the other individuals.

5.   The Defendant did not have to testify against _____ _____, _____, and _____ because they all plead guilty and have been sentenced.

6.   On _____, ___, 200___, the Defendant wrote a letter to the Assistant United States Attorney _____ and requested his Rule 35(b) motion that he was supposed to get after the case against _____, _____, and _____ was resolved. As of this date, the Assistant United States Attorney Mr. _____ has not responded to this letter. **See Exhibit " "** Defendant's _____, ___, 200___ letter to _____ _____.

7.   On _____, ___, 200___, the Defendant mailed a second letter to the Assistant United States Attorney, _____ _____, explaining in detail what was stated at sentencing and that it was represented to this Defendant that he would receive a Rule 35(b) sentencing reduction, instead of a USSG §5K1.1 downward departure, because he might have to testify in the other case. **See Exhibit "B"** Defendant's _____, 200___. As of this date, Mr. _____ has not responded or answered either of the defendant's letters.

A more precise set of facts are stated in this motion to compel.

_____ § _____

MEMORANDUM OF LAW

First, the Defendant argues that his plea agreement mandates that the United States file a Rule 35(b) motion to reduce defendant's sentence. The United States stated at sentencing that the defendant provided substantial assistance and qualifies for a downward departure pursuant to USSG §5K1.1 then choose to wait and give the defendant a sentence reduction pursuant to Rule 35(b). **See Sentencing Transcripts**.

Second, the Defendant argues that because the United States represented that it would file a Rule 35(b) motion for the defendant's pre-sentence substantial assistance, instead of a 5K1.1 motion because he might have to testify against the other parties shows bad faith on behalf of the United States for failing to honor its word. The Assistant United States Attorney, Mr. _____, failure to honor its plea agreement and to keep his word that he would file a Rule 35(b) motion to award, Mr. _____ for his substantial assistance that occurred prior to sentencing violates due process in light of **Santobello v. New York, 404 U.S. 257, 262, 92 S.Ct. 495, 499, 30 L.Ed.2d 427 (1971)**.

Third, the Defendant argues that the prosecutor's decision must have some rational relationship to a legitimate government interest. **See United States v. Wilson, 390 F.3d 1003, 1009 (7th Cir. 2004); Wade v. United States, 504 U.S. 181, 112 S.Ct. 1840, 118 L.Ed.2d 524 (1992)**. There is no known government interest in advising the Court that this Defendant qualifies for a USSG §5K1.1 sentencing departure because of his substantial assistance and then deciding to wait until after the other case is resolved in case the defendant has to testify to give the defendant his departure. **See Sentencing Transcripts**.

The prosecutor's decision not to file a Rule 35(b) motion to reduce defendant's sentence must have some rational relationship to legitimate government interest. **See Wade, 504 U.S. at 186, 112 S.Ct. 1840**. In **United States v. Anzalone, 148 F.3d 940 (8th Cir. 1998)**, the Court held that the government may not withhold a motion for a downward departure for reasons unrelated to whether the defendant provided substantial assistance. Additionally, the United States has failed to honor its plea agreement in the instant case. Due process requirement that prosecutor's promise must be fulfilled if a plea rests in any significant degree on it is limitation on discretionary power to file motion for departure sentence based on defendant's substantial assistance. **See United States v. De La Fuente, 8 F.3d 1333, 1340-41 (9th Cir. 1993)**. The government's discretionary power to file a substantial assistance motion "is subject to constitutional limitations that district courts can enforce." **Wade, 112 S.Ct. at 1843**. It should be obvious that among these constitutional limitations is the due process requirement that "when a plea rests in any significant degree on a promise or agreement of the prosecutor . . . such promise must be fulfilled." **Santobello v. New York, 404 U.S. 257 262, 92 S.Ct. 495, 499, 30 L.Ed.2d 427 (1971)**.

The court's power to order specific performance of a plea agreement is well-established. **See id.** In **Wade**, the Supreme Court implicitly acknowledged that enforcing the terms of a plea agreement overrides the requirement of a government substantial-assistance motion by noting that Wade made no claim "that the condition is superseded in this case by any agreement on the Government's behalf to file a substantial-assistance motion." **Wade, 112 S.Ct. at 1843; see also United States v. Delgado-Cardenas, 974 974 F.3d 123, 1235 (9th Cir. 1992)** (similarly pointing out that case involves no government promise to move for departure).

Furthermore, under the rule established in **Wade**, the district court may order relief "if the prosecutor's refusal to move was not rationally related to any legitimate Government end." **Wade, 112 S.Ct. at 1844**. Breaching the terms of a plea agreement— and, in doing so, violating the due process requirement established in **Santobello** is not **legitimate** governmental purpose. When the government persists in its refusal to make a substantial-assistance motion, the district court may remedy the breach of an executed plea agreement by sentencing the defendant below the statutory minimum. **See De La Fuente, 8 F.3d at 1341**.

The aforementioned facts and authorities stand for the proposition that this Court has the power to compel the United States to file its Rule 35(b) motion to reduce the Defendant's sentence based on his substantial assistance which was made known to this Court at sentence by the United States. It was agreed to by the parties that the United States would file a Rule 35(b) motion to reduce Defendant's sentence after the other case was resolved. The other case has been resolved.

WHEREFORE, based on the above, _____, urges this Honorable Court to issue an order enforcing the parties plea agreement and verbal agreement to reduce defendant's sentence pursuant to Rule 35(b) based on his substantial sentence. Alternatively, issue an order to compel the United States to file its Rule 35(b) motion to reduce sentence.

Respectfully submitted on this ____ day of _____ 20____.

_____
PRO SE REPRESENTATION

CERTIFICATE OF SERVICE

I HEREBY CERTIFY that a true and correct copy of this foregoing instrument has been deposited in _____ Correctional Institution prison internal legal mailing system with first class postage affixed thereto on this ____ day of _____ 20___, correctly addressed to: (insert opposing parties attorney's name and address).

The undersigned hereby executes this certificate under penalty of perjury pursuant to 28 U.S.C. §1746.

_____
Your Name

IN THE CIRCUIT COURT OF THE
_____ JUDICIAL DISTRICT
IN AND FOR _____ COUNTY, _____

STATE OF _____,

VS.   Case No. _____
                                       Criminal Division

_____,

Defendant.

MOTION TO CORRECT TYPOGRAPHIC ERROR IN JUDGMENT

TO THE HONORABLE JUDGE OF SAID COURT:

COMES NOW _____, the defendant, pro se, and respectfully moves this Honorable Court to correct typographic error in the judgment pursuant to Florida Rules of Criminal Procedure, Rule 3.800(a), through a non pro tunc order. The Defendant will show this Court as follows:

1.   The State of Florida, County of _____, initially charged the defendant _____ with Aggravated Battery.

2.   On or about _____ ___, 20___, the defendant _____'s, defense counsel _____, and the Assistant District Attorney, for the State of Florida entered into a plea negotiations. The State of Florida, County of _____, Assistant District Attorney offered to allow the defendant _____ to plead guilty to a misdemeanor Simple Battery charge. The defendant _____ accepted the plea offer.

3.   On that same date, the defendant _____ entered the guilty plea and this Court imposed a _____ (__) year sentence. **See Exhibit "__" Judgment** dated _____ ____, 20___.

4.   After sentencing on that date, the defendant _____, contacted his lawyer _____ and advised him to file a motion to withdraw his guilty plea because he agreed to enter a guilty plea to a misdemeanor Simple Battery, not to the felony Aggravated Battery charge. Counsel _____ advised Mr. _____ to sit tight that he would get the problem corrected.

5.   On _____ ___, 20___, the defendant _____, defense counsel _____, and the Assistant District Attorney for the State of Florida, appeared before this Court and the matter was explained to this Court that defendant _____ plead guilty to Simple Battery, not to Aggravated Battery. On that

same date, this Court reduced Mr. _____ charge and sentence to 364 days. **See Exhibit "___" Judgment** dated _____ ___, 20___.

      6.   The defendant _____ recently obtained a copy of the Judgments in this case, and learned that the record in this case is **still incorrect** and erroneously shows that Mr. _____ was convicted of Aggravated Battery. While on _____ ___, 20___, this Court did correct the sentence to reflect that Mr. _____ plead guilty to a misdemeanor and reduced his sentence to 364 days. Nevertheless, the judgment still shows that he was convicted of Aggravated Battery a felony. This matter has caused Mr. _____ some problems in his federal sentencing. Therefore, in the interest of justice, Mr. _____, respectfully urges this Honorable Court to issue a **non pro tunc** order correcting the judgment to reflect that Mr. _____ was convicted on **Simple Battery**.

      WHEREFORE based on the above, _____,urges this Court to correct the judgment by issuing a non pro tunc order correcting the judgment to reflect that Mr. _____ was convicted of **Simple Battery**.

      Respectfully submitted on this ____ day of September 20___.

_____

PRO SE REPRESENTATION

CERTIFICATE OF SERVICE

      I hereby certify that a true and correct copy of this foregoing Motion to correct typographic error in judgment has been mailed postage prepaid on this _____ ___, 20___, to the following:

_____

VERIFICATION

      I, _____, hereby verify that I have read this motion and the facts stated herein are true and correct under penalty of perjury.

_____

STATE OF _____

_____ COUNTY

       SWORN AND SUBSCRIBED TO BEFORE me the undersigned, a person known to be _____, who swears and declares under penalty of perjury pursuant to 28 U.S.C. §1746 that he has read the above document and that the facts stated therein are true and correct.

                             _____
                             Notary Public

[CAPTION]

MOTION TO SET ASIDE ORDER AND FINAL JUDGMENT

TO THE HONORABLE JUDGE _____:

    COMES NOW_____, the petitioner, pro se, and respectfully moves this Honorable Court to set aside the Order and Final Judgment denying petitioner's **28 U.S.C. §2255** motion dated _____ ___, 20___, pursuant to **Federal Rules of Civil Procedure, Rule 60(b),** for failure to comply with **Rule 11(a)** governing **28 U.S.C. §2255** proceedings.

    Rule 11(a) governing **§2255** proceedings provides:

> **Rule 11(a) Certificate of Appealability.** The district court **must** issue or deny a certificate of appealability when it enters a final order adverse to the applicant. Before entering the final order, the court may direct the parties to submit arguments on whether a certificate should issue. If the court issues a certificate, the court must state the specific issue or issues that satisfy the showing required by **28 U.S.C. §2253(c)(2).** If the court denies a certificate a party may not appeal the denial but may seek a certificate from the court of appeals under Federal Rule of Appellate Procedure 22. A motion to reconsider a denial does not extend the time to appeal. (Effective December 1, 2009).

    This Court's Order and Final Judgment does not comply with Rule 11(a), governing 28 U.S.C. §2255 proceedings and affects the integrity of the proceedings which requires the Court to set aside the Order and Final Judgment entered, and to reissue an Order and Final Judgment in compliance with Rule 11(a), governing §2255 proceedings.

    WHEREFORE based on the above, _____, urges this Court to grant this motion to set aside order and final judgment and reissue an order and final judgment in compliance with **Rule 11(a)**, governing §2255 proceedings.

    Respectfully submitted on this ____ day of _____, 20___.

_____
PRO SE REPRESENTATION
Address
Town, State & Zip Code

[CAPTION]

MOTION FOR STATUS REPORT OR HEARING

TO THE HONORABLE JUDGE _____:

    COMES NOW_____, the petitioner, pro se, and respectfully moves this Honorable Court, for a status report or hearing on his 28 U.S.C. §2255 motion currently pending before this Court. Petitioner will show the Court as follows:

    1. On or about _____ ____, 20___, the petitioner mailed his 28 U.S.C. §2255 motion to vacate, set aside or correct sentence, to the Clerk's Office for filing with the Court.

    2. On _____ ____, 20___, the Court issued an ORDER directing the government to respond to the petitioner's §2255 motion.

    3. The United States filed a motion for extension of time in which to respond that the Court granted.

    4. On or about _____ ____, 20___, the United States filed its: GOVERNMENT"S RESPONSE TO _____ 28 U.S.C. §2255 MOTION.

    5. On _____ ____, 20___, the petitioner filed his Reply to the Government's Response to _____ 28 U.S.C. §2255 Motion.

    6. All parties briefs and reply briefs have been filed since _____ 20___. Because of the fact that if the Court rules favorable on petitioner's §2255 motion (and it should), Petitioner would be entitled to an immediate release and seeks a status report or hearing.

    7. This motion is made in the interest of justice and not meant to delay the proceedings.

    WHEREFORE, based on the above, _____, urges this Honorable Court to grant this motion or conduct a hearing and appoint counsel.

    Respectfully submitted on this ___ day of _____ 20___.

_____
PRO SE REPRESENTATION

CERTIFICATE OF SERVICE

    I HEREBY CERTIFY that a true and correct copy of this foregoing instrument has been mailed with first class postage prepaid affixed thereto on this ____ day of _____ 201__, by hand delivering a copy of the same to the mailroom staff at the _____ Correctional Institution, _____, _____, for processing through the internal legal mail system address to: Assistant United States Attorney, _____, _____, _____, _____.

    Executed on this ___ day of _____ 20__.

_____

[CAPTION]

MOTION FOR A STATUS CONFERENCE

TO THE HONORABLE JUDGE OF SAID COURT

      COMES NOW_____, the defendant, pro se, and respectfully moves this Honorable Court, for a status conference on his "Motion _____." The defendant will show this Court as follows:

      1. On _____ ____, 20___, the defendant and _____ were arrested and charged with theft by taking and theft by receiving. This Court should dismiss the case because: (1) _____ plead guilty to the charges in 20____; (2) the State of _____, County of _____, has known of the defendant's whereabouts in _____ custody for years and failed to prosecute; and (3) it's high unlikely that the State can locate any of its witnesses. The Defendant seeks a status conference by telephonic communication through authorities at the _____ Correctional Institution, _____ _____, _____, _____, concerning this matter at the Court's earliest convenience.

      2. On _____ ____, 20___, the Defendant filed a "Motion to dismiss the failure to prosecute, violation of the speedy trial and interstate agreement on detainers acts." Alternatively, the Defendant requested a fast and speedy disposition of this elderly case which stemmed from _____ ____, 20___, arrest. The State of _____, County of _____, has failed to respond to the defendant's motion to dismiss. It is obvious by the State actions that it has no interest in prosecuting this case.

      3. This Court should grant a status conference on this matter as soon as possible to resolve this elderly case.

      WHEREFORE based on the above, _____, urges this Honorable Court to grant a status conference to resolve this elderly case. Alternatively, issue an order dismissing the case..

      Respectfully submitted on this ___ day of _____ 20___.

_____

Name

PRO SE REPRESENTATION

CERTIFICATE OF SERVICE

      I HEREBY CERTIFY that a true and correct copy of this foregoing instrument has been mailed with first class postage prepaid affixed thereto on this ____ day of _____ 201__, by hand delivering a copy of the same to the mailroom staff at the _____ Correctional Institution, _____, _____, for processing through the internal legal mail system address to: _____, _____, _____, _____.

      Executed on this ___ day of _____ 20__.

_____

Name

CITY OF _____   MUNICIPAL COURT OF _____
VS.   Docket _____
                              Docket _____

_____,
          Defendant.

MOTION TO ENTER GUILTY PLEA IN ABSENTIA
FOR TIME SERVED ON TRAFFIC TICKETS

TO THE HONORABLE JUDGE OF SAID COURT:

    COMES NOW_____, the defendant, pro se, and respectfully moves this Honorable Court to enter a verdict of guilty and sentence defendant to time served for traffic ticket violations in the above styled and numbered causes. Upon consideration of the time the defendant has accumulated since the filing of the charge and grant a sentence of time served in exchange for the defendant's guilty plea in absentia. In support, the Defendant will show this Court as follows:

I. CONFINEMENT

    Defendant is currently being held in the _____ Department of Correctional, in _____, _____. Defendant was arrested on _____ _____, 20___, and has acquired all days since the date of his arrest as flat time served.

II. PLEA IN ABSENTIA

    Defendant knowingly and voluntarily enters a plea of guilty in absentia in exchange for credit time served in the above said causes.

III. PRAYER FOR RELIEF

    WHEREFORE, all considered, defendant prays that the Honorable Court grant defendant's motion and enters a plea of guilty in absentia in exchange for credit time served in all things which the defendant is entitled.

    Respectfully submitted on this ____ day of _____ 20___.

                      _____

                      Your Name
                      PRO SE REPRESENTATION
                      Your Address
                      Town, State & Zip Code

<u>UNSWORN DECLARATION</u>

    I, _____, #_____, am presently incarcerated in _____ Department of Correction, _____, _____, and hereby declare under penalty of perjury that the foregoing is true and correct.

    Executed on this ____ day of _____ 20___.

                      _____

                      Your Name

[CAPTION]

MOTION FOR RETURN OF SEIZED PROPERTY

TO THE HONORABLE JUDGE OF SAID COURT:

    COMES NOW_____, the defendant, pro se, and respectfully moves this Honorable Court for the return of his seized property to wit: _____, _____ and _____, which was seized by the _____ and held as evidence, in the above entitled action.

    The Defendant will show this Court that the State of _____, County of ____, dismissed the charges and has not provided the Defendant with any notice of intent to initiate forfeiture proceeding on the seized property, in violation of due process. Therefore, in the interest of justice the seized property described above should be returned to its rightful owner _____.

    A memorandum brief in support of this motion is attached hereto and made part of this motion by reference herein.

    Respectfully submitted on this ___ day of _____ 20___.

_____
PRO SE REPRESENTATION

[CAPTION]

MEMORANDUM BRIEF IN SUPPORT OF MOTION
FOR RETURN OF SEIZED PROPERTY

TO THE HONORABLE JUDGE OF SAID COURT:

The defendant, _____, files this memorandum brief in support of his motion for the return of seized property, to wit: _____, _____, and _____, which was seized by the _____, and held as evidence, in the above entitled action.

The State of _____, County of _____, dismissed the charge and has not provided the Defendant with any notice of intent to initiate forfeiture proceedings on the seized property. Therefore, in the interest of justice the seized property should be returned to its rightful owner, _____, since it is no longer needed as evidence.

The State of _____, County of _____, has known of the defendant, _____, whereabouts and of his current and past addresses at all times and have not served the Defendant with any type of notice to initiate forfeiture proceedings.

A district court in a criminal case has both the jurisdiction and the duty to ensure the return of property seized from the defendant, _____, which is not stolen, contraband, or otherwise forfeitable and which is no longer needed as evidence. See ***United States v. Bryant*, 684 F.Supp. 421, 423 (M.D.N.C. 1988)**. The general rule is that seized property other than contraband should be returned to its rightful owner once the criminal proceedings have terminated. See ***United States v. LaFatch*, 565 F.2d 81, 83 (6th Cir. 1977)**, cert. denied, 435 U.S. 971, 98 S.Ct. 1611, 56 L.Ed2d 62 (1978), quoted in ***United States v. Farrell*, 606 F.2d 1341, 1343 (D.C. Cir. 1979)** (emphasis added).

The Fifth Circuit in ***Hunt v. United States Department of Justice*, 2 F.3d 96 (5th Cir. 1993)**, held that "Plaintiff did not have an adequate alternative remedy at law in state forfeiture proceedings and therefore the district court's dismissal of his motion warranted reversal." **id.** at **96**. If the government seeks to forfeit property, proper proceedings must be instituted. See ***United States v. Wilson*, 540 F.Supp. 502, 506 (D. Md. 1980)**. The exact same scenario applies to defendant _____ case.

There has been no formal forfeiture proceedings by the State of _____, County of _____, in relation to the Defendant's seized property. Therefore, the seized property should be returned to the Defendant. See ***United States v. Sharp*, 655 F.Supp. 1348, 1352 (W.D. Mo. 1987)**. The ***Sharp*** Court held that a delay of 20 months in initiating forfeiture proceedings constitutes a violation of the claimant's due process rights. **id.** The State of _____, failed to initiate any forfeiture proceedings against his property, in violation of the defendant's due process rights. See ***Sharp*, 655 F.Supp.**

at 1352. Therefore, the seized property should be returned to the Defendant. See ***United States v. Estevez*, 845 F.2d 1409 (7th Cir. 1988)**.

WHEREFORE, based on the above foregoing facts and application of the law, the defendant, _____, urges the Court to issue an **ORDER** directing that the State of _____, County of _____, to return his seized property.

Respectfully submitted on this ___ day of _____ 20___.

_____
Your Name   Prison Number
PRO SE REPRESENTATION
Address
Town, State and Zip Code

No. _____

IN THE

_____ CRIMINAL COURT OF APPEALS

_____ * _____

In re _____,

Petitioner.

Petition For Writ of Mandamus
For the _____th Judicial District of _____ County
_____ Code of Crim. P. _____ and _____
District Court Criminal No. _____

PETITION FOR WRIT OF MANDAMUS

<u>Name</u>   <u>#Prison Number</u>
PRO SE REPRESENTATION
Address
Town, State & Zip Code

CERTIFICATE OF INTERESTED PERSONS AND CORPORATE DISCLOSURE

The undersigned Petitioner, pro se, of record certifies that the following listed persons and entitles have an interest in the outcome of this case. These representations are made in order that the judges of this court may evaluate possible disqualifications or recusal.

_____, the Petitioner,
Pro se Representation
Address _____
Town, State & Zip Code

The State of _____, County of _____ and its
counsel _____
District Attorney
Address _____
Town, State & Zip Code

Delivery of Copy to District Judge

The petitioner, _____, certifies that he has mailed first class postage prepaid on this _____ day of _____ 2011, to the ___th Judicial District of _____ County through the Clerk of said court addressed correctly.

Respectfully submitted on this ____ day of _____ 2011.

Name

TABLE OF CONTENTS

TABLE OF AUTHORITIES

App. No._____

IN THE

_____ CRIMINAL COURT OF APPEALS

_____

In re _____,

Petitioner.

PETITION FOR WRIT OF MANDAMUS

TO THE HONORABLE JUDGES OF THE COURT OF CRIMINAL APPEALS:
    COMES NOW _____, the petitioner, pro se, and respectfully moves this Honorable Court to issue a writ of mandamus and order the "District Court ____ th Judicial District of _____ County, _____, Criminal No. _____," to either grant or deny Petitioner's "Motion for return of the defendant's seized $_____ in United States Currency."

I.
JURISDICTION STATEMENT

    Jurisdiction of this Court is invoked pursuant to _____ Code of Criminal Procedure, Sections _____ and _____ or whatever applicable _____ Code of Criminal Procedure, statute or rule necessary to invoke jurisdiction of this Court. Petitioner is currently in federal custody and has no access to _____ State Law books and requests that this Court liberally construe his pleadings in light of *Haines v. Kerner*, **404 U.S. 519, 521 (1972).**

II.
STATEMENT OF THE CASE

    1. On _____ ___, 20___, the Petitioner was stopped by a _____ Department of Public Safety Officer in _____ County, _____. The _____ Department of Public Safety Office seized $_____ in United States Currency from Petitioner as evidence and charged Petitioner with illegal investment in the "State of _____ v. _____, in the District Court ____th Judicial District of _____ County, _____, Criminal No. _____."

    2. On _____ ___, 20___, the _____ County grand jury returned a two count indictment against _____. Count one charged that _____, and various other codefendants with the intent to establish, maintain, and participate in a combination and in the profits of said combination, did commit an unlawful delivery of controlled substance, to wit: aggravated delivery of more than two hundred (200) pounds but less than two thousand (2,000) pounds of marijuana. Count two charged _____

421

and various other defendants with intentionally and knowingly financed and invested funds they knew and believed were intended to further the commission of the offense of aggravated possession of more than two hundred (200) pounds but less than two thousand (2,000) pounds of marijuana. See **Exhibit "A"** attached hereto a copy of the indictment.

    3. On _____ ___, 20___, the State of _____, County of _____, District Attorney's office moved in the District Court ___th Judicial District of _____ County, _____, Criminal No. _____, for an order to dismiss the indictment. The Court granted the motion and dismissed the indictment. See **Exhibit "B"** a copy of the order dismissing the indictment.

    4. On _____ ___, 20___, the Petitioner _____, filed a "MOTION FOR RETURN OF THE DEFENDANT"S SEIZED $_____ IN UNITED STATES CURRENCY." See **Exhibit "C"** attached hereto "MOTION FOR RETURN OF THE DEFENDANT"S SEIZED $_____ IN UNITED STATES CURRENCY. The district court has refused to issue a show cause order or respond to petitioner's motion in anyway.

    5. On _____ ___, 20___, the Petitioner mailed to be filed in the district court a "NOTICE FOR HEARING AND REQUEST FOR SUBMISSION OF DEFENDANT'S MOTION FOR RETURN OF THE DEFENDANT'S SEIZED $_____ IN UNITED STATES CURRENCY." See **Exhibit "D"** attached hereto.

    6. Petitioner has wrote several letters of inquires of the status of his MOTION FOR RETURN OF THE DEFENDANT'S SEIZED $_____ IN UNITED STATES CURRENCY" to the ___th Judicial District of _____ County, _____, Clerk's Office and received no responses whatsoever.

IV.
ARGUMENTS: REASONS WHY WRIT SHOULD ISSUE

A. MANDAMUS SHOULD ISSUE BECAUSE PETITIONER HAS NO OTHER ADEQUATE REMEDY

Petitioner has no other remedy of law in order to obtain his $_____, in United States Currency from the State of _____, County of _____. The Fifth Circuit in ***Hunt v. United States Department of Justice*, 2 F.3d 96 (5th Cir. 1993)**, addressed a similar issue and held that: "Plaintiff did not have an adequate remedy at law in state forfeiture proceedings and therefore the district court's dismissal of his motion warranted reversal." **id. at 96.**

B. THE STATE FAILED TO INITIATE FORFEITURE PROCEEDINGS

The State of _____, County of _____, dismissed the criminal charges against _____, and failed to initiate forfeiture proceedings on Defendant's $_____ in United States Currency. If the government seeks to forfeit property, proper proceedings must be instituted. See ***United States v. Wilson*, 540 F.2d 1100, 1104 (D.C. Cir. 1976)**. "It is fundamental that due process requires that a property interest not be divested . . . without some kind of a hearing." ***Davis v. Fowler*, 504 F.Supp. 502, 506 (D. Md. 1980)**.

C. THIS COURT HAS JURISDICTION OVER THE ___th JUDICIAL DISTRICT COURT OF _____ COUNTY, _____.

Petitioner, _____, explained to the arresting officer seizing his $_____ in United States Currency, that the funds were from his legitimate business and for the purchase of business machinery. There has been no formal forfeiture proceedings by the State of _____, County of _____, in relation to petitioner's $_____ in U.S. Currency. See *United States v. Sharp*, **655 F.Supp. 1348, 1352 (W.D. Mo. 1987)**. The *Sharp* Court held that a delay of 20 months in initiating forfeiture proceedings constitutes a violation of the claimant's due process rights. **id.** The States of _____ failed to initiate any forfeiture proceedings against petitioner's $_____, which violates his due process rights. See *Sharp*, **655 F.Supp. at 1352**. Thus, the funds should be returned to Petitioner. See *United States v. Estevez*, **845 F.2d 1409 (7th Cir. 1988)**.

    D. A WRIT OF MANDAMUS SHOULD BE ISSUED

    A "writ of mandamus is an order directing a public official or public body to perform a duty exacted by law." *United States v. Denson*, **603 F.2d 1143, 1146 (5th Cir. 1979)**. It "is an extraordinary remedy for extraordinary causes." *In re Corrugated Container Antitrust Litig. Mead Corp.*, **614 F.2d 958, 961-62 (5th Cir. 1980)**. To obtain the writ, the petitioner must show "that no other adequate means exist to attain the requested relief and that his right to issuance of the writ is "clear and indisputable." *In re Willy*, **831 F.2d 545, 549 (5th Cir. 1987)**. The issuance of the writ is within the Court's discretion. *Denson*, **603 F.2d at 1146**.

    WHEREFORE, based on the above, _____, urges this Honorable Court to issue a writ of mandamus directing the ___th Judicial District Court of _____ County, Criminal No. _____, to issue a ruling either granting or denying his motion to return of the $_____ in United States Currency.

    Respectfully submitted on this ___ day of _____ 2011.

_____
Name   # Prison Number
PRO SE REPRESENTATION
Address
Town, State & Zip Code

<u>CERTIFICATE OF SERVICE</u>

    I HEREBY CERTIFY that a true and correct copy of this foregoing instrument has been mailed with first class postage prepaid affixed thereto on this _____ ___, 20___, by hand delivering a copy of he same to the mailroom staff at the Federal Correctional Institution, _____, _____, for processing through the internal legal mail system address to: _____ _____ _____ _____.

    Executed on this ____ day of _____, 2011.

_____
Name

IN THE UNITED STATES DISTRICT COURT
FOR THE _____ DISTRICT OF _____
_____ DIVISION

UNITED STATES OF AMERICA

VS.   Case No. _____

_____

Defendant.

MOTION TO TERMINATE SUPERVISED RELEASE
WITH MEMORANDUM OF LAW

TO THE HONORABLE JUDGE_____:

    COMES NOW_____, the defendant, pro se, and respectfully moves this Honorable Court, pursuant to 18 U.S.C. §3583(e)(1), to terminate the term of supervised release and discharge the defendant.

THE FACTS

    1.   The Defendant was released in _____ 201__, from the federal correctional institution, _____, _____.

    2.   The Defendant has completed the drug treatment program and the drug treatment aftercare, and has been on supervised release for over 20 months.

    3.   The Defendant has worked consistently since his release and complied with the conditions and terms of supervised release.

    4.   The Defendant seeks to terminate supervised release so that he may travel and seek employment and education in different parts of the United States. The Defendant asserts that a change in towns and state will best serve his interest and provide him with a better opportunity in life.

    5.   The United States Probation has agreed with the Defendant that the term of supervised release should be terminate and ask the Court to terminate the supervised release.

    6.   This motion is made in the interest of justice.

MEMORANDUM OF LAW

    18 U.S.C. §3583(e)(1) provides that the court may "terminate a term of supervised release and discharge the defendant released at any time after the expiration of one year of supervised release pursuant to [Rule 32.1] if it is satisfied that such action is warranted by the conduct of the defendant and the interest of justice." **Id.**

    Under this provision, the defendant may move for early termination and discharge after completing one year of supervised release. This requires the court to proceed with a

424

"conduct-based inquiry into the continued necessity for supervision." ***United States v. Pregent*, 190 F.3d 279, 283 (4th Cir. 1999)**. The "interest of justice" language allows the court board discretion to consider a range of factors in addition to the defendant's conduct. The court may terminate supervised release after one year even if defendant has not completed a longer mandatory minimum supervised release required by the substantive statute. ***United States v. Spinelle*, 41 F.3d 1056, 1059-60 (6th Cir. 1994); *United States v. Rodriguera*, 954 F.2d 1465, 1469 (9th Cir. 1992)**.

  WHEREFORE based on the above, _____, urges this Honorable Court to terminate the term of supervised release and discharge Defendant.

  Respectfully submitted on this ___ day of _____ 2011.

_____

PRO SE REPRESENTATION

CERTIFICATE OF SERVICE

  I HEREBY CERTIFY that a true and correct copy of this foregoing instrument has been mailed postage prepaid on this _____ day of _____ 201__, to the Assistant United States Attorney, _____ _____ at _____ _____, _____, _____.

  Executed on this ___ day of _____ 201__.

_____

THE POST-CONVICTION CITEBOOK is the ultimate shortcut quick reference for ineffective assistance of counsel and other constitutional claims. A research reference book with favorable case law on almost any subject in the field of post-conviction remedies. The contents have been designed to assist the individual user in finding favorable case law by topic and in chronological order as a criminal trial or proceedings may unfold.

The Federal Court system has created an extremely narrow road in the field of post-conviction for State & Federal prisoners designed to prevent an individual from obtaining relief from a constitutional violation based on the procedural default rule. The pitfalls created by the procedural default rule require a criminal defendant to show "cause" for failure to raise the issue at trial or on direct appeal and "actual prejudice" resulting from the error. This book has been designed to assist the user in showing "cause" for procedural default. Prejudice must be shown based on the individual facts of each case.

The book provides the user a 16 page Table of Contents with over 740 quick reference topics covering: Ineffective Assistance of Counsel, Pretrial Ineffectiveness, Motions, Defenses, Guilty Pleas, Trials, Jury Selections, Vior Dire, Opening Statements, Defense/Evidence related claims, Objection related claims, Mistrial, Witnesses, Expert Witnesses, Impeachment, Cross-examination, Testifying claims, Closing Arguments, Jury Instructions, Jury Notes, The Right to Counsel, Ineffectiveness v. Strategic Decisions, Conflict of Interest claims, Ineffectiveness caused by the court or the government Miscellaneous Ineffectiveness claims, the court or the government, Miscellaneous Ineffectiveness claims, Denial of Counsel, Probation Revocation, Evidentiary Hearings, Counsel's Cumulative Errors, Legal Standards/Reviews For Ineffectiveness claims, Sentence Ineffectiveness, Death Penalty related claims, United States Sentencing Guidelines Ineffectiveness, Appellant Ineffectiveness, Anders requirements, Post-Verdict, Cause for Procedural Default, Habeas Corpus Miscellaneous and much, much more.

A review of the Table of Contents will assist the individual user in finding and recognizing errors which occurred in his/her case with favorable case law supporting that specific constitutional claim. This book is a great guide for use in a criminal trial/proceeding.

The Clock is Ticking

The book was designed to assist State & Federal Prisoner's and Lawyers in meeting the filing deadlines created by the enactment of the Antiterrorism and Effective Death Penalty Act of 1996 for **28 U.S.C. Sections 2254 and 2255** Motions. **See Pub. L. No. 104-132, 110 Stat. 1214 (April 24, 1996).** See also **28 U.S.C. Sections 2244, 2254**, and **2255**. The deadlines apply to both State and Federal prisoners seeking post-conviction relief in the federal court system.

This book is a valuable asset to any law library and will save the user countless hours on research.

ORDER FROM:

Infinity Publishing.Com
1094 New Dehaven Street
Suite 100
West Conshohocken, PA 19428-2713

OR BUY ONLINE AT:

www.BuyBooksOnTheWeb.com

Toll Free (877) 289-2665

Cost: $59.45
Price includes postage and handling.
Pennsylvania residents
add 6% sales tax.

DO YOU HAVE A
LOVED ONE WHO
HAS BEEN WRONGLY
CONVICTED OR
UNJUSTLY
SENTENCED?

ARE YOU IN TROUBLE
OR DO YOU KNOW
SOMEONE WHO IS?

THEN YOU NEED
THIS BOOK!!!

Made in the USA
Middletown, DE
15 October 2023

40854510R00250